Marzena Rochoń

Optimality in Complexity

416 294 999 900 18

studia grammatica

Herausgegeben von Manfred Bierwisch

unter Mitwirkung von

Hubert Haider, Stuttgart
Paul Kiparsky, Stanford
Angelika Kratzer, Amherst
Jürgen Kunze, Berlin
David Pesetsky, Cambridge (Massachusetts)
Dieter Wunderlich, Düsseldorf

studia grammatica 48

Marzena Rochoń

Optimality in Complexity: The Case of Polish Consonant Clusters

Akademie Verlag

Die Deutsche Bibliothek – CIP-Einheitsaufnahme

Rochoń, Marzena:
Optimality in complexity : the case of Polish consonant clusters /
Marzena Rochoń. – Berlin : Akad. Verl., 2000
(Studia grammatica ; 48)
Zugl.: Berlin, Humboldt-Univ., Diss., 1999
ISBN 3-05-003519-6

ISSN 0081-6469

Das eingesetzte Papier ist alterungsbeständig nach DIN/ISO 9706.

Druck und Bindung: GAM Media GmbH, Berlin

Printed in the Federal Republic of Germany

“Język polski [...] najtwardsze nam i najmiększe, chropawe i płynne stawi na wybór dźwięki;
i pienia lutni, i szumy wichru, i twarde zbroje, i stal chrzęszczącą równie dobitnie wyrazi.”

“The Polish language gives us the choice of the hardest and the softest sounds; it will express with equal clarity the singing of a lute and the rustling of a gale, the hard armors as well as the crunching steel.”

Aleksander Tyszyński
(1837:185)

Acknowledgments

Not every one has the opportunity to develop in the environment of people who not only are professionals but are also constantly ready to discuss one's ideas, to provide constructive criticism and to help. Being fully aware of the fact that I had the great fortune to meet such people, I would like to express my gratitude to them.

First of all, I owe an immense debt to my advisors, Peter Eisenberg, Tracy Alan Hall, and Bernd Pompino-Marschall for discussing various topics of the thesis, helpful comments, and constructive criticisms as well as leaving me freedom to develop my ideas. I appreciate both their help and the way in which we worked together very much.

I am also very grateful to all the people from our Graduiertenkolleg "Economy and complexity in language" at Humboldt University and the University of Potsdam who have contributed to my linguistic development. I am indebted to Professors Manfred Bierwisch, Ria de Bleser, Rainer Dietrich, Monika Doherty, Karin Donhauser, Peter Eisenberg, Gisbert Fanselow, Tracy Alan Hall, Gerda Haßler, Peter Kosta, Jürgen Kunze, Ewald Lang, Bernd Pompino-Marschall, Peter Staudacher, Jürgen Weissenborn, and Chris Wilder for ensuring that my linguistic knowledge was not limited to my main interests, i.e. phonetics and phonology, but also expanded to other linguistic fields. This multidimensional linguistic perspective allowed me to comprehend how complex and exciting linguistics can be.

I wish to extend my sincere appreciation to Professor Norbert Fries whose interesting lectures sparked my interest in linguistics when I was a student at Humboldt University.

Furthermore, I am very grateful to my professors from abroad, John McCarthy, Bruce Hayes, and Jaye Padgett, for deepening my interest in Optimality Theory. Thanks to their classes I was convinced that Optimality Theory is the framework I would adopt for my dissertation.

I am also indebted to my fellow students from Graduiertenkolleg (the so-called Gradukls) Jens Ahrens, Heiner Drehnhaus, Sylke Eichler, Susann Fischer, Peter Gebert, Dorothee Käsler, Jürgen Manowsky, Theodor Marinis, Diana Pili, Eva Schlachter, Stephan Schmidt, and Jochen Trommer for 'doing' linguistics together in a friendly atmosphere. A special thanks goes to Joanna Błaszczak for her help and for setting a good example of perseverance in work.

To Professor Ewald Lang and all the members of the Research Center of General Linguistics (ZAS) in Berlin I owe a special word of gratitude for letting me work in a hyper-linguistic environment and in excellent working conditions. I thank Antony

Dubach Green, Peter Janker, Ursula Kleinhenz, Sylvia Löhken, and Christine Mooshammer for helping me with my phonetic/phonological problems as well as Jörg Dreyer and Frank Heinsberg for always being ready to solve my technical problems.

I acknowledge with thanks the financial support from Deutsche Forschungsgemeinschaft (DFG) which allowed me not only to develop my ideas in the Graduiertenkolleg but also to present them at conferences abroad as well as to participate at the Linguistic Institute at Cornell University and to stay some weeks at the University of Massachussets.

Furthermore, I would also like to thank Ania, Jola L. and Jola S., Marta, Jacek, Józek, Zdzisław, Zygfryd and all the members of the Polish Catholic Community for their friendship and constant support. Closer to home, I am deeply grateful to my family who have always been a source of encouragement and support. I want to express my warmest thanks to my parents Barbara and Stanisław and my sister Małgosia for their consistent love. I dedicate this dissertation to them.

Jestem głęboko wdzięczna mojej rodzinie za nieustanne wsparcie i dodawanie mi odwagi. Chciałabym złożyć gorące podziękowania moim rodzicom Barbarze i Stanisławowi oraz mojej siostrze Małgosi za ich nieustajacą miłość. Dedykuję Wam tę dysertację.

Pan moją mocą i tarczą!
Moje serce Jemu zaufało
Doznałem pomocy więc moje serce się cieszy
i pieśnią moją Go sławię.
Ps 28,7

Marzena Rochoń

Table of contents

0 Introduction

0.1 Main goals of the study

The aim of the present study is to show how the complexity of linguistic structures relates to the economy of elements and principles in the organization of language and to illustrate what role this relation plays in language development.

The focus of the investigation is placed on the principles determining the phonetic component of lexical entries. It will be shown that one of the underlying forces of the phonetic component is the minimization of articulatory effort, which manifests itself in the optimization of the segmental and the prosodic level. As the study reveals the minimization of one level is possible to a certain extent since it is mostly connected with the increasing complexity of another level. This observation reveals that the phonetic representation is constrained not only by principles applying to the segmental and the prosodic level but also by principles determining their relationship. Furthermore, it will be demonstrated that the optimization of the phonetic component can be blocked by connections with the grammatical and the semantic components. This network of various dependencies leads to a conclusion that a direct consequence of a particular sound change cannot be a global improvement of a phonetic representation. Instead it will be shown that visible results of a sound change are local, i.e., they pertain only to one level of a representation. In light of this conclusion the question arises as to whether a global optimization of a language design exists. The longitudinal perspective of the study allows to draw a conclusion that in the case of Polish global economy of the phonetic component manifests itself in the shortening of the speech signal.

As the subject of my investigation I choose Polish consonant clusters. The motivation for taking this subject is manifold. First, the enormous complexity of consonantal sequences in Polish constitutes not only a challenge per se but also questions the role of economy in determining linguistic structures. It poses a question whether changes in languages lead to a more optimal language design. In addition, Polish clusters are still poorly understood and little investigated. This follows from the fact the natural expectation of linguists to find regularities with respect to clusters is fated to fail because of the complexity of consonantal sequences along various dimensions. One has to propose either a considerable number of exceptions or to postulate highly general statements. The strategy I take in the present study is to investigate the causes of this complexity before approaching the subject from the synchronic point of view. I start my investigation by examining the loss of semi-vowels, the so called jers, which began in the 10th century. The result of this sound change caused complex consonantal sequences to emerge. I mainly investigate the causes of their emergence as well as changes they underwent immediately after their emergence. This diachronic perspective leads to a detailed study of present-day Polish clusters with respect to syllable structure as well as some processes such as voicing assimilation, degemination, palatalizations and others.

Finally, I discuss the instability of clusters occurring in present-day Polish in terms of optional deletions, mergers, and assimilations. The investigation of these simplification processes opens a perspective for the future development of clusters.

0.2 Theoretical Framework

For my analyses I employ the framework of Optimality Theory (OT) (Prince and Smolensky 1993, McCarthy and Prince 1993) with the modifications proposed in Correspondence Theory (McCarthy and Prince 1995). I choose Optimality Theory since this is the only theory that is able to express the linguistic system as a system of conflicting requirements. Furthermore, OT reflects the complexity of language by integrating constraints that refer to different dimensions of language into one system. For example, a lexical entry is determined by constraints referring to its phonetic, grammatical, and semantic components as well as the connection between them. Further, the phonetic component, the main subject of the present study, is defined by constraints referring to the segmental and the prosodic level as well as the relation between them. Optimality Theory offers a unified system that is potentially able to express this complexity.

A remarkable achievement of Optimality Theory is that it dispenses with abstract stages in a derivation by evaluating only surface representations. Most earlier studies on Polish phonology assumed such abstract stages. In the course of this study I show that they are unnecessary.

OT also offers new possibilities for modeling the mechanism of sound change. It shows what constraints are responsible for sound change and how they can be encapsulated in a unified system. Furthermore, this theory is able to express individual variations as well as variations attested in language as a whole, cf. 1.3.

Finally, since constraints in OT are violable, it is possible to account not only for the generally attested facts of the given language but also to integrate 'the exceptional' cases in its system.

0.3 Organization of the study

The study is divided into six chapters.

In the first chapter I shall introduce the theoretical underpinnings of my investigation. First, the concept of optimality will be discussed and its application into various sciences will be shown. The focus will be placed on recent linguistic theories such as Optimality Theory (Prince and Smolensky 1993, McCarthy and Prince 1993) and Correspondence Theory (McCarthy and Prince 1995). In addition to the most important assumptions of these theories, the concepts of Generalized Alignment and Local Conjunction will be presented. Further, the models of diachronic change within the framework of OT such as 'Free-Variationist Model' (Bermúdez-Otero 1996 and others) and 'Promotion of the Optimal' (Green 1997) will be compared and discussed. The last section of chapter 1 is a presentation of the main assumptions concerning a lexical entry as well as the main characteristics of the lexicon within OT. Finally, I shall show what strategies used in OT lead to the optimization of the lexicon.

In the second chapter of my thesis I shall approach consonant clusters from a diachronic point of view. It will be shown that the large number of consonant clusters occurring in present-day Polish is a reflex of the loss of 'semi-vowels', the so-called jers, that took place in Late Common Slavic. It will be argued that the emergence of complex consonantal sequences is a result of constraints referring to both the prosodic and the segmental level. It will be shown that it was the loss of 'semi-vowels' that directly caused the consonant clusters to arise, while the driving force behind the deletion of jers had an exclusively prosodic character. Furthermore, various consequences of the processes to be investigated will be discussed (the so-called Period of Trial and Error). The focus will be placed on the multiplication of consonant clusters and their impact on syllable structure. It will be shown that the optimization of prosodic representations is possible only to a certain extent: the reduction of syllables as a direct consequence of the loss of jers was blocked by the increased complexity of consonant clusters. Furthermore, many cases treated previously as exceptions will be integrated into the linguistic system without their 'exceptional' status since the constraints responsible for their development also refer to their morphological representations. Finally, various processes attested exclusively in clusters such as simplifications, metathesis, and epenthesis will be examined.

In the third chapter of my thesis I shall discuss consonant clusters attested in present-day Polish. First, I shall provide a detailed presentation of word-initial and word-final clusters by grouping them into sets of two-, three-, four-, and five-member clusters. The systematization will be based on sonority distinctions between sonorants and obstruents, i.e., all attested combinations between sonorants and obstruents will be shown. In addition, I shall provide a number of lexical items in which each cluster is attested. The generalizations I shall draw with respect to the Polish syllable are based on sonority distinctions, the frequency of occurrence of single clusters as well as the syllabification patterns provided by native speakers. In other words, I shall consider a syllable solely as a surface construct. Based on the surface representation I shall investigate how the proposed structure relates to phonological processes attested in language.

My account of Polish clusters differs considerably from previous approaches which I will also present and discuss in chapter 3. While previous approaches, cf. Rubach and Booij (1990a,b), Gussmann (1991), Bethin (1992), assume abstract levels of derivation and make use of rules creating 'abstract' syllables which are then turned into 'surface' syllables by virtue of later rules, I shall assume one concrete level of representation, which is evaluated by violable constraints. It will be shown that the interaction of appropriate constraints leads not only to a correct syllabification pattern but it also captures variation in syllabification provided by native speakers. I shall also argue that certain consonants are not associated with the syllable but instead with other prosodic constituents such as the foot and the prosodic word. The correctness of the proposal will be supported by processes such as voicing assimilations and degemination.

In chapter 4 I shall also investigate consonant clusters with respect to one particular process, namely palatalization. Effects of palatalizations on labials, coronals, and velars when they are followed by other consonants will be analyzed. For comparison purposes the behavior of all three natural classes in onset and coda position will also be examined with respect to palatalizations. This strategy will show that palatalization is dependent on both its target as well as the positions in which the targets occur, i.e., onset, coda or consonant clusters.

In chapter 4 I shall also investigate palatalizations from a diachronic point of view, which gives an important insight not only into the asymmetry between labials, coronals, and velars but also into the nature of principles determining the development of language. Finally, I shall also present the realization of palatalization in different dialects of Polish. All analyses provided in chapter 4 will be illustrated by means of various constraints determining not only the phonetic component of a lexical entry but also its connections to other components such as the grammatical or semantic ones.

Chapter 5 is intended to open a perspective for the further development of clusters. Since the variations attested in spontaneous speech are commonly interpreted as indicators of an ongoing change in language, the optional processes clusters undergo in present-day Polish will be examined. The focus will be placed on the most frequent processes such as deletion, the merger of consonants, and assimilation. It will be shown that the attested variations are far from arbitrary but are contingent upon various factors that will be examined in detail. The study will reveal that the investigated processes have a common denominator: they lead to a simplified structure from the articulatory point of view.

Finally, I shall provide a summary of the main conclusions of the previous chapters and draw conclusions with respect to the role of complexity and economy in language. These conclusions will be discussed in light of the optimality concept.

0.4 Transcriptions

In prevailing number of cases I shall transcribe only the segments of the word that are relevant for discussion. The remaining segments of the same word will be rendered in Polish orthography.

In the following orthography as well as IPA and Slavic transcriptions are given.

orthography	IPA transcription	Slavic transcription
ó u	u	u
ę	ẽ/en	ę/en
ą	ã/om	ą/om
ł	ɫ	ɫ
ń	ɲ	ń
c	t͜s	c/t^{s}
ć, ci	t͜ɕ	ć/t^{ś}
cz	t͜ʂ (t͜ʃ)	č/t^{š}
dz	d͜z	ʒ/d^{z}
dź, dzi	d͜ʑ	ʒ́/d^{ź}
dż	d͜ʐ (d͜ʒ)	ǯ/d^{ž}
ś, si	ɕ	ś
sz	ʂ (ʃ)	š
ź, zi	ʑ	ź
ż, rz	ʐ (ʒ)	ž
w	v	v

In the present study I shall use transcriptions commonly used in the Slavic tradition. As far as affricates are concerned the second option of the Slavic transcription will be taken, i.e., t^{s}, t^{ś}, t^{š}, d^{z}, d^{ź}, d^{ž}. I shall also normalize direct quotations from other studies according to the proposed transcription system.

The feature matrix of all Polish consonants is given in 7.1 in the appendix.

0.5 Symbols and abbreviations

In the present study I shall use the following symbols and abbreviations. Most of them are introduced separately in the course of the study.

SYMBOLS:

/ /	underlying representation
[ ]	phonetic representation
*	violation of a constraint
!	fatal violation
☞	optimal candidate

☞	selected but not attested candidate
▒	irrelevance of the constraint to the fate of the candidate
│	crucial constraint ranking
⋮	no crucial constraint ranking

ABBREVIATIONS:

C	consonant
V	vowel
R	sonorant
O	obstruent
adj	adjective
adv	adverb
nom	nominative case
gen	genitive case
dat	dative case
acc	accusative case
instr	instrumental case
loc	locative case
voc	vocative case
sg	singular
pl	plural
ps	person
fut	future tense
pres	present tense
past	past tense
imp	imperative
masc	masculine
fem	feminine
neut	neuter
augm	augmentative
pej	pejorative
perf	perfect
imper	imperfect
comp	comparative
sup	superlative
OT	Optimality Theory
CT	Correspondence Theory
LC	Local Conjunction
PF	Phonetic Form
SF	Semantic Form
LE	Lexical Entry

1 CHAPTER ONE: Optimality

Optimality is one of the most attractive and pervasive concepts in present science. It appears to rank with economy and simplicity as a driving force in scientific inquiry. The attractiveness of this concept comes from the belief that optimality and optimizing processes afford us insight into reality. Further, it is often claimed that optimality unites various principles and functions which are often in mutual competition with each other, cf. 1.1.1., and which express contradictory axioms, cf. 1.3.3. In addition, it seems that optimality is also able to reflect the dynamics of the circumstances under which the object under examination exists in a most insightful way. From a formal point of view such a concept must contribute to the elegance of theories in a significant way.

As we will see below optimality is strongly favored by economists, physicists, chemists, biologists, linguists and many others, who are, voluntarily or not, involved in search of optimal solutions because most of them are intuitively aware of the correctness of optimality concept.

Assuming that optimality offers the right direction to pursue, we are approaching the central question. What is optimality? What does it mean that the subject under investigation is optimal? Are optimality concepts reflected in language? How are they used? These and other questions will be discussed in this chapter.

The chapter is organized as follows. Starting with the presentation of various definitions of *optimality*, I try to find the root of this term and its original application. Next, in 1.1.2, I provide some examples from various sciences in order to show how pervasive the optimality principle is in the scientific world. Nevertheless, the popularity of optimality does not exempt it from some inconvenient questions which I also intend to raise. Further, I discuss the incorporation of this principle into recent linguistic theories, focusing on Optimality Theory (OT), a kind of a revolution in phonological theory, cf. McCarthy and Prince (1993a), Prince and Smolensky (1993). In 1.2.1, I present the basic assumptions of OT approaching its latest outgrowth, i.e., Correspondence Theory in 1.2.2, cf. McCarthy and Prince (1995). Further, I review the main concepts of diachronic sound changes proposed in OT, which are based on models like 'Free-Variationist Model' (Bermúdez-Otero 1996 and others) and 'Promotion of the Optimal' (Green 1997). This comparison leads to my own proposal discussed in 1.3.3. Finally, in 1.4 I present main assumptions on Lexical Entry which I adopt for purposes of my dissertation. I also demonstrate the main OT characteristics of the phonological lexicon and show how it is optimized.

1.1 The concept of optimality

The flexibility of optimality that manifests itself inter alia by a wide range of subjects to which it refers, does not help to formulate its definition. Optimality principles are claimed to play a crucial role when similar subjects are in a mutual competition with each other, as for example in biology, and when subjects do not undergo selection at all, as for example in physics, cf. 1.1.2.

Another difficulty arising in defining optimality is caused by the dynamics of the circumstances under which optimality principles are found. The principles might be valid only on one level while other levels of the same subject under investigation undergo different principles. There are also cases attested in which several optimal solutions are available, not just one, cf. models presented in 1.1.1.

Examples which illustrate the flexibility of optimality can be multiplied but it suffices for our purposes to be aware of the difficulty in revealing the optimality per se, its complexity and applicability to various domains. Hence, there is no other way of defining optimality than pertinent investigation of individual subjects. Only the latter way will enable us to find a common denominator of optimality, provided it exists at all.

Before we discuss different models of optimality in detail, let us try to define the term *optimality*.

1.1.1 The term optimality

At the onset of this subsection we examine what terms such as *optimal* and *optimize* are intended to express when they are used in everyday life. Interestingly, they are not used in a homogenous way. The following examples from a German newspaper, 'Frankfurter Allgemeine Zeitung' (FAZ), illustrate the everyday use of the terms *optimal* and *optimize* in different contexts.

> "Die Gymnasien, [...], liefen zunehmend Gefahr, wichtige Elemente der heutigen Wirklichkeit nicht ausreichend abzubilden und die Schüler nicht optimal auf das Leben vorzubereiten." (FAZ, 18.3.1998:4)
> "High schools were in increasing danger of not sufficiently reflecting elements of present-day reality and of not optimally preparing students for life."

> "Dafür würde die Industrie ihre künftigen Fahrzeuge erheblich steifer und schwerer konstruieren müssen, damit zumindest Fahrer und Beifahrer optimal geschützt sind." (FAZ, 17.03.1998:3)
> "For this reason, industries would have to construct considerably stronger and heavier vehicles so that at least drivers and passengers will be optimally protected. "

> "Wir haben erkannt, daß wir unsere Planungs- und Arbeitsabläufe durch einen verbesserten Informationsfluß innerhalb des gesamten Unternehmens wesentlich optimieren können', sagt Eberhard Haag." (FAZ, 17.03.1998:29)
> "We have realized that our planning and working can be greatly optimized by a better flow of information throughout the whole company', says Eberhard Haag."

"Durch flexible Organisation von Arbeitszeit optimieren Unternehmen das Verhältnis von Arbeitskraft und nachgefragter Leistung." (FAZ, 17.03.1998:14)
"Through a flexible organization of work schedules businesses are optimizing the relationship between employees and requested services."

"Die nächste Herausforderung besteht darin, den hohen Service quasi zu automatisieren. Die Netzgeräte werden dahingehend entwickelt, daß sie mitteilen, wenn sie optimal nicht arbeiten, daß sie selbst Fehler diagnostizieren und sogar Empfehlungen für weitere Optimierungen ausgeben." (FAZ, 17.03.1998:14)
"The next challenge involves the virtual automatization of high performance. Mains adaptors are being developed to be able to announce when they are not functioning optimally, diagnose errors themselves and even make recommendations for further optimizations."

These citations show that by using *optimal (optimally)* we usually mean 'best', 'ideal' or 'perfect'. There is, however, an essential difference between *optimal (optimally)* and 'the best', which we sometimes seem to be not aware of, cf. discussion below. However, if we use the verb *optimize* we think of improving the existing situations under given circumstances. The common usage of the word *optimize* appears to approach the idea of optimality.

Before we discuss different optimality concepts let us examine how different words belonging to the *'optimal-family'* are characterized in dictionaries and encyclopedias.

In Webster's New College Dictionary (1995:769) *optimal* is defined as most desirable or favorable. *Optimum* on the other hand, is characterized in the following way:

"1. The best or most advantageous condition, degree, or amount;"
"2. The most favorable conditions for growth and reproduction."

In the same dictionary under *optimize* we find:

"1. To improve or develop as far as possible."
"2. To make the most effective use of <optimize our energy sources>"

The Compact Edition Of The Oxford English Dictionary (1987:2000) defines *optimal* as 'best' or 'most favorable'.

In The Collins Thesaurus (1984) no term such as *optimal* is available. Instead, one can find *optimum* with labels like 'best', 'choicest', 'flawless', 'highest', 'ideal', 'most favorable' or 'advantageous', 'optimal', 'peak', 'perfect', 'superlative.'

Before we proceed let us look to the etymology of the words belonging to the '*optimal*-family.' All *optimal* words are derived from English *optimism*. *Optimism* came into the English from the French *optimisme*. Its origin unsurprisingly comes from Latin *optimus*, where the root *optim* means 'best' and *-us* is an adjectival suffix. As far as the meaning of *optimism* is concerned, we find two definitions in Webster's New College Dictionary (1995:769). First, *optimism* is defined as a 'disposition to expect the best possible outcome or to emphasize the most positive aspects of a situation.' Second, from a philosophical point of view, optimism is (a) *the doctrine, asserted by Leibniz, that our world is the best of all possible worlds*, and (b) *the belief that the universe is* *improving and that good ultimately triumphs over the devil.* Leibniz' doctrine is referred to in the last chapter of this thesis.

Since the main subject of our interest is the optimality principles in scientific inquiry, in the following, some contexts in which optimality was firstly recognized are presented. The usage of the terms optimal, optimum, etc. dates back to the end of the nineteenth century when optimal principles were found in a wide range of phenomena. In (1) some contexts in which these words were used are presented according to The Compact Edition Of The Oxford English Dictionary (1987:2000).

(1) a. "There is probably an optimal[1] temperature, or one at which the process proceeds most rapidly or most favourably." Sibley 1890. Rep.Brit.Assoc.Nature 20 Nov. 70/1.

b. "This may be briefly designated as the optimum of food." 1879 tr. Semper's Anim. Life 43.

c. "An increase of the amount of carbonic acid present in the air, up to a certain limit, optimum, increases the evolution of oxygen." 1882 Vines tr. Sachs' Bot. 747.

d. "For the most rapid circulation of protoplasm there must be a definite amount of water, - the optimum. " 1885 Goodale Phys. Bot (1892) 210.

e. "The minimum or zero point is the point at which the performance is just possible; the optimum point, at which it is carried on with the greatest activity." 1885 Vines Lect. Physiol. Plant 276.

f. "Experience alone can tell us the optimum temperature to a given-kind of micro-organism." 1896 Allbutt's Syst. Med. 1.513.

From both sets of examples, i.e., those found in the present-day use and those from the end of the last century, we can conclude that optimality is understood in at least two different ways. First, we use *optimal* as 'the best'. Second, we understand optimal as 'most favorable under the given circumstances'.

According to mathematical models on optimality the meaning 'best' is only correct if there is only one function or one criterion that is subject to maximization or minimization. In this sense *optimal* means maximal or minimal which appears to be 'the best'. In (2) a formal description of maximization is provided.

(2) A formal description of maximization

maximization = max f(x) subject to $x \in X$

f( ) the objective function (criterion)

x the vector of control variables (attributes characterizing the option, alternative or choice)

X a set to which alternatives x are restricted

In this description just one function is involved. If we want to include such cases in the optimization concept, we have to conclude that maximal or minimal is optimal only under specific circumstances, i.e., in cases where there is only one criterion or one objective function which ought to be maximized. Minimization can similarly be defined. In this model both a criterion and a fixed set of decision alternatives are given.

1 Bold faces are mine (MR).

What remains to be identified is an optimal solution. Such cases are extremely rare in reality, if they occur at all. It is much rather the case that real-life situations are more complex and involve many criteria/functions. Therefore by using the word *optimal* we often do not mean 'the best' but rather 'the most favorable under given circumstances.'

In light of these observations the question arises as to how an optimal solution can be achieved if one considers all criteria/functions at play.

Mathematical models on optimality require that all participating functions be balanced or harmonized. Functions often conflict with each other, compete for their attention and assignments of importance. Such an optimization, however, is not to be understood in terms of a superfunctional aggregation, like the one presented in (4), since there would not be any detectable difference between optimization and a single objective maximization.

(3) Maximization

functions: f1(x), f2(x), ... fk(x)
a superfunctional aggregation: U(f1(x), f2(x), ... Fk(x))

What is hidden beyond balancing or harmonizing (optimizing) different functions? How should we understand optimization in this sense?

In order to keep all functions meaningful and functional it is proposed to treat them in the non-scalarized vector-sense, in mutual competition with each other. Since it is beyond the scope of this section to deal with highly complex mathematical models,[2] we limit ourselves to list different kinds of optimization in order to get more insight into the complexity and flexibility of this phenomenon. In the following, three different kinds of optimization concepts are presented, cf. Warner (1996:3772–3780). For purposes of clarification, each of them is exemplified by real-life cases. In the first two concepts, functions (criteria) are given a priori, as opposed to the last one in which functions (criteria) themselves are to be selected. This is schematically presented in (4).

(4)

Name of a model	Criteria	Alternatives
Multi-Objective Optimality	Yes	Yes
Optimal System Design	Yes	No
Pattern Matching Concept	No	No

In the first concept dubbed Multi-Objective Optimality, both a set of functions (f1, f2, etc) and a set X of alternatives are given. Thus, it is relatively easy to select an optimal solution from a given set X determined by given functions. We can compare this to selecting the cheapest (Min f1) and the safest (Max f2) vacation destination from a given list of places (X).

[2] Models on optimality from the mathematical point of view can be found e.g. in Warner (1996:3767–3781).

The next concept called Optimal System Design lacks a subset X of alternatives. What is given is a set of functions. Therefore, in the optimization process a subset X is to be designed. In reality we often try to construct an optimal system of decision alternatives designed with respect to existing criteria. This concept can be exemplified by designing an affordable list of places (X) which are the cheapest (Min f1) and the safest (Max f2) for vacations.

The last concept of optimality, Pattern Matching Concept, is the most complex one since neither functions nor a subset X of alternatives are given. The crucial difference between previous concepts and Pattern Matching Concept is that in the former the decision criteria were given, while in latter they have to be created. If we consider how human decision-making processes are carried out, we come to the conclusion that it is indeed not always the case that decision criteria are given. On the contrary "different criteria are being tried and applied, some are discarded, new ones added, until a proper balanced mix (...) of both quantitative and qualitative criteria is derived." (Warner 1996:3776). In other words, Pattern Matching Concept seems to mirror certain processes occurring in real life in the most adequate way. If we want to compare this concept to a real-life situation we would have to select necessary criteria (f1, f2, ... fk) such as safety, entertainment, education, cost, and design an affordable list of places (X) which assure the most satisfying or fulfilling (through Max f1 and Min f2) vacations. In order to select functions we need fundamental values which are broadly accepted and cannot be optimized. These values present a kind of criteria used for selecting functions. They are needed for avoiding infinite regress (criteria for selecting criteria for selecting criteria).

The models described above are the most popular concepts of optimality in scientific inquiry. In the following subsection we will consider how they are mirrored in various sciences.

1.1.2 Optimality in science

As mentioned in the introductory section, optimality principles belong to the most pervasive concepts in the scientific world. In the following some selected examples reflecting optimal solutions found in biology, social sciences, economics, and physics are presented.

Biology
In biology the optimality approach is widely used, e.g. for explaining behavioral strategies and natural selection. This line of reasoning goes back to the well-known Darwinian ideas, which maintain that only the candidate which best fits into the environment, survives. Present research bears out the explanatory power of optimality principles to such an extent that a new theory, Optimality Theory, was founded. It argues that natural selection ought to favor the 'fittest' organisms. Moreover, the fitness of organisms will always increase towards some maximum level. In Optimality Theory

of animal behavior all behaviors are claimed to ultimately have costs and benefits which can be translated into effects on fitness.[3]

Social science
If we analyze our behavior in various situations, we come to the conclusion that the primary operative principle is that of rationality, narrowly connected with an optimality concept. We strive to organize our time in the best way. If we plan something, we usually want to achieve it by the least effort and in the shortest possible time. This strategy is suggested to us by our ratio which includes prima facie an optimizing machinery, cf. Schoemaker (1991).

Further, if we are to make a decision, we automatically make a cost-benefit analysis and decide for the optimal solution. At this point the cornerstone idea of optimality shows up, namely, its flexibility and relativity. What is an optimal solution in a given situation often varies with different people. (We ourselves often make different decisions with respect to the same subject, based on many factors which cannot be involved in mathematical models 'producing' optimality.)

In decision-making not only does the cost/benefit ratio play an important role, other factors like individual preferences, the ability to discern the spectrum of options, and the ability to foresee possible consequences are also crucial. We presumably enhance our decisions by learning from the past (another argument for optimality!), which is clearly a very individual factor. In sum, there exists obviously more than a single form of optimality with respect to human behavior, decision making, judgment, etc. Therefore, it is safe to conclude that we optimize, trying to do our best under given circumstances, but the spectrum of optimal choices is a multi-choice set.

Economics
We can also hardly imagine economics functioning without optimality principles. Almost every step in economics is calculated so as to achieve optimal solutions. The whole business organization reflects a mathematical model which – roughly speaking – is presumed to maximize its profits by minimizing costs, effort, etc. In this model also risk components are encountered.

Also worth stressing is the fact that economics abounds in examples in which optimal solutions are found only on one level (mostly on the micro-level) of the subject or situation, but not on the macro-level. In other words, local optima seem to be much more plausible than those of global optimality, which are rather a kind of utopia. This observation is strongly confirmed in other sciences.

Physics
One of the well-known optimality examples in physics is the principle of least time founded by Pierre Fermat (1601–1665). This principle roughly says that light, when passing from air to water, travels the quickest route which is invariably the minimum distance.

---

[3] The reader who is interested in Optimality Theory of animal behavior may obtain more information under the following web address: http://www.soton.ac.uk/~kpa/stu/BY311/1optim.html .

We will not go into detail here but an explicit comment on this principle can be found in Feynman et al. (1964). What we can notice is that this kind of optimality crucially differs from that found in biology or social sciences. In nonliving systems, as opposed to living ones, no competition or selection is involved. In other words, in nonliving systems we can merely contend that we are not able to imagine any other better solution. In order to differentiate between living and nonliving systems with respect to optimality, we should differentiate between *optimization* and *optimum*. The former seems to refer to a process of teleological nature, while the latter can be viewed as a state which cannot be optimized any more because the final goal has been achieved. In the case of optimization the subject is not given a priori but undergoes selection and can be further optimized.

As we conclude from the examples presented above, optimality principles are found in different branches of science. In many of them they play a pivotal role. Optimality can be seen as a kind of metastrategy applied to environments which vary in their complexity and degrees of freedom. It can also be regarded as a kind of a heuristic, albeit some doubt may still surround this claim.

Although the arguments in favor of optimality seem to be very convincing, we cannot forget that reality is a nexus between our mind and a presumed outside reality. Therefore, it is almost impossible to understand optimality independently of its investigator, who as a human being is apt to optimize. This observation leads to some relevant questions. Does optimality help us to understand the real nature of the subjects in question? Does not the optimality heuristic create an illusion of understanding by describing rather than explaining? Answers to these questions are, by no means, easy. And they might not be optimistic considering the fact that we cannot be sure that we fully know the subject and the circumstances under which the subject is investigated. Our optimal solutions proposed today could be seen as merely satisfactory or – even worse – unsatisfactory tomorrow. On the other hand, this is the main characteristic of scientific progress. And scientific progress is most probably possible only to a certain extent if one considers the fact that human beings cannot objectively perceive the surrounding world (cf. principles of quantum mechanics). Our sense-awareness obtains just one of several possible representations of outside reality and with our visual abilities we are far from attending the whole visual field, cf. Schoemaker (1991:208), etc. This leads to the following question that will be not answered: How can we prove that a given solution is really an optimal one and not suboptimal or simply satisfactory?

With all the problems and questions posited so far, I do not intend to deny the importance of optimality in scientific inquiry. What I want to stress is that the optimality game is a difficult one to play with.

In light of the facts presented above, one might posit a plausible question whether we need optimality at all. Again, this question cannot be completely answered. But we should be at least aware how hard it is to get rid of optimality and how hard it is to falsify it. More importantly, we do not have a serious substitute for it thus far. And it is still better to propose an elegant theory than another one, at least we and Ockham think so ...

1.1.3 Optimality in language[4]

Considering multiple-function optimality approaches presented in 1.1.1, one comes to the conclusion that other principles can be easily translated into optimality concepts by postulating functions like, e.g., minimizing the number of elements, minimizing the number of operations, minimizing redundant elements, etc., that is, by formulating those principles in a more concrete way. Such a homogeneous concept would essentially contribute to the elegance of the theory – a highly desirable feature of any good theory – by keeping a variety of factors involved.

This line of reasoning is broadly pursued in linguistics in recent linguistic research. Let us consider concrete examples.

In the Minimalist Program (Chomsky 1993 and 1995), as the name already indicates, a considerable number of examples illustrating different kinds of reductions can be found. One of them is a crucial reduction of levels of representation. In Government and Binding Theory (GB) (Chomsky 1981) four levels of representation are assumed, viz. Deep Structure (D-Structure), Surface Structure (S-Structure), Phonetic Form (PF) and Logical Form (LF). Further investigations, cf. Minimalist Program, have shown that just two levels of representation are necessary, namely PF, an abstract representation of the sound, and LF, an abstract representation of the meaning, because these two are the only levels of representation related to external systems, the articulatory-perceptual (A-P) and the conceptual-intentional (C-I), respectively. They have external motivation and therefore are ineliminable.

The S-Structure assumed in GB is a level linking each of the other levels, viz. D-Structure, PF and LF. Its properties, however, can be reduced to independent conditions holding for PF and LF representations. Therefore, S-Structure representation can be eliminated and replaced by an optional 'Spell-out' rule which may apply at any point of the derivation splitting off phonological information from the structure derived up to this point. The elimination of D-Structure results in accomplishing derivation via the lexicon and two operations, Merge and Move. The former, applying to two objects, α and β, creates a new object K, and the latter takes a phrase constructed as a tree and concate-nates it with the tree.

Minimalist Program illuminates central notions of optimality which are also found in other theories such as Optimality Theory (OT) presented below, namely, competition and selection of an optimal candidate in terms of an optimal derivation (at this intermediate step of derivation) which is constrained by various economy conditions.

As already mentioned, one of central tenets of Optimality Theory, cf. McCarthy and Prince (1993a), Prince and Smolensky (1993), which makes it highly 'optimal' is its assumption about competition and selection of the optimal candidate. The candidate which fares on the constraints in the best way, i.e., violates them minimally, is selected as an optimal one, cf. 1.2 for details. Since I wish to discuss Optimality Theory in the next subsection, I limit myself here to presenting one example which illustrates the optimization strive of OT in phonology. (Optimality Theory has also been adopted for

---

[4] Some ideas presented here can be also found in Błaszczak and Rochoń (1998).

syntactic and morphological analyses, cf. e.g. Grimshaw (1994), Pesetsky (1997), Russell (1997), Speas (1997)).

In Correspondence Theory (McCarthy and Prince 1995), a subtheory of Optimality Theory, faithfulness constraints such as PARSE and FILL are replaced by MAX and DEP. MAX and DEP express correspondence between two related strings. Hence, not only input-output but also output-output relations, i.e. relations between morphologically related words, or relations between prosodic heads can be evaluated by MAX and DEP. In other words, the narrow domain of application of FILL and PARSE is abandoned and some domain-specific constraints are reduced to two general constraints which capture general relations but still leave room for specific differences. For other consequences of this change see also 1.2.2.

The simplicity (and therefore optimality) trend of present-day linguistics is clearly recognizable in another phonological theory, namely, Radical cv Phonology (van der Hulst 1996). This is a theory of phonological categories at the segmental and syllabic level, i.e., phonological features (e.g., [continuant], [round]) and syllabic constituents (e.g., onset, nucleus). While in most other frameworks these categories have been postulated as theoretical primes, in Radical cv Phonology both can be derived from two primitives such as V and C that are claimed to be the most basic atoms. The cost of such a drastic reduction is a considerably larger set of operations and principles, e.g. a head-dependency relation.

The examples presented above may suffice to illustrate the concept of optimality and optimization in present linguistic research, although many other examples could be presented here as well, e.g., the lexicon organization from a minimalist point of view proposed in Bierwisch (1996).

1.2 Optimality Theory

Optimality Theory (Prince and Smolensky 1993, McCarthy and Prince 1993a) is undoubtedly one of the most pervasive linguistic theories of the 1990s. This radical departure from rule-based analyses has its origin in phonology, where rules are replaced by constraints that evaluate surface representations. In standard generative phonology, rule ordering allows rules and generalizations to be postulated which can hold at 'abstract' stages in the derivation that do not necessarily correspond to the surface. The output of one rule may be changed by subsequent rules and the generalizations made earlier must be abandoned.

Since Optimality Theory does not postulate intermediate stages, such unnecessary generalizations are systematically avoided. Instead, constraints on well-formed representations are not claimed to be true on a representational level. On the contrary, constraints are violable and therefore they do not have to be surface-true. In light of the fact that constraints are highly conflicting and make contrary claims about the well-formedness of most representations, their violability seems to be a very plausible assumption, for details cf. 1.2.1.

Not surprisingly, this new approach to phonological explanation has opened vast possibilities of improved analyses for various phenomena. The importance of this theory for linguistic explanations has been recognized and adopted by other linguistic disciplines such as morphology and syntax, cf. Archangeli and Langendoen (1997) and the references therein.

1.2.1 Central tenets of Optimality Theory

The goal of this section is neither to describe Optimality Theory in every detail nor to demonstrate its superiority over a rule-based phonology. The interested reader is advised to download the electronic data base of Rutgers Optimality Archive (ROA)[5] from the Internet, where various papers in OT are available. In the following only core ideas of OT relevant for this study as well as the necessary conventions used in subsequent analyses are presented. Furthermore, the relationship between phonological activity and markedness in OT is examined. Finally, the nature of input in OT is discussed.

One of the most attractive features of Optimality Theory is the way it deals with universal and language specific requirements imposed on every linguistic theory. OT postulates a set of constraints (CON), which is assumed to be part of Universal Grammar (UG). Hence, these constraints must be highly general and express a universal well-formedness along all linguistically relevant dimensions. Since the ranking of constraints in various languages is different, various grammars in the languages of the world are attested.

Basically, two types of constraints have been assumed, namely, *markedness constraints*, generally prohibiting marked structures, and *faithfulness constraints*, which militate against deviations from input forms. We will discuss these constraints in more detail below. Apart from markedness and faithfulness constraints, there are also so-called hard constraints which are never violated. Since they are not interesting for phonological analyses, they are generally excluded in the subsequent analyses.

Another important assumption of OT is that constraints are violable. This is a crucial difference between Optimality Theory and other constraint-based approaches which require certain strategies in order to satisfy constraints, cf. Constraint and Repair Theory (Paradis (1988)). Violation in OT is *minimal*, i.e., the candidate which best satisfies a strict hierarchy of constraints is chosen as optimal. It incurs the fewest violations in the strict domination sense, i.e. the higher a constraint is, the more selective power it has. Therefore, multiple violations of a lower ranked constraint cannot override a single violation of a higher ranked constraint.

Another important idea of OT is constraint interaction. Since constraints refer to many different linguistic dimensions, they are often in conflict with each other. It is often the case that outputs cannot fulfill different phonotactic requirements and be faithful to the input at the same time. In order to resolve different types of conflicts, constraints are crucially ranked with respect to each other.

---

[5] The ROA address is: http://ruccs.rutgers.edu/roa.html

Evaluation of linguistic outputs is conventionally presented in form of a tableau, as shown in (5).

(5)

	Input	A	B	C	D	..
	$cand_1$		*!			
☞	$cand_2$				*	
	$cand_3$			*!		

A, B, C	constraints
*	violation of a constraint
!	fatal violation
☞	optimal candidate
(shaded cell)	irrelevance of the constraint to the fate of the candidate

In the tableau presented in (5) three candidates compete. The first one is excluded because of a violation of the high-ranked constraint B. The candidates worth considering are $cand_2$ and $cand_3$ because both of them satisfy the high-ranking constraints A and B. Since $cand_2$ fares better on the next constraint in the ranking, the constraint C, it is selected as the optimal output.

The selection of the optimal candidate is indicated by the pointing hand '☞'. When a constraint is violated, an asterisk (*) appears in the appropriate cell. A fatal violation is indicated by an exclamation mark '!'. This is the point where the candidate in question loses against other more successful candidates. A shaded cell indicates the irrelevance of the constraint to the fate of the candidate. After the fatal violation the loser's cells are shaded; the winner's cells are shaded when the selection is carried out.

The scheme presented in (6) illustrates how the machinery of OT works. Apart from the constraint set (CON), there are two functions, Gen and Eval, which play an important role in OT. Taking input as a basis, Gen produces a potentially infinite set of output candidates. The candidates produced by Gen are simultaneously evaluated on the basis of a language-specific ranking by another function called Eval. Eval selects an optimal candidate from the set of possible candidates.

(6)

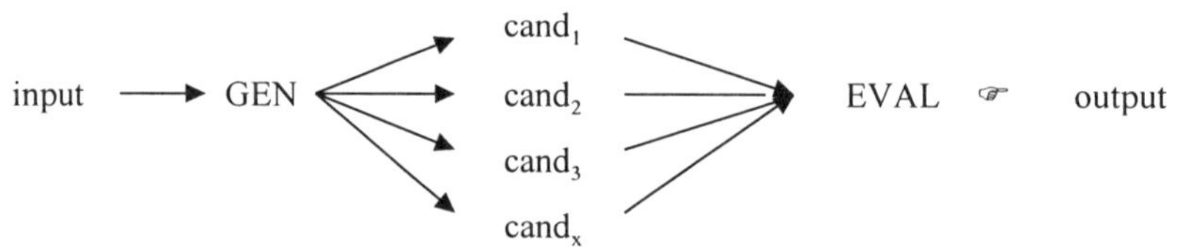

Best-satisfaction of the constraint hierarchy is computed over the whole candidate set. As stated above, the optimal output, even though it may contain violations, still satisfies the ranking in the best way because it fares better on higher-ranked constraints than its contestants.

Originally, three principles underlay Gen. They are presented in (7).

(7) Underlying principles of Gen (cf. McCarthy and Prince (1993a:20, 1993b:88f.)

a. Freedom of Analysis
"Any amount of structure may be posited."

b. Containment
"No element may be literally removed from the input form. The input is thus contained in every candidate form."

c. Consistency of Exponence
"No changes in the exponence of a phonologically-specified morpheme are permitted."

According to Containment, Gen can only add structure not already present in the input but not remove it. Thus, the deleted segments, while not visible in the output form, are nonetheless still present. This view has been considerably modified in Correspondence Theory, cf. 1.2.2.

In sum, the core principles of OT are summarized in the following way:

(8) Principles of OT (McCarthy and Prince 1993a:5)

(i) *Violability*
Constraints are violable; but violation is minimal.

(ii) *Ranking*
Constraints are ranked on a language-particular basis; the notion of minimal violation (or best-satisfaction) is defined in terms of ranking.

(iii) *Inclusiveness*
The candidate analyses, which are evaluated by the constraint hierarchy, are admitted by very general considerations of structural well-formedness; there are no specific rules or repair strategies with specific structural descriptions or structural changes or with connections to specific constraints.

(iv) *Parallelism*
Best-satisfaction of the constraint hierarchy is computed over the whole hierarchy and the whole candidate set.

Since the idea of markedness plays a central role in OT and is also crucial to the present study, a few important remarks concerning this notion are in order.

As mentioned earlier, constraints, being universal, are claimed to express markedness statements. In order to establish markedness statements we need criteria which determine the selection of marked structures or elements. In the following, some of them, which are independent of OT assumptions, are listed.

One of the most important criteria traditionally refers to factorial typology. Structures are considered to be marked if they are found less frequently in inventories across languages, as opposed to unmarked structures, which are present in nearly every language. There are several reasons why certain structures are consistently absent in contrast to others, e.g., the complexity of structures along different dimensions (production, comprehension, cognitive functions, etc.). Another markedness criterion pertains to implicational universals, according to which the presence of a marked segment implies the presence of its unmarked counterpart, e.g., the presence of palatalized labials like [p^j b^j] implies the presence of plain ones, i.e. [p b] in the same inventory. Implications of several types can be found not only on the segmental level but also in other domains. Furthermore, a marked structure crucially differs from an unmarked one with respect to the order of acquisition, i.e., children acquire marked structures considerably later than unmarked ones. From a diachronic point of view, a marked segment or structure is lost earlier than an unmarked one, assuming the same circumstances, cf. Jakobson (1971).[6]

From all the criteria mentioned above, we can correctly draw the conclusion that marked structures are disfavored in inventories across languages. Paradoxically, they are widely present in inventories of languages. In light of this fact the question arises as to how marked structures are dealt with in Optimality Theory, in which constraints are postulated which militate against markedness.

As mentioned above, constraints can be violated, allowing for marked structures. Put differently, marked structures are those which violate structural constraints. For example, secondarily palatalized sounds are attested in many languages and they violate constraints militating against articulatorily complex sounds, cf. 4.2.

Markedness constraints can be 'context-free', prohibiting any occurrence of marked structures (e.g. *No palatalized coronals*) or they can be contingent upon the context, referring to a particular position or sequence (*No palatalized coronals in coda position*). Because of violations, the marked structures are also visible to the phonology of a given language, as opposed to unmarked structures which – not being subject to constraints – are consequently invisible to phonology despite their presence. Unmarkedness can also be expressed in terms of 'harmony'. Unmarked segments are more harmonic[7] than marked ones. In this sense, more harmonic elements are less likely to undergo phonological processes, cf. Smolensky (1993) for details. Moreover, the (un)markedness of structures is directly encoded in a ranking of constraints. The higher ranked constraints, which are rarely violated, reveal the dimensions along which the language is unmarked. The lower ranked constraints, being often violated, indicate the ways in which the language shows its markedness.

Finally, let us consider the notions of input and underlying representation. In the following, we focus on the original understanding of input and underlying representation, cf. Prince and Smolensky (1993), which I adopt for purposes of my study.

---

[6] For the concept of markedness cf. also Trubetzkoy (1931), Chomsky and Halle (1968), Stampe (1972), Bailey (1973), Dressler (1982), (1985), Mayerthaler (1981), Dressler, Mayerthaler, Panagl, Wurzel (1987), Vennemann (1983), (1988a), Wurzel (1984),(1998).

[7] *Harmonic* cannot be equated with *well-formed* because the former is gradient and the latter binary.

In most OT studies, a traditional view concerning underlying representation is assumed, i.e., each morpheme has an underlying representation in the lexicon. The representation contains only contrastive (unpredictable) properties occurring in the morpheme. Properties which are predictable are not present in underlying representations.

In OT, all underlying representations are derived from surface forms by principles of grammar. And this is a crucial assumption because language-particular underlying forms can be stated without any restrictions on input.[8] Potentially, inputs are as infinite as the candidate set which increases the range of possible variations. This phenomenon is known as Richness of the Base, cf. Prince and Smolensky (1993:§8), or Freedom of the Input (FOTI). As far as the content of the input is concerned, it has been assumed that some kind of phonological information creates the input for each morpheme.

OT provides a formal mechanism for deriving the underlying representation of morphemes. As mentioned above, one of the main ideas of OT is that a language-particular grammar is a result of a particular ranking of the universal constraints. Hence, a language-learner has to 'deduce' from surface representations how the constraints are ranked. If some property is contrastive, the language-learner 'deduces' that this property is designed in the underlying representation. For example, plain and palatalized labials in pairs like [p]asek 'belt' nom.sg. and [p']asek 'sand' nom.sg. provide evidence that a faithfulness constraint demanding a faithful parse of palatalized labials is ranked above a markedness constraint prohibiting palatalized labials: Faith [Lab, PAL] >> *[Lab, PAL]. If some phonological property is predictable it cannot be fixed in the underlying representation because predictable properties follow from markedness and not from faithfulness constraints. For example, in Polish a velar plosive is always palatalized when it is followed by i ([k'i], [g'i]). This is due to a high-ranking constraint demanding velars to be palatalized when they are followed by a vowel /i/. This constraint is ranked above the faithfulness constraint prohibiting plain velars followed by i (*ki>>Faith(ki)). Although it is predictable that velars are palatalized in a particular position, several inputs may converge on the optimal output. Hence, we encounter a serious problem. How can we decide which input is the appropriate one considering the fact that it is possible to construct multiple inputs which converge on the same single output?

The answer is provided by an algorithm called Lexicon Optimization, cf. Prince and Smolensky (1993), and Itô, Mester and Padgett (1995), which I shall discuss in detail in 1.4.3. This algorithm evaluates the mapping between the winning output and each competing input. The pair which incurs the fewest violations is the optimal one, and the desired input of the optimal mapping can be selected. Lexicon Optimization is also very important in the case of diachronic development, where changes of underlying forms have to be accounted for, cf. also 4.1.5.

8 Notice that there is a crucial diference between inputs and underlying forms.

1.2.2 Correspondence Theory

Correspondence Theory (McCarthy and Prince 1995) is a subtheory of Optimality Theory which was originally devised to account for facts from reduplication in various languages. The theory posits unified identity relations between input-output as well as a base and its reduplicant with faithfulness constraints that account for both kinds of correspondence. Further, the correspondence relation was recognized between independent but phonologically related words, e.g. in truncation, affixation, compounding and other types of word formation. Since this kind of correspondence refers to a relation between two 'surface' forms, as is the case of a base-reduplicant relation, constraints which are responsible for this identity are called Output-Output (O-O) correspondence constraints, and the relation between two words Output-Output correspondence, respectively.

Hence, the main difference between IO- and OO-correspondence is that the former relates two parts of a single word, while the latter refers to two separate output words. But the relation per se remains the same. Formally, all kinds of correspondence can be captured by the definition presented in (9).

(9)

Correspondence (cf. McCarthy and Prince 1995:262)
Given two strings S_1 and S_2, correspondence is a relation $\Re$ from the elements of S_1 to those of S_2. Elements $\alpha \in S_1$ and $\beta \in S_2$ are referred to as correspondents of one another when $\alpha \Re \beta$.

Since in my analyses IO- and OO-Correspondence play an important role, I illustrate both identity relations with two selected examples. In (10) there is an IO-Correspondence between the input /mak/ 'poppy-seed' nom.sg. (the underlying representation in a traditional sense) and the output [mak]. The same relation occurs between /mak+u/ 'poppy-seed' gen.sg. and [maku] and therefore it is evaluated by IO-faithfulness constraints. Further, between the two output forms [mak] and [maku] a kind of a faithfulness relation exists since both are morphologically related. This is evidenced by the fact that both words contain the root with the underlying representation /mak/ and are derived by grammar of Polish. Evidently, the OO-constraints that evaluate this relation express a traditional concept of 'paradigm leveling' according to which words belonging to the same paradigm display the same form, cf. Kenstowicz and Kissberth (1979: 199).[9]

(10)

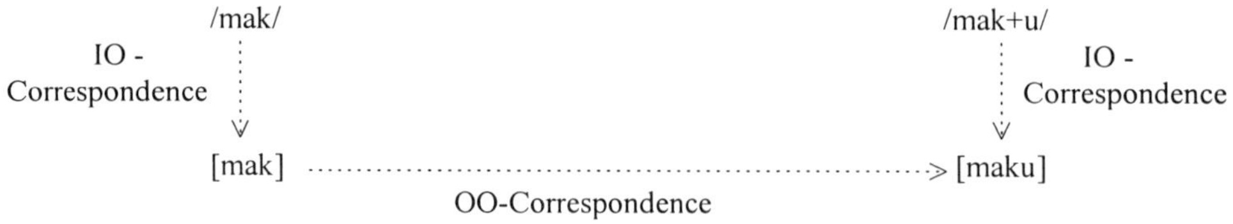

[9] For details see 4.1.5.

In correspondence between segments two constraint families play a leading role, viz. MAX, which prohibits phonological deletion and DEP which militates against epenthesis. Both approximate the function of PARSE and FILL in the original version of OT, respectively, cf. Prince and Smolensky (1993). This approximation, however, should be understood very carefully, i.e., in the PARSE/FILL model deletion of segments is understood as a non-parsing. Hence, the unparsed segment is still available to the phonology for constraint enforcement, even if unpronounced. PARSE militates against such segments. FILL militates against empty prosodic nodes posited by GEN, since the inserted segment, under the assumption that no segments can be literally added by GEN, must consist of an empty node only. Its phonetic content is determined by principles of 'phonetics' which are independent of the system of constraints. As expected, there are some questions and problems which arise by assuming the PARSE/FILL model. First, featural composition of epenthetic segments has to be subject to constraints that embody markedness. Second, GEN has to be able to posit full segments, no just empty nodes, in order to deal with reduplicative phonology. Further, violations in the featural domain cannot be expressed by means of PARSE/FILL constraints since they refer to segments and not to features.

The Correspondence Model, in which MAX and DEP are involved, is considerably simplified and has more explanatory power. First of all, deleted segments are present in the input but not in the output and consequently no empty nodes or unparsed elements are found in the output. The constraint MAX prohibits deleted segments. Inserted elements are present in the output and they do not have correspondents in the input since DEP militates against them. Furthermore, inserted segments are phonologically active and undergo evaluation by constraints because their insertion is literal. Features can be treated in a similar way.

The correspondence parallels between input and output, base-reduplicant, and other related words can be captured by the same kinds of constraints. Moreover, the problems with respect to GEN mentioned above do not exist any more. Superfluous notions, such as Consistency of Exponence, cf. (7)c, can be abandoned.

As we can conclude from the examples presented above, the fact that two elements correspond does not guarantee identity between them. We need various faithfulness constraints which demand complete correspondence between strings. In the following such constraint families are presented.

The general schema of MAX Constraint Family and its specific instantiation for input-output relations are shown in (11), cf. McCarthy and Prince (1995: 264).

(11)

General Schema
Every segment of S_1 has a correspondent in S_2.

Specific Instantiations
MAX-IO
Every segment of the input has a correspondent in the output.

The DEP Constraint Family which prohibits phonological epenthesis is presented in (12).

(12)

General Schema
Every segment of S_2 has a correspondent in S_1.
(S_2 is 'dependent on' S_1.)

Specific Instantiations
DEP-IO
Every segment of the output has a correspondent in the input.

Correspondence relations are found not only between segments but also between features. Therefore another constraint family is required in order to account for the identity relations between features. This family is called IDENT(F) and demands correspondent segments to be featurally identical to one another. Its general schema and specific instantiation are shown in (13), cf. McCarthy and Prince (1995: 264).

(13)

General Schema
Let α be a segment in S_1 and β be any correspondent of α in S_2.
If α is [γF], then β is [γF].
Correspondent segments agree in the value for feature F.

Specific Instantiations
IDENT-IO(F)
Output correspondents of an input [γF] segments are also [γF].

There are also other constraints which express different aspects of the correspondence relation than those presented above. Since they will generally not be referred to in the present study, they will only be mentioned here briefly. For example, the function of a constraint I-CONTIG can be abbreviated as 'No Skipping' and O-CONTIG is interpreted as 'No Intrusion.' Both constraints belong to CONTIGUITY family. Further, LINEARITY is understood as 'No Metathesis,' UNIFORMITY as 'No Coalescence' and INTEGRITY as 'No Breaking.' For the application of these constraints, see McCarthy and Prince (1995).

In Correspondence Theory surface patterns of related words can be predicted by a ranking of OO-Identity, IO-Faithfulness, and markedness constraints. OO-Identity constraints require identity of outputs in words in paradigms in the same way that IO-Faithfulness constraints demand identity in input-output pairs or BR-Identity constraints require identity between a base and its reduplicant. By means of OO-Identity constraints intermediate stages in word formation are eliminated and identity of morphologically-related words is directly evaluated, cf. Benua (1997:5). The Trans-derivational Correspondence Theory proposed by Benua (1997) is related to earlier studies in which the concept of analogy was used, cf. Schuchardt (1885), Sturtevant (1907), Hermann (1929), Harris (1973), Hock (1973), Hooper (1976).

In the following, various constraint interactions examining this correspondence will be presented and exemplified.

The interaction between OO-Identity, IO-Faithfulness and markedness constraints (Phono-Constraints) can result in three different patterns expressing three kinds of phonological application between two paradigmatically related words, viz. Underapplication, Overapplication,[10] and Normal Application.

The first pattern, Underapplication, occurs when the phonological process is conditioned but fails to apply. OO-Identity constraints on a derivational output-output relation take precedence over markedness requirements or faithfulness to the underlying form.

In the following, I illustrate on the basis of diachronic data from Polish a case of Underapplication, in which OO-Identity constraints demanding two related words to be identical take precedence over markedness requirements and faithfulness to the underlying form. This is schematically shown in (14) where an output-output relation is found between *Blizka* 'Blizk' a proper name of a town in gen.sg. and *Blizk* nom.sg.

(14)

/blizk+a/ /blizek/

IO-Correspondence ↓

[blisk+a] ⟶ [blisk]

OO-Correspondence

The tableau in (15) illustrates how the interaction of constraints leads to the emergence of *Blisk*. The Phono-Constraint that plays an important role in this process is *CC]$_\sigma$, which prohibits complex codas. The high-ranking constraints DEP-OO and MAX-OO demand a faithfulness relation between the genitive and the nominative form. Since the basis for evaluation is constituted by a root in the genitive case, *Blisk*, only one candidate in (15) does not violate DEP-OO and MAX-OO. This is exactly the candidate *Blisk* that displays a complex coda.[11]

(15)

Blizk	DEP-OO	MAX-OO	*CC]$_\sigma$	DEP-IO	MAX-IO
☞ Blisk			*		*
Blizek	*!				
Blis		*!			*

The example in (15) illustrates the effect of the precedence of OO-Identity over a markedness constraint prohibiting complex codas and input-output faithfulness con-

[10] The terms Under- and Overapplication come from Wilbur (1973).

[11] I do not consider voicing assimilations here, cf. 3.3.1.

straints. The Phono-Constraint $*CC]_\sigma$ remains invisible in the sense that it does not have influence on the optimal candidate that emerges with its complex coda. The crucial ranking accounting for this Underapplication is presented in (16).

(16)

DEP-OO, MAX-OO >>$*CC]_\sigma$ >> DEP-IO, MAX-IO

The ranking in (16) accounts for morphologically related words that show irregular phonology in order to preserve their faithfulness to source bases. Examples similar to these will be provided in the course of this study.

The second pattern, Overapplication, is found in cases in which a phonological process applies but is not conditioned. For example, in Madurese nasality spreads from primary nasal consonants onto following vocoids. In reduplicated words, however, the prefixed reduplicant is nasalized, although it is not preceded by a nasal. Consider examples shown in (17) cf. McCarthy and Prince (1995:282).

(17) Nasalization and Reduplication in Madurese

/neat/	ỹãt-nẽỹãt	'intentions'
/moa/	w̃ã-mõw̃ã	'faces'

The examples in (17) show that nasal spreading overapplies since it operates outside its domain. There is no independent word in Madurese which could have the form *ỹãt* or *w̃ã*. The existence of nasalized vocoids in these words is possible due to the reduplication effect: a constraint requiring featural identity in nasality between a base and its copy (IDENT-BR(nas)) has to be high-ranked. Similarly, a constraint militating against the sequence [+nas][-nas, +vocalic], i.e. $*NV_{oral}$, should be high-ranked and additionally it cannot be crucially ranked with respect to IDENT-BR(nas), otherwise its influence on the reduplicant would be blocked. The tableau presented in (18) illustrates the selection of the optimal candidate, cf. McCarthy and Prince (1995:283). Note that $*V_{nas}$, which militates against nasal vowels, and $IDENT\text{-}IO_{(nas)}$, which demands faithfulness between input and output with respect to [nasal], do not have influence on the selection of the optimal candidate.

(18)

/RED+neat/	IDENT-BR $_{(nas)}$	$*NV_{oral}$	$*V_{nas}$	IDENT-IO $_{(nas)}$
☞ ỹãt-nẽỹãt			*****	**
yat-nẽyat		*!	*	*
yat-nẽỹãt	*!		***	**

The tableau in (18) shows that in the case of Overapplication both IDENT-BR and the markedness constraint $*NV_{oral}$ have to be higher ranked than IDENT-IO. In the same vein, Overapplication attested in various output-output related words is accounted for if OO-Identity constraints and Phono-Constraints are ranked above IO-Faith constraints.

The third pattern, Normal Application, accounts for cases in which a phonological process always applies when it is properly conditioned. Normal Application indicates disruption between identity of related words, i.e., a phonological process applies in one word where it is properly conditioned but not in its correspondent word. In this case a Phono-Constraint takes precedence over OO-Identity (or IDENT-BR) and IO-Faith constraints. The Normal Application is exemplified by the third candidate in (18), i.e. yat-nẽỹãt. The nasal vocoids are not present in the reduplicant since there is no trigger of [nasal]. This candidate would be selected as optimal if $*V_{nas}$ were ranked above $\text{IDENT-BR}_{(nas)}$, cf. McCarthy and Prince (1995:284).

In sum, different constraint rankings are responsible for a variety of application of phonological processes. They are shown in (19), cf. Benua (1997:43).

(19)

a. Overapplication
OO-Identity, Phono-Constraint>>IO-Faith
b. Underapplication
OO-Identity>>Phono-Constraint>>IO-Faith
c. Normal Application
Phono-Constraint>> OO Identity, IO-Faith

1.2.3 Generalized Alignment

Generalized Alignment (McCarthy and Prince 1993b) is a subtheory of OT. The essence of Alignment is the idea that all the diverse ways in which constituents may share the edge of a phonological or morphological constituent can be captured under a single family of well-formedness constraints. In other words, general combinations of any pair of prosodic or morphological constituents are evaluated by so-called Alignment constraints. A general schema for Align is demonstrated in (20).

(20)

Generalized Alignment (McCarthy and Prince (1993b:80))
Align (Cat1, Edge1, Cat2, Edge2) $=_{def}$
$\forall$ Cat1 $\exists$ Cat2 such that Edge1 of Cat1 and Edge2 of Cat2 coincide.

Where
Cat1, Cat2 $\in$ PCat $\cup$ GCat
Edge1 and Edge2 $\in$ {Right, Left}

In (21) below, Alignment[12] is exemplified by a constraint which demands that the right edge of a stem coincide with the right edge of a final syllable-edge.

[12] Note that Align is not a constraint. This is a kind of schema for creating constraints which directly follows from the definition.

(21)

Align (Stem, R, σ, R)
Align $]_{STEM} =]_{\sigma}$
Every final stem-edge matches to a final syllable-edge.

Note that according to the definition of Generalized Alignment, for all instances of Category 1 there exists some instances of Category 2. Hence, Align (Stem, R, σ, R) quantifies universally over stems but existentially over syllables. It requires every final stem-edge to match with a final syllable-edge. Reversing the arguments, i.e. (σ, R, Stem, R), would lead to a different result, because the constraint would demand every final syllable edge to coincide with a final stem edge.

Alignment constraints are similar to other constraints in the sense that they are violable. They allow, however, gradient violation. In (22) the constraint Align (Stem, R, Ft, R) is formally stated and exemplified by a stem consisting of six syllables. (The foot consists of two syllables and is shown in parentheses).

(22)

Align (Stem, R, Ft, R): the right edge of every stem coincides with a right edge of a foot.

$[\sigma\sigma\sigma\sigma\sigma\sigma]_{STEM}$	Align (PrWd, R, Ft, R)
$[\sigma(\sigma\sigma)(\sigma\sigma)\sigma]_{STEM}$	*!
$[(\sigma\sigma)(\sigma\sigma)\sigma\sigma]_{STEM}$	*!*
☞ $[(\sigma\sigma)(\sigma\sigma)(\sigma\sigma)]_{STEM}$	

The tableau in (22) shows that the first candidate is more harmonic than the second in terms of satisfying Align (Stem, R, Ft, R). This is because there is just one intervening syllable between the right edge of a foot and the right edge of a stem rather than two, as in the second candidate. The winner of the contest is, however, the third candidate whose right edge of the stem perfectly corresponds to the right edge of a foot.

In summary, the discussion above shows how Generalized Alignment is able to express the mutual interaction of prosodic and morphological constituents in linguistic structures. Examples of such interaction will be also given in the further part of the study.

1.2.4 Local Conjunction

Since the idea of Local Conjunction (LC) will also be used in the following chapters of this study, this subsection is devoted to introducing the underlying assumptions of LC.

In Optimality Theory, phonological representations are usually expressed by the ranking of single constraints, e.g., *Lab>>Ident(Lab). Further investigations, however, have argued that there are cases in which single constraints do not suffice to account for the data. Therefore, the possibility of conjoining two (and more) single constraints has been taken into consideration. Such conjoined constraints are called a Local Conjunction, cf. Smolensky (1993), (1997) Alderete (1997), Fukazawa and Miglio (1996), Hewitt and Crowhurst (1995), Kirchner (1996), £ubowicz (1998) and McCarthy (1996).

Formally, Local Conjunction is constituted by a universal operator '&' which takes at least two arguments (A, B) within a domain D (segment, adjacent segments, syllable, etc.) on a language-particular basis and creates a conjunction of type A&B. This is illustrated in (23).

(23) Local Conjunction

&(A, B, D) =A&B

&	universal operator	A, B	constraints
D	domain of conjoining constraints		

Local Conjunction A&B can be violated in one single case, i.e., if and only if A and B are both violated somewhere in domain D. It is very important that this operation be considered as a kind of last resort operation, i.e., only in cases in which all rankings of single constraints fail to explain the data can LC be used.

The main idea behind this proposal is that constraint interaction can be stronger locally than non-locally. Therefore, Local Conjunction accounts for cases in which multiple constraint violations in a local domain are avoided, while the same violations in a nonlocal context are allowed. In other words, multiple constraint violations in a local context are categorically worse than the same violations in a nonlocal context. This can be schematically presented by means of the following ranking, cf. (24). (A, B, C= constraints).

(24)

A&B >> C >> A, B

Note that single A and B constraints, which are ranked lower than the constraint C, can be violated so as to satisfy C. But if they are conjoined and hence higher ranked than C, then the violation of the conjunction may result in a fatal violation. Moreover, A&B may even force the violation of the constraint C.

Let us illustrate how LC works when applied to Polish. In Polish, palatalized labials occur in the onset but not in the coda, although they are sometimes present in the underlying representations. Thus, a constraint *No palatalized labials* (*[Lab, Pal]) does not suffice to account for Polish data because it incorrectly predicts that palatalized labials do not occur in the onset. What is needed is a constraint that prohibits palatalized labials in coda position. Such a constraint is possible with a conjunction of two markedness constraints, namely, **[Lab, Pal]&NoCoda* applying to the domain of a segment. The implementation of the conjunction into the ranking is illustrated in (25).

(25)

[*[Lab, Pal]&NoCoda]$_{SEGMENT}$>> IDENT [Lab, Pal]>> *[Lab, Pal], NoCoda

*[Lab, Pal]:	No palatalized labials.
NoCoda:	Codas are prohibited.
IDENT [Lab, Pal]:	Palatalized labials present in the input are also present in the output.

The application of LC is demonstrated in (26).

(26)

a. Palatalized labials in coda: gołąb 'pigeon' nom.sg.

/gołąb'/	*[Lab,Pal]&NoCoda	IDENT [Lab, Pal]	*[Lab, Pal]
☞ gołą[p]		*	
gołą[p']	*!		*

b. Palatalized labials in onset: piasek 'sand' nom.sg.

/p'asek/	*[Lab,Pal]&NoCoda	IDENT [Lab, Pal]	*[Lab, Pal]
☞ [p']asek			*
[p]asek		*!	*

As we may conclude from the examples in (26)a and b, Local Conjunction allows palatalized labials to be present in the onset, on the one hand, but prohibits them in the coda, on the other hand. Thus, LC offers an adequate analysis for Polish.

In the following, some remarks concerning the universal operator '&' are in order. As mentioned above, the operator '&' which is present in UG combines the universal constraints A and B (or more) on a language-particular basis. It plays an important role in UG since it offers a possibility of conjoining constraints. Otherwise, all local conjunctions must be present in UG, putting thus a large burden on it. For example, instead of *[Lab, Pal]&NoCoda we could postulate an additional constraint *[Lab, Pal]σ prohibiting palatalized labials in codas. But such a constraint seems to be redundant since there are constraints that have been already present in the language and their conjunction leads to the same restriction as *[Lab, Pal]σ does. Hence, the operator '&' is an extremely economic tool. However, considering the number of possible conjunctions and being aware of the costs of operations, the power of the operator should be considerably restricted. Therefore, LC is allowed just in cases in which other tools do not suffice to account for the data without exceptions. It is also restricted to certain well-defined domains, as mentioned above.

The power of LC might be further reduced by imposing restrictions on types of constraints which are allowed to be conjoined by it. Several cases examined thus far result in different proposals. One of them (Fukazawa and Miglio 1996) suggests that two constraints may be conjoined only if they belong to the same constraint family.

This proposal derives additional support from other studies which prove that the conjoined constraints come from the same family, e.g., *PARSE[Low]&*PARSE [ATR] (Kirchner 1996), IDENT[+ATR]&IDENT[HI] (Miglio 1996). Alderete (1996) proposes however to conjoin two identical markedness constraints No long vowel&No long vowel so as to account for Obligatory Contour Principle effects in Wellagga. This idea is generally called Self-Conjunction and is used for expressing OCP effects. Further development of LC has shown the usefulness of conjoining a faithfulness constraint with a markedness constraint. £ubowicz (1998), who introduced this idea, argues that by conjoining a markedness constraint with a faithfulness constraint, the markedness constraint is active in triggering a phonological process only when the faithfulness constraint is violated. This proposal is assumed to capture all effects of the Strict Cycle Condition, cf. Mascaró (1976), Kiparsky (1982b), Rubach (1984).[13]

In sum, the question of limiting LC power by restricting the types of constraints that can be conjoined is still under discussion. It seems, however, that such restrictions do not exist at all.

1.3 Sound change in Optimality Theory

Since diachronic changes of phonological structures constitute a significant part of this thesis, different concepts of sound change proposed in framework of Optimality Theory are presented and discussed in this subsection. Of special interest will be both a formal way of expressing sound change in terms of constraint interactions, as well as an evaluation of their explanatory adequacy.

The section is organized as follows. First, I present a model which makes use of the unranking of certain constraints by accounting in free variation, the so-called Free-Variationist Model, as proposed by Antilla (1995), Bermúdez-Otero (1996), Cho (1995), Löhken (1995), Zubritskaya (1994). Second, I examine a model called 'Promotion of the Unmarked' proposed by Green (1997). Finally, in 1.3.3 I discuss both models and present my assumptions concerning sound change.

1.3.1 Free-Variationist Model

Traditionally, in accounting for sound change we differentiate three stages. The first stage should be regarded as a starting point where just one output of an underlying representation is produced. In the next stage the homogeneity of one possible output is disturbed by speakers who begin to produce another variant of the same input. In some cases there might be three or more outputs of the same input. This stage is called a variation stage, which is also referred to as a free variation stage. Further, at some point one of the possible outputs is going to be preferred, ceteris paribus. Finally, such a

[13] Opacity cases are also accounted for in a new proposal called Sympathy Theory, cf. McCarthy (1998).

situation leads to the selection of the preferred candidate as the only possible one.[14] In most cases, the selected candidate is different from the output in the first stage, resulting in sound change. In (27) examples illustrating the three stages are provided, cf. Löhken (1997:216).

(27)

Old High German	Middle High German	New High German	
tu.ri	tü.rə : tür	tür (Tür)	'door'
ma.gad	ma.gət : magt	magt (Magd)	'maid'
mennis.ko	men.schə : men.sch	men.sch (Mensch)	'man'
mer.zo	mer.zə : merz	merz (März)	'March'
ei.ne:st	ei.nəst : einst	einst	'once'
hen.gist	hen.gəst : hengst	hengst (Hengst)	'stallion'

In Middle High German there existed a variation between forms containing a schwa (ə), which was derived from Old High German full vowels, and forms in which a schwa was deleted. As the data from New High German indicate, forms without a schwa were selected.

However, there are also cases attested in which variation leads to the selection of the original candidate, i.e., the candidate which had been produced before variation started. For example, variation in Middle High German between *bəlangən* : *blangən* 'to concern' or *bəroubən* : *broubən* 'to rob' led to the selection of *bəlangən* and *bəroubən* (later *berauben*), which is accounted for by phonotactic restrictions in New High German, cf. Löhken (1997:212).

The concept of sound change in terms of variation and selection was already known in the nineteenth century, cf. Müller (1892:32) and Paul (1966:32).[15] In Optimality Theory the whole process of sound change is analyzed by means of constraints. In the following two models of sound change which differ primarily in the way they account for the variation stage will be presented and discussed. One of the concepts postulates that there is a free-variation, which is expressed by resolving a crucial ranking between two (or more) constraints which are responsible for variation. The main idea behind this proposal is that the unranking of constraints results in a selection of two or more candidates that 'tie', i.e., they incur the same number of violations of unranked constraints. Since these candidates are equally good (equally optimal under given circumstances), both of them are selected. This model was proposed by Antilla (1995), Bermúdez-Otero (1996), Cho (1995), Löhken (1995, 1997), Zubritskaya (1994), among others. Bermúdez-Otero refers to this proposal as the Free-Variationst Model. In the remainder of this section the Free-Variationist Model will be formally presented.

---

[14] Different factors might contribute to variation. They are usually divided into external and internal factors. It is beyond the scope of this subsection to describe them in detail. Therefore, it may suffice to mention just some of them, like differences in age, in social status, in the manner of speaking (formal vs. colloquial style), dialectal differences, influence from other languages, etc. It has to be stressed that some linguists reject free variation for sociolinguistic reasons, cf. Weinreich, Labov and Herzog (1968), Labov (1972).

[15] The first edition of Paul's work appeared in 1880.

In the first stage, presented in (28), all constraints are crucially ranked with respect to each other, which results in one optimal output, cf. also Löhken (1997: 85f).

(28) 1st stage: crucial ranking of constraints
A>>B>>C>>D

	A	B	C	D
candidate i		*!		*
☞candidate ii			*	*
candidate iii	*!			

Candidate (iii) is excluded due to a violation of the high-ranked constraint A. The second candidate in (28) fares better on B than the first candidate. Therefore it emerges as optimal. This is the only possible output produced by speakers under the same circumstances.

In the next stage, the two constraints B and C shift from being crucially ranked B>>C to being unranked. This stage is shown in (29), where a dotted line expresses unranked constraints.

(29) 2nd stage: unranking of constraints → free variation

A>>B;C>>D

	A	B	C	D
☞candidate i		*		*
☞candidate ii			*	*
candidate iii	*!			

In (29) both candidates, candidate (i) and candidate (ii), are equally good. Hence, both are selected as optimal. The unranking of the two constraints B and C results in free-variation.

Finally, in the third stage, the two constraints B and C become ranked again. Since two possibilities of constraint ranking are possible, i.e. B>>C or C>>B, the optimal output can be either the original one, candidate (ii), or a new one, candidate (i). Both cases are exemplified in (30)a and (30)b, respectively.

(30) 3rd phase: selection of the winning candidate

a. A>>B>>C>>D

	A	B	C	D
candidate i		*!		*
☞candidate ii			*	*
candidate iii	*!			

b. A>>C>>B>>D

	A	C	B	D
☞candidate i			*	*
candidate ii		*!		*
candidate iii	*!			

In (30)a the candidate (ii) is selected as optimal. This is exactly the same candidate as in (28). The reason for such selection is motivated by the crucial ranking between C and B which is also attested in (28). A different situation is shown in (30)b, where candidate (i) emerges as optimal. The reversal of constraints B and C is responsible for the selection of the new candidate.

We postpone discussion of the Free-Variation Model to 1.3.3, where main arguments in favor and against it are provided in comparison with the model discussed in the following subsection.

1.3.2 Promotion of the Unmarked

Another OT approach to diachronic sound change, proposed by Green (1997), is an outgrowth of the theory of the Emergence of Unmarked (McCarthy and Prince 1994). The latter assumes that constraints which are violated in a given language as a whole might be exactly obeyed in particular domains of this language. Therefore their effects can still be observed in certain domains and under certain conditions.

The main idea behind *Promotion of the Unmarked* is that a constraint which militates against markedness, hence favoring unmarked structures, is promoted up the constraint hierarchy, thereby passing other constraints. According to Green (1997:13) "phonological change results when an unmarked pattern comes to predominate in phonology."

In light of the fact that a language-specific ranking consists of many constraints, the promoted constraint does not have to pass just one constraint but often several so as to achieve its goal. The cost of this promotion might result in violation of different constraints at different stages and it is to be reflected in different sound changes; the teleological character of the changes remains the same.

Green (1997:14) exemplifies his approach with the so-called Open Syllable Law of Proto-Slavic. Proto-Slavic underwent several phonological changes such as the loss of word-final obstruents, the reduction of consonant clusters to only those that were permissible onsets, the change of short unnasalized vowels to long nasalized ones, metathesis (in West and South Proto-Slavic) or epenthesis (in East Proto-Slavic). *Promotion of the Unmarked* captures these seemingly unrelated phonological changes with one generalization, namely, the markedness constraint prohibiting closed syllables (NoCoda) was consequently promoted over other constraints throughout Proto-Slavic.

Green (1997) rejects analyzing constraints in such a way that they are unranked, as in the Free-Variation Model. According to Green (1997:20), free variation in terms of variants which are equally harmonic and available to every speaker of the language at all times is highly unlikely, cf. ftn 14. In order to account for a variation stage, Green (1997) assumes multiple grammars with varying constraint rankings. This means that "speakers may have different grammars from each other (with correlations of age, social status, geographical location, etc.), or even that a single speaker may have different grammars in his competency (with correlations of a speaking style)," Green (1997:22). In other words, the principle "one grammar for one language" is abandoned here. This proposal is discussed in 1.3.3.

1.3.3 Discussion

This subsection is devoted to a discussion of both the Free-Variationist Model and Promotion of the Optimal presented in the previous subsections.

The main argument against the *Free-Variationist Model* is that it fails to capture the fact that speakers prefer one variant over another depending on sociolinguistic factors. In other words, it is highly improbable that a speaker produces two nonpreferential outputs under the same circumstances. Rather, there exists a strong division in preferences between speakers with respect to sociological, geographic, generational, context situative and other factors.

The second objection raised against the Free-Variationist Model (see Green 1997) is that undominated constraints are responsible for free variation and "undominated constraints are never violated by surface forms" according to the assumption in OT (Green 1997:20). But even if they are dominated, "it is general practice in OT to say that when two candidates tie on a set of constraints, the tie is broken by a lower constraint " Green (1997: 20).

As far as the second objection is concerned, I think that it is extremely difficult to decide whether the constraints we posit on the top of *our* hierarchies are indeed undominated or not. In other words, there might be other constraints we do not discuss that are ranked ahead of the constraints we propose in our rankings. Second, there is no restriction in OT assumptions hindering the violation of highly ranked constraints, although it is true that in most cases the lower-ranked constraints are violated so as to satisfy higher-ranked constraints. Third, as Green (1997:20) correctly notes, in the case of a tie between higher ranked constraints, the competition between candidates is resolved by means of lower ranked constraints. However, the main idea behind the *Free-Variationist Model* is just a tie of violations of *unranked* constraints that are directly responsible for free variation, i.e. selected candidates fare on lower ranked constraints equally well. And if constraints which are responsible for all differences between optimal candidates are unranked with respect to each other, then there exists no possibility of selecting just one of them. In other words, the underlying assumption of unranked constraints leading to the emergence of more than one candidate is theoretically correct.

An alternative solution called *Promotion of the Unmarked*, as presented in 1.3.2, proposes multiple grammars with varying constraint rankings. In contrast to the *Free-Variationist Model,* this approach accounts for the sociolinguistic factors that determine variation in language. On the other hand, the multiple grammars proposal seems to be a highly uneconomical solution since it allows for redundancies in terms of multiplying the same sequences in constraint rankings which are not responsible for particular variation. Further, I will show in chapter 3 that only by unranking certain constraints one can account for certain phenomena, e.g. variations in syllabification, cf. also examples given below.

In sum, there are pro and contra arguments regarding both models.

In the following, I present my assumptions, which differ slightly from the two models presented above. My model is based primarily on OT assumptions and the previous proposals presented above as well as my own conclusions drawn from investigation of diachronic changes in Polish.

First of all, I assume one language-specific ranking (general ranking) which allows a certain 'flexibility.' [16] This flexibility allows for various variations in a language as a whole, i.e., it mirrors all individual differences found in a language. In other words, we can present language variation by means of constraints being unranked so as to gain a general picture of formal variations in a given language. In case of individual speakers, I assume crucial rankings between constraints that prevent variations. If a variation is also attested in the speech of an individual speaker then certain constraints must be unranked in his grammar. For example, in Polish the word *matka* 'mother' nom.sg. may be syllabified either as *ma.tka* or *mat.ka* by the same speaker, cf. also examples provided in 3.1.1 and 3.2.2. This indicates that constraints responsible for syllabification are unranked with respect to each other in the grammar of a single speaker. However, the variation in individual grammars occurs not very often for sociolinguistic reasons mentioned above. Therefore, the ranking of individual speakers does not allow such a flexibility in terms of the unranking of constraints as the general ranking does. In other words, the variation in individual rankings is minimal. General ranking can be viewed however as a kind of mirror that reflects all rankings attested in a given language.

Let us illustrate this idea with an example. The tableau in (31) presents rankings of individual speakers. In the case of the speaker X it is *candidate i* that emerges as optimal, cf. (31)a. The crucial ranking between constraints C and D is responsible for this selection. On the one hand, the optimal output selected by Eval from the ranking of the speaker Y, who speaks the same language as the speaker X, is *candidate ii*, cf. (31)b. This optimal output is a direct consequence of the domination of constraint D over constraint C.

(31) a. speaker X

	A	B	C	D	E	F
☞candidate i				*	*	
candidate ii			*!			*
candidate iii	*!					*

[16] Cf. also the approach to mobile constraints proposed by Reynolds (1994).

b. speaker Y

	A	B	D	C	E	F
candidate i			*!		*	
☞candidate ii				*		*
candidate iii	*!					*

The rankings of individual speakers indicate that there is variation in a language which, according to my assumptions, has to be mirrored in a general ranking. In (32) it is shown that the constraints which were differently ranked in individual grammars, i.e. C and D, are unranked in the grammar of the language as a whole. As a consequence two candidates, candidate (i) and candidate (ii), are selected as optimal.

(32)

	A	B	C	D	E	F
☞candidate i				*	*	
☞candidate ii			*			*
candidate iii	*!					*

I assume that the selected outputs, i.e. *candidate i* and *candidate ii*, do not have to be considered as 'free-variants' since it is very seldom the case that speakers use the same output as a free-variant of another. Instead, I assume that the optimal candidates in (32) are *attested outputs* in a given language.

In sum, I do not assume multiple rankings because the flexibility of a general ranking allows me to capture variations in the language. I also do not assume a free-variation stage as proposed in the Free-Variationist Model because such stage is rarely attested for sociolinguistic reasons.

As far as language change is concerned I assume that linguistic structures are the output of a dynamic system of conflicting functions, subject to constraints, each of which strives to take precedence over the other. These functions refer to the mental systems, i.e., the Articulatory-Perceptual and the Conceptual Intentional system, as well as to internal connections between Phonetic Form and Logical Form, as presented in 1.4.1.

For example, PF is determined by functions like, e.g., Minimization of articulatory effort (Min f1) on the one hand, and Maximization of perception (Max f2) on the other hand. Each of them is again very complex and consists of a set of other functions. Some of them are exemplified in (33). Again, these functions often compete against each other and against functions referring to other components.

(33) Examples of various competing functions determining PF component, cf. Boersma (1997a: 28-40).

Min f1: Minimizing of articulatory effort
a. energy

Minimization of covered distance: "An articulator moving away from the neutral position prefers to travel a short distance."
Minimization of extension: "An articulator likes to stay near the neutral position. "
Minimization of duration: "A non-neutral position x should be maintained as short as possible."
Minimization of speed: "Faster gestures are disfavored."

b. number of gestures
Minimization of the number of contours

c. precision
Minimization of precision "In a certain environment, a certain articulator does not work up the precision to put itself in a certain position."
d. coordination
Maximization of making use of available features and their combinations.

Max f2: Maximizing of perception, cf. Boersma (1997a: 42f).

Minimization of distortion: "A less distorted recognition is preferred over a more distorted recognition. "
Maximization of recognition: "The corresponding feature value for every acoustic feature value should be recognized. "

The functions in (33) show that the phonetic component of lexical entries is determined by an enormous set of competing functions. Therefore, changes should be understood as a result of the precedence of one function over another at some point in the development of the language. But such a precedence cannot occur independently and without interactions with other functions involved in language development. For this reason, the emerging structures are unmarked only with respect to the function(s) that take(s) precedence over other functions.

As the development of Slavic languages shows, open syllables were created on the basis of the promotion of NoCoda,[17] cf. Green (1997). Hence, the emerging outputs were unmarked with respect to NoCoda. But as will be shown in chapter 2 these outputs were quickly abandoned and structures with complex codas emerged. In other words, Promotion of the Unmarked should be regarded as a kind of promotion restricted to certain domains, i.e., as a kind of local promotion because phonological change is a dynamic outcome of multiple, often conflicting, promotions which determine language components. This idea receives support in analyses of phonological structures of Polish from both a diachronic point of view, cf. chapter 2 and 4, and a synchronic point of view, cf. chapter 3.

[17] In Optimality Theory functions are expressed by means of various constraints.

1.4 Lexicon

This section presents assumptions about the lexicon which play a crucial role in the present investigation. The notion of lexicon and lexical entry will be taken in a narrow focus based on conceptual requirements of the organization of language. The assumptions presented below are considered to be a kind of extension of the phonological lexicon proposed in Optimality Theory, c.f. Itô and Mester (1995, 1998) Fukazawa (1997), Fukazawa, Kitahara and Ota (1998). Since we are looking for principles or functions governing phonological changes, this extension seems to be indispensable. It shows, namely, that the phonological representation of a lexical entry is connected with other components which might block its optimization. The leading concept of the organization of a lexical entry is presented in 1.4.1. In 1.4.2 the main emphasis is put on the organization of the phonological aspect of the lexicon. It will be shown how lexical strata which display different phonological behaviors can be accounted for by means of multiple faithfulness constraints integrated into one invariant ranking. Finally, in 1.4.3 the algorithm of Lexicon Optimization, a useful tool for the present study, will be demonstrated and exemplified.

1.4.1 Lexical Entry

Traditionally, a lexical entry is conceived of as a complex structure which consists of a representation of signals (Phonetic Form) and a conceptual representation (Logical Form), i.e. representation of sound and meaning, respectively. This correspondence is both arbitrary (in the Saussurean sense) and fixed, which means that (i) there is no motivation for such relation and that (ii) this relation is controlled and cannot be freely changed. This is approximately reflected by a simple function of a type y=f(x) according to which pairs x_1, y_1, x_2, y_2,...x_n, y_n are constituted, leaving aside exceptions in a sense of homophony.

In the following we try to answer the question how the description presented above is to be understood in terms of basic conceptual requirements of the organization of language. For this reason, a fundamental concept of language organization will be presented, following proposals made by Chomsky (1991) and Bierwisch (1997).

First, we assume following Chomsky (1986) that Intentional-Language (I-Language) provides a mapping between Phonetic Form (PF) and Logical Form (LF), i.e. between structures of expressions and their interpretations. Both PF and LF are organized by mental systems such as Articulatory-Perceptual System (A-P) and Conceptual-Intentional System (C-I), respectively. A-P determines motoric and perceptual patterns of signal processing, while C-I is responsible for integrating subsystems of conceptual organization of experience and the establishment of intentional relations to the environment. These systems are constrained by extralinguistic principles on the one hand and are accessed by the language capacity on the other hand. The architecture of language organization is presented in (34), cf. Bierwisch (1997: 229).

(34)

Expression Content

A-P <===> PF --- LF <===> C-I

I-Language

PF: Phonetic Form
LF: Logical Form
A-P: Articulatory-Perceptual System
C-I: Conceptual-Intentional System

As already mentioned, the correspondence between A-P and C-I is possible by means of interfaces with these domains, viz. PF and LF, which are organized in terms of configurations of discrete primes or basic dimensions. But such a correspondence would not be possible without fixed connections between configurations of PF and LF, which cannot be mapped on structural analogy for the reasons presented above. Therefore, fixed connections between the configurations of both domains are required; they constitute lexical items of a given I-language.

This concept clearly illustrates why a lexical entry consist of PF and LF and why the relation between PF and LF is both arbitrary and fixed. In (35) the formal representation of a Lexical Entry is provided, cf. Bierwisch (1996: 231).

(35) A Lexical Entry (LE)

$<PF_{LE}, LF_{LE}>$

Logical Form can be further split into two components, namely, the Semantic Form (SF), and the Grammatical Form, (GF), as proposed by Bierwisch (1996:233). SF is narrowly connected with C-I, while GF consists of the syntactic and morphological information which is to be interpreted within I-Language. Thus, the schema in (35) can be further modified by that presented in (36).

(36)

$<PF_{LF}, <GF_{LF}, SF_{LF}>>$

The representation in (36) will be adopted for purposes of the present study.

In conclusion of this presentation let us point to some observations that are of primary relevance to the thesis. First, considering the fact that there are 'connections' between components of a lexical entry, optimization of PF cannot occur freely. As it will be shown in 4.1.4, the optimization of PF is also dependent on other components (to a certain extent). Second, PF displays a linear ordering, as opposed to the abstract-hierarchical organization of LF. This difference is reflected by principles or constraints which govern these components. Evidently, the optimization of PF can be connected with linearity of PF. Finally, the optimal output is determined by various, at best partially understood, extra- and intralinguistic functions, subject to constraints. Hence, linguistic structures are to be interpreted as outcomes of competitions between complex sets of functions referring to two different systems.

1.4.2 Phonological Lexicon

In Optimality Theory, which primarily investigates phonological properties of lexical items, the term 'lexicon' is usually restricted to the phonological component, i.e., PF in a sense of the model presented in 1.4.1, while other components of lexical entries are generally not taken into consideration. This is adequately reflected in the term Phonological Lexicon, cf. Itô and Mester (1998).

Generally, it is assumed that the Phonological Lexicon (PL) of a given language comprises phonological representations of all its lexical entries. Since they display different phonological behaviors, they can be further divided into different subsets (strata, sublexicons). This asymmetry follows from the etymology of these words. Hence, we can differentiate between a subset of native words, a subset of established loans, a subset of assimilated foreign words, a subset of unassimilated foreign words and others.

In light of this observation, the question arises as to how it is possible to account for these differences in terms of OT which assumes only one language-specific ranking. It seems to be very problematic to evaluate different, often conflicting, phonological behaviors of linguistic structures with respect to the same markedness constraint in the same ranking of constraints.

Some proposals concerning this problem have been made. For example, a model of lexical stratification proposed by Itô and Mester (1995) allows faithfulness constraints to be reranked depending on the sublexicon they referred to. The most recent model, however, proposed by Fukazawa (1997) and further developed by Fukazawa, Kitahara and Ota (1998), adheres to the fundamental premise of OT, namely, the concept of one language-specific invariant ranking and fully corresponds to other assumptions of OT. This model will be adopted for purposes of this thesis.

Following Fukazawa's proposal, we assume an Input-Output Correspondence for each sublexicon relation. In other words, each sublexicon displays a unique Input-Output Correspondence relation which is evaluated by its stratum-specific faithfulness constraints. All kinds of faithfulness constraints are integrated into one ranking. Since they occur in different positions with respect to markedness constraints, different stratum-specific phonological phenomena are possible.

This proposal will be illustrated by means of an approximate division of the Polish lexicon, which also displays some stratification. For purposes of illustration, we assume four strata whereby each stratum is posited to have its own Input-Output Correspondence relation evaluated by a set of the stratum specific IO-faithfulness constraints, cf. (37).

(37)

I-O Polish native (P) {Max -IO-P, Dep-IO-P, Ident[F]-P,...}
I-O Polish established loans (L) {Max -IO-L, Dep-IO-L, Ident[F]-L,...}
I-O Polish assimilated foreign words (A) {Max -IO-A, Dep-IO-A, Ident[F]-A,...}
I-O Polish unassimilated foreign words (U) {Max -IO-U, Dep-IO-U, Ident[F]-U,...}

For purposes of simplification we analyze only two strata of the Polish lexicon with respect to palatalization. We limit ourselves to palatalization expressed by a secondary articulation.

In Polish, there are no native words in which coronals with secondary articulation are attested.[18] Historically, all coronals underwent palatalization processes by changing their place of articulation or place and manner of articulation. Moreover, in present-day Polish there is a constraint which causes the retraction of /i/ to /ɨ/ after 'hard' dental/alveolar and retroflex coronals, i.e. after /t, d, s, z, t^s, d^z, r, š, ž, $t^{\check{s}}$, $d^{\check{z}}$/.[19] But there is a group of foreign words which are systematically exempt from this generalization. Some of them are shown in (38).

(38)

[s']inus 'sinus'nom.sg.
[s']inologia 'Sinology'nom.sg
[r']ing 'ring' nom.sg.
[r']isotto 'risotto'nom.sg.
[d']inosaur 'dinosaur' nom.sg.
[d']iploid 'diploid'nom.sg.
[t']ik 'tic'nom.sg.

On the other hand, these words display correct morphological behavior in the sense that they undergo different declension according to the declension system of Polish, cf. (39). Therefore, we assume that these words belong to assimilated foreign words, i.e. the A-stratum.

(39)

	dinozaur, sg.	dinozaury, pl.
Nom.	dinozaur	dinozaury
Gen.	dinozaura	dinozaurow
Dat.	dinozaurowi	dinozaurom
Acc.	dinozaura	dinozaury
Instr.	dinozaurem	dinozaurami
Loc.	dinozaurze	dinozaurach
Voc.	dinozaur	dinozaury

[18] Phrase-level Palatalization will be not considered here, cf. 4.1.8.
[19] Cf. also a rule called Retraction in Rubach (1984:33) discussed in 4.2.1.

In order to account for the palatalization of coronals we establish the following ranking, cf. (40).

(40)

Ident- [di]-A>>*di>> Ident [di]-P

The ranking in (40) correctly predicts that words like those in (38) are no longer problematic for an invariant constraint ranking in Polish because there is a family of faithfulness constraints, which, when appropriately ranked, cause Eval to select the optimal candidate. Consider the tableau in (41).

(41)

dinozaur	Ident[di]-A	*di	Ident [di]-P
☞ [d'i]nozaur		*	
[d^{ź}]nouzaur	*!		
[dɨ]nozaur	*!		

This example shows that it is possible to resolve the conflict between language-internal variability by means of multiple sets of Input-Output faithfulness constraints , without rejecting invariant language-specific ranking.

For other advantages of this proposal and its superiority over the core-periphery organization of the lexicon (Itô and Mester 1995) see Fukazawa, Kitahara, and Ota (1998).

1.4.3 Lexicon Optimization

In this subsection it will be shown how the optimization of the lexicon is formally understood in Optimality Theory. It has to be stressed that the term Lexicon Optimization refers to the phonological/phonetic substance of lexical entries, as presented in 1.4.2.

Lexicon Optimization, introduced by Prince and Smolensky (1993: 191-196) and developed by Itô, Mester, and Padgett (1995: 585-594), is a kind of algorithm used for identifying the most harmonic input. Since one of the OT premises requires no constraints on the input, it is possible to construct multiple inputs that converge on the same output. In order to avoid this situation, an algorithm called Lexicon Optimization evaluates each possible "input-optimal output" pair against constraint violations. A pair which incurs the fewest violations is considered to be optimal and its input is selected as an optimal one. The formal definition of Lexicon Optimization is provided in (42).

(42) Lexicon Optimization

Suppose that several different inputs I_1, I_2, ... I_n when parsed by a grammar G lead to corresponding outputs O_1, O_2, ...O_n, all of which are realized as the same phonetic form Φ - these inputs are all phonetically equivalent with respect to G. Now one of these outputs must be the most harmonic, by virtue of incurring the least significant violation marks: suppose this optimal one is labeled O_k. Then the learner should choose, as the underlying form for Φ, the input I_k. (Prince and Smolensky 1993:192)

To put it in a more informal way, we assume that inputs should be as harmonic to outputs as possible. Note that this leads to maximizing harmony of the grammar striving for minimization of violations, cf. also 1.2.1.

Several important applications of this algorithm can be found. Principally, whenever reanalyses of the surface forms occur, reanalyses of underlying forms by means of Lexicon Optimization are expected. Taking sound change into consideration, we contend that there are no alternations after a change, which allow speakers to continue to posit the original input form unless other high ranked constraints require it. Consequently, speakers choose the new most harmonic input which is due to Lexicon Optimization. Furthermore, in the course of language acquisition, faithfulness constraints are continuously promoted over markedness constraints, contrary to the initial state when markedness constraints outrank faithfulness constraints, cf. Gnanadesikan (1995), Smolensky (1996), Tesar and Smolensky (1996). Hence, the underlying forms are continuously changing until the ultimate underlying form is established. This process is also possible due to Lexicon Optimization.

In the following, the formal way of evaluating inputs by Lexicon Optimization is presented.

The example in (43) illustrates how new underlying forms were constituted after the loss of semi-vowels, so-called jers (ь, ъ), in the last period of Proto-Slavic.[20] As shown in 2.1.1 jers in certain positions disappeared. Some examples illustrating this process are presented in (43), cf. Długosz-Kurczabowa and Dubisz (1993:74f.) and Rospond (1971:72).

(43)

kъto → kto	'who' nom.
dъva → dva	'two' nom.
krajъ → kraj	'country' nom.sg.

The examples in (43) show that the loss of jers caused new output forms to emerge. The selection of new surface forms led to the reanalysis of the input. It was Lexicon Optimization that evaluated all possible candidates.

In the following the selection of the optimal input is illustrated. Taking into consideration the form /kto/, three most serious input candidates presented in the *tableaux des tableaux* in (44) are involved into the competition. They are listed in the left-top corner of each tableaux. Note that the faithfulness constraints MAX-IO and DEP-IO are ranked higher than a markedness constraint prohibiting two segments in the onset $*CC_{ONSET}$.

[20] For illustrative purposes this example is simplified and limited to hard jers, for detailed analyses and discussion see 2.1.

(44)

INPUT	OUTPUT	MAX IO	DEP IO	*CC_{ONSET}
☞ kto ☞	kto			*
	kъto		*!	
	kuto		*!	
kъto ☞	kto	*!		*
	kъto			
	kuto			
kuto ☞	kto	*!		*
	kъto			
	kuto			

Lexicon Optimization examines *tableaux des tableaux* and selects the optimal input-output pair which incurs the fewest and less significant violations, thereby identifying the optimal input, i.e. /kto/. Other candidates /kъto/ and /kuto/ are excluded due to the violation of a high-ranked MAX IO.

The selection of the new input forms automatically leads to grammar optimization, thus avoiding redundant abstractness of underlying forms, cf. footnote (9). This is indeed the ultimate goal of Lexicon Optimization.

2 CHAPTER TWO: Consonant Clusters From A Diachronic Perspective

2.1 The prominent role of jers

The wide variety of consonant clusters occurring in present-day Polish is a reflex of a diachronic process which took place in Late Common Slavic. The vocalic elements, the so-called jers, which created syllable-nuclei disappeared in certain well-defined contexts. Their loss resulted in an abundance of previously unknown consonant clusters. As expected, the new complex clusters underwent various simplification processes but did not adjust to any shape that could be explained exclusively by principles referring to the segmental level.

In this chapter the changes affecting the jers as well as their consequences are discussed in detail. It will be argued that the loss of jers is a result of constraints referring to both the prosodic as well as the segmental level. In other words, the emergence of consonant clusters is a direct and unquestionable consequence of the loss of jers; the driving force for the whole process, however, is to be sought at the prosodic level. The process itself undoubtedly manifests the importance of the segmental-prosodic interaction for the selection of optimal outputs.

The chapter is organized as follows: in 2.1.1 the main stages of the development of jers are sketched. In 2.1.2, the algorithm responsible for the asymmetrical behavior of jers, i.e. either their loss or their reinforcement to full vowels, is presented. This algorithm is generally known as Havlík's Law (1889). In 2.1.3 I interpret the changes affecting the jers as the interaction of constraints referring to segmental and prosodic levels. In the next section, in 2.2, various consequences resulting from the loss of jers are discussed. The focus lies on changes in syllable structure, especially the incorporation of consonant sequences into prosodic representation, analyzed in 2.2.2. Finally in 2.3 various processes attested exclusively in clusters such as simplifications (2.3.1), metathesis (2.3.2) and epenthesis (2.3.3) are discussed.

2.1.1 The development of jers

The origin of jers goes back to Common Slavic short high lax vowels ĭ, ŭ, both inherited from Proto-Indo European. In the eighth century ĭ lost the strong flattening of the lips and ŭ the lip rounding, and at the same time both were lowered, cf. Stieber

(1973:15). The processes resulted in the appearance of two new vowels called jers. The jer that was derived from the short front vowel ĭ is called a front jer (ь) and the one lowered from the short back vowel ŭ is referred to as a back jer (ъ). Both letters (ь,ъ) come from the Cyrillic alphabet, where they are pronounced [jers].[21]

The historical development of jers is shown in (45)[22] in comparison with the development of other vowels, cf. Carlton (1991:98). It is important to note the qualitative and quantitative differences between the large Proto-Indo European vowel inventory and the relatively modest Late Common Slavic system.

(45)

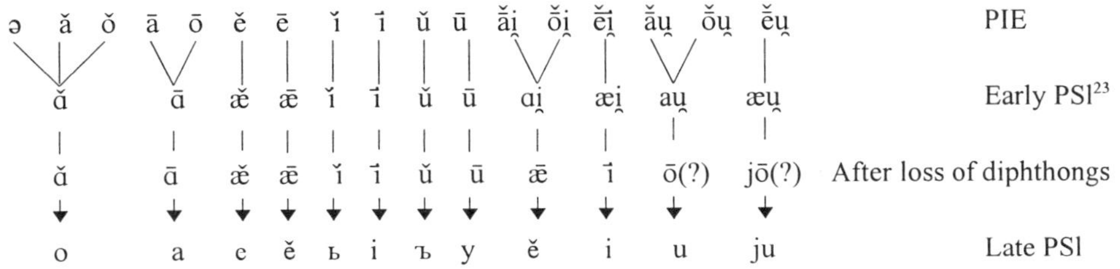

ɑ̄ long back vowel
ɑ̆ short back vowel
ā long central vowel
ă short central vowel
i̯ glide

Although we do not have direct evidence concerning the phonetic specifications of jers, we may assume on the basis of the facts presented above that jers were evidently short vowels, most probably even shorter than their predecessors, cf. Lehr-Spławiński (1978:80); they were articulated lower than ĭ and ŭ. In the Slavic tradition jers are commonly known as *półsamogłoski* 'semi-vowels' because of their shortness. With respect to their quality Zec (1998) assumes that jers were [-tense].

All jers, as well as the vowels from which they were derived, constituted syllable-nuclei and were associated with the mora.[24] Since the vowels from which ь and ъ derived were also dominated by a single mora respectively, the development of jers was a process which took place at the segmental level. This is illustrated schematically in (46).

---

[21] In the English literature these vowels are spelled as *yers*, while in the Slavic literature the spelling *jers* is more common.

[22] I have not provided additional indices that indicate differences between the same sound derived from different sources, e.g. $ě_1$ and $ě_2$, since such indices would require further explanation and comments deemed beyond the scope of this presentation. Evidently this simplification bears no effect on the subject under investigation.

[23] PSl is an abbreviation of ProtoSlavic, another term for Common Slavic.

[24] It is far from established whether moras were associated with jers. In the present study jers are assumed to be a mora-bearing unit because they existed as a syllable nuclei for a long period of time, and syllable nuclei were associated to moras, cf. (55).

(46)

In the next stage of their development, in approximately the tenth century, jers started to show an asymmetrical behavior: they either became gradually shorter and finally disappeared, or they were reinforced to full vowels, depending on the position in which they occurred. The two-fold development of jers suggest that the process must have been driven by the prosodic force, cf. discussion in 2.1.2.

The changes affecting the jers began in the Bulgarian-Macedonian dialects in the tenth century. The process gradually spread to the North and East. According to Carlton (1991:76), this process did not occur in the Ukraine until the early or mid twelfth century, and it affected the Novgorod area approximately a century later. As far as Northern Common Slavic is concerned, it is assumed that the loss of jers took place in the eleventh century, as is indicated by their absence in manuscripts from the early twelfth century as well as by internal processes which took place before the loss of jers, cf. Długosz-Kurczabowa and Dubisz (1993:81). After the completion of the changes in the jers, separate Slavic languages emerged, cf. also examples given below in (77).

2.1.2 Havlík's Law

In order to account for the changes described above it is commonly assumed that the asymmetry in the behavior of jers depended on the positions in which jers occurred. Generally, jers in 'weak' positions were lost, while jers in 'strong' positions became full vowels. Consider examples shown in (47), where the weak and strong positions are demonstrated, cf. Stieber (1966:14). The front jer in the strong position is marked as ь̥ and in the weak position as ь̯, while the back jer in the strong position is expressed as ъ̥ and in the weak position as ъ̯.

(47)

sъ̥nъ̯	'dream' nom.sg.
pь̥sъ̯	'dog'nom.sg.
tь̥mь̯nica	'darkness' nom.sg.

The algorithm differentiating between jers in weak and strong positions was originally proposed by Havlík (1889), and is now known as Havlík's Law. Havlík (1889:48) exemplified the principles he discovered on the basis of mono-, bi-, and trisyllabic words containing only jers as syllable-nuclei. They are illustrated in (48), where the mark '∪' indicates a jer syllable and the mark '— ' a full vowel syllable.

(48)

1. ∪ ∪	→	— ∪	(dьnь → denь)
2. ∪ ∪ ∪	→	∪ — ∪	(dьnьsь → dьnesь)
3. ∪ ∪ ∪ ∪	→	— ∪ — ∪	(šьvьcьmь → ševьcemь)

Havlík's Law can be summarized as follows:

> The even-numbered jers counting from the right of the word are in the strong position and the odd-numbered jers in the weak position. If any other vowel is encountered, then the first jer to the left of this vowel will be in the weak position.

As mentioned above, the jers in weak positions disappeared and the jers in strong positions were reinforced to full vowels. This is shown in (49), where the odd and even-numbered jers are indicated by the numbers to the right side of each one, cf. Stieber (1966:14) and Rospond (1971:72).

(49)

Common Slavic		Polish	
sъ̥^{2}nъ̯^{1}	→	sen	'dream' nom.sg.
pь̥^{2}sъ̯^{1}	→	p'es[25]	'dog' nom.sg.
tь̥^{2}mь̯^{1}nica	→	t'emnica	'darkness' nom.sg.
lъ̥^{2} bъ̯^{1}	→	leb	'head' (pej.) nom.sg.
sъ̯^{3}jь̥^{2}mъ̯^{1}	→	sjem	'council' nom.sg.

As shown by the examples in (49), jers in strong positions were reinforced to a mid front vowel /e/. This vowel is indeed the most common reflex of jers in Polish.[26] It is worth mentioning that jers displayed a great variety of reflexes depending on the language in which they occurred. This variety was one of the important factors that contributed to the differences among the languages in the Slavic family. Different reflexes of front and back jers are summarized in (50), cf. Carlton (1991:166). (Reflexes of jers in single Slavic languages are presented in (77) where consequences of the changes affecting the jers are discussed.)

(50)

ь̥> o, e, a, ie, ə, ă ā
ъ̥> e, 'e, a, ə, ă ā

As mentioned above, Havlík's Law is commonly taken as a basis to account for the loss of jers in weak positions and their emergence in strong positions.

In the following, we will consider two approaches to the changes in the jers based on Havlík's Law, as recently presented by Bethin (1998). She assumes that "changes in the

[25] The front jer induced palatalization of the preceding consonant. This process is discussed in 4.1.2, 4.1.7, and 4.2.7.

[26] Other possibilities will be discussed below.

jers were prosodic rather than segmental" (Bethin 1998:212). This assumption has the formal consequence that the moraic tier is relevant in the calculation of strong and weak positions of jers.

According to the first approach, called dissociation, all jers in weak positions are to be dissociated from the mora, while all jers in strong positions retaining the association to the mora emerge as full vowels. This is schematically presented in (51), cf. Bethin (1997:212).

(51) Dissociation

The second approach, called re-association, requires all jers to lose their association to moras. In the next step, only jers in strong positions are re-associated with moras under certain prosodic circumstances described below. The individual stages of the entire process are illustrated in (52), cf. Bethin (1998:212).

(52) Re-association

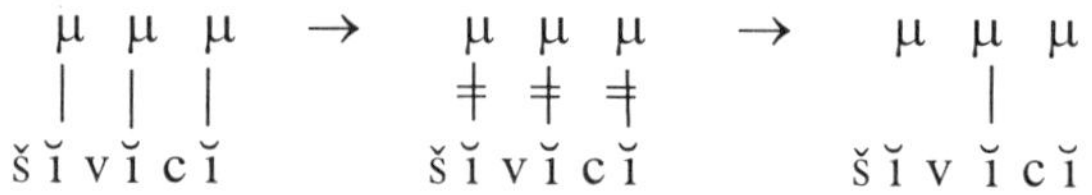

Bethin (1998:213) argues in favor of the second approach. The first approach, she claims, does not differentiate between the prosodic status of non-jer vowels and that of jers in strong positions, and "it would not easily determine that the bisyllabic grouping of (kŭni-) should not be parsed the same as (-žĭkŭ) without reference to segmental features" (Bethin 1998:213). The wrong outcome of the dissociation analysis is presented in (53), where from kŭnižĭkŭ the word konžek emerges, instead of knižek.

(53)

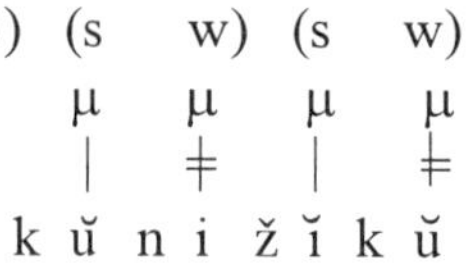

The re-association analysis, according to Bethin (1998:213), correctly predicts the output *knižek,* because moras, deprived of all jers, are finally reparsed according to a trochaic metrical foot. The re-association of the mora is, however, allowed to take place only under the condition that the vowel it associates with is the head of the foot. Consider the analysis shown in (54).

(54)

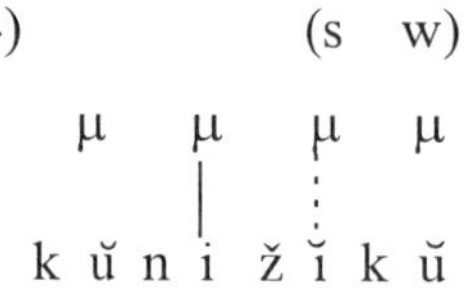

Note that both approaches presented above rely on the assumption that the changes in the jers were prosodic, cf. Bethin (1998:212). Since the reference to segmental features is abandoned, the subject of the re-association parsing is always an unassociated mora. However, the condition under which a mora is allowed to be associated refers directly to the heads of prosodic feet. If the parsing recognizes the prosodic feet only, it must treat moras associated with full vowels which constitute prosodic heads and unassociated moras in a homogeneous way. Otherwise, false outputs are predicted. Thus, it seems that the parsing does not differentiate between associated and unassociated moras. If this is indeed the case, then the first approach presented by Bethin is to be preferred. But as pointed out above, cf. also Bethin (1998:213), by adopting the first approach another serious problem arises.

The re-association analysis can probably account for the changes affecting the jers by including some additional although arbitrary assumptions, for example, the parsing recognizes only unassociated moras. Moras, albeit unassociated, have to be linearly ordered, and the parsing associates only a mora that is above a jer in strong position.

2.1.3 An OT approach to the changes in the jers

In this section an alternative approach to the changes affecting the jers will be proposed. My treatment differs crucially from both analyses presented above. First, it employs constraints referring to the surface representation. Second, it refers not only to prosodic constituents, but also to segmental features. Third, like the analyses proposed by Bethin, it recognizes the strong-weak pattern before the loss of jers. The last assumption follows from the fact that Havlík's Law, cf. (48), evidently differentiates between weak and strong positions, which conditioned the asymmetrical development of jers, i.e., either their disappearance or their emergence. In other words, the bisyllabic domain is to be assumed before the changes in jers.[27] Furthermore, the prosodic system of Late Common Slavic presented in (55) suggests that the bisyllabic domain was mostly arranged in a strong-weak pattern, cf. Bethin (1993:233) and Bethin (1998:124).

All representations in (55) except for (55)e display a strong-weak pattern, in which the prominence, i.e. the strong element is expressed by stress (*) or length. Stress and tone (H) are assumed to be different but potentially related entities: while the former is a property of syllables, the latter is characteristic of moras. In contrast to tone, stress is not an autosegment but it marks the strong element in a strong-weak grouping. However, stress depends on the location of a high-tone (H) because it occurs on the syllable with a high tone in a word and in the case when there was no high tone in a given word, stress is assigned to the initial syllable by default (*). Bethin (1998:122) represents the underlying accent as a high tone (H) on a given mora.

---

27 This assumption is directly supported by some processes in Late Common Slavic which are interpreted as prosodic adjustments to the strong-weak pattern, e.g. the shortening of syllables under original acute accent and the so-called neo-acute retraction, which caused retraction of the ictus. Both processes took place before the changes in the jers, cf. Bethin (1998:125). The neo-acute retraction is discussed below.

In the representations in (55) the first member of the prosodic group is either long (pretonic longs), cf. (55)d, or stressed (initial stress by default on short vowels), cf.(55)c. Quite often it is both stressed and long: stress on long vowels in rising, cf. (55)a, and in other cases the default stress falls on initial longs in falling, cf. (55)b. (Rising and falling contours are the phonetic implementation of tone and/or stress. Stress in atonic forms, i.e. stress assigned by default, is realized as falling pitch, while high tone is interpreted as rising pitch only if it occurs on nonfinal long vowels, cf. Bethin (1998:123)).

(55) The prosody of bisyllabic forms

(a) rising (long) (b) falling (long) (c) falling (short) (d) pretonic long

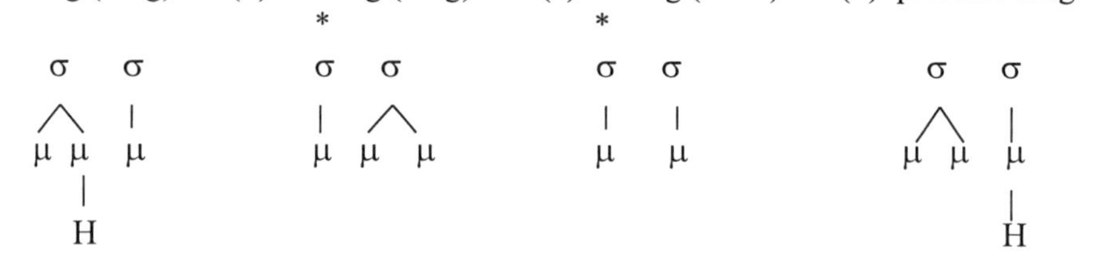

*līpa 'linden' *zǫ̂bŭ 'tooth' *uȍzŭ 'cart' *sǫdŭ̏ 'judgment'

(e)
pretonic short

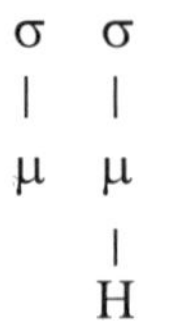

* stolŭ̏ 'table'

H high tone
* stress prominence
ŭ short high lax vowel (jer)
^ (long) falling intonation
¯ (long) raising intonation
˵ (short) falling intonation

The representations in (55)a, b, c, d show the strong-weak pattern in which the prominence is manifested by stress and/or length. Interestingly, there was only one exception to the metrical strong-weak pattern constituted by the pretonic short vowels in (55)e. This prosodic group exhibited a weak-strong pattern in terms of stress without compensation on the moraic level. However, if the root vowels lengthened then the metrical relationship [s-w] might have been possible in this domain. In the next step of its development this group indeed conformed to the metrical [s-w] pattern by the lengthening root vowels. This process is commonly known as neo-acute retraction or pretonic lengthening of short vowels. This is illustrated in (56), cf. Bethin (1993:235).

Moras in parenteses indicate that not every North Central Slavic dialect retained length distinction in terms of moras. In Polish moras disappeared.[28]

(56) Neo-Acute retraction onto Lax (Short) Vowels in North Central Slavic

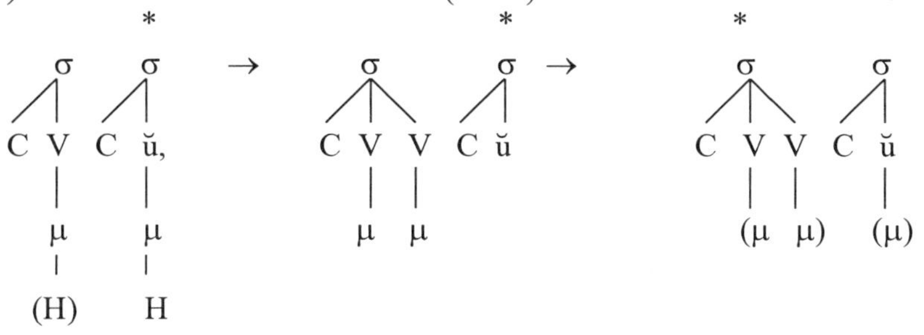

s t o l ŭ 'table'

In sum, the strong-weak pattern expressed either by length or by stress (with the one exception of pretonic short vowels) describes the prosodic relations in Common Slavic and Late Common Slavic. The strong-weak pattern was undoubtedly the prerequisite for a trochaic metrical foot. North Central Late Common Slavic is assumed to have generalized the trochaic metrical foot as a prosodic grouping at the time of the neo-acute retraction, i.e., before the loss of jers, cf. Bethin (1998:145).

In the following we will model the situation in terms of constraints. First, we assume that the algorithm responsible for establishing the strong-weak pattern took the right edge of the word as a starting point, cf. Havlík's Law in (48). Thus, the algorithm was determined by a constraint requiring the right edge of every foot to coincide with the right edge of the prosodic word. This constraint is formally expressed in (57), cf. McCarthy and Prince (1993b:94).

(57)

ALIGN-FT
Align (Ft, R, PrWd, R)
Every foot stands in final position in the Prosodic Word.

The fact that all syllables are parsed to feet, is expressed by means of the constraint PARSE-SYLL presented in (58), cf. McCarthy and Prince (1993b:91).

(58)

PARSE-SYL: All syllables must be parsed by feet.

Furthermore, the parsing algorithm requires a constraint, called FT-BIN, ensuring that all feet are binary. FT-BIN is formulated in (59), cf. McCarthy and Prince (1993b: 90).

---

28 Note that the process occurred before the changes in the jers and affected not only jers but also tense vowels. For this reason it cannot be considered to be compensatory lengthening of vowels before a weak jer as proposed by Klemensiewicz (1954) and Timberlake (1983), cf. discussion in 2.2.

(59)

FT-BIN: Feet must be binary under syllabic or moraic analysis.

Let us illustrate the selection of optimal candidates with concrete examples. Taking a word consisting of three jer-syllables such as šьvьсъ 'shoemaker' nom.sg., the algorithm selects the form with a final binary foot, i.e. šь(vьсъ), which neither violates ALIGN-FT nor FT-BIN. Both šь(vьсъ) and its most serious competitor (šьvь)съ incur a single violation of PARSE-SYL. This tie is, however, resolved by the next constraint, ALIGN-FT, in favor of the winning candidate šь(vьсъ). This situation is illustrated by the tableau in (60). Note that the ranking of constraints in (60) is crucial (FT-BIN>> PARSE-SYL>>ALIGN-FT) because any other order would lead to the selection of incorrect outputs. For the motivation of the crucial ranking between PARSE-SYL and ALIGN-FT cf. the tableau in (67).

(60)

šьvьсъ	FT-BIN	PARSE-SYL	ALIGN-FT
šьvьсъ		*!**	
☞ šь(vьсъ)		*	
(šьvь)съ		*	*!
šьvь(съ)	*!	**	
(šьvь)(съ)	*!		
šьvь(съ)	*!	**	
(šь)(vьсъ)	*!		
(šьvьсъ)	*!		

Recall that according to Havlík's Law the full vowel has the force to break the parsing of jer-syllables into the strong-weak pattern. But this restriction corresponds to the trochaic pattern, namely, the weak position of a jer is possible if the preceding vowel is a full vowel. In other words, the bisyllabic domain CVCь is allowed because it resembles the strong-weak pattern. If we assume that jers are differentiated from full vowels by segmental features as, e.g., by being [-tense], then it seems that the parsing algorithm is sensitive not only to the moraic level but also to the segmental level.

Now it becomes clear why the algorithm above rejects the parsing of the jer-syllable followed by a full vowel syllable into one foot. The potential foot would result in a 'semi-vowel' in the strong position followed by a syllable with a full vowel in the weak position. The impossibility of the parsing of a jer-syllable followed by a full vowel-syllable as a single foot was recognized by Zec (1998:8) and formulated in terms of the constraint presented in (61) in which 'ь' means a jer-syllable and 'V' a full vowel-syllable.

(61)

*(ь.V): Feet of the (ь.V) shape are prohibited.[29]

[29] Zec (1998:8) calls this constraint FtForm. Since this name is used for another constraint, it will be replaced here by *(ь.V).

The constraint in (61) prohibits a jer to emerge as a foot head. Importantly, sequences such as two jer-syllables (ь.ь), two full-vowel-syllables (V.V) and a full vowel-syllable followed by a jer-syllable (V.ь) do not violate *(ь.V) and therefore can be parsed into feet. It is important to stress that the main task of the constraint in (61) is to prohibit potential iambic feet and to create a basis for optimal trochaic feet. Theoretically, it would be possible to postulate a constraint directly responsible for the trochaic pattern. It is usually called FOOT-FORM TROCHAIC and requires the first syllable of the foot to be strong in comparison to the second syllable which is supposed to be weak: Ft→ $\sigma_s\sigma_w$, cf. McCarthy and Prince (1993b: 91). In the case at hand the constraint FOOT-FORM TROCHAIC would require an additional restriction that the form (ь.V) does not satisfy this constraint. For this reason I propose to implement the constraint presented in (61) into the ranking because it immediately excludes feet which are not optimal candidates for trochaic feet. The ranking of *(ь.V) above FT-BIN leads to the expected results. Words with full vowels are treated in a two-fold way depending on the positions in which the full-vowel syllables occur with respect to the syllables containing a jer. If the full-vowel syllable occurs word-finally, it cannot be parsed with the preceding jer-syllable into a foot. Such a form would violate the high-ranking *(ь.V). This is shown by the second candidate in (62).

(62)

šьvьca	*(ь.V)	FT-BIN	PARSE-SYL	ALIGN-FT
šьvьca			**!*	
šь(vьca)	*!		*	
☞ (šьvь)ca			*	*
šьvь(ca)		*!	**	
(šьvь)(ca)		*!		
šьvь(ca)		*!	**	
(šь)(vьca)	*!	*		
(šьvьca)		*!		

The optimal candidate with the initial foot, i.e. (šьvь)ca 'shoemaker' gen.sg., emerges as optimal since it incurs violations of neither the high-ranking *(ь.V) nor FT-BIN. Its violation of ALIGN-FT is inconsequential due to the low-ranking of this constraint.

Bisyllabic words with a jer-syllable followed by a full-vowel syllable such as e.g. dъva 'two', tьma 'moth'nom.sg., or kъto 'who'nom.sg. cannot be parsed into one foot because of the high-ranking *(ь.V). This is illustrated by the tableau in (63).

(63)

kъto	*(ь.V)	FT-BIN	PARSE-SYL	ALIGN-FT
☞ kъto			**!	
(kъto)	*!			
kъ(to)		*	*	
(kъ)to		*	*	*!

Unfortunately, the winner in (63), kъto, is not attested. It is a candidate in which syllables remain unparsed. A universal constraint which militates against such candidates is *Headedness*, formulated in (64), cf. Selkirk (1995:443).

(64)

Headedness Any C^i must dominate a C^{i-1} (except if $C^i = \sigma$)
e.g. "A PWd must dominate a Ft."

The constraint in (64) immediately excludes every prosodic word which does not display feet in its prosodic structure. This is shown in (65). Note that Headedness is not violated if a candidate contains an unparsed foot. Such candidates violate ***Exhaustivity***, a constraint discussed in 3.3.

(65)

kъto	Headedness	*(ь.V)	FT-BIN	PARSE-SYL	ALIGN-FT
[kъto]$_{PrW}$	*!			**	
[(kъto)]$_{PrW}$		*!			
☞ [kъ(to)]$_{PrW}$			*	*	
[(kъ)to]$_{PrW}$			*	*	*!

In (65) the faithful candidate without a foot, *kъto*, is immediately excluded because of the violation of Headedness. The two candidates *kъ(to)* and *(kъ)to* display a tie on both FT-BIN as well as PARSE-SYL, since each of them violates both constraints once. The deciding role is played by ALIGN-FT, which correctly predicts that the former candidate is the optimal one.

If a syllable containing a full vowel is followed by a jer-syllable as e.g., konь 'horse' nom.sg., kostь 'bone'nom.sg., or t'enь 'shadow' nom.sg., then this syllable is parsed into a single foot. Consider candidates shown in the tableau in (66).

(66)

konь	Headedness	*(ь.V)	FT-BIN	PARSE-SYL	ALIGN-FT
[konь]$_{PrW}$	*!			**	
☞ [(konь)]$_{PrW}$					
[ko(nь)]$_{PrW}$			*!	*	
[(ko)nь]$_{PrW}$			*!	*	*!

The second candidate in (66), (konь), emerges as optimal since it forms a binary foot that does not contain a jer in its first syllable. Instead its full vowel is potentially able to function as the prosodic head of a foot. Other candidates are excluded due to a violation of Headedness or FT-BIN.

Finally, let us consider how the ranking proposed thus far deals with the critical candidate kъnižьkъ discussed in (53) and (54). Note that this four-syllable word contains only one full vowel syllable which cannot constitute a foot with the preceding jer-syllable. In (67) it is shown how potential candidates fare on the relevant constraints.

(67)

kъnižьkъ	Headedness	*(ь.V)	FT-BIN	PARSE-SYL	ALIGN-FT
[kъnižьkъ]$_{PrW}$	*!			****	
[(kъni)(žьkъ)]$_{PrW}$		*!			*
[kъ(ni)(žьkъ)]$_{PrW}$			*!	*	*
[(kъ)ni(žьkъ)]$_{PrW}$			*!	*	*
☞[kъni(žьkъ)]$_{PrW}$				**	
[(kъni)žьkъ]$_{PrW}$		*!		**	*!
[(kъ)nižь(kъ)]$_{PrW}$			*!*	**	*
[(kъ)(nižь)(kъ)]$_{PrW}$			*!*		**
[kъ(ni)žь(kъ)]$_{PrW}$			*!*	**	*

The optimal candidate kъni(žьkъ) contains a final foot and two unparsed syllables. Hence, it does not incur any violations of FT-BIN. Its most serious competitor (kъni)(žьkъ) is excluded due to a violation of the high-ranking *(ь.V).

The optimal forms presented above, cf. (60), (62), (63), (66), (67), had already existed before the changes affecting the jers. The bisyllabic domains constituted bases for further changes. Hence, in the next stage of their development, the algorithm, taking the winners presented above as underlying forms, selected the new optimal candidates according to the constraints that started to play a decisive role in determining outputs.

According to Havlík's Law jers in strong positions were reinforced to full vowels, while jers in weak positions were lost. The reinforcement process can be interpreted as the strengthening of jers occurring in positions of potential prosodic heads. Jers could not, however, create prosodic heads because of their featural content, cf. the discussion below. In order to become a prosodic head a jer had to change its featural content, i.e., it had to become a full vowel. This suggests a crucial difference between the first and the second stage of the development of jers, namely the position of faithfulness in the ranking: while MAX and IDENT had to be undominated at the former stage, the same constraints after some time lost their higher positions in the ranking and were dominated by other constraints at the later stage.

The driving force behind the emergence of prosodic heads was confronted with another tendency, namely, the tendency to reduce syllables.[30] Without taking this tendency into consideration, the whole process of the changes in the jers would remain unexplained. In several words prosodic heads were created but they were not followed by another syllable, i.e. the well-formedness of a bisyllabic foot was abandoned and in many cases a monosyllabic foot was created. Clearly, syllables in weak positions were more likely to disappear than ones in strong positions.

Let us consider which constraints expressing the conflicting tendencies played a decisive role in selecting the optimal outputs. First, the algorithm had to be determined by a constraint that disallows the emergence of prosodic heads of feet. This constraint is presented in (68). Recall that the bisyllabic domain had already existed before the changes affecting the jers. Note that the constraint in (68) does not express any requirement concerning the quality of the vowel in the strong position of the foot.

(68)

Faith Head ϕ: No eliding of vowels in a strong position.

Although jers were syllabic, they were insufficient to be foot-bearing units. According to Zec (1998:8), their insufficiency is connected with the fact that they were [-tense]. Since we do not know the exact featural content of jers, I propose that the head of a foot must be a full vowel (i.e. a non jer vowel) without further specification. This is expressed by the constraint in (69).[31]

(69)

ϕ [V]: A head of a foot must be a full vowel.

The constraints presented above contributed to the emergence of full vowels in strong positions. But there was another constraint which forced the dropping of jers. It directly expresses the tendency to reduce the number of syllables in the word. Implicitly, only syllables in weak positions could be lost because jers in strong positions were required by Head ϕ and ϕ [V]. Formally, the constraint militating against jers is stated in (70). It implies that jers are unstable unless they fulfill other high-ranking constraints, cf. also the constraint *SCHWA proposed by Raffelsiefen (1995:11) which militates against schwas.

---

[30] It is important to stress that the tendency to minimize the number of syllables expresses a general function of language, namely, its tendency to minimize the articulatory effort, cf. 1.3.3.

[31] Jers behaved in a similar fashion as [ə] in German or English, because they cannot bear stress.

(70)

*ъ (ь): No jer

In the following we will consider how the algorithm worked. The representative examples, which were previously selected as optimal candidates, created the basis for further changes. Their development was caused by some constraints introduced above. In the tableau in (71), competition among several candidates is presented. Since there is only one candidate, i.e. š(vec), that incurs no violations of the high-ranking constraints as opposed to its competitors, it is selected as optimal.[32] The last two candidates in (71) violate Faith Head ϕ because they drop the first syllable of their feet, cf. also (60).

(71)

šь(vьcъ)	Faith Head ϕ	ϕ [V]	*ь(ъ)
šь(vьcъ)		*!	***
☞ š(vec)			
še(vьcъ)		*!	**
šь(vec)			*!
šь(vcъ)	*!	*	**
šь(vcъ)	*!	*	**

Since the same invariant ranking affected other words, the new optimal outputs appeared with full vowels in previously strong positions and without jers. Note that each word containing at least one jer was reduced by one syllable. Pronouns constituted an exception, as discussed below. In the tableau in (72) the selection of the optimal candidate from the underlying input (šьvь)ca is shown, cf. also (62).

(72)

(šьvь)ca	Faith Head ϕ	ϕ [V]	*ь(ъ)
(švь)ca	*!	*	*
(šve)ca	*!		
(šьvь)ca		*!	**
(ševь)ca			*!
☞ (šev)ca			

The optimal candidate in (72), (šev)ca, in contrast to its competitors, does not incur any violations of the high-ranking constraints. It displays a faithful parse of a prosodic head which is constituted by a full vowel. Additionally, it does not contain a jer. This example clearly illustrates that MAX constraint, which prohibits deletions, and the IDENT constraint which requires faithful parsing of features had to be ranked lower

[32] Note that a constraint requiring faithful parsing of prosodic brackets, i.e. a foot, must be an undominated one.

than the constraints in (72) because the selected candidate does not contain jers. The featural content of jers is either changed or they are entirely dropped.

Furthermore, in bisyllabic words containing an unparsed jer-syllable, the jer was dropped. This is illustrated by the tableau in (73), cf. also (65).

(73)

kъ(to)	Faith Head φ	φ [V]	*ь(ъ)
kъ(to)			*!
☞ k(to)			

This example, like the output shown in (71), illustrates how the loss of jers caused the emergence of consonant clusters. Significantly, a large number of three or four consonant clusters emerged word-initially. As will be shown in 2.2.2, the consonants did not belong directly to the initial syllable but were linked either to a foot or to a prosodic word. Word-internally the consonants were parsed in syllable-initial or syllable-final position.

Since syllables were generally open in Late Common Slavic, after the loss of final jers, consonants occurring previously in the onset emerged in the coda. Consider the example shown in (74), cf. also (66).

(74)

(konь)	Faith Head φ	φ [V]	*ь(ъ)
(konь)			*!
☞ (kon)			

Finally, words consisting of at least three syllables, such as as kъni(žьkъ), presented in (67), became significantly shorter because of the constraint *ь(ъ). The selected optimal candidate, is shown in (75), cf. also (67).

(75)

kъni(žьkъ)	Faith Head φ	φ [V]	*ь(ъ)
kъni(žekъ)			*!*
kъni(žek)			*
kni(žk)	*!	*	
kni(žkъ)	*!	*	*
kъni(žьkъ)		*!	***
☞ kni(žek)			
kni(žekъ)			*!

The optimal output *kni(žek)* consists of two syllables, each of which contains a full vowel. In the next stage of the development the restructuring of prosodic constituents must have taken place. Since the strong-weak pattern was the only possible one and two full vowels could create such patterns. Therefore, kni(žek) was restructured to *(knižek)*.

The same holds for forms such as (šev)ca, presented in (72). This form contains a prosodic head in the prominent first position, but the second syllable remains unfooted. Hence, the restructuring from (šev)ca to (ševca) took place.

In summary, the development of jers played an enormous role in the segmental and prosodic structure of Slavic languages. The present study interprets the asymmetrical behavior of jers, i.e., either their loss or their reinforcement to full vowels, predicted by Havlík's Law (1889), as an interaction of both prosodic as well as segmental constraints. Since the bisyllabic domain was recognized as a basis for different processes in Late Common Slavic, the same domain is argued for the changes affecting the jers. Their development is determined by the force behind the emergence of prosodic heads on the one hand, and the tendency toward the reduction of syllables, on the other. Consequently, jers in strong positions of bisyllabic domains emerged as foot heads, and jers occurring in other positions, i.e. weak positions, disappeared. This process resulted in the emergence of the previously unattested consonants clusters. This and other consequences of the changes in the jers will be discussed in the next section in detail.

2.2 Consequences of the changes affecting the jers

The changes in the jers are commonly recognized as triggers of a 'phonological revolution' in the history of the Slavic languages, since their consequences had a significant impact on morphological and phonological dimensions such as the emergence of new syllable structures, the reorganization of prosodic relations, changes in the phonemic inventories, etc. These consequences will be summarized in this section, specifically with respect to the main subject of the present study, i.e., consonant clusters.

The loss of jers reduced the vocalic inventory by two segments, i.e., the front jer (ь) and the back jer (ъ). This reduction was, in a sense, recompensed by the increased frequency of jer reflexes, i.e., full vowels. In different Slavic dialects, jers in strong positions were reflected by various vowels, cf. discussion below. In Polish the most frequent jer reflex was a mid-vowel /e/, whereby the /e/ emerging from the front jer displayed additional palatalizing properties.

In restricted contexts other vowels such as /i/ and /ɨ/ are found as reflexes of jers. Their presence is attested in the adjacency of the glide /j/ in word-initial, word-medial and word-final position. The examples in (76) are provided for illustrative purposes only; an irregular development of jers in this context precludes one from stating generalizations, cf. Rospond (1971:76).

(76) Reflexes of jers in Polish

a.word-initially

jь → i	/jь/dą → [i]dę	'to go' 1ps.sg.pres.

	/jь/skra → [i]skra	'spark' nom.sg.
jь → ∅	/jь/mieć → ∅mieć	'to have' inf.
	/jь/gra → ∅gra	'play' nom.sg.
jь → ji→je[33]	/jь/go →[ji]go → [j]ego	'he' gen.sg.
b.word-internally		
ьj →ij	b/ьj/ą → b'[ij]ę	'to hit' 1ps.sg. pres.
	v/ьj/ą → v[ij]ę	'to plait' 1ps.sg. pres.
ьj →ij →ɨj	s/ьj/a → s[ij]a →s[ɨ]ja	'neck' nom.sg.
	č/ьj/a → č[ij]a → č[ɨ]ja	'whose' nom.sg.fem.
c. word-finally		
ъjь → ɨ	dobr/ъjь/ → dobr[ɨ]	'good' masc.nom.sg.
	star/ъjь/ → star[ɨ]	'old' masc.nom.sg.
ьjь → i	tan/ьjь/ → tan[i]	'cheap' masc.nom.sg.
	kost/ьjь/ → kost[i]	'bone' gen.pl.

In various areas of Common Slavic the changes affecting the jers in strong positions had different results. In (77) the most commonly encountered reflexes of strong jers in different Slavic dialects are illustrated, cf. Carlton (1991: 231-333). The single contexts, as well as reflexes of jers occurring adjacent to the glide /j/, are discussed in Carlton (1991).

(77)

	Czech	Slovak	Upper Lausatian	Lower Lausatian
ъ	e	o, a, ā, e	'e, 'o	'e, 'a
ь	e	e, 'a, ie, o	e, o	e

	Ukrainian	Russian	Belorussian	Bulgarian
ь	e	'e	'e	e
ъ	o	o	o	ə

	Slovene	Macedonian	Serbian	Croatian
ь	a, ə	e	ǎ ā	ǎ, ā
ъ	a, ə	o	ǎ ā	ǎ, ā

'e palatalizing e
ā long back vowel
ǎ short back vowel
a central vowel

The summary in (77) shows that different reflexes of jers must have directly contributed to the deepening of the dialectal differences in Common Slavic in a significant way. They are indeed one of the major dimensions along which the Slavic languages diverge.

---

[33] This change is attested only in the accusative singular of pronouns.

They also constitute one of the most important reasons as to why the loss and the vocalization of jers is considered as the last change to affect speakers of Common Slavic, cf. Carlton (1991:76).

Another consequence of the changes in the jers was the appearance of the 'mobile vowel,'[34] which appears in some forms of the same paradigm and disappears in others. The behavior of fleeting vowels therefore causes many vowel-zero alternation. In Polish it is the vowel /e/ that alternates. In (78) it is shown that the presence or absence of /e/ is directly motivated by the changes in the jers. Note that front jers caused palatalization of the preceding consonant. In the case of *pies* 'dog' nom.sg. palatalization is indicated orthographically by the vowel /i/, cf. the first example in (78). The lack of palatalization in *psa* 'dog' gen.sg. (i.e. *p'sa) is motivated by the loss of secondary palatalization in clusters. For a detailed discussion, see 4.1.7.

(78)

pies	pьsъ	'dog' nom.sg.
ps-a	pьsa	'dog' gen.sg.
ps-em	pьsъmъ	'dog' instr.sg.
sen	sъnъ	'dream' nom.sg.
sn-u	sъnu	'dream' gen.sg.
sn-em	sъnъmъ	'dream' instr.sg.

This alternation is considered to be fairly productive in Modern Polish, where not only proper names but also relatively new borrowings such as sin[g'el] vs. sin[gl]a 'single' nom./gen.sg. show the same pattern as native words.

Another direct consequence of the loss of jers was the reduction of the number of syllables in the word. Each word consisting of jers in weak positions reduced the number of its syllables. A considerable number of bisyllabic words became monosyllabic. Words consisting of three syllables were reduced to bi- or monosyllabic ones. Four-syllable words often became bisyllabic. The emergence of the new shape was clearly dependent on the prosodic and segmental organization of input forms. Some selected examples are illustrated in (79).

(79)

a. 2 syll. → 1 syll.	
dъ.va.→ dva	'two'nom.
lъ.nu.→ lnu	'flax'gen.sg.
domъ → dom	'house' nom.sg.
b. 3 syll. → 2 syll.	
pь.sъ.ka. → p'es.ka	'doggie' gen. sg.
šь.vь.ca. → šev.ca.	'shoemaker' gen.sg.

[34] Another term used for a mobile vowel is *fleeting* or *floating* vowel.

c. 3 syll. → 1 syll.
pь.sъ.kъ. → psek 'doggie' nom.sg.
šь.vь.cь → šviec 'shoemaker' nom. sg.
d. 4syll. → 2 syll.
měrьnъjь → m'ěrny 'mediocre' nom.sg.

The reduction of syllables is a strong argument for the optimization of Phonetic Form (PF), cf. 1.4.1. Since the PF of a lexical entry is linearly ordered, as opposed to Semantic Form, its optimization in terms of the shortening of a speech signal is not far from being expected. More importantly, the process described above is a convincing example of optimization, since it was accomplished without the loss of morphological information. However, as will be argued in the course of this thesis, cases of cost-free optimization almost never occur. Optimization at one level is nearly always accompanied by different compensatory phenomena at the same or another level. In the case at hand, there are some processes of a compensatory nature attested. For example, morphological information was not lost but the loss of jers in weak positions caused a lengthening of vowels in the preceding syllable. This process, commonly known as compensatory lengthening, manifested itself in various Late Common Slavic dialects in different ways, cf. Bethin (1998:96-104). In the following, we limit our discussion to the compensatory lengthening taking place in Polish, one of the Northern West Slavic dialects.

In Polish, this process is mainly found in bisyllabic words containing a word-final jer. As argued in several studies, the compensatory lengthening was additionally conditioned by segmental constraints, i.e., by the presence of a following voiced consonant. If the following consonant was voiceless, the lengthening of the preceding vowel did not take place. Relevant examples are provided in (80)a, where the vowel /o/ is lengthened, and in (80)b, where no lengthening occurs.

(80)

a.
wozъ → wóz[35] 'cart'nom.sg.
konь → kóń 'horse'nom.sg.
nogъ →nóg 'leg'gen.pl.
stolь → stól 'table'nom.sg.
b.
bokъ→bok 'side' nom.sg.
mrokъ→mrok 'darkness' nom.sg.
nosъ→nos 'nose' nom.sg.

As expected, within the same paradigm the words differ with respect to vowel length. The distinction is also retained in Modern Polish in which ó is pronounced as u. In most paradigm forms, however, the lengthening of the vowels did not occur, which is

[35] The lengthening is indicated by the diacritic < ´ > above the vowel.

motivated by the presence of the full vowel in the next syllable. Consider the paradigmatic forms of *wóz* 'car' nom.sg., provided in (81).

(81)

Nom.	wóz
Gen.	woza
Dat.	wozu
Acc.	wóz
Instr.	wozem
Loc.	wozie
Voc.	wóz

Formally, compensatory lengthening can be viewed as a dissociation of the mora from the jer – if one assumes a jer to be associated with mora – and its association to the preceding full vowel. This is shown in (82). Recall that not every North Central Slavic dialect as e.g. Polish retained length distinction in terms of moras.

(82)

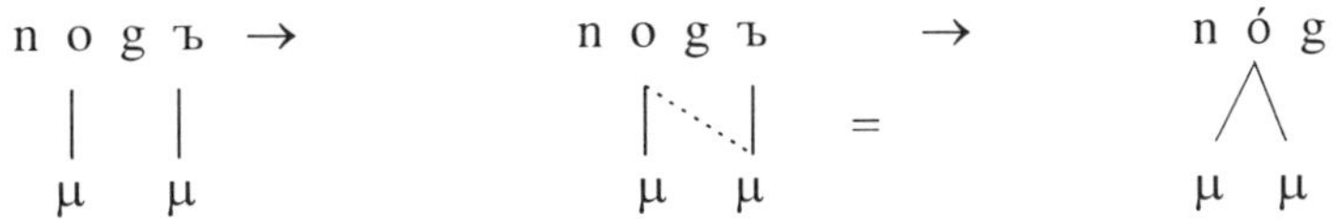

If compensatory lengthening is to be explained as a disassociation of moras associated with jers in the weak position, i.e. in a bisyllabic domain, the question arises as to why this process is conditioned only by voiced consonants and sonorants. In other words, the phonological explanation provided in (82) predicts the lengthening in items shown in (80)b which did not happen. Hence, it requires the stipulation that **compensatory** lengthening is sensitive to a segmental feature, i.e. [+voice]. Alternatively, one could postulate the deletion of jers and the lengthening of full vowels before voiced segments.

Additionally, it has to be stressed that there are also cases attested in which lengthening is found before voiceless consonants, e.g. *wrota* vs. *wrót* 'gate' nom.pl./gen.pl., *cnota* vs. *cnót* 'virtue' nom.sg./gen.pl., *siostra* vs. *sióstr* 'sister' nom.sg./gen.pl., *ręka* vs. *rąk*[36] 'hand'nom.sg/gen.pl. cf. Rozwadowski (1915:323ff.). Rozwadowski considers such cases as outputs of the lengthening under neo-acute before a jer in the weak position, cf. 2.1. In other words, the lengthening in these words was caused by retraction of a raising pitch contour from the last jer-syllable to a preceding full-vowel syllable. The process occurred before the changes in the jers and therefore cannot be considered as compensatory, cf. also discussion in 2.1.3.

An important epiphenomenon of the compensatory lengthening is that it provided distinctions between minimal pairs emerging after devoicing. Consider the examples shown in (83), cf. Długosz-Kurczabowa and Dubisz (1993:135).

[36] The lengthening is expressed by a change from /em/ to /om/ in Modern Polish, spelled as ę → ą.

(83)

róg [rʊk]		rok	[rɔk][37]	'year' nom.sg./ 'horn' nom.sg.
płód [pwʊt]		płot	[pwɔt]	'fence' nom.sg./ 'fetus' nom.sg.

In summary, compensatory lengthening, being a consequence of the loss of jers in weak positions, was subject to both prosodic as well as segmental constraints. It straightforwardly supports the claim that optimization does not occur without compensation which often manifests itself in a visible way.

A different way of compensating for the loss of jers is attested by the changes in syllable structure. As will be shown below, the optimization of the prosodic level in terms of the reduction of the number of syllables resulted in an increased complexity of structures on the other level, i.e., in the emergence of consonant clusters. This phenomenon, being the most important consequence of the loss of jers for the purposes of the present study, will be treated separately in the next subsection.

2.2.1 The Period of Trial and Error

The enormous changes triggered by the changes in the jers caused a kind of linguistic chaos. After the whole process was accomplished various ambiguities and variations arose invoking uncertainty among speakers.

The evidence from manuscripts shows that the process under consideration resulted in serious consequences for the morphophonemic system. The emergence of new complex syllable structures containing unknown clusters intensified the articulatory difficulties. Many forms showing an irregular development deepened the chaos. For this reason, this period, which is very interesting from the linguistic point of view but 'noisy' from the speaker's point of view, was dubbed the *Period of Trial and Error* by Isačenko (1970: 91).

In the following, we will discuss the most important issues connected with the Trial and Error period, focusing on consonant clusters. Let us first analyze apparent counter-examples with respect to the loss of jers in weak positions and their emergence as full vowels in strong positions.

One of the most important written sources from the first half of the twelfth century is 'Bulla Gnieźnieńska' 'Bull of Gniezno', dated 1136-1147, which was issued by Pope Innocent III for the Archbishopric of Gniezno. Although written in Latin, the Bull contains about four hundred Polish geographic and personal names, providing an important source of linguistic material. There is no single word in this document which contains a jer that would have indicated that the loss of jers was accomplished in the first half of the twelfth century.

The names attested in the Bull show a predominantly unified behavior, i.e., the jers are lost in weak positions and reinforced to full vowels in strong positions. Some of the relevant examples are presented in (84).

---

[37] The transcription provided resembles the pronunciation of present-day Polish.

(84)

Brodic (129)[38], Dobron (183), Dancowo (298), Parno (212), Pricuna (218), Radenta (68), Sirac (68), Trebna (132).

Most of the forms presented in (84) contained jers in weak positions. Consider the examples in (85).

(85)

Brodicъ → Brodic
Dobronь → Dobron
Danъcovo → Dancovo

However, a significant number of forms found in the 'Bulla Gnieźnieńska' (1136-1147) must apparently be treated as exceptions, since they lost jers in strong positions. Some examples are provided in (86). (The letter c is pronounced as [k].)

(86)

Blizc (192), Datc (360), Darcs (175), Domc (74), Crusc (147), Plastc (120), Potr (123), Razc (140), Rezc (141), Sodlc (142), etc.

The names provided in (86) crucially differ from those listed in (84) since the latter display complex codas. In most cases the codas also violate Sonority Sequencing Generalization (SSG),[39] cf. Selkirk (1984) as well as Sievers (1901), Jespersen (1904), Selkirk (1984), Prince and Smolensky (1993a).

Thus the obvious question arises as to why the words in (86) did not display the regular development and emerged with complex codas in violation of SSG. If they had developed in a predicted way, i.e., conforming to Havlík's Law, they would have emerged in the shapes presented in (87).

(87)

Blizъcъ → Blizec
Datъcъ→Datec
Sodlъcъ → Sodlec

An explanation for the aberrant behavior of the words under consideration can be seen if one considers the development of other forms constituting the same paradigm. In (88) the genitive and the dative case of the forms *Blizc*, *Datc*, and *Sodlc* are shown. The inflectional suffixes are separated by a hyphen (-). It is important to stress that other forms of the paradigm display the same root as the genitive and dative forms presented below.

---

[38] The numbers in parentheses indicate the verse number (taken from Rozwadowski (1909:432-82)).

[39] Sonority Sequencing Generalization (SSG) says : 'In any syllable, there is a segment constituting a sonority peak that is preceded and/or followed by a sequence of segments with progressively decreasing sonority values.' Selkirk (1984:116), cf. also discussion in 3.1.

(88)

gen. Blizъc-a → Blizc-a
dat. Blizъc-u → Blizc-u
gen. Datъc-a → Datc-a
dat. Datъc-u → Datc-u
gen. Sodlъc-a → Sodlc-a
dat. Sodlъc-u → Sodlc-u

If we take into account the commonly attested phenomenon that noun paradigms tend to have the same roots, we can offer an explanation for the facts described above. The new outputs with complex codas, i.e. *Blizc*, *Datc*, *Sodlc*, etc., do not have to be treated as exceptions but as forms identical to the roots of the regularly developed oblique forms. For example, *Brodicъ* nom.sg. emerged as *Brodic* since the genitive case of this form was *Brodic+a*, cf. examples in (84).

Accounting for the apparent exceptions in (86), we state that a constraint requiring root homogeneity in paradigms[40] took precedence over a constraint prohibiting complex codas as well as a constraint requiring the well-formedness of the syllable structure in accordance with the Sonority Sequencing Generalization. In Correspondence Theory, cf. 1.2.2, we can directly express the relationship between two related forms by means of constraints evaluating the Output-Output correspondences.

In 1.2.2 correspondence relations between the input and the output as well two output forms are presented schematically. The root of the genitive form *Datca* constitutes a basis for the nominative form *Datc* [datk]. As a consequence, the faithfulness between the underlying nominative form /datek/ and the output form [datk] is not of predominant importance. In other words, the constraints requiring a faithful relation between the input and the output must be low-ranked.

(89)

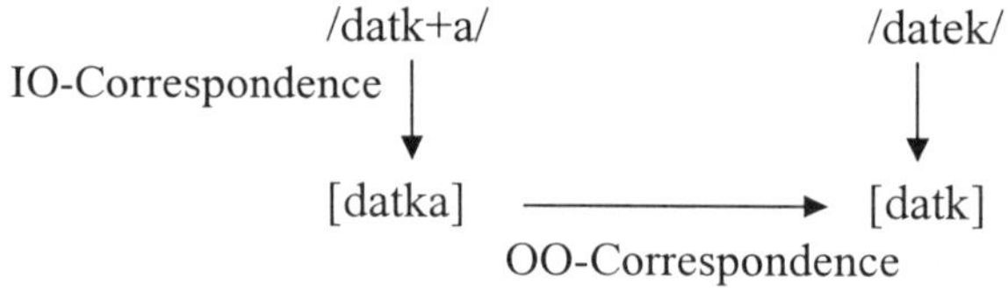

The IO-constraints evaluating the faithfulness between the input and the output, i.e. between /datek/ and [datk], are MAX-IO and DEP-IO, cf. the formulation of MAX-IO and DEP-IO in 1.2.2. Constraints requiring a faithful relation between related output forms, i.e., the output of the genitive form (root) and the output of the nominative form are MAX-OO and DEP-OO. Recall that MAX-OO prohibits deletions and DEP-OO militates against epenthesis in two phonologically related representations. In other words, MAX-OO and DEP-OO demand two related words to be identical.

[40] Recall that this constraint is based on a traditional concept of 'paradigm leveling' according to which words belonging to the same paradigm display the same form, cf. Kenstowicz and Kissberth (1979: 199); cf. also 1.2.2 and 4.1.5.

Another important constraint is NO COMPLEX CODAS presented in (90), that militates against complex codas, cf. Prince and Smolensky (1993a: 85f.).

(90)

$*CC]_\sigma$: NO COMPLEX CODAS[41] Syllables must not have complex codas.

In order to predict the selection of the optimal outputs, constraints requiring the faithfulness between the input and the output as well as the constraint militating against complex codas had to be lower ranked than constraints demanding a faithful parse between the output forms. This is illustrated in the tableau in (91) in which the candidate *Datk* that does not incur any violations of high-ranked DEP-OO and MAX-OO emerges as optimal.

(91)

Datek	DEP-OO	MAX-OO	$*CC]_\sigma$	DEP-IO	MAX-IO
☞ Datk			*		*
Datek	*!				
Dat		*!			*
Dtek	*!				*

The optimal candidate in (91) is a convincing example of the precedence of morphological requirements over phonological ones. The tendency for the homogeneous root of a paradigm proved stronger than the tendency against complex codas.

Generally, cases where the output-output relation takes precedence over markedness requirements or faithfulness to the underlying form are called Underapplication, as opposed to Overapplication and Normal Application, cf. 1.2.2. In the case at hand the optimal candidate has a complex coda and therefore violates the markedness requirement $*CC]_\sigma$.

In (92) a general schema of Underapplication as well as the specific instantiation derived from the case discussed above is provided.

(92)

Underapplication
OO-Identity>>Phono-Constraint>>IO-Faith
DEP-OO, MAX-OO >>$*CC]_\sigma$>> DEP-IO, MAX-IO

Before we proceed, let us posit the legitimate question as to why it was the nominative case that adjusted its form to the oblique cases and not vice versa. The question becomes more interesting if we consider the hypothetical examples emerging as outputs of the adjustment of the forms in oblique cases to that of the nominative case. These potential candidates are shown in (93).

[41] This constraint crucially differs from NoCoda, which prohibits simple codas, i.e., codas consisting of one consonant, cf. Prince and Smolensky (1993a: 85f.). Cf. also 3.2.2.

(93)

nom.	Blizъcъ →	Blizec
gen.		Blizec-a
dat.		Blizec-u
nom.	Datъcъ →	Datec
gen.		Datec-a
dat.		Datec-u
nom.	Sodlъcъ→	Sodlec
gen.		Sodlec-a
dat.		Sodlec-u

The adjustment of the oblique forms to the nominative forms has the same favorable effect as the adjustment of the nominative forms to the oblique forms presented above, namely, the homogeneity of the root in the paradigm. Moreover, the new forms such as *Blizeca*, *Blizecu*, etc., do not display codas at all since the single-consonant codas are resyllabified as onsets. Additionally, since there are no coda clusters, words like the ones in (93) vacuously satisfy the SSG. Hence, the potential candidates in (93) seem to be the more preferred ones than the attested outputs in (86). The problem is illustrated by the tableau in (94). The regular genitive form *Blizc+a* emerges incorrectly as *Blizeca*, since it changes its form according to the nominative form. Both output-output faithfulness constraints, DEP-OO and MAX-OO, are satisfied by the selected candidate, *Blizeca*, which is not faithful to its underlying form incurring a violation of DEP-IO. Its contestant, the intended winner *Blizca*, is incorrectly ruled out due to a violation of the high-ranking MAX-OO.

(94)

Blizc+a	DEP-OO	MAX-OO	$*CC]_\delta$	DEP-IO	MAX-IO
☞ Blizeca				*	
Blizca		*!			

These examples indicate that there needs to be an explanation for why the nominative forms adjusted to the oblique forms and not vice versa.

Let us consider the differences between the attested outputs, cf. (88), and the incorrect candidates, cf. (93). The only crucial difference, apart from those already observed, is the number of syllables. The forms presented in (88) consist of two syllables, whereas the incorrect forms in (93) consist of three. This simple observation has important consequences in explaining the phenomenon under consideration. At the time of the development of new outputs two strong tendencies existed. On the one hand the language tended to unify its paradigms, and on the other it tried to reduce articulatory effort by reducing the number of syllables. In many cases, but not in all, the outputs affected by the constraint requiring a minimal number of syllables resulted in a well-formed trochaic foot. In other words, if the oblique forms had adjusted to the nominative form, they would have been not only longer than the attested forms but they would also have had an unparsed syllable, i.e., *Bli.(ze.ka.)*.

As mentioned above, the emergence of the optimal (bisyllabic) trochaic foot could not be considered as the strongest tendency occurring at that time since there are many forms which do not display an optimal trochaic foot. Some relevant examples are discussed below.

Thus, in order to account for the nonadjustment of oblique forms to the nominative basis, a general constraint requiring a minimal number of syllables will be postulated. This constraint was previously proposed by Verhijde (1995:197) and Zoll (1997:193), and is a specific instantiation of a general constraint demanding no structure, as stated in (95), cf. Prince and Smolensky (1993a). This constraint is violated whenever a syllable is attested in the output. In its most radical application, it is satisfied when there are no syllables.

(95)

*Struc-σ: Have no syllables.

The constraint *Struc-σ expresses directly one of the main functions determining the development of the language, i.e., the minimization of the articulatory effort. This function, as shown in 1.3.3, is determined by many subfunctions, subject to several constraints. For example, Kirchner (1995:7) formulates a general constraint called LAZY that can be expressed in a different way, cf. the formulations given in (96). LAZY requires minimization of the articulatory effort, which can be manifested e.g. by the minimization of the number of articulatory gestures.

(96)

'LAZY': Minimize articulatory effort. (cf. Kirchner (1995:7)
Any gesture is more effortful than no gesture. (cf. Kirchner Internet OT-discussion from 10.05.97)

In the following we implement *Struc-σ into the ranking established thus far. If *Struc-σ is ranked above DEP-OO and MAX-OO, candidate *Blizeca* cannot emerge as optimal. It fares worse than its contestant *Blizca* with respect to the high-ranking *Struc-σ. This is illustrated in the tableau in (97).

(97)

Blizc+a	*Struc-σ	DEP-OO	MAX-OO	*CC]$_\delta$	DEP-IO	MAX-IO
Blizeca	**!*				*	
☞ Blizca	**		*			

In the following we consider other cases which are similar to the examples presented above in the sense that the force striving for root homogeneity in the paradigm was stronger than the faithfulness to underlying forms emerging after the changes affecting the jers. The forms under consideration displayed two variants within a paradigm. In (98) three representative examples are provided, cf. Łoś (1922:27). The shape of the root in the nominative form is the same as in the accusative and the vocative case, while the root form occurring in the genitive form is also representative for the dative, the instrumental and the vocative case.

(98)

a.		
nom.	sъ̯jь̥mь̯ → sjem	‘council’ nom.sg
gen.	sъ̥jь̯ma → sejma	‘council’ gen.sg.
b.		
nom.	šь̯vь̥cь̯→ šviec	‘shoemaker’ nom.sg.
gen.	šь̥vь̯ca→ ševca	‘shoemaker’ gen.sg.
c.		
nom.	pь̯sъ̥kъ̯→ psek	‘doggie’ nom.sg.
gen.	pь̥sъ̯ka → p’eska	‘doggie’ gen.sg.

Modern Polish does not display variations within the paradigms of words presented in (98). The nominative form was replaced by a root in genitive. But in the fifteenth and sixteenth centuries a considerable number of variable forms is still attested, cf. (98). For example, the title of the well known satire from 1586 written by Marcin Bielski is *Sjem niewieści* ‘Women’s council’ where the form *sjem* occurs in the nominative case. In present-day Polish this form is ungrammatical. Instead, the nominative case has the shape *sejm* which was adopted from the genitive case. In *Biblia Królowej Zofii* ‘The Bible of Queen Zofia’ from the mid fifteenth century we find the form *psek* ‘doggie’ nom.sg. in the following sentence “Agdisz tak szedl thobyas, a psek byezal gego zanym”, cf. Vrtel-Wierczyński (1963:83). In present-day Polish only the form *piesek* pronounced as [p’esek], is attested.

A similar leveling process took place in many other forms whose representative examples are shown in (98). If we compare the potential candidates for paradigm leveling, we come to the conclusion that both forms are monosyllabic, i.e., *sjem* and *sejm*, *šviec* and *ševc*, *psek* and *p’esk*. Hence, the constraint requiring a minimal number of syllables did not play a decisive role by selecting the optimal base for a paradigm root. What the winning forms have in common is the complex codas and noncomplex onsets. Since in most forms of a paradigm one of the last consonants constituting the complex codas was immediately resyllabified as the onset of the next syllable, the complex codas remained in two or three cases, depending on the properties of the word (animate/inanimate), e.g. *sejm* nom. vs. *sej.mu* ‘council’ gen. and *sej.mem* ‘council’ instr. Thus, it seems that complex codas were necessary outputs which the language allowed to emerge in order to permit other processes to occur. In terms of constraint interaction, it can be hypothesized that violations of $*CC]_\sigma$ were allowed in order to satisfy a higher ranking constraint.

In light of this observation the question arises as to which constraint outranked $*CC]_\sigma$. The account that will be presented here directly refers to the vowel-zero alternation presented above. As was shown in (78), in the monosyllabic words, the alternation of the vowel /e/ is a reflex of the presence of the jers. This alternation is also exemplified in (99).

(99)

sen	sn-u	'dream' nom.sg./gen.sg.
len	ln-u	'flax' nom.sg./ gen.sg.
pień[42]	pni-a	'trunk' nom.sg./ gen.sg.
wieś	ws-i	'village' nom.sg./ gen.sg.
pies	ps-a	'dog' nom.sg./gen.sg.
owies	ows-a	'barley' nom.sg./gen.sg.
mgieł	mgł-a	'fog' gen.pl./ nom.sg.
pcheł	pchł-a	'flea' gen.pl./ nom.sg.
szkieł	szkł-o	'glass' pl.gen./ sg.nom.

All words shown in (99) have at least one feature in common, namely, that the alternating vowel is followed by a single consonant. The vowel can be preceded, however, by one or two consonants, cf. the three last examples in (99). This observation leads us to the conclusion that the appearance of an alternating vowel is not only a diachronic reflex of a jer but it is conditioned by a segmental constraint, i.e., the alternating vowel must be followed by a single consonant.

In Modern Russian this condition is regarded as a rule. According to Isačenko (1970:91) "in present-day Russian there exists a very strict rule which precludes vowel/zero alternations within a given paradigm, if the vowel/zero alternation is followed by more than a single consonant." Isačenko (1970:91) also points out that in Russian an alternating vowel that was a diachronic reflex of a jer was regularly replaced by a 'steady' vowel if it was followed by two or more consonants. This rule, called the Single Consonant Rule, operates only within a given paradigm, i.e., in the presence of grammatical and not derivational morphemes. It is stated formally as in (100), cf. Isačenko (1970:92).

(100)

{#} → {V}/_ CC(C) before grammatical morphemes
where # marks the vowel/zero alternation

Most probably, this rule became operative in Polish as well, since words displaying vowel/zero alternation do not contain two consonants in root-final position, cf. the examples shown in (99). Hence, the reason why the roots having two consonants in the coda finally became a basis for a paradigm leveling can be motivated by the avoidance of vowel/zero alternation.

The insertion of a 'steady' (nonfleeting) vowel seems to be the ultimate goal of the changes presented above. However, it still has to be explained why the vowel-zero alternation is avoided. The relevance of this question is strengthened by a considerable number of monosyllabic words in Modern Polish that do display vowel/zero alternation, cf. the examples in (99). All forms in the right-hand column in (99) display initial clusters, since the root-final consonant becomes adjacent to the initial consonant(s) after

[42] Recall that the letter *i* following the consonant indicates its palatalization. The variation in pronunciation is discussed in 4.2.

the disappearance of the vowel. This observation provides an answer to the question posited above: if language economy had opted for *sjem*, *švec*, and *psek,* the oblique forms would most probably have changed to *sjma*, *švca*, and *pska*, analogously to the forms shown in (99). Such a possibility was certainly undesired for reasons to be discussed below and therefore the forms with two final consonants were more preferred as bases for paradigm levelings than forms containing one final consonant.

These observations lead us to propose a constraint which prohibits complex onset clusters in word-initial position. However, considering the fact that there is a considerable number of words in present-day Polish with three-member word-initial consonants and some words with four consonants in word-initial position, it would not be plausible to postulate a constraint prohibiting *any* three- of four-member clusters. In other words, the constraint prohibiting quantitaive complexity does not explain why sequences like *sjm*, *švc*, or *psk* were avoided and clusters such as *mgł* or *pstr* were allowed. The answer to this question is by no means easy and requires a very detailed phonological/phonetic explanation.

To the best of my knowledge Cyran and Gussmann (1999) are the first phonologists who attempt to show that Polish clusters are not totally accidental but they can be systematized (at least partially) according to segments constituting clusters. Important generalizations they found are inter alia that (i) in two-member word-initial clusters homorganic stops (/tt/, kk/, /pp/) are not possible, (ii) in two-member word-initial r+sonorant, n+consonant, j+consonant are not attested, (iii) three or four-member sequences consisting solely of obstruents – apart from sequences involving /s/ – do not occur (iv) in three-member onsets the first position is filled by a coronal obstruent and the second by a velar (the reversal order of the two segments is not present). Although Cyran and Gussmann (1999) make an attempt to give an account of word-initial clusters in the framework of Government Phonology, the data still required a detailed investigation. However, it seems to be appropriate to analyze the sequences from an articulatory or perceptive point of view in order to substantiate the generalizations concerning possible/impossible clusters independently of theoretical framework

Following Cyran and Gussmann (1999) I conclude that consonantal sequences in present-day Polish are not arbitrary but obey certain restrictions. Therefore, I assume that the restrictions were also active when after the loss of jers new clusters were created. This assumption also follows from many simplifications of clusters discussed in 2.3.1. as well as the irregular development of jers discussed below.

In the following I propose a constraint prohibiting complex clusters in the onset in a highly general way, cf. (101), whereby ‘complex’ is to be understood in articulatory rather than quantitative terms. I do not formalize this constraint by listing possible/ impossible clusters since the list would be incomplete. However, the attested simplifications of consonant clusters as well as not regular development of jers suggest that sequences such as e.g. *dsk*, *tsk*, *t͡šst*, *t͡śśt͡ś*, *vr’b*, *vr’x*, *śrp*, *vln*, *klb*, *xlm* are to be considered as ‘complex’, cf. also discussions in 2.2.3. and 2.3.1.

(101)

*Complex$_{\text{onset}}$ No complex consonant clusters in the onset

Another constraint that played a role in the selection of the paradigm bases is presented in (102).

(102)

*# : No vowel/ zero alternation

The constraint in (102) prohibits vowel-zero alternation and is satisfied if the floating vowel is followed by two consonants. Such a constellation blocks vowel-zero alternations.

Let us consider how the constraint interaction led to the selection of the optimal paradigm base.[43] In the tableau in (103) an evaluation of the nominative form *šv'ec* is provided.

(103)[44]

šv'ec	*Struc-σ	*#
☞ ševc	*	
šv'ec	*	*!

Since both candidates *šv'ec* and *ševc* (the genitive form) are monosyllabic, *Struc-σ alone cannot determine the winner. The decisive role was played by a constraint that prohibited the vowel-zero alternation by favoring two consonants in root-final position. Hence, the faithful parse is excluded due to the violation of *#, and *ševc* is selected as the optimal output.

The two final consonants in the optimal form *ševc* block the vowel/zero alternation. If *šv'ec* had been selected as optimal, an epiphenomenon would have emerged, i.e., the emergence of complex consonant clusters in the genitive form resulting in the total restructuring of these forms. The potential candidates are displayed in the tableau in (104), where the high-ranking *Complex$_{onset}$ immediately excludes the form with a complex cluster *švca* from consideration. Since the remaining candidates tie on *Struc-σ, the optimal input is selected by *#, which favors the root with two final consonants.

(104)

šv'ec	*Com$_{onset}$	*Struc-σ	*#
švca	*!	*	*
šv'eca		**	*!
☞šev'ca		**	

The tableau in (104) shows that the parsing consequently preferred the existing genitive forms as bases for paradigm levelings. If this solution is correct, then we are still faced with a few apparent counterexamples, such as *cześć* [t^{ś}eśt^{ś}] vs. *czci* [t^{ś}t^{ś}i] 'worship'

[43] Recall that the paradigm-levelings we discuss took place mostly in the fifteenth and sixteenth century.

[44] The motivation for a crucial ranking between Struc-σ and *# follows from the subsequent tableaux.

nom.sg./gen.sg. Although the nominative form contains two consonants in root-final position, it displays a vowel/zero alternation. However, the consonant cluster in the onset is simplified, cf. [t^{š}eśt^{ś}] 'worship' nom.sg., emerges in the genitive case as [t^{š}t^{ś}i] and not as [t^{š}śt^{ś}i]. Consequently, the form [t^{š}t^{ś}i] does not violate the high-ranking $^*CCC_{onset}$ and is still selected as the optimal candidate. This is illustrated in the tableau in (105).

(105)

t^{š}eśt^{ś}i	$^*Com_{onset}$	*Struc-δ	*#
t^{š}śt^{ś}i	* !	*	*
☞ t^{š}t^{ś}i		*	*
t^{š}eśt^{ś}i		*!*	

The examples presented above show that the constraint requiring the minimization of the number of syllables was outranked by a constraint prohibiting complex consonant clusters. This observation has a more general application, namely, the minimization of syllables is possible only to a certain extent because it is countered by increasing complexity on another level. The degree of complexity, however, is limited. In the case at hand, the appearance of complex consonant clusters was a reflex of the reduction of syllables, but this reduction was allowed unless more than three consonants appeared in the syllable onset. In this situation language economy decided not to allow to the emergence of complex clusters by favoring paradigms with two consonants in the coda that block vowel/zero alternation and its effects. If, however, clusters emerged, they were simplified, cf. also. 2.3.1. Not coincidentally that both strategies express the tendency of language to minimize the articulatory effort, although in a different way and in referring to different levels.

2.2.2 New syllable structure: emergence of new consonant clusters

One of the most important consequences of the loss of jers described in 2.1 was the increase in the number of consonant clusters in both onset and coda position. Their emergence had not only what I refer to below as 'external' consequences but also 'internal' ones.

By external consequences of the loss of jers I mean all results which do not refer to the internal organization of clusters, e.g. the influence of consonant clusters on syllable structure. Since jers in word-final position were said to be in weak positions, their loss caused the consonants in the onset to emerge in final position of the word, thus creating a closed syllable. If jers occurred in weak positions in the initial syllable of the word, new word-initial clusters emerged, cf. examples given below. The loss of jers in word-internal syllables created new clusters in word-internal position. Almost every cluster was new with respect to the possible combination of consonants. Furthermore, the clusters influenced the morphological system considerably and triggered various kinds of changes, cf. 2.2.1.

The external consequences were accompanied by 'internal' processes such as various kinds of assimilations, e.g., assimilation with respect to voicing, to the place of articulation, or to palatalization. Furthermore, certain complex consonant clusters, evidently constituting a burden for speakers, were simplified in different ways.

The direct consequences of the processes described above are by no means homogeneous. They displayed ambiguities and variations underlying the Period of Trial and Error.

In the following we analyze these consequences in detail. First, let us consider the onset clusters attested at the end of Common Slavic. According to Carlton (1991:101) the following consonants existed at that time, cf. (106).

(106)

Two-member clusters	Three-member clusters
1. b, p + r, l	1. s + p + r
2. d, t + r, l, v	z + b + r
3. g, k + l, v, n	2. s + t + r, v
4. s + l, v, n, m, p, t, k	z +d + r, v
z + l, v, n, m, b, d, g	3. s + k + r, v, l
5. x + r, l, v	z + g + r, v, l

The two-member clusters in (106) generally conform to the Sonority Sequencing Generalization, cf. ftn 39 and the discussion in 3.1. The only exception to the SSG based on the Sonority Hierarchy proposed by Selkirk (1984) are clusters that have an initial /s/ and /z/, since both fricatives can be followed by the plosives p, b, t, d, k, and g. Three-member clusters always contain /s/ or /z/ as their first member. Their second and third members together create a sequence that does not violate the SSG. (In 3.1 and 3.2 I argue that in Polish there is no difference between fricatives and stops with respect to sonority.)

If we assume the 'special' status of /s/ and /z/, then we contend that Common Slavic clusters generally conformed to the SSG as proposed by Selkirk 81984). Although they underwent different modifications, such as those resulting from palatalizations (discussed in chapter 4), their quantitative shape was principally retained until Late Common Slavic. It was the loss of jers that caused the emergence of quantitatively and qualitatively new consonant clusters. They emerged in different positions, i.e., word-initially, word-internally, as well as word-finally. In the following we will discuss some representative examples illustrating these changes.

Let us first consider clusters that appeared word-initially. In (107) the appearance of consonant clusters in bisyllabic words is demonstrated. In the left-hand column the changes in the shapes of syllables are shown, while in the right-hand column they are illustrated with concrete examples.[45]

---

45 The back jer (ъ) in the left-hand column is a cover symbol for either a front or back jer, as illustrated in the examples in the second column.

(107)

Cъ.CV. → CCV	kъto → kto	'who' nom.sg.
Cъ.CCV. → CCCV	mьgła → mgła	'mist' nom.sg.
Cъ.CCCV. → CCCCV	pьstry → pstry	'colorful' nom.sg.masc.
CCъ.CV→ CCCV	krъwi → krwi	'blood' nom.sg.
CCъ.CCV. → CCCCV	stьblo → st'blo	'stalk' nom.sg.

The new consonant sequences frequently created clusters that at first glance appear to violate the SSG. This observation, however, is only valid if one assumes that all consonants were incorporated into a syllable. But assuming that the SSG was still operative as a high constraint in the syllable domain after jers were deleted, the question arises as to what is the adequate representation of consonants that violate it. There are arguments that will be provided below and in chapter 3, that suggest a possible solution, namely, the incorporation of certain consonants into the higher prosodic constituents such as a foot or a prosodic word. This follows from the organization of the prosodic hierarchy that requires the following order of prosodic constituents: mora > syllable> foot> prosodic word, cf. Nespor and Vogel (1986:11), Selkirk (1995:442), cf. also 3.3. The idea of incorporation of the extrasyllabic segments into higher prosodic structure was proposed e.g. by Rubach and Booji (1990b), Rubach (1997), and Green (1997, 1998).

Consider the different prosodic representations of the intial sonorant /m/ shown in (108)a, b, and c.

(108)

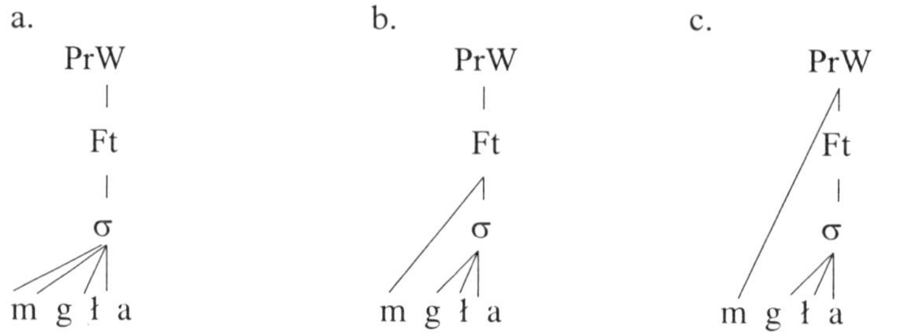

In (108)a all consonants belong to the same syllable, while in (108)b the sonorant /m/, the onset of the former jer-syllable, is linked to the foot, which constitutes the next level of the prosodic hierarchy. In (108)c the sonorant /m/ is adjoined directly to the prosodic word, skipping the foot level. I argue in 3.3 that the representation provided in (108)b is the most adequate one, since it conforms to both the segmental (sonority requirements) and the structural requirements (organization of the Prosodic Hierarchy).

The correctness of this analysis is independently supported by the word-internal syllabification of intervocalic sonorants. As I show in 3.1, word-internal syllabification plays a crucial role by determining 'true' syllable clusters. It determines whether the consonant cluster that occurs word-initially is a true syllable onset and whether the consonant cluster occurring word-finally is a true syllable coda, cf. 3.2.2. For example, if a word has an initial sonorant+obstruent+sonorant cluster, it can be shown that the first sonorant in the medial sequence consisting of sonorant+obstruent+sonorant is invariably syllabified as a coda, while the last two segments are syllabified as an onset of the following syllable: a word such as *kołdra* [kowdra] 'cover' nom.sg. is syllabified as *koł.dra* and never as *ko.łdra* or *kołd.ra*. This leads to the conclusion that only /dw/ is a 'true' syllable onset and hence can be syllabified as in (108)a. If a sequence sonorant+ obstruent+sonorant occurs *only* word-initially then only the final two consonants belong to the syllable, while the final is licensed by a higher prosodic constituent.

What the representation of the new word-initial consonant cluster shows is that there are licensing principles applying on single levels of the prosodic hierarchy. The new clusters were not incorporated into the syllable if the syllabic level did not license them. Hence, the unlicensed consonant skips the syllabic level and is attached to the level where it is licensed,[46] cf. the discussion in 3.3.

Word-internal clusters do not require further comment. As shown below, they were mostly heterosyllabified and incorporated into a syllable. Consider the examples provided in (109). The syllabification of clusters illustrates the reason why there were only a few cases where more than two consonants emerged in the onset, cf. also 3.2.2.

(109)

CCV.Cъ.CV.→ CCVC.CV	pravьda → pravda	'truth' nom.sg.
CCV.Cъ.CCCV. → CCVC.CCCV[47]	glupьstvo → glupstvo	'nonsense' nom.sg.

If a sonorant emerged between the obstruents it could not be syllabified either as the coda or as the onset since it would violate the SSG. The relevant example is provided in (110). In Modern Polish *piosnka* 'song' dim.nom.sg. displays a variation in syllabification; it can be syllabified as *pios.nka* and *piosn.ka*, cf. Rubach and Booij (1990b: 438).

(110)

CV.CCъ.CV → CVC.CCV or CVCC.CV   pěsnъka → pěsnka 'song' dim.nom.sg.

In 3.3 I will provide arguments for adjoining these consonants to a prosodic word. This conclusion directly follows from analyses of assimilatory voicing phenomena and degemination.

Finally, single consonants as well as consonant clusters emerged in syllable-final as well as in word-final position. With the loss of jers the period of the open syllables can therefore be considered to be accomplished.[48] Consider the examples shown in (111).

(111)

CV.Cъ.→ CVC	rybъ → ryb	'fish' gen.pl.
CV.CCь → CVCC	čestь → čest'	'worship' nom.sg.

[46] A similar situation is attested in Irish, cf. Green (1997:203f).

[47] For other possible syllabifications of words of a similar type cf. 3.2.2.

[48] In West Slavic moraic sonorants occurred in coda position.

In the prevailing number of cases the new codas arose from former onsets, which generally conformed to the SSG. Hence, they could not display decreasing sonority values required for elements following syllable peaks, and therefore they violated the SSG.

The requirements for word-final clusters, similar to word-initial clusters, suggest that the new clusters were not directly incorporated into the syllable but rather into the prosodic foot. The investigation of phonological processes such as voicing assimilation and degemination I discuss in 3.3 suggest that certain word-final consonants (the so-called extrasyllabic consonants) are licensed by the prosodic word. This is illustrated in (112).

(112)

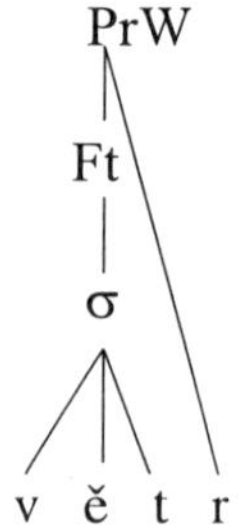

In summary, a direct consequence of the loss of jers was the emergence of complex consonant clusters which usually arose word-initially and word-finally. Most often they were not directly incorporated into the syllable but they had to be licensed by higher prosodic constituents such as the foot or the prosodic word in contrast to word-internal clusters which were licensed by the syllable. The only exception to the final generalization are medial clusters containing sonorants that could not be incorporated into the syllable but were licensed by the prosodic word.

2.2.3 Consonant clusters and the exceptional development of jers

As it was shown in 2.2.1, the algorithm responsible for the changes in the jers was in some cases blocked by higher ranked constraints. For example, output-output constraints requiring the paradigm root to be homogeneous had the power to override the regular development of jers. Furthermore, a high-ranking constraint prohibiting complex consonants clusters forced the avoidance of vowel/zero alternation, cf. the evaluations provided in (105) and (106).

In this subsection further examples are provided which straightforwardly indicate that the complexity of consonant clusters constituted a serious burden for the regular development of jers. Therefore, different strategies were undertaken in order to avoid segmental complexity.

Starting with monosyllabic words, let us consider the forms before and after the loss of jers provided in (113), cf. Łoś (1922:26). The expected but not attested shapes are given in parentheses.

(113)

dъ̯ska → [desk]a	(*dska)	'board' nom.sg.
tъ̯skny → [tesk]ny	(*tskny)	'longing' masc.nom.sg.
tъ̯skliwy → [teskl]iwy	(*tskliwy)	'sickly' masc.nom.sg.
čь̯stny → [t$^{\check{s}}$estn]y	(*čstny)	'noble' masc.nom.sg.
čь̯stovati → [t$^{\check{s}}$est]ovati	(*čstovati)	'to treat sb to sth' inf.

What these examples show is the unexpected reinforcement of jers to full vowels in weak positions. Such a development was, however, not surprising since it avoided the highly marked complex clusters shown in parentheses in (113). What seems to be more interesting is the reason why the clusters in the final column in (113) did not emerge while various free and four-member word-initial consonant clusters were created and not simplified, e.g., in [pstr]y 'colorful' nom.sg.masc. In other words, why did *pьstry* not emerge as *pestry* and *čь̯stovati* as **čstovati*?

As mentioned in 2.2.1, in order to answer this question a systematic investigation of all phonotactic restrictions is required. However there is not enough data in the literature which shows the exceptional development of forms like those presented above. Therefore we may only tentatively assume that the sequence such as čst [t$^{\check{s}}$st] was more complex than pstr from the articulatory point of view.

That articulatory economy was crucially involved in the processes described above, is confirmed by the forms presented in (114). These are derived from the same inputs as the forms provided in (113). Hence, both outputs constituted variations of the same form. The new words shown in (114) cannot be considered to be regular forms, since they display simplified clusters with respect to the original forms. Interestingly, a consonant was not elided, but instead the fricative /s/ and the preceding stop merged into an affricate. Note that in the first example in (114) voicing assimilation occurred. Other processes are discussed in 2.3.1.

(114)

dъ̯ska → [t^{s}k]a	'board' nom.sg.	cf. Łoś (1922:26)
tъ̯skny → [t^{s}kn]y	'longing' masc.nom.sg.	cf. Łoś (1922:27)
tъ̯skliwy → [t^{s}kl]iwy	'sickly' masc.nom.sg.	cf. Łoś (1922:27)
čь̯stny → [t$^{\check{s}}$n]y	'noble' masc.nom.sg.	cf. Łoś (1922:27)

Furthermore, groups of the type /trVt/ and /tlVt/,[49] which have always been of interest to Slavic phonologists, contained jers, i.e., sequences such as trъt, trьt, tlъt, tlьt were attested. According to Carlton (1991:250) their development occurred in Polish fairly regularly. If a jer was in a weak position, it disappeared, and if it was in a strong position, it was reinforced to /e/. Consider the examples shown in (115).

(115)

krъvь → [kr]ew	'blood' nom.sg.
krъvi → [krf]i	'blood' gen.sg.

[49] In these groups, /t/ denotes a plosive, /V/ a vowel and /r/ and /l/ represent r and l respectively.

plъtь → [pw]eć	'sex' nom.sg.
plъti → [pwt^{ś}]i	'sex' gen.sg.
drъžati → [drž]eć	'to shiver' inf.
grьmeti → [gžm']ieć	'to peal' inf.
slьza → [swz]a → [wz]a	'tear' nom.sg.

A different situation took place in sequences of the type tъrt, tьrt, tъlt, tьlt. Here we find many exceptions to the regular development of jers. For example, if /r/ in the sequence tъrt was followed by a velar or a labial, the jer was always realized as a vowel despite its position. The reinforcement to a full vowel also took place when /l/ occurred after labials and before dentals in the formula tьlt. Also when a labial preceded ъl, a full vowel appeared. Consider the examples shown in (116), cf. Carlton (1991:249f).

(116)

vьr'ba → vierzba	(*v'r'ba)	'willow' nom.sg.
vьr'xu → vierzxu	(*v'r'xu)	'surface' nom.sg.
sьrpa → sierpa	(*śrpa)	'sickle'nom.sg.
vъlna → welna	(*vlna)	'wool' nom.sg.
kьlbasa → kielbasa	(*klbasa)	'sausage' nom.sg.
xъlmu→ helmu	(*xlmu)	'helmet' nom.sg.

What the irregular development of these words suggests is the avoidance of certain consonant clusters. However, it does not seems possible to define the exact phononactic restrictions from the diachronic point of view because of the inconsistency of the sources. To be more concrete, the same cases as those presented above are explained by Stieber (1973:22) in a different way, namely by postulating a syllabic consonant. He represents *vъlna* as *vl̥na* or *kьlbasa* as *kl̥basa*. The syllabic liquids, according to Stieber (1973:22), developed further into -el, leading to the emergence of the forms *welna* and *kielbasa*. Adopting Stieber's proposal does not, however, cause us to the reject the solution proposed here. On the contrary it provides direct evidence that the development of syllabic liquids into a sequence of a vowel and a liquid was triggered by the high-ranking constraint leading to the avoidance of complex clusters.

2.3 Processes affecting clusters

This subsection is intended to show what kinds of processes took place within the 'new' consonant clusters. On the basis of some examples it will be illustrated that the emergence of clusters was followed by processes that in many cases constitute a basis for the phonology of Modern Polish. The focus of the following presentation will be placed on simplifications of consonant clusters discussed in 2.3.1; other processes such as metathesis and epenthesis are analyzed in 2.3.2 and 2.3.3, respectively. Two other important processes, voicing assimilations and palatalizations, are discussed at length in chapter 3 and chapter 4, respectively.

2.3.1 Simplifications of consonant clusters

The new complex clusters required much articulatory effort on the part of speakers in order to accurately pronounce new clusters. Data reveal that complex articulatory sequences were avoided by speakers by eliding consonants. This strategy had a straightforward perceptive consequence, namely, hearers not parsing the missing consonants started to pronounce their simplified version. The restructuring of underlying lexical forms followed suit.

Unsurprisingly, this phenomenon was by no means regular; the deleted consonants as well as the environment in which simplifications were attested differed from case to case. For this reason it is almost impossible to establish generalizations and draw reliable conclusions. However, it seems that in the processes of simplification of clusters, constraints requiring the faithful parsing of clusters were ranked lower than constraints prohibiting complex articulatory sequences, cf.(101). In other words, the attempt to minimilize the articulatory effort was stronger than other tendencies.

Let us proceed to the examples. Simplifications generally took place in three-member consonant clusters. In many cases it was the medial plosive that underwent deletion. Consider the examples shown in (117), cf. Klemensiewicz et al. (1955:155) and Rospond (1971:126f).

(117)

stn → sn	milostьnъ → milosny	'love-' masc.nom.sg.
rdn → rn	milosr̥dьnъ → miłosierny	'merciful' masc.nom.sg.
rgn → rn	stargnąć → targnąć	'to pluck' inf.
zdn → zn	Gniězdьno → Gniezdno → Gniezno	'Gniezno' nom.sg.
stb → zb	istba → izba	'room' nom.sg.

Clusters containing sequences of two fricatives such as /žs/, /šs/, /zs/ after the assimilation to /ss/ as well as the original /ss/ sequences elided the first fricative. Simplifications of that type are attested in word-medial position. Relevant examples are shown in (118), cf. Rospond (1971:125). Interestingly, word-initial clusters of the type /ss/ did not undergo simplification, and they still occur in Modern Polish, e.g. /ss/ać 'to suck' inf., /ss/ak 'mammal' nom.sg.

(118)

žьsk → šsk → ssk → sk	božьsk- → boski	'divine' masc.nom.sg.
lšьsk → ssk → lsk	volšьsk- → włoski	'Italian' masc.nom.sg.
sьsk → ssk → sk	nebesьsk- → nebesьski	'blue' masc.nom.sg.
zьsk → ssk → sk	lazьsk-→ łaski	'£azy's' masc.nom.sg.

Furthermore, sequences of the type fricative+liquid+fricative were avoided in different ways. First, the first fricative was dropped and the following sequence, although not preferable in view of sonority requirements, was retained. Sometimes simplifications proceeded to the extent that even the following liquid was elided, so that a single consonant from a three-member cluster emerged. Relevant examples are provided in (119), cf. Klemensiewicz et al. (1955:155).

(119)

slьsk → s	permyslьskъ	→ przemyski	'Przemyśl's' masc.nom.sg.
slьz → lz	slьza → łza		'tear' nom.sg.

Simplifications also took place in two-member clusters. Especially striking are examples in which the plosive (the first member of the cluster) was deleted word-finally. Hence, only one consonant, predominantly a sonorant, remained in word-final position. This process is understandable if one considers the fact that the only possible codas in Late Common Slavic were sonorants (l and r).[50] The same strategy, i.e., avoidance of the first plosive of a two-member cluster is found in word-medial position. This led to an even more favorable situation than in the case of word-final simplifications, namely, codas were entirely dropped and an open syllable was created. Both simplification types are illustrated by the examples in (120), cf. Rospond (1971: 126).

(120)

pn → n	sъpnь →sen	'dream' nom.sg.
dm → m	dadmь →dam	'to give' 1 ps.sg. fut.
bn → n	gybnąti → ginąć	'to die' inf.

As mentioned earlier, an expected simplification took place in cases when the dental plosive /t/ or /d/ preceded /s/ after the loss of jers. The fricative, instead of being pronounced as a separate sound, coalesced with the plosive to form an affricate. When /s/ followed /d/, its change to a secondary articulation was preceded by a voicing assimilation, i.e., /d/ became voiceless. The examples in (121) illustrate these developments, cf. Klemensiewicz et al. (1955:155).

(121)

dьs → ds → ts → [t^s]	sosědьstvo→ sosě[t^s]tvo	'neighbourhood' nom.sg.
tьs → ts → [t^s]	bogatьstvo → boga[t^s]tvo	'richness' nom.sg.

In sum, the cases presented above illustrate that the new clusters constituted a serious burden for speakers, and therefore they were avoided by them in different ways. The question what was the exact articulatorily (or other) reasons for these simplifications I leave open for further research.

2.3.2 Metathesis

Another phenomenon attested after the loss of jers was an exchange in the order of consonants in clusters, i.e. metathesis. This process occurred fairly rarely.

---

[50] In Late Common Slavic sonorants in coda position were moraic in contrast to sonorants occurring in other positions.

Examples illustrating metathesis seem to show a better adjustment to the universal sonority profile of the syllable, which is a common explanation for cases of metathesis, cf. e.g. Ultan (1978), Hock (1991). But considering the enormous number of forms in Polish violating the SSG, the examples presented below are to be considered as exceptions rather than examples illustrating a regular development. Consider the examples illustrating metathesis in (122).

(122)

blъxa → płxa → pxła	'flea'nom.sg.	Łoś (1922: 27)
dvьri → dvři → džvi	'door' nom.sg.	Rospond (1971: 128)

In the first example the order plosive+liquid+fricative was changed to plosive+fricative +liquid, a sequence that shows a better sonority profile than the one before the metathesis. In the second example in (122) the motivation for the exchange of consonants is less clear, namely the sequence plosive+labio-dental voiced fricative+fricative trill changed to the sequence of plosive+dental voiced fricative+voiced fricative after the fricative trill became a voiced fricative, cf, also 4. 2.7.

Another example of metathesis is found in documents from the fifteenth century, cf. Łoś (1922: 196). Consider examples provided in (123), in which the sequence /vš/ was metathesized to /šv/.

(123)

všemi→švemi→svemi	'one's (sth)' pron.instr.pl.
všemu→švemu→svemu	'one's (sth)' pron.dat.sg.

Since there is only a handful of examples illustrating exchange of consonants, we conclude that metathesis was not a productive process after the loss of jers. It is to be considered as exception which is a rather an expected phenomenon in the process of sound change.

2.3.3 Epenthesis

In this subsection we finish the discussion of the processes taking place in the clusters by considering a rather unexpected phenomenon, namely, epenthesis of a consonant in the existing clusters. The epenthesis of the consonant usually created a three-member cluster from a two-member one.

Let us consider the cases presented in (124), cf. Łoś (1922: 194f).

(124)

zr→zdr[51]	zrada → zdrada	'treason' nom.sg.
sr→ str	srąčiti → stręczyć	'to pander' inf.
sk → stk	klęska → klęstka	'defeat' nom.sg.

[51] This is an example of prothesis, i.e. epenthesis in word-initial position.

mn → mpn	nieskromność → nieskrompność	'immodesty' nom.sg.
ml →mpl	pomłocił → pompłocił	'to tresh' inf.perf.
nr → ndr	Henryk → Hendryk	'Henryk' nom.sg.

What the examples presented in (124) have in common is the agreement in place assimilation between the first consonant in the cluster and the epenthesized one. Such a feature is characteristic for the so-called intrusive stops, e.g., English pri[ns] 'prince' is pronounced as pri[nts] and Sa[ms]on as Sa[mps]on, where the epenthesized dental and labial plosive have the same place of articulation as the preceding consonants.[52] This phenomenon is sometimes explained as an epiphenomenon of articulatory transitions from the place of articulation of one consonant to another. Counterexamples, however, show that such an explanation cannot always be accepted. This is also the case in Polish, e.g. sk → stk. It must be stressed, however, that epenthesis is attested in only a handful of words and is therefore not to be considered as a regular development of clusters. Moreover, most forms that displayed an epenthetic consonant after the loss of jers in Old Polish do not have it in Modern Polish, e.g., klę[stk]a or nieskro[mpn]ość are pronounced as klę[sk]a and nieskro[mn]ość, respectively. As stressed by £oś (1922: 194ff), epenthesis in clusters was in most cases irregular and sporadic.

It is, however, still interesting to see that the development of language cannot be exclusively encapsulated in systematic schemes. Rather, the attested irregularities and exceptions indicate individual dynamics of linguistic forms which were strongly evidenced by the Period of Trial and Error.

52 Epenthesis in English and German is different from the ones presented in (124) because in both languages a stop is epenthesized after a homorganic nasal or lateral but not after r and before a fricative.

3 CHAPTER THREE: A Synchronic Approach To Polish Consonant Clusters

> "Polish paradox: speakers tolerate extraordinarily consonant clusters except when they do not" (Bethin 1992:14).

The reason why Polish tolerates marked consonant clusters has never been adequately explained. Their complexity refers to different dimensions and therefore does not allow one to find any regular patterns that they follow. This is, however, not surprising. The vast majority of clusters, as shown in chapter 2, arose as a by-product of prosodic changes. Constraints determining prosody were higher ranked than constraints referring to the segmental level. For this reason regularities concerning segmental sequences were, in a sense, sacrificed in order to fulfill stronger prosodic requirements. This leads to the conclusion that any attempt to systematize clusters from a synchronic point of view is forced either to admit a significant number of exceptions or to postulate additional mechanisms, strategies or constructs such as empty vowels, cf. 3.1.2. But as shown in the previous chapter, a sacrifice of segmental regularities was possible only to some extent, and therefore we might still be able to make generalizations with respect to the segmental level. This is the main task of the present chapter, which is outlined as follows.

First, I shall give a brief introduction to the clusters attested in present-day Polish, whose complexity is illustrated when one examines universal requirements governing clusters and syllable structure. Against this background I will provide a detailed presentation of the data by grouping them into two-, three-, four-, and five-member clusters with respect to both the sonority of the elements constituting clusters and the positions in which they occur, i.e., word-final and word-initial positions. Although the focus of the presentation is placed on word-initial and word-final clusters, word-internal consonant sequences also will be discussed. Taking into consideration sonority distinctions, the number of possible consonant sequences in single sets (sonorant+ obstruent, obstruent+obstruent, etc.), the frequency of occurrence of single clusters, as well as syllabification provided by native speakers, I formulate some generalizations concerning Polish syllable structure.

The main difference between my approach and the previous accounts presented in 3.1.2 is that I consider the syllable to be solely a *surface* construct. The earlier analyses, cf. Rubach and Booij (1990a,b), Gussmann (1991), Bethin (1992), assume various abstract derivational levels and make use of rules which create 'abstract' syllables thatare then changed into surface syllables by later rules. In addition, rules are determined by constraints in order to prevent the emergence of undesired structures. In my approach I assume a single (concrete) level of representation and consequently I dispense with abstract rules in a derivation. Instead, I use constraints that evaluate the surface representation. Most, but not all, of the constraints, as opposed to rules, are violable and therefore are able to account for variations of syllabification with one invariable model of grammar.

In order to determine the well-formedness of the Polish syllable I will try to draw as many conclusions as possible from the facts referring to the surface. Based on the surface representation I will show how syllable well-formedness is reflected in phonolo-gical processes.

In 3.2 I will propose an account of consonantal sequences and syllable structure which makes use of universal markedness constraints. The proposed analysis evaluates clusters against universal constraints posited in clusters (3.2.1) as well as syllabification (3.2.2). It will be shown that an analysis within the framework of Optimality Theory correctly accounts for syllabification patterns and captures all attested variations provided by native speakers. Against this background a novel treatment of extrasyllabic consonants will be presented in 3.3. Finally, the correctness of the proposed syllable structure (including extrasyllabic consonants) will be supported by voicing phenomena (3.3.1) as well as degemination (3.3.2).

3.1 The complexity of consonant clusters

> "The one uncontroversial fact about Polish syllables is that their number in a word equals the number of vowels" (Gussmann 1992b:37).

Agreement among linguists with respect to the structure of the Polish syllable is limited to the observation that a syllable must consist of at least one vowel. Hence, the number of syllables in a given word corresponds to the number of vowels which it contains. Admittedly, this is not a very enlightening observation. Another uncontroversial fact concerns syllabification; it is namely undeniable that a sequence of vowel+conso-nant+vowel (VCV) is always syllabified as V.CV, cf. the discussion in 3.2.2.

All other issues concerning syllable structure are a matter of debate and are therefore explained by sometimes drastically different accounts. A modest illustration of this discrepancy is provided in 3.1.2. One might wonder what triggers such controversies. My answer is straightforward: the enormous complexity of consonant clusters along different dimensions (quantity, violations of sonority) as well as various *abstract* ways to approach it is the main reason for the existing disagreement. As a consequence the proposed principles/generalizations concerning the segmental and prosodic require-ments are in conflict, which leads to differences in their representation.

Let us first have a glance at this complexity by observing the quantitative range of possible consonant sequences attested in one-syllable words. In (125) it is shown that a single Polish syllable may consist at one extreme of a single vowel and at the opposite extreme of one vowel and seven consonants.[53] Word-initial onsets may have as many as four consonants, but they may also remain empty. The same is true for codas with the subtle difference that even five consonants may occur in word-final position.

(125)

Coda / Onset	O member	1 member	2 members	3 members	4 members	5 members
O member	[a] 'but'	[ix] 'they' gen.pl.	[ɔśt^{ś}] 'fish-bone' nom.sg.			
1 member	[tɔ] 'this'nom. sg.neut.	[mak] 'poppy' nom.sg.	[sɛrt^{s}] 'heart' gen.pl.	[baršč] 'borscht' nom.sg.	[źɛmstf] 'district' gen.pl.	
2 members	[stɔ] 'hundred' nom.	[ptak] 'bird' nom.sg.	[skarp] 'treasure' nom.sg.	[spɔlšč] 'to polonize' 2ps.sg.imp.	[gwupstf] 'stupidity' gen.pl.	[skɔmpstf] 'stinginess' gen. pl.
3 members	[mgwa] 'fog' nom.sg.	[krtań] 'larynx' nom.sg.	[stwamś] 'to crush' 2.ps.sg.imp.		[sknɛrstf] 'stinginess' gen.pl.	
4 members	[źd^{ź}bwɔ] 'stalk' nom.sg.	[pstšɨt^{ś}] 'to speckle' inf.	[pstrɔŋk] 'trout' nom.sg.			

The quantitative complexity of the one-syllable words presented in (125) is accompanied by qualitative richness; it seems that all possible combinations of consonants are attested in various positions. In light of sequences such as plosive+sonorant+plosive in word-initial position, e.g., /krt/ in [krt]ań 'larynx' nom.sg. or nasal+plosive+fricative+plosive+fricative in word-final position as /mpstf/ in sko[mpstf] 'stinginess' gen. pl. the adjacency of two plosives in [pt]ak 'bird' nom.sg., which is undoubtedly a marked structure cross-linguistically, is not surprising in Polish. The few restrictions indicated by the blank cells in (125) do not allow one to derive any generalizations either; on the contrary, they may even further blur the potential generalizations, if they exist at all.

If one hopes to find any kind of agreement among consonants constituting clusters such as identity with respect to place of articulation, continuance, nasality, etc., one must be satisfied with the fact that Polish consonant clusters only agree with respect to voicing with some exceptions, of course. This issue is discussed in 3.2.1 and 3.3.1.

In light of these facts the question arises whether there exists a construct called *syllable* in Polish at all and if so, whether it shows any kind of regularities. The positive answer to the first question is provided for instance by the ability of native speakers to syllabify words; although the results of syllabification often differ from each other, there are a few instances that are never violated by dividing words into syllables, these

[53] Note that not every word in the tableau is a lexical one; [a] and [to] are functional words.

are discussed in 3.2.2. More importantly, there are phonological rules that indicate the impossibility of parsing of certain consonants into syllables, cf. 3.3. Before we answer the question concerning regularities of clusters, let us briefly repeat the universal requirements posited for syllable structure that constitutes the first level of the organization of consonant clusters along the prosodic hierarchy.

One indispensable concept governing syllable structure is sonority. Although there is no ultimate definition of sonority in phonetic terms, it is commonly understood as "the degree of openness of the vocal apparatus during production or the relative amount of energy produced during the sound" Goldsmith (1990:110). Because it is difficult to find exact phonetic correlates of sonority of single sounds, many phonologists try to define this principle on the basis of abstract representations, cf. Clements (1990), Rice (1992), Selkirk (1984). They operate with abstract notions of a sonority scale that orders natural classes of segments from the most sonorous to the least sonorous. The most sonorous segments are claimed to create the peak of a syllable, which is surrounded by less sonorous segments, cf. also the concept on Consonantal Strength discussed below.

The concept of sonority is one of the oldest concepts concerning syllables. The first observations about sonority appear in Sievers (1901) and Jespersen (1904).[54] More recent studies on this issue include e.g. Hooper (1976), Murray and Vennemann (1983), Selkirk (1984), and Clements (1990). For illustrative purposes we will consider the Sonority Sequencing Generalization as proposed by Selkirk (1984), cf. (126).

(126)

> Sonority Sequencing Generalization (SSG): "In any syllable, there is a segment constituting a sonority peak that is preceded and/or followed by a sequence of segments with progressively decreasing sonority values" (Selkirk 1984:116).

Selkirk assigns sonority indices to selected segments; their function is to express the sonority relations between the sounds to which they are assigned. In (127) a 'provisional version' of the sonority hierarchy of English is shown in which sounds are provided with their sonority indices, cf. Selkirk (1984:112). Selkirk leaves the question open where other sounds fit into the hierarchy in (127).

(127)

> a (10), e, o (9), i, u (8), r (7), l (6), m, n (5), s (4), v, z, ð (3), f, θ (2), b, d, g (1), p, t, k (.5)

The sonority indices in (127) characterize the natural classes of segments that can be associated with a particular position in the syllable. They are intended to express the sonority *relations* between the natural classes rather then to reflect the absolute integer value of sonority.

In addition, Selkirk (1984:115) proposes a syllable template schema presented in (128), in which O denotes an onset element and R a rhyme; the subscript integers stand for the first position, second position, etc.

---

[54] For a historical overview concerning sonority, cf. Clements (1990: 284-287).

(128)

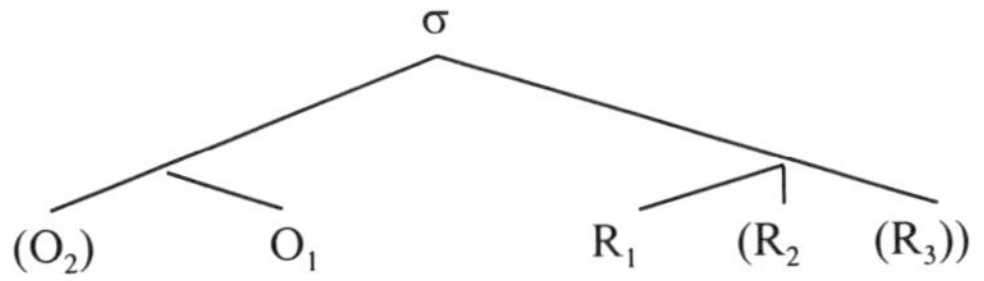

This template schema stands for a set of separate templates containing the following order of terminal positions O_1R_1, $O_2O_1R_1$, $O_1R_1R_2$, $O_2O_1R_1R_2$, $O_1R_1R_2R_3$, $O_2O_1R_1R_2R_3$. Each terminal position is expressed in terms of sonority indices (SI) that condition the association of a class of segments to particular positions in the syllable structure in a given language. Selkirk (1984:116) exemplifies the template in (128) in the following way, cf. (129). (SI = Sonority Index).

(129)

a. If x is associated with O_1, then SI (x) $\leq$ 8.
b. If x is associated with O_2, then SI (x) $\leq$ 3.
c. If x is associated with R_1, then SI (x) $\geq$ 8.

The first condition in (129) states that the O_1 position must be associated with *i* or *u* or any segment with a sonority index less then 8, while the second condition states that O_2 position must be filled by either *v*, *z*, ð, or *f*, θ, or *b*, *d*, *g*, or *p*, *t*, *k*. The last condition in (129) states that the first position in the rhyme has to be filled by a vowel.

It has to be stressed that all conditions in (129) are language particular conditions for English. The universal condition imposed on the syllable is expressed by SSG, cf. (126), that indicates that consonant clusters display increasing sonority from their syllable-initial position to the peak (nucleus) and decreasing sonority from the peak to the coda.

In contrast to Selkirk (1984), Vennemann (1988), following Hooper (1976), takes into consideration "a phonetic parameter of degree of deviation from unimpeded (voiced) air flow" and orders sounds according to this phonetic correlate. The proposed scale is presented in (130), cf. Vennemann (1988:8). Note that in Vennemann's model 'sonority' is accounted for with the inverse order, i.e. 'segmental strength.' In (130) it is shown that the low vowels have the least consonantal strength as opposed to voiceless plosives, which have the most strength.

(130)

↑ increasing Consonantal Strength

voiceless plosives
voiced plosives
voiceless fricatives
voiced fricatives
nasals
lateral liquids (l-sounds)
central liquids (r-sounds)
high vowels
mid vowels
low vowels

As in the case of SSG, the scale of 'Consonantal Strength' is claimed to be universal.

In light of universal concepts like SSG or the scale of 'Consonantal Strength,' the question arises whether they are operative in Polish. The data presented in (125) suggest that sonority does not play any role in the organization of the Polish syllable what-soever. For example, the word [mgwa] 'fog' nom.sg. contains an [m] as the first member of an onset and a [g] as the second member. Thus, it clearly violates SSG and the scale of 'Consonantal Strength.' However, this tentative conclusion can be only accepted if one presumes that all consonant sequences occurring at word-edges, as e.g. /krt/ in [krt]ań 'larynx' nom.sg., belong to a syllable.

In the following I argue that Sonority Sequencing Generalization plays a very important role in the organization of Polish syllable but the sonority hierarchy in (127) and the scale of 'Consonantal Strength' in (130) do not operate in Polish. Instead I propose an appropriate hierarchy for Polish. I discuss the syllabification of word-medial consonant clusters in order to gain an insight into the nature of the phonetic syllable. Furthermore, I expect that the results of the investigation will help to determine syllable onsets and syllable codas. This is an important point considering the fact that word-initial or word-final clusters cannot always be equated with syllable onsets or syllable codas, respectively. Interestingly, earlier analyses such as Kuryłowicz (1952) and Wierzchowska (1971) make the word-internal syllabification dependent on word-initial or word-final clusters, i.e., medial syllable onsets and syllable codas are defined in terms of word-initial and word-final clusters. A sequence such as $C_1VC_2C_3V$ will be syllabified as $C_1V.C_2C_3V$ if C_2C_3 is an attested word-initial consonantal sequence. This generalization however does not hold for Polish and more importantly, it leads to false predictions. For example, a word like *pałka* 'stik' nom.sg. is syllabified as *pał.ka* although the existing word-initial łk cluster in *łkać* 'to sob' predicts the unattested syllabification *pa.łka*, cf. also Bethin (1992:28); *korty* is syllabified as *kor.ty* 'tennis-court' nom.pl. and not as *ko.rty* albeit the word-initial cluster /rt/ exists in *rtęć* 'mercury' nom.sg.

According to the Law of Initials, cf. (131)[55] word-medial syllable onsets are a subset of word-initial syllable onsets and the better the word-medial syllable onsets, the less they differ from word-initial syllable onsets.

(131)

Law of Initials
"Word-medial syllable heads are the more preferred, the less they differ from possible word-initial syllable heads of the language system" (Vennemann 1988:32).

I assume that according to the Law of Initials the preferred syllabification of the word *pałka* 'stick' nom.sg. would be *pa.łka* since *łk* does not differ from the word-initial cluster in *łkać* 'to sob' inf. However, if one considers *łk* as an impossible initial *syllable* onset, then the only possibility would be the syllabification *pał.ka*, cf. 3.2.2. A correct generalization that can be made with respect to the syllabification of *pał.ka* is that whenever a sonorant is followed by an obstruent word-medially, only the obstruent is syllabified as onset and the sonorant is syllabified as coda. This strict syllabification pattern creates adjacent syllables that obey the Contact Law, cf. (132).

(132)

Contact Law
"A syllable contact A$B is the more preferred, the less the Consonantal Strength of the offset A and the greater the Consonantal Strength of the onset B; more precisely - the greater the characteristic difference CS(B)-CS(A) between the Consonantal Strength of B and that of A" (Vennemann 1988:40).

Although the Contact Law accounts for the correct syllabification of *pał.ka*, it does not predict the correct syllabification of all medial sequences attested in Polish. As will be shown below words like *dobry* 'good' masc.nom.sg. are syllabified either as *do.bry* or *dob.ry*, cf. 3.2.2. In order words, the Syllable Contact Law holds for Polish only to a certain extent. In 3.2.2 I will argue that the Syllable Contact Law is incorporated in a 'sonority constraint' that prohibits the incorporation of certain clusters into the syllable while allowing the parsing into the syllable of others.

More recent studies, such as Halle and Vergnaud (1980), Steriade (1982), Rubach and Booij (1990a, 1990b), and Green (1997, 1998), show that in some languages more complex consonantal sequences are allowed at word-edges than in word-medial position. More importantly, consonants occurring at edges do not count from the point of view of the SSG because they are *word-inital* or *word-final clusters* and not *syllable-initial* or *syllable-final* ones.

If word-initial or word-final sequences occur word-medially, they are heterosyllabified. For example the cluster in *łk* occurs in word-inital position in *łkać* and it is heterosyllabified in *pał.ka*. Hence, it is plausible to claim that word-internal syllabification provides viable evidence for showing which clusters are syllable-initial clusters. Using this strategy, some consonants occurring at word-edges, as for example *ł*

[55] In Vennemann's terminology *head* refers to the traditional onset and *onset* to the first consonant in the syllable; *offset* indicates the last consonant in the syllable.

in *łkać* remain unsyllabified; they do not correspond to medial consonantal sequences. As will be shown in 3.3, these consonants are licensed by higher prosodic constituents such as a foot or a prosodic word. Additionally, it has to be stressed that word-internal syllabification may be dependent on the morpheme-boundary. Evidently, this instance has to be taken into consideration by investigating syllabification, cf. discussion in 3.2.2.

Since syllable-initial and syllable-final clusters, products of internal syllabification, will be used for defining syllable onsets and codas, the remaining question is what principles underlie word-internal syllabification. Is it the Sonority Sequencing Generalization that governs the parsing of syllables, or are there any other principles responsible for syllabification?

The answer to this important question can be obtained only after a detailed study of possible word-initial and word-final consonants as well as word-internal syllabification. This issue is the subject of the next subsection.

3.1.1 The Data

In this subsection we will consider clusters occurring word-initially and word-finally. In order to predict 'true' syllable onsets and syllable codas we will also examine word-medial syllabification of clusters.

Both word-internal and word-final clusters are discussed quantitatively (two-, three-, four-, five-member clusters) as well as qualitatively in terms of sonority; sonority differences are limited to the distinction between obstruents and sonorants.

The examination of clusters leads to the conclusion that sonority plays a crucial role in the organization of a Polish syllable. However, the sonority scale I propose for Polish differs considerably from the ones proposed by Selkirk (1984), cf. (127), or Vennemann (1988a) cf. (130), as it does not require sonority differences between some groups of sounds. Thus, Polish treats obstruents, regardless of their manner of articulation or voicing specifications, in a unified way; it therefore allows sequences of plosives and fricatives in onsets and codas in either order. As far as sonorants are concerned it appears that the requirement of increased sonority is fulfilled in a Polish syllable onset. This condition is of no relevance for the coda, in which sequences of two or more sonorants are prohibited. All above observations lead to the conclusion that the sonority scale for Polish has the shape as shown in (133).

(133) Sonority Hierarchy for Polish

obstruents < nasals < liquids < glides < vowels

The hierarchy in (133) is identical to the Universal Sonority Hierarchy proposed by Clements (1990). In the following sections I justify the Sonority Hierarchy in (133) and show that apparent violations, e.g. *r* in [rt]ęć 'mercury' nom.sg., are stray and are licensed by higher prosodic constituents such as a foot or a prosodic word.

3.1.1.1 *Onset*

Before presenting the data some remarks concerning the way in which they were obtained and how they are presented here are in order. First, all clusters are provided in their phonetic representation, which serves to avoid ambiguity and controversy. Second, all onset consonant sequences occurring in word-initial position are attested in words collected in a three-volume *Słownik Języka Polskiego* "Dictionary of the Polish Language" (Szymczak 1995). A few items that are not cited in Słownik Języka Polskiego but which occur in colloquial speech are also provided under the label 'colloquial speech.' Many clusters are presented with a subscript on their right side that indicates in how many lexical items the given cluster is attested. If the cluster occurs in some words that belong to the same semantic family but differ in grammatical category (which has the same cluster) or in the kind of suffix that is attached to the stem, it is counted as a single cluster. The frequency indicated is restricted to three items, i.e., if a cluster occurs in more than three items the index is not given. The motivation for providing the frequency of clusters follows from the fact that frequency plays a crucial role in formulating generalizations on syllable structure. Furthermore, I have marked morpho-logical boundaries by <+>, although boundary determination was sometimes difficult to establish. This uncertainty, however, does not bear in any significant way on the results of the present study since, as we will see below, there are many clusters that occur both tauto- as well as heteromorphemically.

For a few clusters I have given the label 'optional pronunciation', which refers to clusters with a palatalized final consonant that are pronounced with a secondary articulation or optionally with a glide /j/.[56] Finally, I have marked clusters that are attested only in foreign words by a star <*>. In the appendix in 7.4 all word-initial clusters are provided together with an example of a word in which they occur.

A Two-member word-initial clusters

Let us consider two-member consonant clusters. In (134) obstruent+sonorant, obstruent +obstruent, sonorant+obstruent, sonorant+sonorant clusters occurring in word-initial position are shown. Note that a handful of obstruent+obstruent clusters consists of identical consonants, i.e. geminates. They are marked in bold letters.

(134) Two-member consonant clusters

a. Obstruent+sonorant[57]

pl	pl'	*pl'	pw	pr	*pr	*pr'$_2$	pn$_2$	*pn	pń$_1$
tl$_1$	tl'$_1$	tw	tr	*tr	tń				
kl	*kl	*kl'	kw	kr	*kr	*kr'$_1$	kn	*kn	kń
*kń	km'$_3$								
bl	bw	br	*br'	bń$_1$					

56 For example [zm']ana 'change' nom.sg. can be pronounced as [zmj]ana. This optionality is disussed in 4.1 and 4.1.3.

57 All affricates are treated as single segments as opposed to a sequence of stop+fricative, cf. Rubach (1994).

dl$_3$	dw	dr	*dr’	dn$_1$	dm$_1$					
gl	*gl	gw	gr	gn	*gn	gń	gm$_3$	gm’$_1$		
t^{s}w$_1$	t^{s}n$_1$	t^{s}m$_2$								
t^{š}w$_3$	t^{š}m$_1$									
t^{ś}m$_1$	t^{ś}m’$_1$									
vl	v+l	v+l’	vw	v+w	vr	v+r	v+m	vn	v+n	
vń	v+ń									
*fl	*fr									
*sj	*sl	sr	sw	sn	sm					
šl	*šl	*šl’	šr	šw	*šn$_3$	šm	*šm	šm’		
śl	śl’	śr	śń	śm’						
zj	z+j	zl	z+l	z+l’	*z+l’	zw	z+w	z+r	zn	
z+n	zń									
z+ń	zm									
z+m	zm’	z+m’								
žl$_1$	žw$_2$	žr$_1$	žń$_1$	žm$_1$	žm’					
źl	źr									
xl	*xl	xl’	xw	xr	*xr	xm$_3$	xm’$_1$			

b. Obstruent+obstruent

pt$_1$	*pt	pt’$_2$	ps$_3$	*ps	pš	pś$_3$	px$_1$			
tk$_2$	tt$^{\text{š}}_1$	tš	tf	tf’	tx					
t^{s}f$_2$	*t^{s}f$_1$	t^{š}t$_1$	t^{š}t$^{\text{ś}}_2$	**t^{š}t$^{\text{š}}_1$**	t^{š}k$_1$	t^{š}f$_1$				
t^{ś}p$_1$	t^{ś}f’									
kp’$_1$	kt	kt$^{\text{ś}}_1$	kf	*kf	kf’	*ks	kś	kš		
bz$_2$	bź$_1$	bž								
db$_1$	dv$_3$	dv’$_1$	dž							
d^{z}v$_1$	d^{z}b$_1$									
d^{ź}g$_1$	d^{ź}v’$_1$									
d^{ž}d$^{\text{ž}}_2$										
gb$_1$	gd	gd$^{\text{ź}}_1$	gv	gv’	gz	*gz	gź$_3$	gž		
f+p	f+p’	fk	f+k	ft	f+t	f+t$^{\text{s}}_3$	ft^{s}	ft^{ś}	f+t^{ś}	ft^{š}
f+t^{š}	fs	f+s	f+ś	fš	f+š	f+x$_1$				
sp	*sp	s+p	sp’	*sp’	s+p’	sk	*sk	sk’	s+k’	st
*st	s+t	st^{s}	*st^{s}	s+t^{s}	s+t^{š}	**ss$_1$**	**s+s**	s+š	sf	s+f
s+ś	sx	*sx	s+x	*sx’	*s+x’					
šp	šp’	št	*št	št^{š}	šk	šk’	šf			
śt^{ś}	ś+t^{ś}	śp’	śf’							
v+b	v+b’$_2$	vd	v+d	vd^{ź}	v+d^{ź}	v+g’$_1$	v+g$_1$	**v+v$_1$**	v+v’	vz
v+z$_3$	vź	v+ź	vž	v+ž$_3$						
zb	z+b	zb’	z+b’	zd	z+d	z+d^{ź}	zg	z+g	z+g’	zv
z+v	z+v’	zz$_2$	z+ź$_3$	z+ž						
źd$^{\text{ź}}_1$										
žg										
xt$^{\text{s}}_2$	xš	xf	xf’							

c. Sonorant+obstruent

lv_1	lv'_1	$lž_2$		
wk_1	wb_1	wg_1	wz_1	
rt_1	rd_1	$rd^z{}_2$	rv_3	$rž_2$
mg'_1	mž	mš	mx_1	

d. Sonorant+sonorant

mn_3	mń	ml	mr	mw
ln_2	$lń_1$			

Optional: *lj

The data presented in (134) give us valuable insights into the nature of word-initial two-member clusters. First of all, it appears that that stating phonotactic restrictions in terms of possible or impossible consonantal sequences and systematic and accidental gaps would not lead to any significant conclusions. Rather, what seems to be adequate in light of the complexity of the clusters are observations made on the basis of possible sonorant and obstruent combinations as indicated in (134). This systematization of clusters leads to the conclusion that the sequences of obstruent and sonorant in (134)a as well as sequences of two obstruents in (134)b constitute a significant majority of word-initial onsets. Sonorant+obstruent sequences in (134)c are unique in two respects: (i) there are far fewer sonorant+obstruent sequences attested than obstruent+sonorant or obstruent+obstruent and (ii) sonorant+obstruent clusters are usually restricted to one item. The smallest set of word-initial two-member clusters is presented in (134)d. Note that this group consists of only eight sonorant+sonorant sequences; one of them occurs in one item, one in two items and one in three items.

Assuming that frequency plays a role in stating generalizations, we have to conclude that the number of attested clusters as well as the number of items in which they occur is significantly larger in (134)a,b than in (134)c,d. Consequently, two-member word-initial clusters in which the first consonant is a sonorant are more marked in Polish than ones in which the first consonant is an obstruent.

Leaving frequency aside, let us now evaluate (134)a,b vs. (134)c,d with respect to sonority. The clusters in (134)a satisfy SSG since they consist of an obstruent followed by a sonorant. The clusters in (134)b, however, do not show a rising sonority: a plosive is followed by another plosive, a fricative is followed by another fricative or a plosive; similar combinations are attested with an affricate. If we assume that fricatives are more sonorous than plosives as in the Sonority Hierarchy in (127), then we are able to account only for sequences of plosives followed by fricatives. If we postulated that obstruent onset clusters also tolerate segments of the same sonority, then fricative +fricative and plosive+plosive sequences would be correctly considered to be possible onsets. However, over half of the set in (134)b consists of fricative+plosive clusters, which would violate the Sonority Hierarchy in (127). This indicates that if one wants to account for all two-member obstruent clusters, one has to assume that the Sonority Hierarchy in (127) does not hold in Polish since Polish treats all obstruents equally with respect to sonority; there seems to be no difference between fricatives, plosives, and affricates since all obstruents may occur in either order in a two-member word-initial clusters. In other words, Polish tolerates a sonority plateau with respect to obstruents.

In light of this conclusion the question arises as to the position of Polish in comparison with other languages with respect to word-initial two-member obstruent clusters. The most recent studies on the typology of obstruent clusters proposed by Morelli (1998a,b) show that the most unmarked type of clusters consists of a fricative followed by a plosive and not vice versa. In her cross-linguistic study of consonant clusters Morelli (1998b) investigates about 25 typologically diverse languages with respect to two-member obstruent clusters in word-initial and word-final position. Morelli differentiates between six types of languages according to the number of possible combinations such as fricative+stop, stop+fricative, stop+stop, and fricative+ fricative that they allow. Although Morelli's study does not specifically include Polish clusters, Polish undoubtedly belongs to the few languages of Type 6, to which Georgian, Tsou, and Yateé Zapotec belong. Consider the tableau in (135), cf. Morelli (1998a:3).

(135) Patterns of occurrence of obstruents in onsets

	FS	SF	SS	FF
Onset Type 1	√			
Onset Type 2	√			√
Onset Type 3	√	√		
Onset Type 4	√	√		√
Onset Type 5	√	√	√	
Onset Type 6	√	√	√	√

F: fricative

S: stop

On the basis of this typology Morelli (1998a) states various markedness relations and implicational universals concerning onset obstruent clusters. She claims that fricative+ plosive clusters are the least marked sequences, while the most marked sequences are plosive+plosive clusters because the presence of the latter implies both the presence of fricative+plosive clusters and also plosive+fricative clusters in the same language. There is, however, no implication between fricative+fricative sequences on the one hand and plosive+fricative or plosive+plosive sequences on the other. Consider the schematic representation of implication and markedness relations shown in (136)a and b. ('⇒' indicates an implication in implication relations and '→' in markedness relations)

(136)a. Implication relations

SS
⇓
SF
⇓
FF ⇒ FS

b. Markedness relations

FS → FF
↓
SF
↓
SS

The schemes presented in (136) show that Polish obstruent clusters confirm the markedness relations that are attested in other languages. The crucial point, however, is that the clusters collected by Morelli (1998a,b) are attested in word-initial position, exactly as the Polish clusters in (134) are. In other words, the implications stated in (136) do not necessarily refer to syllable onset clusters. In order to state whether the clusters under consideration belong to a syllable in Polish, we will make use of word-internal syllabi-fication.

B The syllabification of intervocalic consonant clusters

Rubach and Booij (1990a) report on the basis of a test conducted on students of the University of Warsaw[58] that two consonants occurring word-internally show variation with respect to syllabification. For example, *dobry* 'good' nom.sg.masc. was syllabified as *do.bry* (29)[59] or as *dob.ry* (19), *Tatry* 'Tatra' nom.pl. was syllabified as *Ta.try* (39) and *Tat.ry* (26) and *patrzeć* [patšet^{ś}] 'to look' inf. as *pa.trzeć* (36) and *pat.rzeć* (20). What these examples show is a slight preference for complex onsets regardless of whether the given cluster displays rising sonority or if it consists of two obstruents.

With these facts in mind the question arises as to whether a similar optionality is attested with respect to the third and the fourth set in (134) when occurring word-internally. Is it possible that sequences of sonorant+obstruent (RO) and sonorant+ sonorant (RR) can be parsed as onsets (V.ROV), (V.RRV) and also be heterosyllabified (VR.OV), (VR.RV) ?

The syllabification of such sequences was also investigated by Rubach and Booij (1990a), who came to the conclusion that the sequences of sonorant+obstruent are always heterosyllabified.[60] For example, *kontakt* 'contact' nom.sg. was syllabified as *kon.takt* (45) and never as *ko.ntakt* (0); *konserwa* [konserva] 'can' nom.sg. was syllabified as *kon.ser.wa* (45) and neither as *ko.nser.wa* (0) nor *kon.se.rwa* (0). Hence, the statistics show unambiguously that the only possible syllabification of sonorant+ obstruent clusters is VR.OV. This implies that the initial sonorant in sonorant+obstruent clusters does not belong to the syllable onset.

Furthermore, the results of the experiment show that sequences of two medial sonorants which violate SSG were heterosyllabified, e.g., the medial /rn/ cluster in *korniszon* 'gherkin' nom.sg. is parsed *kor.ni-* (46) and not as *ko.rni-* (0); *kormoran* 'cormorant' nom.sg. was syllabified as *kor.mo-* (46) and not *ko.rmo-* (1), cf. Rubach and Booij (1990a:127). As will be shown below, Polish does not tolerate sonorants from the same natural class either: *karmnik* 'feeder' is syllabified as *karm.nik* or *kar.mnik* whereby the medial *m* belongs neither to the onset not to the coda, cf. Rubach and Booij (1990b:438). This point will be discussed below.

These and other examples provided below show that the Polish syllable does not

[58] The students were read a list of words and were asked to syllabify them without any time to consider their options. The test was repeated one or more times with a different group of students if the results were not clear. Moreover, in instances of particular interest for the authors the test was repeated three times with the same group of students in at least one week intervals.

[59] The number in parentheses indicates the number of students with the syllabification for a given word.

[60] It has to be stressed that the syllabified strings occur morpheme-internally and therefore the influence of a morpheme-boundary for syllabification has to be excluded.

tolerate a sonority plateau with respect to sonorants because a medial sonorant sequence which violates the hierarchy nasals<liquids<glides is heterosyllabified.

C Generalizations/conclusions

The facts concerning two-member word-initial clusters such as the number of possible combinations of obstruents and sonorants, cf. (134), the number of items in which clusters are attested, cf. (134), as well as word-internal syllabification shown in the previous subsection indicate that Polish has two-member syllable onsets that consist either of obstruent+sonorant sequences or two obstruents; plosives and fricatives are treated equally with respect to sonority. The first member of a cluster that displays crucial sonority violations, cf. (134)c, is not parsed into a syllable. As far as word-initial sonorant clusters are concerned, cf.(134)d, it appears that the sonority requirements posed on sonorants are finer than in the case of obstruents: only a very restricted number of combinations with an initial *m* or *l* is attested in the word-initial position; sequences of sonorants that violate the hierarchy nasals<liquids<glides are hetero-syllabified, cf. also 3.2.2.

In (137)a,b,c,d sample representations for the four groups presented in (134) are provided. Note that the representations in (137)c,d are incomplete. In 3.3 we will discuss possible representations of consonants that are not parsed into the syllable.

(137)

a. Obstruent+sonorant

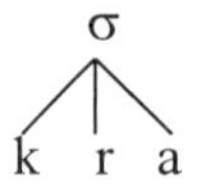

'ice float' nom.sg.

b. Obstruent+obstruent

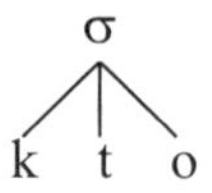

'who' nom.sg.

c. Sonorant +obstruent

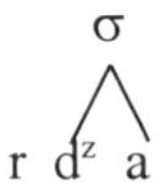

'rust' nom.sg.

d. Sonorant+sonorant

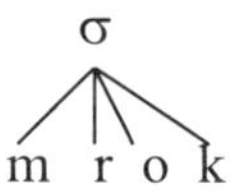

'darkness' nom.sg.

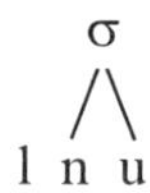

'flax' gen.sg.

The investigation reveals that the Polish syllable is governed by the sonority hierarchy in (133) which I have repeated in (138) for convenience.

(138)

obstruents < nasals < liquids < glides < vowels

D Word-initial clusters with three- or more members

Since three-member clusters constitute a significantly larger group than two-member clusters, their presentation is divided in two sets. Consider first all possible combinations of obstruents and sonorants in (139).

(139) Three-member clusters

a. Obstruent+sonorant+obstruent
plf$_1$ pwć$_1$
trf$_2$
krf'$_1$ krf$_1$ krt$_1$
brd$_1$ brv'$_1$
drg$_2$ drv$_1$ drv'$_1$ drž$_1$
grd$_1$
b. Obstruent+sonorant+sonorant
kln$_2$ klń$_1$ krn$_1$ *krj$_1$
brn$_1$ brń$_1$ *brj$_1$
*prj$_1$ *trj *drj
zmr$_1$ z+mr$_2$ z+mń$_1$
smr$_2$
colloqial speech: z+mn$_1$ z+mw$_1$
optional: dvj$_1$ kmj$_1$ knj$_3$ gvj$_1$ zmj z+mj śmj
xmj$_1$ t^{ś}mj$_1$
c. Sonorant+obstruent+sonorant (obstruent)
lgn$_1$ lgń$_1$ lśń$_1$
mdl$_1$ mdl'$_1$ mdw$_1$ mkn mkń$_1$ mkl'$_1$ mgl'$_1$ mgw$_1$ mgń$_1$ mśt$^ś_1$
ržn$_1$ ržń$_1$
d. Sonorant+sonorant+sonorant (obstruent): not attested

The common denominator of the clusters presented in (139) is their limited frequency. All of them are found in only one or two lexical items except for five clusters repeated in (140).

(140)

trj, drj, zmj, z+mj, śmj

The first two clusters in (140), *trj* and *drj* are attested only in foreign words, while others *zmj*, *z+mj*, and *śmj* display an optional pronunciation of two-member clusters such as *zm'*, *z+m'*, and *śm'*, respectively.

The crucial observation concerning clusters in (139) is that apart from a few clusters in the obstruent+sonorant+sonorant set, all other clusters violate sonority; they display a sonority drop from their first to their last member, i.e., towards the peak of a syllable.

Against this background let us now consider consonantal sequences that constitute the majority of attested three-member clusters. They consist either exclusively of obstruents or of two obstruents followed by a sonorant, cf. (141a) and (141b), respectively.

(141) Three-member clusters

a. Obstruent+obstruent+obstruent
pšt$^š_1$

tkf'$_1$
džv'$_1$
tšp'$_2$ tšt$^{ś}_1$
kšt$_2$
bzd$_2$ bžd$_2$
gžb'$_1$ gžd$_1$
f+pš$_2$ fsp f+s+p f+s+p'$_2$ f+st f+sk f+s+x$_1$ fšt$^{š}_2$ fśt$^{ś}_3$
v+zb v+zb'$_2$ v+zv$_2$ vzg$_2$ vzd$_2$ vžd$_1$
s+ps$_1$ spš s+pš s+pś$_1$ s+tf s+tf' stš s+tx skf s+kf skf'
skš sk+š s+st s+xf št^{š}f
z+bź$_1$ z+bž$_2$ z+dv$_1$ z+dž$_1$ z+gv zgž z+gž
Colloquial: s+xš$_1$
b. Obstruent+obstruent+sonorant
pxw$_1$ pxl'$_1$ pxn$_1$ pxń$_1$
tkn$_1$ tkń$_1$
tkl'$_1$ txn$_1$ txń$_1$
tšn tšm'$_1$
bžm'
gžm$_1$ gžm'$_1$
t^{s}kl'$_1$
t^{š}kn$_1$ t^{š}kń$_1$
d^{ź}gn$_1$ d^{ź}gń$_1$
f+pl$_1$ f+pw$_3$ f+pr f+tw f+tr fkl$_1$ f+kl fkw f+kw f+kr f+tr
f+śl$_1$ fśr$_1$
f+śr f+sw f+sn$_1$ f+xw$_1$
vbr v+dr$_3$ v+dm v+gw vgl$_1$ v+gr$_1$ v+gń$_1$ v+z+l$_1$ vzr$_3$ v+z+r
v+z+n$_3$ vzń$_3$ vzm'$_1$ v+zm
s+pw s+pl *spl *spl' s+pl' spr s+pr s+tw s+tl
str s+tr s+tš *st^{s}j skl s+kl skw s+kw
skr s+kr s+kl$_1$ skn sk+n$_2$ sfl s+fr s+xw$_2$ s+xl s+xr
s+xn sxń
*špr$_3$ *štr$_1$ škw$_1$ škl$_1$ škl'$_1$
^{x}št$^{ś}_1$ ^{x}št$^{š}_1$
z+bw z+bl z+br zdj$_2$ z+dw$_1$ zdr z+dr z+dm$_1$ z+gw zgl$_2$ zgr
z+gr z+gn$_3$ z+gń z+vw z+vl z+vr
źgn$_1$ źgń$_1$
žgn$_1$ žgń$_1$
Colloquial: f+tš s+pś$_1$

Apart from the obvious fact that the number of possible consonant combinations in the group in (141) considerably exceeds the number of clusters in the first group in (139), the crucial difference between both is the frequency of occurrence in lexical items. The clusters exemplified in (139) are mostly attested only in single items, while many clusters presented in (141) occur in more than three lexical items (in most cases the number of items is considerably higher than three). The difference between (139) and (141) is also supported by the sonority relation between both groups. As already mentioned, almost all clusters presented in (139) crucially violate the SSG while those in (141) do not. (Recall that a sonority plateau with respect to obstruents is tolerated in Polish.)

Let us now consider how the three-member onsets are syllabified intervocalically. In the experiment described in Rubach and Booij (1990a:127) the following preference patterns are obtained. Words having three medial consonants show syllabification preferences such as VC.CCV [l'is.tfa] (40), VCC.CV [l'ist.fa] (11), and V.CCCV [l'i.stfa] (8). Hence, three-member word-internal clusters have the preferred syllabification VC.CCV. Although the syllabified cluster is found word-initially in e.g. [stf]arzać 'to create' inf. it does not give us a reason to conclude that /str/ is not a true syllable onset. The uncertainty is eliminated if one considers the medial syllabification of four-member clusters in sko[mpstf]o whose one of possible syllabifications is sko[m.pstf]o, cf. Rubach and Booij (1990a:126). The syllabfication sko[mp.stf]o and not the presence of a cluster *stf* in [stf]arzać provides an evidence that [stf] is a syllable-onset cluster.

The observations made thus far lead to the conclusion that Polish allows three-member clusters in syllable onset position. This quantitative restriction governs only certain consonant types. All combinations of obstruents are allowed in onsets, which confirms again that Polish tolerates a sonority plateau with respect to obstruents. What is not allowed in the onset is a sequence of consonants in which a sonorant is followed by obstruents; if a sonorant is followed by obstruents the sonorant is not parsed into a syllable. Three-member sequences with two initial sonorants are not attested in word-initial position.

In (142) four-member consonant clusters occurring word-initially are presented. What is striking about these clusters is that all except /s+trf/ are attested in no more than three items. Nine clusters occur in one item, one in two items and three in three items. Furthermore, eight clusters are morphologically complex.

(142) Four-member consonant clusters

drgń$_1$	drgn$_1$		
pstr$_3$	pstš$_1$		
s+trf	s+krf$_1$		
źd^{ź}bw$_1$			
fstr$_1$	f+s+tš$_3$	f+s+kš$_1$	f+s+kr$_1$
v+z+dw$_1$	v+z+dr$_3$	v+z+gl$_2$	

If we adopt our conclusions drawn thus far for word-initial four-member onsets in Polish, we contend that they consist of syllable onsets and other elements that do not belong to the syllable. This is confirmed by medial syllabification, by which the last three consonants, provided they do not violate the hierarchy in (133), are usually syllabified as the syllable onset and the first of these as the coda. As shown in Rubach and Booij (1990a: 126), *skąpstwo* [skompstfo] 'meanness' nom.sg. can be syllabified as *skom.pstfo* and *abstrakt* [apstrakt] 'abstract' nom.sg. as *a.bstrakt*. Taking the occurrence of the four-member onsets in word-medial position as evidence for their syllable onset status, word-initial clusters shown in (142) are claimed to be true syllable onsets. An exception is constituted by the clusters drgń, drgn, s+trf, s+krf, in which a medial sonorant occurs. These sequences violate the Sonority Hierarchy in (133) because a sonorant is followed by an obstruent. Since they do not occur in word-medial position, their syllabification cannot be examined. Similar to the syllabifications of other strings which contain an obstruent+sonorant+obstruent cluster, the sonorant is not parsed into a syllable, cf. examples given below

F Conclusions

Let us now summarize our observations made thus far. The systematization of the data reveals that the onset of a Polish syllable may consist of as many as four segments. The additional condition imposed on onset strings is that they display either rising sonority (from obstruent to sonorant) or a sonority plateau, whereby the latter is tolerated only as far as obstruents are concerned.

3.1.1.2 *Coda*

In the following, we will consider clusters attested in the coda. They are systematized with respect to the number of consonants of which they consist (two-, three-, four-, five-member clusters) and with respect to sonority. As far as the latter condition is concerned I restrict my generalizations to the division in obstruents and sonorants. In collecting the data I used *Index a tergo* (Grzegorczykowa and Puzynina 1973), which considers the data collected in *Słownik języka polskiego* 'Dictionary of the Polish Language' (Doroszewski 1958-1969). Additionally, I used the data collected by Takatori (1997), who provides a list of two-member word-final clusters. What I did not consider was the frequency of the occurring clusters. This was mainly because in *Index a tergo* only lexical items in the nominative case (nouns) and in the infinitive form (verbs) are given. It is often the case that the additional seven cases of nouns as well as various verb forms, depending on the person, number, tense, modus, take various declensional and conjugational desinences. Thus the frequency of final clusters would be incomplete without taking into consideration all desinences. Although I tried to include all desinences, I decided to omit the frequency.

A Two-member word-final clusters

Let us start with the two-member clusters provided in (143), which show the sequences consisting of obstruent+sonorant (a), obstruent+obstruent (b), sonorant+obstruent (c), and sonorant+sonorant (d) in word-final position.

(143) Two-member clusters

a. Obstruent+ sonorant

pw	pr	pn	pń	
tw	tr	tm		
kw	kl	kr	*km	*kn
$t^{ś}$m	$t^{š}$m	t+w		

*fl *fr fn
sw sm
śl śń śm
šm šn
x+w xr xn *xm

b. Obstruent+obstruent

*pt pt^{š} pt^{ś} pš ps
tf tš
kt kf *ks
t^{ś}p t^{š}p t^{š}t št^{š}
ft ft^{s} ft^{ś}
sp st sk sf
šp *št šx
śp śt^{ś} śf
xt xt^{ś} xf

c. Sonorant+obstuent

*mp mt^{ś} *mf *ms mš mś
nt nk nt^{s} nt^{ś} *nt^{š} *nf *nš *ns
ńp ńt^{š} ńt^{ś} ńt^{s}
lp lt lk lt^{s} *lf lx
rf rp rt rk rt^{s} rt^{š} rt^{ś} rf rs rš rś
rx
jp jt *jk jt^{s} jt^{š} jt^{ś} jf *js jš
wp wt wk wt^{š} wf ws wš

d. Sonorant+sonorant

ml mn
*jl jm jn jń
lm lń
rm rl rn r+w rń
*wl wm wń

What the systematization of word-final clusters shows is a similar asymmetry as in the case of word-initial clusters. First, sonorant+obstruent clusters in (143)c constitute the largest set of word-final clusters. Second, obstruent+obstruent sequences in (143)b and obstruent+sonorant in (143)a do not differ considerably from each other with respect to the number of clusters. However, it has to be stressed that the number of both groups as well as sonorant+obstruent clusters might be almost twice as large if one considers the underlying representation: a voiced consonant loses its voicing under the influence of a following voiceless consonant. Since final devoicing is operative in Polish, it triggers the devoicing of the final consonant, which in turn causes the devoicing of the preceding sound. The smallest group of possible word-final clusters comprises sequences consisting of two sonorants, cf. (143)d. As far as the frequency is concerned we conclude that while there is no considerable difference in number of sonorant+ob-struent, obstruent+obstruent and obstruent+sonorant clusters, sonorant+

sonorant clusters constitue a significat minority of all possible two-member clusters in word-final position.

Word-medial syllabification shows that sonorant+obstruent as well as obstruent+ obstruent sequences can be syllabified in the coda. For example, *kurtka* [kurtka] 'jacket' nom.sg. is syllabified either as *kurt.ka* or as *kur.tka*. Furthermore, *skąpstwo* [skompstfo] 'stinginess' nom.sg. is syllabified either as *skomp.stfo* or as *skom.pstfo.*[61] These as well as other syllabification patterns discussed in 3.2.2 indicate that syllable codas may consist either of sonorant+obstruent sequences or of obstruent+obstruent sequences. Both cluster types do not violate the SSG. Clusters consisting of obstruent+sonorant sequences in *piosnka* 'song' nom.sg. are syllabified either as *pios.nka* or *piosn.ka*, cf. Rubach and Booji (1990b:438). But in this case the syllabification types do not give us an insight into a syllable. As was shown in (137)c, clusters of the type sonorant+obstruent are not licit in the syllable onset because they violate SSG. For the same reason, obstruent+sonorant sequences are not parsed in the coda. Since the /n/ in *piosnka* belongs neither to onset nor to coda both syllabification types *pios.nka* (31) and *piosn.ka* (31) are found equally frequently, cf. Rubach and Booij (1990b:438). As will be proposed in 3.3 the sonorant /n/ in this and similar words is extrasyllabic and it is licensed by a higher prosodic constituent such as prosodic word.

Furthermore, two sonorants are prohibited in the coda. This is directly expressed by the well-known Coda Constraint stated, e.g., by Rubach and Booij (1990a:124), cf. (144). This constraint follows from phonological and morphological processes, cf. 3.1.2.

(144) Coda Constraint

Two sonorants are prohibited in the coda.

The phonetic evidence for this constraint comes from the syllabification of word-medial strings. Again, the variation in syllabification of three medial sonorants indicates that the medial sonorant does not belong to any syllable; the /m/ in *karmnik* 'feeder' nom.sg. belongs neither to the coda nor to the onset, which is supported by the fact that both syllabifications *kar.mnik* (57) and *karm.nik* (46) are equally frequently, cf. Rubach and Booij (1990b:438).

As in the case of word-initial clusters there is no sonority difference between plosives and fricatives because both sets of sounds occur in the coda in either order in Polish. This confirms again the correctness of the Sonority Hierarchy in (133).

Cross-linguistically the most frequent word-final clusters are plosive+fricative and fricative+plosive sequences, cf. Morelli (1998b:4). Unlike word-initial sequences there is no cluster such as fricative+plosive that is always present in word-final position. Morelli shows that the presence of a plosive+plosive cluster implies the presence of a fricative+plosive cluster in the same language, while the occurrence of the fricative+ plosive cluster presupposes the occurrence of the plosive+fricative cluster. These implications determine the markedness relations between different types of obstruent clusters in word-final position. This is demonstrated in (145), cf. Morelli (1998b:5).

[61] A detailed analysis of these cases is proposed in 3.2.2.

(145) Markedness relations

a. FS → SS
b. SF → FF
(F=fricative, S=stop)

The markedness relation in (145) expresses that both fricative+plosive and plosive+ fricative sequences are more marked than plosive+plosive and fricative+ fricative sequences. Furthermore, Morelli (1998b) differentiates between eight types of languages, which show different types of obstruent clusters in word-final position. If Polish were taken into consideration, it would belong to the eighth type, which captures languages allowing all types of obstruent clusters, as in the case of Georgian.

B Three- and more member clusters

Three-member word-final clusters create a smaller group than two-member consonantal sequences. Consider word-final clusters consisting of three members in (146).

(146) Three-member clusters

a. Obstruent+obstruent+obstruent
p+sk
*kst
t+^{s}tf[62]
+stf stš
št^{š}p
b. Obstruent+obstruent+sonorant
stm str
štr
xtr
c. Sonorant +obstruent+obstruent
*mpt mst
ntš ntf
*nks *nkt nkf nšt ńt^{ś}p ń+sk ńśt^{ś}
lšt^{š}
rpt^{s} rst rsk ršt ršt^{š} rśt^{ś}
jst jśt^{ś} jsk
d. Sonorant+obstruent+sonorant
mpr *mpl
ntn ntr ntr nkr
*ltr lśń
e. Obstruent+sonorant+ sonorant: not attested
f. Obstruent+sonorant+ obstruent: not attested

The frequency of occurring of clusters indicates that sonorant+obstruent+obstruent sequences in (146)c constitute the largest group of three-member word-final clusters. Smaller groups are those of obstruent+obstruent+obstruent in (146)a and sonorant+

[62] The suffix is /stv/ but its first segment and the stem-final consonant constitute an affricate.

obstruent+sonorant in (146)d. The smallest set consists of four obstruent+obstruent+sonorant sequences in (146)b. However, as the experiment by Rubach and Booij (1990a) reveals, there are no examples in which three-member codas would result from medial syllabifications. For example, *skąpstwo* [skompstfo] 'stinginess' nom.sg. is never syllabified as **skomps.tfo* nor is *abstrakt* [apstrakt] 'abstract' nom.sg. parsed as **abst.rakt*. This indicates that Polish allows only two-member codas that do not violate the SSG, which is based on the Sonority Hierarchy presented in (133).

In Polish there are also four-member clusters occurring in word-final position. Their number is limited to eleven. Consider the data shown in (147). Note that all clusters are divided by a morpheme-boundary.

(147) Four-member clusters

a. Obstruent+obstruent+obstruent+obstruent

p+stf $t^{ś}$+stf f+stf

b. Sonorant+obstruent+obstruent+obstruent

m+psk m+stf n+stf nt+^{s}tf ń+stf l+stf r+stf j+stf

All clusters in (147) obey the SSG. For the reasons mentioned above the last two consonants cannot be syllabified as codas.

There is only one five-member cluster in word-final position. This cluster is shown in (148). It is worth stressing that it contains the cluster [stf], which is a suffix in the genitive case. Hence, there is a morpheme boundary between the first two consonants and the [stf].

(148) Five-member clusters

mp+stf

An examination of the clusters above leads to the conclusion that sonority plays a crucial role in the organization of a Polish syllable. However, the sonority scale attested in Polish in (133) differs considerably from the ones proposed by Selkirk (1984) or Vennemann (1988a), since it does not require sonority differences between particular groups of sounds. Thus Polish treats obstruents, regardless of their manner of articulation or voicing specifications, in a unified way; it therefore allows sequences of plosives and fricatives in onsets and codas in either order. As far as sonorants are concerned it appears that the requirement of increasing sonority is fulfilled in a Polish syllable onset. This condition is of no relevance for the coda in which sequences of two or more sonorants are prohibited. All above observations lead to the conclusion that the sonority scale for Polish has the following shape: obstruents<nasals<liquids<glides< vowels. Consonants which violate this hierarchy are not parsed into the syllable. As will be shown in 3.3 they are parsed into higher prosodic constituents such as the foot or the prosodic word.

Furthermore, there are quantitative restrictions that allow for as many as four consonants in the onset and two in the coda. These restrictions are stated in terms of the constraints in 3.2.2, where it is shown how their interaction leads to the selection of optimal syllabifications. Before turning to these analyses, let us consider how the clusters discussed above have been analyzed in previous accounts.

3.1.2 Previous accounts

In this subsection previous analyses of consonant clusters in Polish as well as Polish syllable structure are presented and discussed.

The following studies will be considered: Kuryłowicz (1952), Booij and Rubach (1990a,b), Gussmann (1991) and Bethin (1992). Since other studies such as e.g. Bargiełówna (1950) and Sawicka (1974) have rather a descriptive character, they will be not taken into consideration here.

Kuryłowicz (1952)

Kuryłowicz' study was the first attempt to provide generalizations concerning the complexity of consonant sequences. His interesting conclusions rely on the observation that consonants constituting clusters are interchangeable. For example, if an onset consists of two consonants C_1C_2, then C_2C_1 also occurs. Consider the examples shown in (149).

(149)

dr : rd	[dr]oga vs. [rd]est	'road' nom.sg. / 'water-papper' nom.sg.
xm : mx	[xm]ura vs. [mx]u	'cloud' nom.sg./ 'moss' gen.sg.
lv : vl	[lv]a vs. [vl]ec	'lion' nom.sg. / 'to draw' inf.

Furthermore, Kuryłowicz (1952) claims that sequences of consonants are to be considered as a result of different combinations of *elementy* 'elements' and *zbitki* 'clusters'. 'Elements' are single consonants, while 'clusters' consist of two or maximally three consonants. By postulating such categories violations of Kuryłowicz' equivalent of the SSG are avoided. Based on these assumptions Kuryłowicz restricts the possible combinations of elements and clusters in the onset to the following sequences:

1. element+(element)[63], e.g. [w+g] in [wg]ać 'to lie' inf.
2. (element)+two- or three-member cluster, e.g. [m+gw] in [mgw]a 'fog', nom.sg.
3. two- or three-member cluster+(element), e.g. [kr+t] in [krt]ań 'larynx'nom.sg.
4. two-member cluster+two-member cluster e.g. [dr+gn] in [dr+gn]ąć 'to wince' inf.

Kuryłowicz claims that most two-member clusters usually consist of two elements that are interchangeable. Consequently, words containing the same two consonants in word-initial position are analyzed as onsets with two identical elements, e.g. [ss]ak 'mammal' nom.sg. has two /s/ elements.

Furthermore, Kuryłowicz observes that most three-member consonant clusters have as their first member *f*, *v*, *s*, or *z*, which are diachronic reflexes of prefixes. This is the main reason why he proposes to isolate the prefixes from clusters. As a result two-member clusters are extracted from the original three-member groups. The 'new' two-member consonantal sequences are systematized into three groups presented in (150), cf. Kuryłowicz (1952:223).

---

[63] Parentheses denote the optionality of the element.

(150)

I	pr	tr	kr	xr
	br	dr	gr	
	pš	tš	kš	xš
	bž	gž		
	pw, pl	tw, tl	kw, kl	xw
	bw, bl	dw,	gw, gl	
			gn, gń	
		t^{ś}m	xm	
		dm	gm	
		tf, tf'	kf, kf'	xf
		t^{ś}f		
		dv, d^{ź}v	gv, gv'	
II	śp'	st, śt^{ś}	sk	št^{š}
III	śr sw	śl, sn,	sm, sf'	

w=ł[64]
t^{š}=č
t^{ś}=ć

The first group consists of a plosive or an affricate or the fricative /x/ and the 'sonorants' *r*, *l*, *ł*, *n*, *m*, *ž/š*, *v/f*. Kuryłowicz regards *ž/š* and *v/f* as sonorants since they were derived historically from sonorants. The second group differentiates itself from the third by its second member; in the second group it is a plosive or an affricate that follows *s/ś*, while in the third group the fricative *s/ś* is followed by a sonorant.

Three-member clusters that do not exhibit a syllable boundary are claimed to consist of an element followed by a two-member cluster, e.g. *v/br*, *z/br*, *p/xl*, *m/dl*, *m/gl*, *l/gn*, or of a two-member cluster followed by an element, e.g. *tr/f*, *kr/f'*, *kr/n*, *br/v*, *dr/g*, *dr/v*, *gr/d*. There are also some clusters such as *str*, *spr*, *skr*, *stš*, *skš*, *pšč*, *xšč*, *sxl*, *skn*, *skf*, and *skf'*, which display optionality; they can be interpreted either as an element and a two-member cluster or as a two-member cluster and an element.

Kuryłowicz stresses that the morphological boundary does not to have to coincide with the phonological boundary. For example, clusters such as *str* or *stx* in [str]acić 'to lose' inf. or [stx]órzyć 'to get cold feet' inf. have a morphological boundary after the first consonant (*s/tr*, *s/tx*) while the phonological boundary falls after the second consonant (*st/r*, *st/x*), since only the first two consonants might constitute a cluster. Four-member clusters consist of an element and a three-member cluster, e.g., *f/str*, *p/str*, *v/zgl*. Only one cluster *źd^{ź}bw* attested in a single word *źdźbło* 'stalk' nom.sg., is divided into two two-member clusters: *źd^{ź}/bw*.

In sum, Kuryłowicz (1952) interprets onsets in Polish as bipartite groups, each of which consists of a two-member cluster that might be reduced to one element or

[64] The symbols ł, č and ć were used in the original text. Here they have been changed according to the transcriptions employed in the present study.

entirely deleted. By postulating internal structures of clusters he avoids violations of sonority in single components of consonantal sequences.

Codas according to Kuryłowicz (1952) consist of elements (single consonants), onset clusters (prevocalic clusters) and coda clusters (postvocalic clusters). Coda clusters might be mirror images of onset clusters. For example, a coda of the type obstruent+sonorant is a reflex of a sonorant+obstruent onset sequence. Similar to onset structures, codas in Polish display bipartite structures, which are presented in (151), cf. Kuryłowicz (1952:230).

(151)

1. element+element, e.g. [čp] in li[čp] 'number' gen.pl.
2. coda cluster+element, e.g. [nks] in sfi[nks] 'sphinx' nom.sg.
3. (element)+ two- or three-member onset cluster, e.g. [kst] in te[kst] 'text' nom.sg.
4. coda cluster+onset cluster, e.g. [mpstf] in skom[mpstf] 'meanness' gen.pl.

In summary, Kuryłowicz' observations made about possible sequences of consonants lead him to propose a general bipartite structure of Polish consonant clusters that consists of no more then two well-formed units, i.e. elements or clusters.

Kuryłowicz' insight into the complex structure of consonants inspired further studies on this topic, cf. the presentations given below. However, one of the most serious critiques of this proposal is its lack of restrictions, cf. Gussmann (1991:208). In other words, the generalizations made by Kuryłowicz predict the occurrence of consonants clusters that are not attested, since there are no constraints favoring or penalizing certain combinations. Thus, in Kuryłowicz' approach *any* combination of elements is allowed. If this were the case, then, as observed by Gussmann (1991:208), we would expect 1225 onsets in Modern Polish and 2500 four-consonantal groups derived from over 50 biconsonantal clusters, instead of the 231 and 15 that are actually attested in Modern Polish.

Furthermore, a very important generalization has been omitted, namely the frequency of a given cluster. As shown in 3.1.1 many clusters are found only in one or two lexical items. Others, as for example the obstruent+sonorant onset cluster, occur in many words. Such asymmetries raise the question of whether generalizations may be made without taking into consideration the frequency of occurrence of clusters in lexical items. For other critiques of Kuryłowicz' proposal, see also Gussmann (1991) and Bethin (1992).

Rubach and Booij (1990a,b)

In the framework of Lexical Phonology Polish consonant clusters are discussed by Rubach and Booij (1990a,b). In the following a brief summary of the results relevant for the present study is provided.

Rubach and Booij (1990a) propose the Syllable Structure Algorithm of Polish (SSA), which organizes X slots into syllables. The organizing principle of a syllable, to which SSA is sensitive, is the Sonority Sequencing Generalization, which is additionally restricted by the Obstruent Sequencing Principle presented below. SSA is constituted by various rules applying in the order shown in (152).

(152)

N-placement
CV Rule
Polish Onset
Polish Coda
Complex Coda

The SSA applies in a cyclic manner.[65] N-placement is an X-bar projection of the primitive category N, which constitutes the nucleus of the syllable as proposed by Levin (1985). The CV rule parses a single C into the onset (onset = N'' in (153)). In contrast to the Polish Onset rule, see below, the CV rule is universal and obligatory, i.e., it applies regardless of whether there is material to be included in the onset or not. For example, a syllable like [a] is represented as in (153)b. The motivation for the obligatory parsing comes from the fact that N''corresponds to the syllable node and must be projected even if the onset consonant is not available. The application of the CV rule is shown in (153), cf. Rubach and Booij (1990a:124).

(153)

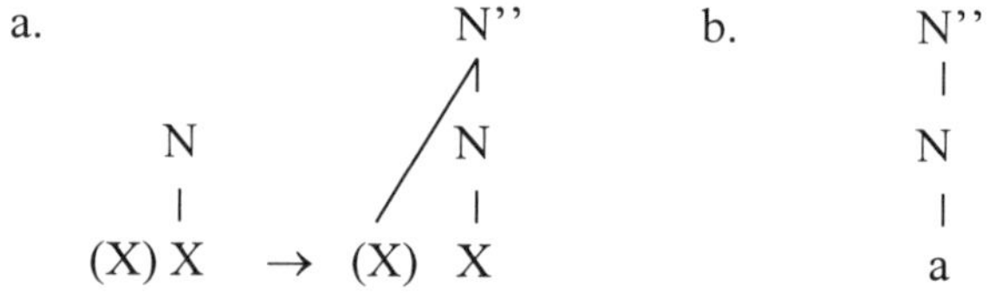

The Polish Onset rule adds a single consonant to the single consonant that is the output of the CV rule, as in (154).

(154) Polish Onset

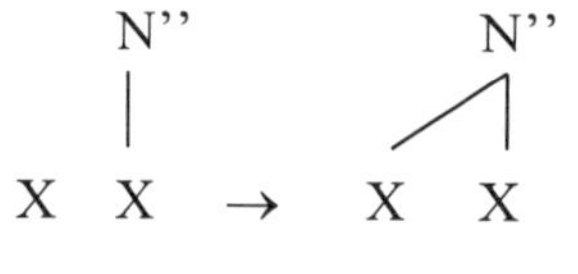

The Polish Onset rule is optional, i.e., the sequence VCCV can be syllabified as V.CCV, but it does not have to be. The parsing of consonants by the Polish Onset depends on their sonority since, as mentioned above, it is argued that the Polish syllable does not violate the Sonority Sequencing Generalization, and therefore the sonority of segments defined in the order vowels>liquids>nasals>fricatives>stops decreases towards the edges of a syllable. It is also claimed that this hierarchy only plays a role word-internally. Although Rubach and Booij (1990a:123) consistently refer to SSG in their analyses, they also observe that Polish does not require a sonority distinction between obstruents. This distinction is expressed by the so-called Obstruent Sequencing

[65] Rubach and Booij (1990a) assume that there is a rule called Coda Erasure which reorganizes syllable structure when new material is added in the course of derivation.

Constraint which says "With non-identical obstruents there is no requirement of sonority distance." This constraint allows the Polish Onset rule to incorporate a sequence of obstruents such as plosives and fricatives into the onset in either order.

The Polish Coda rule as well as the Complex Coda rule, cf. (155)a and (155)b respectively, are ordered after the CV rule and the Polish Onset rule. They are obligatory since all consonants 'left over' by the onset rules must be incorporated into the prosodic structure. While the Polish Coda rule creates the N' node by attaching one consonant, the Complex Coda rule incorporates any extra X-slots which do not violate SSG to the N' node. (N' denotes the rhyme of a syllable.)

(155) a. Polish Coda b. Complex Coda

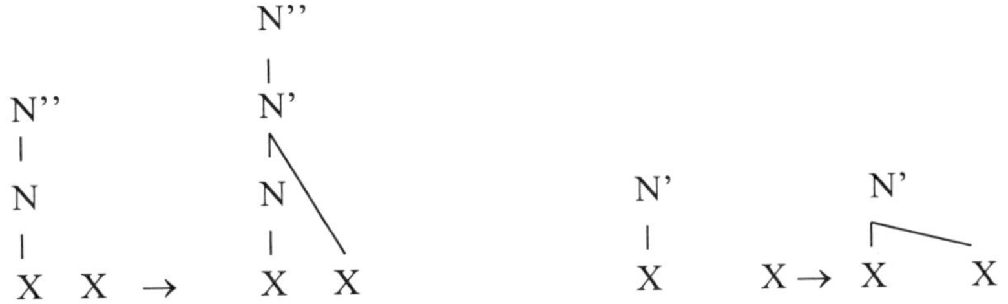

In addition, the N' node cannot contain two sonorants which is due to a Coda Constraint (recall (144)), which is restated in Levin's (1985) model in (156), cf. Rubach and Booij (1990a:124).

(156) Coda Constraint

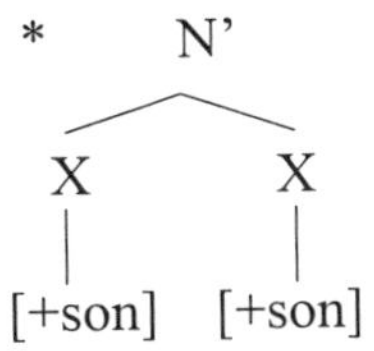

Finally the syllables erected by the SSA are incorporated into mots, cf. Liberman and Prince's term (1977).[66]

Rubach and Booij (1990b) develop their derivational approach proposed in Rubach and Booij (1990a) by investigating consonants that are not parsed by the Syllable Structure Algorithm of Polish into a syllable because of principles that underlie SSA such as SSG, Obstruent Sequencing Constraint[67] or Coda Constraint. They argue for an asymmetry between word-initial and non-word-initial unsyllabified segments on the basis of processes such as voicing assimilations and degemination. This asymmetry is

---

66 The term *mot* can be equated with *prosodic word*.

67 Obstruent Sequencing Constraint in Rubach and Booij (1990a) slightly differs from Obstruent Sequencing Constraint proposed in Rubach and Booij (1990b). The latter says: "With obstruents there is no requirement for sonority distance" Rubach and Booij (1990b:431). Hence, geminates are excluded from the constraint stated in (1990a), since "it is probably universally true that intervocalic geminates are never syllabified together" Rubach and Booij (1990b:431).

reflected by the Initial Adjunction rule which incorporates extrasyllabic consonants into the mot postcyclically and by the Housekeeping Adjunction rule, which incorporates extrasyllabic consonants to the mot postlexically. Both rules are discussed in 3.3.1, when voicing phenomena are analyzed.

The account proposed by Rubach and Booij captures many facts concerning Polish syllable structure in an adequate way. In order to account for these facts it make use of rules that are additionally determined by constraints, cf. Obstruent Sequencing Constraint and Coda Constraint. According to such assumptions an abstract syllable structure is created on every level of derivation on which constraints apply. Finally, Rubach and Booij do not show how optionality in syllabification is accounted for in Polish.

Gussmann (1991)

In his article on a Polish syllable structure Gussmann (1991) observes that the majority of clusters do not violate sonority.[68] There are only some clusters occurring in single words that violate sonority. For example, the cluster /wb/ occurs only in the paradigm of the word *łeb* [wep] 'head' pej. nom.sg., which in the genitive case deletes the vowel and emerges as [wb]a; the cluster /mx/ in *mchu* [mxu] 'moss' gen.sg. is attested only in the oblique forms of one word, namely *mech* 'moss' nom.sg. Again, the cluster is created because of the deletion of the vowel /e/. Gussmann argues that the violations of sonority in such cases should be regarded as an exception rather than the rule.

Rejecting the interchangeabilty of clusters proposed by Kuryłowicz (1952), he postulates the template for the onset presented in (157), cf. Gussmann (1991:209).

(157)

/S/+Obstruent + Sonorant

Since /S/ in this sequence denotes a coronal spirant, consonants such as *s, z, ś, ź, š, ž*, are allowed in this position. A coronal spirant is followed by an obstruent which in turn is followed by a sonorant. The order of elements is inviolable but the presence of every element is optional. Clusters such as /str/ in [str]ona 'page' nom.sg., /sp/ in [sp]ać 'to sleep', inf., or /sr/ in [sr]oka 'magpie' nom.sg. strictly adhere to the template in (157), which shows that not all elements have to be present; single consonants conform to it as well. By attributing a special status to the coronal spirant, Gussmann relates the well-formedness of the template to sonority requirements. Hence, the proposed syllable structure does not violate sonority.

As far as codas are concerned Gussmann claims that the only possible consonant in this position is a sonorant since first, Polish displays a tendency towards open syllables and second, this tendency is violated in a certain case, i.e., when the sonorants follow nuclei. Gussmann (1991:212) supports his claim by syllablifications of words such as *pa.no.wa.li* 'to rule' 3ps.pl.past, *pra.wo.sła.wie* 'Orthodox church' nom.sg., *war.ta* 'guard' nom.sg., *sej.my* 'parlament' nom.pl., *pal.to* 'coat' nom.sg., although he points out

[68] In his article Gussmann uses the term sonority without referring to a particular concept such as 'SSG' or 'Consonantal Strength'.

that cases displaying final obstruents such as wido[k] 'sight' nom.sg., de[šč] 'rain' nom.sg., spó[jš] 'to look' 2ps.sg.imp. require explanation. He postulates that all such words have an underlying V slot (empty vowel) that indicates a specific grammatical case or category, e.g. widokV. The empty vowel V is the exponent of the nom. sg, gen.pl. and the imperative; it also occurs in a number of derivational suffixes such as Vny, -Vski, -Vk. On the surface the vowel is deleted, "which accounts for the majority of the surface violations of our syllable template," cf. Gussmann (1991:212). In some instances, as Gussmann admits, the motivation for a V slot is indirect or it cannot be found.

One of the central ideas of Gussmann's proposal is the notion of extrasyllabicity. All segments that fail to conform to the proposed underlying order, i.e., SCRVR (S=s, z, š, ž, ś, ź, C=obstruent, R=sonorant, V=vowel) remain extrasyllabic in the course of derivation and are only adjoined to the syllable on the surface. The mechanism that erases hierarchical information and collapses all segments into one tier is dubbed *structure flattening*. It is illustrated in (158), (s=syllable). Note that in Gussmann's approach representations are expressed by C and V slots and not X slots as in Rubach and Booij's approach (1990)a, b. In contrast to Rubach and Booij (1990)a, b Gussmann also assumes that the syllable consists of onset and rhyme and not of projecting nodes.

(158)

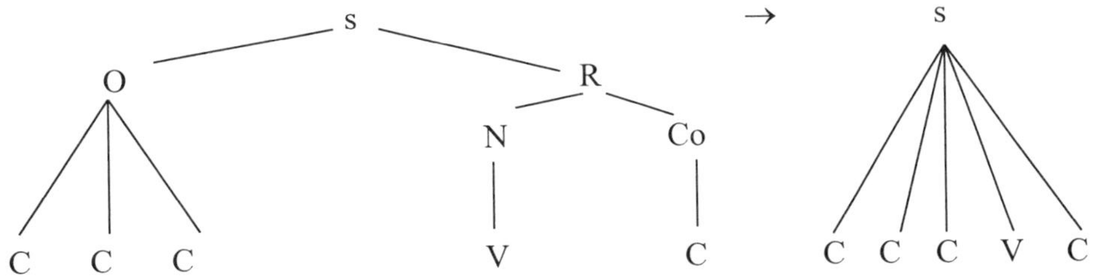

Since the *structure flattening operation,* cf. (158), results in a CCCVC sequence it is difficult to see how codas containing more than one consonant are treated by this mechanism given that positing an abstract vowel is not motivated. Gussmann himself also points out other complications following from his proposal, namely the treatment of certain phonetic obstruents as underlying sonorants. For example, he claims, following Kuryłowicz (1952), that [v] in tra[v]a 'grass' nom.sg. is derived from an underlying glide /w/. After suffixation, as in tra/wk/a 'grass' dim.nom.sg., [v] undergoes devoicing and emerges as [f], cf. tra[fk]a. Hence, there is no underlying difference between phonetic [v] and [f]. A problem arises if we consider words like [f]ala 'wave' nom.sg., and [fl]ądra 'flounder' nom.sg. in which the initial [f] cannot be derived from the underlying /w/ via devoicing since devoicing does not apply syllable- or word-initially. For this reason, Gussmann rejects Kuryłowicz' proposal that all [f] and [v] are derived from un underlying /w/ and claims that "at least in some positions /f/ has to be recognized as an underlying segment, which reopens the question as to whether it makes sense to postulate a sonorant underlying in words such as *woda* and *wlec*" Gussmann (1991:211).

Furthermore Gussmann, similar to Kuryłowicz (1952), treats [š ž] as sonorants. Persuing these lines, clusters of a type obstruent+š(ž) adhere to the template in (157). The motivation for this treatment comes from palatalization processes that change sonorants into obstruents, cf. k[r]a vs. k[š]e 'ice float' nom.sg./loc.sg., g[r]a vs. g[ž]e 'game'nom.sg./ loc.sg. Gussmann also assumes that nonalternating [š ž] in e.g. b[ž]eg 'coast' nom.sg. or k[š]ak 'bush' nom.sg. are derived from an underlying /r'/, cf. also Gussmann (1992a). He does not however extend this assumption to well-formed onsets in which [š ž] appear, cf. (157).

Concluding his investigation Gussmann claims that every Polish syllable conforms to the template shown in (159), whose hierarchical organization is removed by *a structure flattening operation,* presented in (158), cf. Gussmann (1991: 213).

(159)

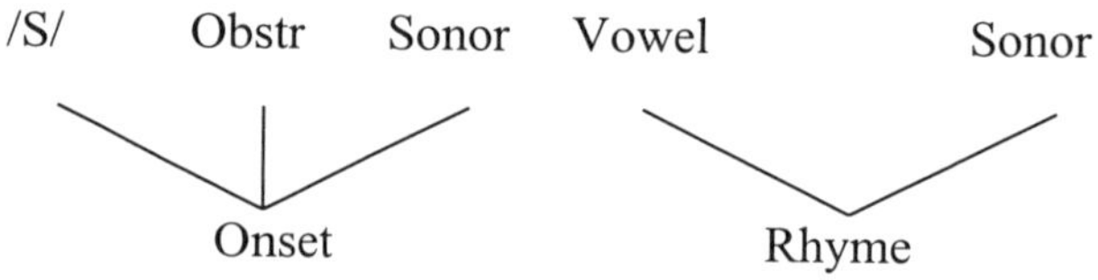

Musan (1994) shows that the restriction concerning codas proposed by Gussmann (1991) as well as Bethin (1992), cf. the presentation given below, is untenable for Polish. Her investigation of *Comparative Allomorphy*, *Nasal Backing*, *Vowel Raising*, and *Jer Vocalization* provides morphological as well as phonological evidence against sonorant-only codas. She argues that Polish allows sonorant-obstruent codas.

Furthermore, the surface structure of a Polish syllable proposed by Gussmann, cf. (158), does not capture all the data provided in 3.1.1. As mentioned above, it is not clear how four-member onsets and codas consisting of two and more consonants, which are not followed by an empty vowel V, are to be represented.

Bethin (1992)

Bethin's proposal concerning Polish syllable structure differs from the approaches presented above in that she assumes that the basic syllable derived by a cyclic application of syllable-building rules has the shape CRVR. (C=obstruent, R=sonorant, V=vowel). Segments that are not syllabified by syllable-building rules or adjunction rules are attached to the mot, i.e. to the prosodic word. Like Rubach and Booij (1990a), Bethin follows Levin (1985) in assuming that the syllable consists of an X-bar projection of the nucleus, which is a primitive category. The syllabification rules she proposes include a rule of Nucleus Assignment, an Onset Rule, a Coda Rule, a Complex Onset Rule and an Initial Adjunction Rule. The Coda Rule incorporates a single sonorant since the basic syllable shape is CRVR. The Complex Onset Rule only syllabifies sequences of rising sonority, i.e. [-sonorant] [+sonorant]. If there remains an unsyllabified element, represented as X' below, it can be syllabified by the Polish Complex Onset Rule under the condition that it is [-sonorant] and the following segment X is [+sonorant], cf. (160).

(160)

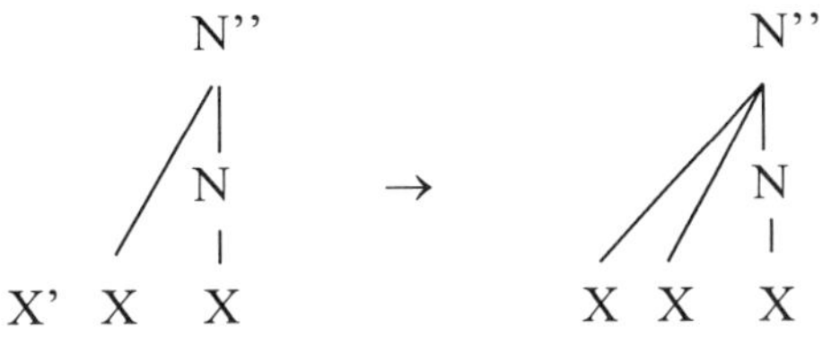

The syllabication rules apply cyclically, starting with a Nucleus Assignment and ending with the Complex Onset Rule (COR). However, after the application of the COR some segments may remain unsyllabified. For example, the second member of the cluster consisting of two plosives like *kt* or *pt* cannot be syllabified by the COR because of its violation of the sonority restriction. In the same vein, *ł* in *łk* and many others segments of clusters which violate sonority remain unsyllabified. In light of the data Bethin (1992) argues that the basic syllable structure CRVR can be changed to CCVC by syllable building rules which lose their language-specific distinctions and reapply at the word level. However, the restructuring of CRVR at the syllable level to CCVC at the word level is further restricted by sonority: sequences of equal sonority such as *db* are syllabified while sequences such as *łk* cannot be incorporated into a syllable because of sonority violation. The initial *ł* is parsed into a syllable by Initial Adjunction after the Complex Onset Rule reapplies at the word-level, cf. (161). In other words, Initial Adjunction is a postcyclic rule of syllabification. In summary, onsets in Polish are created either by syllable incorporation rules or the adjunction rule in case when they violate sonority.

(161)

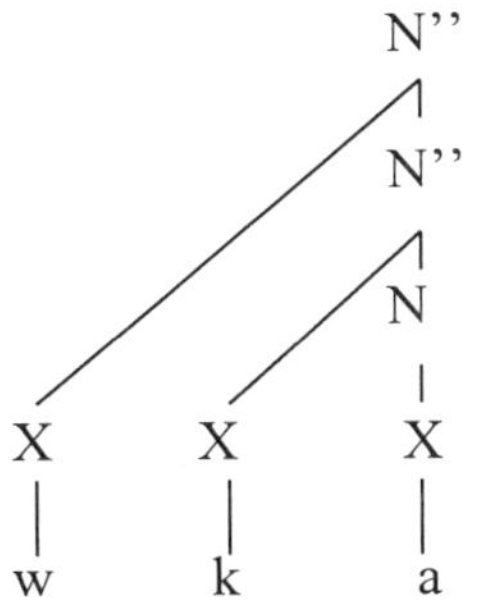

Remaining segments, i.e., those that are not syllabified either by syllable incorporation rules or by adjunction rules such as final or medial unsyllabified consonants, are attached to the mot, since they have to be pronounced. This point will be discussed in 3.3.1.

The arguments in favor of the basic shape CRVR are, according to Bethin, supported by the distribution and frequency of clusters. For example the main argument for the CR onset type, apart from its conformity to SSG, is the fact that they are the most frequent types of onsets in Polish. The strongest argument for the coda consisting of a single sonorant, cf. CRVR, is based on the observation that the most frequent codas that mirror onsets have the shape RC, cf. Kuryłowicz (1952). After isolating clusters that resemble onsets, the remaining cases are prevailingly sonorants. Additional evidence for codas consisting of a sonorant comes from syllabification provided by native speakers, who strongly prefer syllabification of the type VR.CV in sequences such as VRCV.[69]

As it will be shown in 3.2.2 it is indeed the case that native speakers heterosyllabify the medial sequence consisting of a sonorant and an obstruent. But it is not sufficient evidence for postulating codas consisting of one sonorant since sonorant+obstruent sequences are also syllabified as codas, cf. examples in 3.2.2.

Furthermore as shown by Musan (1994), the sonorant-only coda restriction does not hold for Polish. A similar position is also taken by Szpyra (1995). She shows that Nasal Vowel Backing and Raising make crucial reference to consonants in the coda, including obstruents. Her investigation of clipped hypocoristics in Polish shows that there is no evidence for postulating a syllable template in which a coda consists of a single sonorant. She shows that truncated names in Polish end in no more than two consonants of decreasing sonority.

Rubach (1996) points out that the templates postulated by Bethin (1992) are problematic with respect to the voicing specification of segments.[70] Her assumption that unsyllabified obstruents, i.e., those obstruents which do not adhere to templates, lose their voicing specification leads to incorrect predictions. For example, the underlined obstruents in *srebrny* 'silver' adj. masc. nom. sg., *krnąbrny* 'unruly' adj.masc.nom.sg. cannot be syllabified into the onset since the proposed template allows for maximum two elements. As a consequence, the voiced obstruent has to be devoided of its voice specification – which is incorrect.

Concluding this presentation we contend that there is considerable disagreement concerning the structure of the Polish syllable. The investigation of various factors referring to clusters as well as phonological and morphological processes leads to drastically different accounts. It seems to be rather impossible to find an absolute solution in light of the accounts proposed in the literature but as correctly observed by Szpyra (1995:51) "the largest number of arguments have been given to show that Polish follows the most basic version of the SSP[71] in that it disallows R+O sequences in the onset and O+R clusters in the coda. [...] Other aspects of syllable structure have not been justified in a sufficient manner."

The main reason for the lack of a consensus is that phonologists describe an *abstract* construct called 'syllable' on different *abstract* levels of representations. The single derivational syllables is created by means of rules which are additionally determined by constraints.

In the following I will abandon this stategy and will propose a novel account of Polish consonant clusters and a Polish syllable within the framework of Optimality Theory. The new aspect of this proposal is that I will consider the syllable structure as a *surface* object that is determined by different universal constraints. I will show that the

---

69 Cf. also 3.2.2 for other arguments.

70 The same objection pertains to the account proposed by Gussmann (1991).

71 Sonority Sequencing Generalization (SSG) as proposed by Selkirk (1984) is renamed by Szpyra (1995) as Sonority Sequencing Principle (SSP).

constraints alone select which consonants are parsed into syllable while leaving others outside the syllable. Further, other constraints determine into which prosodic category the extrasyllabic consonants are to be parsed. Since they interact with constraints responsible for various phonological processes, the output representations of consonantal sequences have to be optimal, i.e., they must show why certain processes apply and others are blocked.

In the proposed analyses I will take into consideration conclusions drawn from the presentation of clusters in 3.1.1. In particular, I will consider the unquestionable fact about Polish syllables that in the domain of a syllable sonority falls are not attested; external evidence will be gained from variation in syllabification provided by native speakers. I will also show how this variation is obtained by resolving crucial rankings between universal constraints.

3.2 A Polish syllable typology

Polish syllables, as proposed in 3.1.1, may consist of as many as four segments in the onset and as many as two in the coda. The additional condition imposed on strings is that syllable onsets display either rising sonority, i.e. they do not violate the SSG which is based on the sonority hierarchy proposed in (133), or a sonority plateau only with respect to obstruents.[72] In other words, sequences of obstruent+obstruent, obstruent+sonorant, $sonorant_2$+$sonorant_1$ (where $sonorant_2$ is less sonorous than $sonorant_1$), obstruent+obstruent+obstruent, obstruent+obstruent+sonorant, obstruent+$sonorant_2$+$sonorant_1$, obstruent+obstruent+obstruent+obstruent, obstruent+obstruent+obstruent+ sonorant or obstruent+ obstruent+$sonorant_2$+$sonorant_1$ are allowed to occur in onsets. In codas, on the other hand, as many as two consonants may occur (VC_1C_2). While the second consonant has to be an obstruent, the first one may be either an obstruent or a sonorant. Two sonorants may not occur in the coda due to a high-ranking constraint in Polish posited earlier in (144) prohibiting two sonorants in codas.

Before we consider what constraints are responsible for the optimal parsing of consonants (3.2.2.), let us discuss what universal constraints determine consonantal sequences and how Polish clusters behave with respect to them.

3.2.1 Cluster constraints

Universally, clusters are expected to undergo some syntagmatic constraints that impose different kinds of restrictions on their possible sequences of sounds. Generally, such constraints require the identity of consonants along different featural dimensions. Pulleyblank (1997:64) calls them Identical Cluster Constraints. He proposes four different constraints demonstrated in (162).

---

72 An additional restriction concerning identical segments (geminates) is provided in 3.3.2, where degemination is discussed.

(162) Identical Cluster Constraints

PLACE: A sequence of consonants must be identical in place of articulation.
CONTINUANCY: A sequence of consonants must be identical in continuancy.
NASALITY: A sequence of consonants must be identical in nasality.
VOICING: A sequence of consonants must be identical in voicing.

Identical Cluster Constraints directly express one of the most important functions determining language: the minimization of articulatory effort. They impose "articulatory inertia - changes in the positioning of articulators are disallowed" Pulleyblank (1997:64). However, these constraints, by referring excusively to articulatory demands, fail to consider the properties of clusters from a cross-linguistic perspective. It is hardly imaginable that all of the constraints in (162) are high-ranking in the languages of the world, cf. discussion below.

If we want to evaluate Polish consonant clusters with respect to these constraints, we immediately come to the conclusion that PLACE, CONTINUANCY and NASALITY are ranked below the constraints requiring a faithful parse of the relevant consonant sequences. There is namely a considerable number of clusters whose consonants are not identical in place of articulation. So, for example, a velar plosive might be followed by a labial plosive in *gburowaty* 'churlish' nom.sg. or a coronal plosive might be followed by a labial plosive as in *dbać* 'to take care' inf. This means that the faithfulness constraint requiring a faithful parse of place of articulation, $\text{IDENT}_{\text{PLACE}}$, is ranked higher than a constraint demanding identical place of consonants belonging to the same cluster. Consider the tableau in (163), which illustrates this point.

(163)

dbat^ś	$\text{IDENT}_{\text{PLACE}}$	PLACE
☞ dbat^ś		*
dzat^ś	*!	
vbat^ś	*!	

The first candidate in (163) is selected as optimal since it does not violate the high-ranking $\text{IDENT}_{\text{PLACE}}$. Although other candidates satisfy PLACE by having consonants in clusters that have the same place of articulation, they must be excluded from consideration, since they violate $\text{IDENT}_{\text{PLACE}}$.

Not only the constraint requiring a faithful parse of places of articulation is high-ranked in Polish. The constraint that demands a faithful parse of the feature [continuant] must outrank the constraint CONTINUANCY. This follows from the fact that consonants do not change this feature when they occur in clusters; sequences consisting of plosives followed by fricatives and fricatives followed by plosives occur extensively in Polish regardless of the number of consonants belonging to the cluster or of the position in which they occur in the word. Examples are provided in 3.1.1.

It is interesting to observe that according to the recent studies on obstruent clusters by Morelli (1998a,b), the unmarked type of onset sequences is constituted by sequences consisting of a fricative followed by a plosive, cf. also (135). These results strongly suggest that the universality of the constraint CONTINUANCY stated in (162) needs to be reconsidered. In order to account for this universally preferred order, i.e., a fricative followed by a plosive, Morelli (1998b:6f.) proposes three constraints, which are repeated in (164).

(164)

OCP [-cont] ^{Onset}: Tautosyllabic [-continuant] segments are disallowed in the onset.
OCP [+cont] ^{Onset}: Tautosyllabic [+continuant] segments are disallowed in the onset.
*SO^{Onset}: A tautosyllabic sequence containing a stop followed by any obstruent is disallowed in the onset.

The appropriate ranking of these constraints accounts for the markedness relations between obstruents in the onset. The sequence that incurs no violations, i.e., a fricative followed by a plosive, is the unmarked type of obstruent cluster. Sequences consisting of tautosyllabic fricatives or of a plosive followed by a fricative are marked since they violate OCP[+cont]^{Onset} and *SO^{Onset}, respectively. The most marked cluster type consists of two plosives because sequences of that type violate not only OCP[-cont]^{Onset} but also *SO. This is illustrated in (165), cf. Morelli (1998a:7).

(165)

	OCP[+cont]^{Onset}	*SO^{Onset}	OCP[-cont]^{Onset}
a. FS			
b. FF	*		
c. SF		*	
d. SS		*	*

F= fricative
S=stop

If we want to account for Polish obstruent clusters by means of the constraints proposed by Morelli (1998b), we are forced again to rank the identity constraint demanding the faithful parse of the feature [continuant] above all markedness constraints, since Polish allows for all types of sequences. This is indeed proposed by Morelli (1998b:8) for the sixth language type in her systematization, cf. (135).

A similar conclusion pertains to coda clusters. Regardless of whether we assume the constraint CONT or the constraints proposed by Morelli (1998b) which directly follow from her cross-linguistic study, the identity constraint demanding the faithful parse of [continuant] must be ranked above the markedness constraints in order to capture all possible sequences occurring in the coda in Polish.

The next constraint in (162), i.e. NASALITY, cannot be ranked higher than the identity constraint forcing the faithfulness between the input and the output with respect to the feature [nasal]. This follows from the fact that in Polish a sequence of consonants is not identical in nasality. Clearly, sequences like *gn-*, *ml-*, *tń-*, and *mr-* in the onset or *-mp*, and *-nt* in the coda crucially violate NASALITY, although they are perfect onsets and codas in Polish. Again, it is hardly imaginable that there are languages in which all consonant clusters are [+nasal]. It is much more probable that there are languages in which clusters are all [-nasal].

As the analysis shows, syntagmatic constraints such as PLACE, CONTINUANCY and NASALITY are lower ranked in Polish (if they exist at all). They are crucially preceded by constraints demanding faithful parse between features. But the precedence relation IDENT>>Markedness does not hold without exception. The only case where a syntagmatic markedness constraint is ranked above the identity constraint is constituted by voicing agreement. The VOICING constraint stated in (162) requires a sequence of consonants to be identical in voicing. It is however satisfied in Polish only with respect to obstruent sequences. For example, pro/śb/a 'request' nom.sg. is realized as pro[źb]a and li/$t^{š}$b/a 'number' nom.sg. is pronounced as li[$d^{ž}$b]a. Furthermore, gałą/zk/a 'branch' dim.nom.sg. is realized as gałą[sk]a and ły/žk/a 'spoon' nom.sg. as ły[šk]a. More examples are provided in 3.3.1, where the voicing phenomena are discussed. The voicing assimilations show that first, obstruents in clusters agree with respect to voicing, and second, in any given sequence of obstruents[73] voicing is predictable from the rightmost obstruent in the sequence, cf. also Bethin (1992:165).

In order to account for voicing assimilation in Polish, I propose to restrict the constraint VOICING (162) to obstruents, cf. (166).

(166)

$\text{VOICING}_{\text{OBSTRUENT}}$: A sequence of obstruents must be identical in voicing.

In (167) the implementation of the constraint in (166) into the ranking is shown.

(167)

pro/śb/a	$\text{VOICING}_{\text{OBSTR}}$	$\text{IDENT}_{[\text{voice}]}$
prośba	*!	
☞ proźba		*

In sum, Polish consonant clusters obey only the $\text{VOICING}_{\text{OBSTRUENT}}$ constraint, in that sequences of obstruents display agreement in voicing. They violate other syntagmatic constraints proposed by Pulleyblank (1997) such as PLACE, CONTINUANCY, NASALITY. What remains to be analyzed is the activity of a sonority constraint that seems to play an important role in the organizing of consonant sequences in syllable structure. Since the definition of this constraint requires a detailed analysis of syllabification, its formulation will be postponed to the next subsection, where syllabification is investigated.

[73] As will be shown in 3.3.1 in word-medial and word-final position an intervening sonorant does not block the assimilation between obstruents.

3.2.2 Syllabification: constraint interaction

In this subsection I propose constraints in OT that correctly account for Polish syllabification patterns. I show how their interaction captures variations attested in syllabification.

As mentioned in 3.1, VCV sequences are invariably syllabified as V.CV. Two universal markedness constraints are responsible for this pattern, i.e., a constraint requiring every syllable to have onsets and a constraint prohibiting codas. The first one is commonly known as ONS and the second one as *Coda. Both are stated as in (168), cf. Prince and Smolensky (1993:85).

(168)

ONS: Syllables must have onsets.
*CODA: Syllables must not have a coda.

Furthermore, we contend that MAX-IO, which requires a faithful parse of all segments present underlyingly in the surface representation, is a high-ranked constraint in Polish. In (169) the interaction of both constraints markedness constraints, ONS and *CODA, with the faithfulness constraint MAX is presented.[74]

(169)

mama	MAX	*COD	ONS
☞ ma.ma			
mam.a		*	*
ma.a	*!		*

The first candidate in (169), ma.ma, emerges as optimal since it perfectly satisfies MAX, *COD, and ONS. The second candidate, mam.a, which incurs a violation of *COD and ONS, must be trivially excluded from consideration as well as the third candidate, which deletes the medial consonant and therefore violates MAX.

Sequences containing two medial consonants such as CVCCV, i.e. CVOOV or CVORV, are syllabified by native speakers either as CV.CCV or as CVC.CV sequences. Recall the variation in syllabification of the following words: do.bry (29) and dob.ry (19), Ta.try (39) and Tat.ry (26) and pa.trzeć [patšet^{ś}] (36) and pat.rzeć (20), cf. Rubach and Booij (1990a:126). Hence, the question arises how this variation can be accounted for in a constraint-based grammar like Optimality Theory. In the previous accounts of syllable structure and syllabification in Polish this phenomenon has not been explicitly analyzed, cf. 3.1.2. In Rubach and Booij's (1990a) approach the most preferred syllabification pattern was taken as a basis for determining syllabification rules.

The approach to syllabification in Polish in the framework of Optimality Theory that will be proposed here opens new possibilities for accounting for variation. Variation is accounted for within one representational level, which is possible under the assump-

[74] The motivation for a crucial ranking between MAX and *COD follows from subsequent analyses.

tions that (i) constraints are violable and (ii) the crucial ranking of constraints can be resolved.

In the case under consideration the lack of crucial ranking between *Coda and a constraint prohibiting two consonants in the onset, *σ[CC, is responsible for the variation attested in the syllabification of two medial consonants as in *dob.ry* and *do.bry*. The *σ[CC constraint is a specific instantiation of a general constraint *COMPLEX, proposed by Prince and Smolensky (1993:87), which says: "No more than one C or V may associate to any syllable position node." The exact formulation of *σ[CC constraint is provided in (170).

(170)

*σ[CC: Onsets consisting of two consonants are prohibited.

How *σ[CC interacts with ONS and MAX is provided by an illustrative example in (171).

(171)

dobry	MAX	*COD	ONS	*σ[CC
☞ do.bry				*
☞ dob.ry		*		
do.ry	*!			

Both candidates *do.bry* and *dob.ry* emerge as optimal since *COD and *σ[CC are not crucially ranked with respect to each other.[75] The optionality reveals that Polish does not obey the Syllable Contact Law in (132), because apart from a preferred contact *do.bry* it also allows *dob.ry*, which has a 'bad' contact [b.r]. For this reason I reject for Polish a 'syllable contact' constraint as formulated by the Syllable Contact Law, and instead I propose below in (172) a 'sonority' constraint based on the Sonority Hierarchy for Polish which accounts for syllabification patterns in Polish. The example in (171) is also representative for the syllabification of words that contain two medial obstruents. As follows from the ranking in (171), a word like *matka* 'mother' nom.sg. is syllabified either as *mat.ka* or *ma.tka*, cf. Bethin (1992:25).

To sum up, the ranking presented in (171) predicts that every medial consonant cluster consisting of two consonants (obstruent+obstruent or obstruent+sonorant) will be syllabified either as a complex onset or a simple (one-element) onset and a simple coda. A single exception, however, is a pattern in which a sonorant is followed by an obstruent. For example, words like *ramka* 'frame' nom.sg. or *rurka* 'tube' nom.sg. do not exhibit variation. They are syllabified as *ram.ka* and *rur.ka*, respectively. These cases, as well as other syllabification patterns presented below, allow us to posit a constraint that prohibits a sonority fall from a syllable edge towards its peak. It is based on the

[75] Recall that the unranking of constraints means that violations of the unranked constraints are equally important. For example, in order to compute a tie between candidates, the total number of violations of unranked constraints has to be the same for each candidate as presented in (171) and other examples given below.

Sonority Hierarchy for Polish: obstruents<nasals<liquids<glides<vowels, cf. (133). The constraint is based on Sonority Sequencing Generalization but in contrast to SSG it also allows sonority plateau in a syllable, e.g. a sequence of two or more obstruents can be parsed into a syllable. Its formulation is given in (172).

(172)

*Son↘V: No decreasing sonority from the edges of the syllable towards its peak.

The constraint in (172) is satisfied whenever a cluster that does not violate the proposed hierarchy is parsed into a syllable. In tableau in (173) clusters are shown which do not violate *Son↘V when they are parsed into syllable onset.

(173)

Cluster$_{ONSET}$	*Son↘V
obstruent+obstruent	✓
obstruent+sonorant	✓
nasal+nasal	✓
nasal+liquid	✓
nasal+glide	✓
liquid+liquid	✓
liquid+glide	✓
glide+glide	✓

The clusters in (173) perfectly satisfy *Son↘V because they do not display decreasing sonority from the edges of the syllable towards its peak from a point of view of Polish Sonority Hierarchy. A considerable number of clusters would however violate the constraint in (172) if it were based on the hierarchies proposed by Selkirk (1984), cf. (127), or Vennemann (1988), cf. (130). Nevertheless, in (173) there are clusters which do not occur in the syllable onset in Polish such as nasal+nasal, liquid+liquid, glide+glide. Therefore additional constraints are required which prohibit such sequences, cf. constraints presented in (174).

(174)

*NASAL+NASAL$_{ONSET}$: a sequence of two nasals in the onset is prohibited.
*LIQUID+LIQUID$_{ONSET}$: a sequence of two liquides in the onset is prohibited.
*GLIDE+GLIDE$_{ONSET}$: a sequence of two glides in the onset is prohibited.

The constraints presented in (174), similarly to *Son↘V, are highly ranked. If sonorants occur word-medially the constraints are responsible for their heterosyllabification. Consider the tableau in (175) in which the constraint *NASAL+NASAL$_{ONSET}$ contributes to the selection of the optimal candidate.

(175)

manna	*Son↘V	*NASAL+ NASAL$_{ONS}$	*COD	ONS	*σ[CC
ma.nna.		*!			
☞ man.na			*		
mann.a			*	*!	*

The second candidate in (175) is selected as optimal because it does not violate *NASAL+NASAL$_{ONSET}$ and ONS in contrast to other candidates. The role of constraints in (175) is especially visible in the case of geminates ocurring in diffrent positions. This issue is discussed in 3.3.2.

Let us consider how *Son↘V interacts with the other constraints proposed thus far and how this interaction leads to the selection of optimal outputs. The tableau in (176) illustrates the possible syllabifications of the word *ramka* 'frame' dim.nom.sg.

(176)

ramka	MAX	*Son↘V	*COD	ONS	*σ[CC
ra.mka		*!			*
☞ ram.ka			*		
ra.ma	*!				
ramk.a			*	*!	

The battle between the candidates in (176) is won by *ram.ka,* a candidate that violates only one constraint, i.e. *COD, and does not display decreasing sonority towards the syllable peak. Its most serious competitor *ramk.a* is excluded due to a violation of ONS. Other candidates either violate the high-ranking MAX (*ra.ma*) or the high-ranking *Son↘V (*ra.mka*).

Let us proceed to the syllabification of three-member consonant sequences in word-medial position. If the clusters consist of obstruents, they are optionally syllabified in three different ways, namely as VC.CCV, VCC.CV, or V.CCCV. For example, the word *listwa* [listfa] 'board' nom.sg. is syllabified either as [l'is.tfa] (40), or as [l'ist.fa] (11) or even as [l'i.stfa] (8), cf. Rubach and Booij (1990a:126). This variation reveals the existence of other constraints prohibiting complex codas and complex onsets. Both constraints are formulated in (177).

(177)

*CC]σ: Codas consisting of two consonants are prohibited.
*σ[CCC: Onsets consisting of three consonants are prohibited.

Like the constraint in (170), the two constraints in (177) are violable, as I show below. They are also a further specification of the *COMPLEX constraint family. It is important to stress that *CC]σ cannot be replaced by *COD since the latter militates against simple codas and the former against complex codas. If there were no differentiation between *COD and *CC]σ, words of different shapes would be treated in the same way. For example, words exhibiting patterns such as CVC.CVCC. and CVC.CVC. would incur two violations of *COD without further quantitative distinction. In the same vein, *σ[CC cannot be replaced by *σ[CCC, as it is illustrated in the subsequent analysis.

The postulation of *CC]σ and *σ[CCC is motivated by the variation in syllabification. If the constraints were not active, only two candidates would be selected as optimal and one of the intended mappings (lis.tfa) would be excluded from consideration. This situation is illustrated in the tableau in (178).

(178)

listwa	*Son⋭V	*COD	ONS	*σ[CC
lis.tfa		*		*!
☞ list.fa		*		
☞ li.stfa				*
listf.a		*	*!	

Since all candidates in (178) fare equally well on *Son⋭V, the winner can only be decided by the next three unranked constraints. Two candidates *list.fa* and *li.stfa* emerge as optimal, since each of them incurs only one violation of one of the constraints responsible for variation. As follows from the tableau in (178), one attested candidate, i.e. *lis.tfa*, is not selected. The crucial point is that *COD is always violated once regardless of whether a coda consists of one, two or more consonants. For this reason CC]σ, in contrast to *COD, prohibits two consonants in the coda and must therefore be active. Furthermore *σ[CC is violated once regardless of whether the onset consists of two or more consonants. In order to account for such a difference, a constraint prohibiting three consonants in the onset, i.e. *σ[CCC, has to be active. The tableau in (179) illustrates how the implementation of the constraints *CC]σ and *σ[CCC leads to the selection of correct candidates.

(179)

listwa	*Son⋭V	*COD	ONS	*CC]σ	*σ[CC	*σ[CCC
☞ lis.tfa		*			*	
☞ list.fa		*		*		
☞ li.stfa					*	*
listf.a		*	*	*!		

Since the first three candidates fare equally on the unranked constraints, all are selected. Hence, the ranking in (179) accounts for all three attested syllable parsings.

As in the case of two medial consonants, it is not always the case that all syllabification possibilities are attested in every three-member set. Sequences that have sonorants as their first member are syllabified either as CVC.CCV or CVCC.CV, but not as CV.CCCV. The tableau in (180) shows that ranking of constraints assumed in (179) correctly predicts only the first two parsings.

(180)

kurtka	*Son↘V	*COD	ONS	*CC]σ	*σ[CC	*σ[CCC
☞ kur.tka		*			*	
☞ kurt.ka		*		*		
ku.rtka	*!				*	*
kurtk.a		*	*	*!		

The third candidate in (180), ku.rtka, is immediately excluded from consideration due to the violation of *Son↘V. The last candidate, *kurtk.a*, incurs a total of three violations of the unranked constraints, i.e. one more violation than *kur.tka* and *kurt.ka*, and therefore cannot be selected as optimal.

A similar situation obtains when four word-internal consonants are syllabified. If a given sequence does not display a sonority fall, the preferred syllabification pattern of VCCCCV sequences is VC.CCCV. But sequences of the type VCC.CCV and V.CCCCV are also attested. As mentioned above, Rubach and Booij (1990a:126) report that a word like *abstrakt* [apstrakt] 'abstract' nom.sg. is syllabified as *ab.strakt* (20), *abs.trakt* (14) or *a.bstrakt* (6). This means that an additional constraint prohibiting four consonants in the onset, i.e. *σ[CCCC, must become active in evaluating optimal candidates. The tableau in (181) illustrates the effects of the implementation of *σ[CCCC into the ranking postulated above.[76]

(181)

abstrakt	*Son↘V	*COD	*CC]σ	*σ[CC	*σ[CCC	*σ[CCCC
ap.strakt		**	*	*	*!	
aps.trakt		**	**	*!		
a.pstrakt		*	*	*	*	*!
☞ apst.rakt		**	**			
apstr.akt	*!					

Unfortunately, the incorrect prediction is made that *apst.rakt* is the optimal candidate. This candidate differs from the intended winners in that it has a three-member coda. Hence, what has to be additionally active is a constraint prohibiting three consonants in the coda, i.e. *CCC]σ. More importantly, this constraint must be crucially higher ranked than *COD in order to avoid the emergence of *apst.rakt* as an optional variant. This is exactly the situation presented in (182).

[76] Notice that additional violations of COD and *CC]σ are caused by the complex word-final coda.

(182)

apstrakt	*CCC]σ	*COD	*CC]σ	*σ[CC	*σ[CCC	*σ[CCCC
☞ ap.strakt		**	*	*	*	
☞ aps.trakt		**	**	*		
☞ a.pstrakt		*	*	*	*	*
apst.rakt	*!	**	**		*	

Finally, let us consider variations in the syllabification of medial five-member sequences. Unsurprisingly, words that exhibit VCCCCCV patterns are syllabified either as VC.CCCCV or VCC.CCCV, because maximally two consonants are allowed in the coda position. Rubach and Booij (1990a:126) take the syllabification of *skąpstwo* [skompstfo] as a representative example which exhibits the following patterns: VCC.CCCV [skomp.stfo] (28) and VC.CCCCV [skom.pstfo] (19). Since the pattern VCCC.CV [skomps.tfo] is attested only twice it can be considered as an exception. The range of possible syllabifications is shown in (183).

(183)

skompstfo	*Son↘V	*CCC]σ	*COD	*CC]σ	*σ[CC	*σ[CCC	*σ[CCCC
☞ skom.pstfo			*		**	*	*
☞ skomp.stfo			*	*	**	*	
skomps.tfo		*!	*	*	*		
skompst.fo		*!	*	*			
sko.mpstfo	*!				*	*	*

The first two candidates in (183) emerge as optimal, since they perfectly satisfy high-ranking constraints such as *Son↘ and *CCC]σ. In contrast to other candidates, neither of the selected outputs displays a decreasing sonority from the syllable edges towards the syllable peak or has a coda consisting of more than two consonants.

The ranking shown in (183) correctly predicts the surface syllabification in Polish. The crucial advantage of this account over the derivational ones presented in 3.1.2. is that the OT approach accounts for the *surface* syllable structure and not some abstract syllable structure. In addition, most constraints governing Polish syllable structure are violable in contrast to derivational approaches, in which rules are never violable. The violability of universal constraints allows us to account for widely attested variations in syllabification in a simple way, i.e. by resolving the crucial ranking between appropriate constraints.

Furthermore, it must be stressed that the ranking presented in (183) is a ranking that captures facts referring to the Polish language and therefore constitutes a kind of general picture of attested syllabification in Polish. As we might presume, grammars of individual speakers mostly allow only minimal variation. This suggests that in individual rankings constraints are mostly crucially ranked with respect to each other, thus preventing variations. In some instances, however, even individual grammars allow variation by resolving the crucial ranking between constraints. For example, my own grammar allows me to syllabify *matka* 'mother' nom.sg. either as *mat.ka* or as *ma.tka* without any preferences. Other speakers might syllabify the word exclusively as *ma.tka*; others only as *mat.ka*. This means that the ranking between NoCoda and *σ[CC is resolved in my grammar and not in the grammar of other speakers who syllabify the word *matka* in a unified manner. The crucial point is that a general ranking such as that presented in (183) captures all possible syllabification patterns by resolving crucial rankings between some constraints. This flexibility, however, is possible to a certain extent since it mirrors the flexibility found in individual grammars. In other words, a general ranking is a summary of individual rankings, cf. also the discussion in 1.3.3.

3.3 Extrasyllabic consonants

This subsection focuses on consonants occurring in word-initial and word-final position that are not syllabified. The interesting cases are those that would violate the high-ranking sonority constraint *Son↘ proposed in (172) if they were incorporated into the syllable. Examples are provided by word-initial clusters such as /rt/, /rd/, /wb/, /wg/, /mgw/, and /lgn/ and word-final ones such as /kl/, /kr/, /kw/, /str/, and /štr/. In (137) I presented representation of two-member onset clusters, two of which are repeated in (184)a and (184)b. These representations contain a segment which is not syllabified because of the violation of *Son↘.

(184) Extrasyllabic consonants

a. Sonorant +obstruent

σ
/\
r d^z a 'rust' nom.sg.

b. Sonorant+sonorant

σ
/\
l n u 'flax' gen.sg.

The question arises as to how the offending sonorants are incorporated into higher level of prosodic structure, given the fact that they are not subject to Stray Erasure and therefore emerge on the surface.

As was mentioned in 3.1.2, in the derivational approach proposed by Rubach and Booij (1990a) extrasyllabic sonorants are incorporated either by the postcyclic Initial Adjuction to the prosodic word or by the postlexical House-Keeping Adjunction to the same prosodic constituent, i.e. prosodic word. Bethin (1992) proposes to adjoin the extrasyllabic consonants to a syllable by the Initial Adjunction or to the prosodic word depending on the position in which they occur. Both proposals are discussed below.

In the following I will propose a novel account of the unsyllabified segments by adjoining them to the foot rather than to the syllable or to the prosodic word. I will show that of the possible representations in (185) only the one in (185)b is correct.

(185)

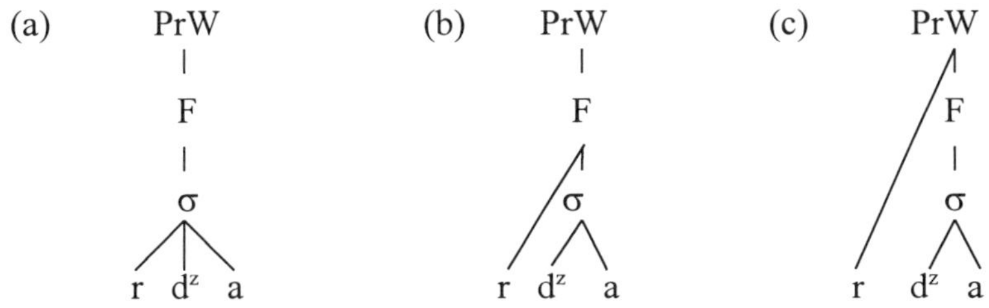

There are at least two reasons for why the representation in (185)b is correct. The first follows from the prosodic organization of morphosyntactic structures and the second from internal requirements of OT. According to assumptions made in Prosodic Phonology, cf. Nespor and Vogel (1986), sentences are organized into the prosodic hierarchy, which consists of the following constituents: the syllable, the foot, the phonological word, the clitic group, the phonological phrase, the intonational phrase, and the phonological utterance, cf. Nespor and Vogel (1986:11). The order of the constituents is not accidental but proceeds from the smallest prosodic unit, i.e the syllable, to the largest one, i.e. the phonological utterance. The hierarchy is shown in (186). It has to be stressed that although the existence of a prosodic hierarchy is unquestionable, there is less agreement concerning the presence of single constituents. For example Selkirk (1984b), (1995) does not postulate clitic group or mora as prosodic constituents.

(186) phonological utterance
|
intonational phrase
|
phonological phrase
|
clitic group
|
phonological word
|
foot
|
syllable

Such a hierarchical organization follows from the constraints on prosodic domination presented in (187), cf. Selkirk (1995:443).

(187) Constraints on Prosodic Domination (where C_n = some prosodic category)

Layeredness No C^i dominates a C^j, $j > i$, e.g. 'No σ dominates a Ft':

* σ
|
Ft

Headedness Any C^i must dominate a C^{i-1} (except if $C^i = \sigma$),
e.g. 'A PWd must dominate a Ft':

PWd
|
Ft

Exhaustivity No C^i immediately dominates a constituent C^j, $j < i-1$,
e.g. 'No PWd immediately dominates a σ' :

* PWd
|
σ

Nonrecursivity No C^i dominates C^j, $j = i$,
e.g. 'No Ft dominates a Ft.'

* Ft
|
Ft

All the constraints in (187) are components of Strict Layer Hypothesis, which can be interpreted as a complex constraint demanding a prosodic constituent of level C^i to dominate only constituents immediate to the next level down in the prosodic hierarchy, C^{i-1}, cf. Selkirk (1995:443). For purposes of the present study we will dub this constraint Strict Layer. Formally, it is stated as in (188).

(188)

Strict Layer (Layer): A prosodic constituent of level C^i immediately dominates only constituents of the level C^{i-1}.

In contrast to assumptions made by Nespor and Vogel (1986) who argue that Strict Layer is not violable, it is assumed that (i) Strict Layer is violable and (ii) violations of Strict Layer are 'gradient' in the sense that a segment linked to a prosodic constituent C^{i+1} (where C^{i+1} = Ft) incurs one more violation of Strict Layer than a segment linked to C^i (where $C^i = \sigma$). Examples are provided in (189).

In the same vein, Strict Layer requires extrasyllabic consonants to be parsed into the syllable. In order to avoid a violation of sonority, cf. (185)b, the offending consonants cannot be adjoined to the syllable but they have to be adjoined to the next prosodic level, i.e., the foot. That the foot is a prosodic constituent in Polish is independently supported by the fact that bisyllabic feet play an indispensable role in Polish prosody by constituting optimal domains for stress assignment,[77] cf. e.g., Rubach and Booij (1985)

---

[77] Feet in Polish are maximally bisyllabic and left-headed. Primary stress falls on the penultimate syllable, while a secondary stress is assigned to every odd syllable starting from the first one on the right edge of the word, i.e. every foot head. Consider the following examples, in which number '1' indicates primary stress, '2' secondary stress and '0' no stress. Parentheses '( )' mark feet. Note that in the final example the middle syllable is 'stray'. This follows from the assumptions mentioned above.

1 0
(gry.mas) 'grimace' nom.sg.

and Kraska-Szlenk (1995). Furthermore, recent studies such as Rowicka and van de Weijer (1994) reveal that the foot as a prosodic domain plays a crucial role in Polish in the formation of the Derived Imperfective. Although the foot exists in Polish as a prosodic category, it is often disregarded even if the prosodic hierarchy plays an important role in the proposed analyses, cf. Bethin (1992) and Rubach (1997). Rubach (1997) justifies the avoidance of the foot by noting that feet play no role in the analysis of segmental phenomena in Polish.

In the present study I will invoke the foot as an active prosodic category in Polish, and I will show that it plays a crucial role in various instances. Specifically, it constitutes the domain for the licensing of extrasyllabic consonants. Such representations are independently confirmed by processes such as voicing assimilations and degemination, discussed in 3.3.1 and 3.3.2, respectively.

As I claimed above word-initial extrasyllabic consonants are linked to the foot and not to the syllable or the prosodic word. The tableau in (189) illustrates why this solution is better than others.

---

0 1 0 gry.(ma.śny)	'fussy' adj.masc.nom.sg.
2 0 1 0 (gry.ma)(śni.ca)	'fussy girl' nom.sg.
2 0 0 1 0 (gry.ma.)śni.(ca.mi)	'fussy girl' instr.pl.

(189)

r d^z a	*Son↘V	Layer
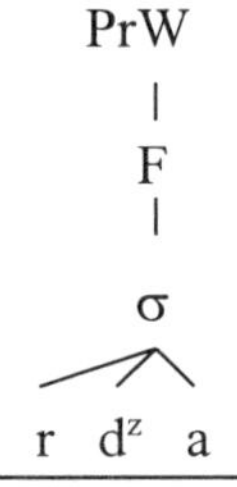	*!	
☞ 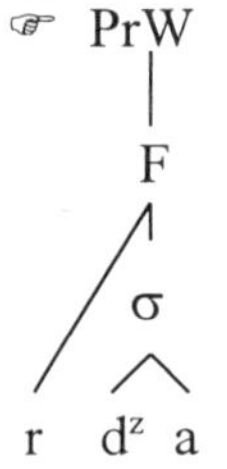		*
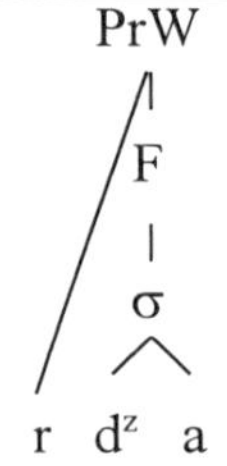		*!*

Although the first candidate in (189) perfectly satisfies Layer by incorporating all consonants into the syllable, it is not selected as the optimal because it violates the high-ranked constraint *Son↘V. The second candidate, however, does not violate *Son↘V because the word-initial sonorant is linked to the foot. Consequently, it violates Layer only once by skipping the syllable level. For this reason it fares better than the third candidate, which incurs two violations of Layer by skipping both the syllable and the foot level.

A mirror image might be potentially obtained for extrasyllabic consonants in word-final codas. For example, the final sonorant in *wiatr* 'wind' nom.sg. could be attached to the foot, thereby avoiding violations of the *Son↘V and incurring a minimal violation of Layer. The same conclusion could be also derived with respect to word-internal sonorants found between obstruents or sonorants. Some selected examples are shown in (190).

(190)

pio[sn̥k]a	'song' dim. nom.sg.
pierwio[sn̥k]i	'primroses' nom.pl.

ździe[pw̥k]o		'stalk' dim.nom.sg.
mę/dr/ek	mę[tr̥k]a	'crafty person' nom.sg. / gen.sg.
Ję/dr/ek	Ję[tr̥k]a	'Jędrek' nom.sg./gen.sg.

In other words, the ranking presented in (189) predicts the representations in (191)a and (191)b for word-final and word-medial extrasyllabic sonorants, respectively.

(191)

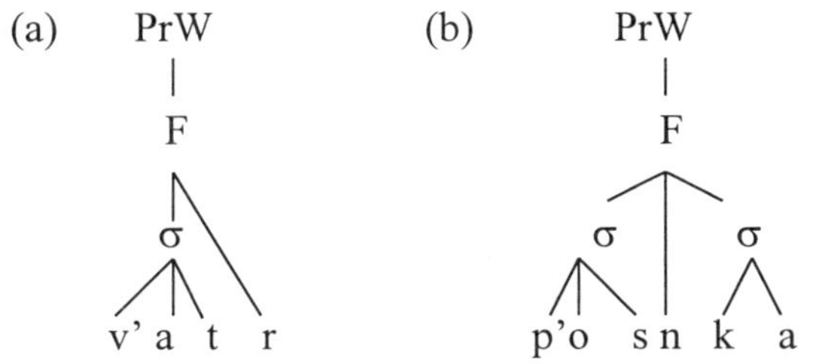

The validity of the solution of incorporating all extrasyllabic sonorants into feet, which follows from structural requirements of the prosodic hierarchy as well as sonority conditions, remains to be proved. This will be a task of the next subsections where it will be shown that the selected representation in (189) is correct, while the structures in (191)a and (191)b are incorrect for independent phonological reasons, such as the behavior of the extrasyllabic consonants in voicing assimilation and degemination.

3.3.1 Voicing assimilations

Before stating generalizations concerning the behavior of extrasyllabic consonants in voicing assimilations, the main facts referring to voicing phenomena in Polish will be summarized.

First, Polish has word-final devoicing that affects obstruents but not sonorants, as shown in (192)a. The data in (192)b illustrate that sonorants also devoice in word-final position when they follow obstruents. In other words, word-final obstruents as well as word-final clusters containing a final sonorant are devoiced. The underlying forms in (192) are motivated by alternations: pró/g/ vs. pro[g]u 'threshold' gen.sg., kate/dr/ vs. kate[dr]a'cathedral' nom.sg., etc.

(192)

a.

pró/g/	pró[k]	'threshold' nom.sg.
gra/d/	gra[t]	'hail' nom.sg.
gołą/b/	gołą[p]	'pigeon' nom.sg.
gła/z/	gła[s]	'stone' nom.sg.

gwó/źd$^{\acute{z}}$/	gwó[śt$^{\acute{s}}$]	'nail' nom.sg.
wó/r/	wó[r]	'sack' nom.sg.
gra/m/	gra[m]	'gram' nom.sg.
pla/n/	pla[n]	'plan' nom.sg.
b.		
kate/dr/	kate[tr̥]	'cathedral' gen.pl.
ka/dr/	ka[tr̥]	'frame' nom.sg.
katechi/zm/	katechi[sm̥]	'catechism' nom.sg.
ja/źń/	ja[śń̥]	'ego' nom.sg.

As I mentioned in 3.2.1, Polish has regressive voicing that applies word-internally, as in (193)a, as well as across word boundaries, as in (193)b. The underlying forms in (193) result from alternations, e.g. li/t^{š}b/a vs. li[t^{š}]+ić 'to count' inf., margine/s/ vs. margine[s]y 'margin' nom.pl.

(193)

a.		
pro/śb/a	pro[źb]a	'request' nom.sg.
li/tšb/a	li[džb]a	'figure' nom.sg.
ko/śb/a	ko[źb]a	'mowing' nom.sg.
b.		
margine/s z/eszytu	margine[z z]eszytu	'margin of an exercise book' nom.sg.
sma/k b/rzoskwini	sma[g bž]oskwini	'peach taste' nom.sg.
no/s z/wierzęcia	no[z zv']rzęcia	'animal nose' nom.sg.
zeszy/t d/o matematyki	zeszy[d d]o matematyki	'mathematics notebook' nom.sg.

These examples indicate that the trigger of voicing assimilation is always the final consonant of the cluster. This is crucially supported by the regressive devoicing that applies to obstruents followed by voiceless consonants. Again, regressive devoicing is attested word-medially and across word-boundaries, cf. (194)a and (194)b, respectively. Similarily to previous examples the underlying forms in (194) are motivated by alternations, e.g. kłó/dk/a vs. kłó[dek] 'padlock' gen.pl., zaprzą/g/ vs. zaprzę[g]i 'span of horses' nom.pl.

(194)

a.		
kłó/dk/a	kłó[tk]a	'padlock' nom.sg.
gałą/zk/a	gałą[sk]a	'branch' dim.nom.sg.
ły/žk/a	ły[šk]a	'spoon' nom.sg.
gwia/zdk/a	gwia[stk]a	'star' dim.nom.sg.
b.		
zaprzą/g k/onny	zaprzą[k k]onny	'span of horses' nom.sg.
opa/d ś/niegu	opa[t ś]niegu	'snowfall' nom.sg.
samochó/d s/ławka	samochó[t s]ławka	'Sławek's car' nom.sg.
pośli/zg s/amochodowy	pośli[sk s]amochodowy	'car skid' nom.sg.

In rule-based phonology, it is often assumed that voice specification of the rightmost obstruent spreads to the neighboring obstruent(s) on its left side. This is illustrated in the spreading rule in (195), where 'v'='voice' and 'L'=laryngeal node, cf. Rubach and Booij (1990b), Rubach (1996).[78]

(195)

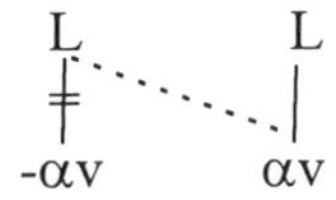

In the following we will examine how extrasyllabic sonorants behave with respect to regressive voicing. Interestingly, if they occur in word-initial position as the first member of a sonorant-obstruent cluster, then voicing assimilation between the obstruent in the onset and the word-final obstruent of the preceding word does not apply. Relevant examples are provided in (196). The underlying forms in (196) result from alternations, e.g. ry/k/ vs. ry[k]u 'roar' gen.sg.

(196)

ry/k lv/a	ry[k lv]a	'roar of a lion' nom.sg.
sma/k rd/estu	sma[k rd]estu	'water-pepper taste'nom.sg.
wielko/śtś łb/a	wielko[śtś wb]a	'size of the head' nom.sg.
obło/k mg/wy	obło[k mg]wy	'cloud of mist' nom.sg.

These examples indicate that word-initial extrasyllabic sonorants block the assimilation of obstruents. In light of these data, the question arises as to how word-internal extrasyllabic sonorants behave with respect to voicing, e.g. the /r/ in *mę[trk]a* 'crafty person' gen.sg. As was shown in (190) medial extrasyllabic sonorants are transparent to voicing assimilation: the medial plosive /d/ in *mędrek* 'crafty person' nom.sg. undergoes devoicing if the following sonorant is adjacent to a voiceless obstruent, as in *mę[trk]a*.

The same conclusion can be drawn with respect to word-final extrasyllabic sonorants. The examples provided in (197) show that word-final sonorants are transparent in the processes of assimilation between obstruents. The underlying forms are motivated by alternations, e.g. ry/tm/ vs. ry[tm]u 'rhythm' gen.sg.

(197)

ry/tm b/razylijski	ry[dm b]razylijski	'Brazilian rhythm' nom.sg.
wia/tr z/achodni	wia[dr z]achodni	'westerly' nom.sg.
ło/tr z/abrał	ło[dr z]abrał	'rascal took (sth) away'
pie/śń g/óralska	pie[źń g]óralska	'mountaineer's song' nom.sg.

In light of these data the question arises as to why extrasyllabic sonorants in word-initial position block voicing, cf. (196), and those in word-medial and word-final

---

78 In these proposals voiced obstruents are specified as [+voice] underlyingly and voiceless obstruents as [-voice].

position do not, cf. (190) and (197). That this discrepancy does not depend on whether or not sonorants are specified for [+voice] or unspecified for this feature follows from the asymmetrical behavior of sonorants in different positions. If all sonorants were specified for [+voice] underlyingly, we would expect blocking of voicing assimilation not only in cases like (196) but also in examples in (190) and (197). This expectation follows from the No-Crossing Constraint which says that association lines may not cross, cf. Goldsmith (1976). In (198) it is shown what effect the No-Crossing Constraint has on the voicing assimilation between /k/ and /d/. The representation in (198) is not correct because, as indicated by the examples in (190) and (197), voicing assimilation between /k/ and /d/ applies.

(198)

*

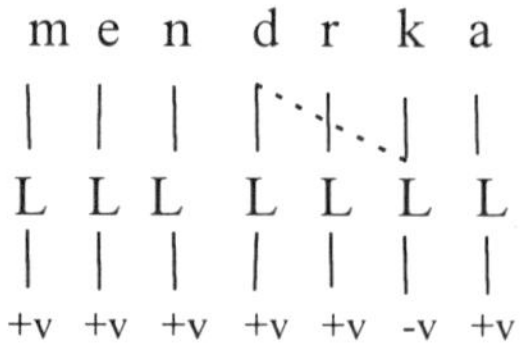

In the opposite case, i.e., if the sonorants were not specified for voicing, they would be transparent in every position. This assumption predicts correct outputs in (190) and (197) on the one hand but does not account correctly for examples provided in (196). For illustration, consider representations shown in (199)a and (199)b, respectively.

(199)

a.

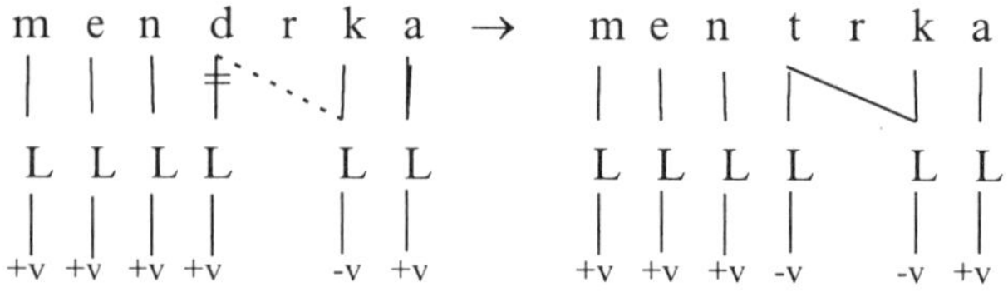

b. *

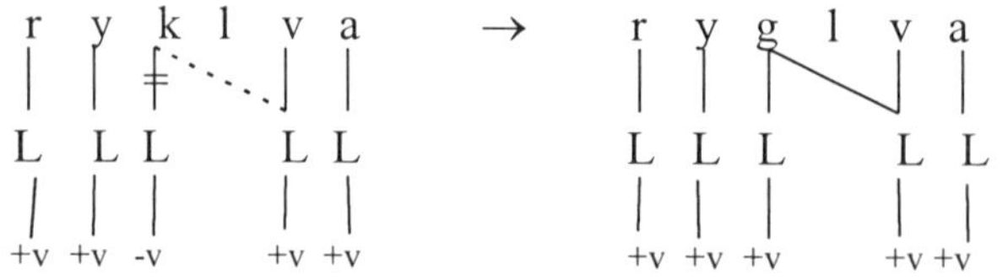

In derivational approaches, cf. Rubach and Booij (1990a,b), Rubach (1996), Bethin (1992), the asymmetry is accounted for by different representations at various derivational stages. For example Rubach and Booij (1990b), as well as Rubach (1996), assuming the adjacency of laryngeal nodes as a condition for [voice] spreading, claim that the offending sonorants are not specified for voicing but receive their voicing specification when they are prosodified. Since initial extrasylabic sonorants are prosodified by the postcyclic Initial Adjunction, cf. 3.1.2, they are able to block the voicing assimilation that applies postlexically. Noninitial extrasyllabic sonorants being prosodified by the postlexical Housekeeping Adjunction, allow the voicing assimilation to apply.

In the approach to OT I am adopting in the present study there are no derivational stages. The attested asymmetry can be therefore not ascribed to derivational stages but it has to be mirrored in representation itself. In the following I discuss Rubach'approach (1997) and make some comments concerning his proposal.

In his constraint-based approach Rubach (1997:562) argues that the initial extrasyllabic sonorants are adjoined to the syllable, while the noninitial ones to the prosodic word. He proposes the constraint Sonorant Default that requires only syllabified sonorants to be [+voice]. This constraint plays a crucial role in accounting for the asymmetrical behavior of extrasyllabic sonorants, i.e., word-initial extrasyllabic sonorants are syllabified, thereby receiving [+voice] specification and blocking voicing assimilation, while noninitial extrasyllabic sonorants are attached to the prosodic word and, being not specified for voicing, allow voicing assimilation to apply. Consider the representations shown in (200), cf. Rubach (1997:562).

(200)

a.

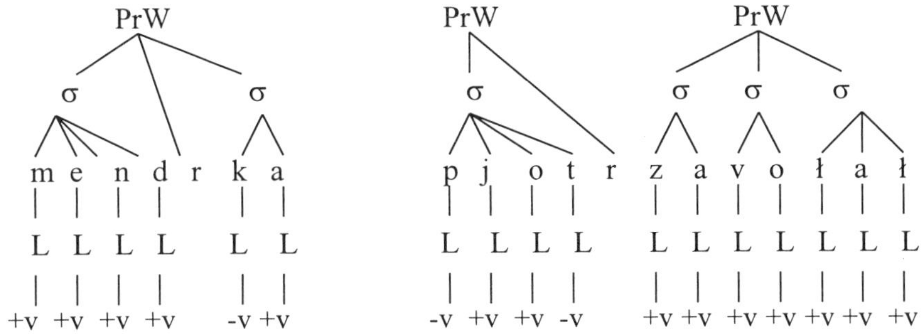

b.

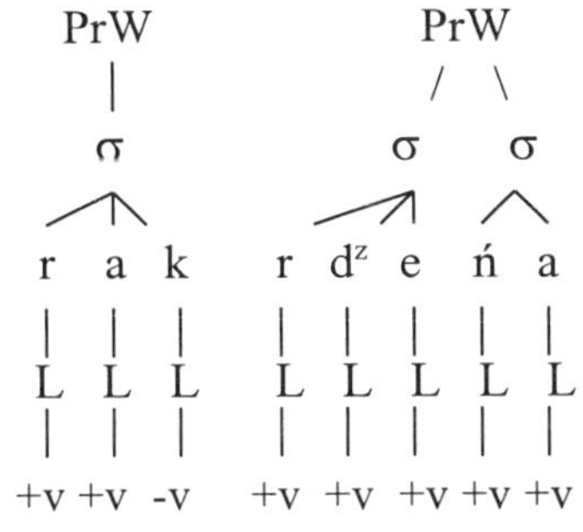

The /r/ in (200)a is specified neither for the laryngeal node nor for voicing because it is not syllabified. Hence, voicing assimilation between /d/ and /k/ applies because the laryngeal nodes of these two segments are adjacent. However, assimilation is blocked in (200)b by the voicing specification of the r because the laryngeal nodes of /d/ and /k/ are not adjacent. According to Rubach (1997) the extrasyllabic sonorants in (200)a receive the specification of [+voice] by phonetic implementation.

One might wonder why the extrasyllabic sonorants in (200)b are linked to the syllable. Rubach (1997:566) justifies this representation by postulating the constraint ALIGN LEFT (stem, σ) that requires a left edge of a stem to coincide with a left edge of a syllable. Although Rubach claims that this solution accounts for regressive assimilation he finally rejects it because it does not account for progressive assimilation. Before we discuss this point let us make some remarks concerning the solution for regressive assimilation presented by Rubach.

First, it is by no means clear why the foot, an existing prosodic constituent in Polish, has been omitted in this account. According to Rubach feet play no role in the analysis of segmental phenomena in Polish and therefore are not taken into consideration. But, as mentioned above, the most recent studies show that the foot plays an important role in the formation of imperatives. Furthermore, prosodic constituents such as feet, prosodic words, etc. may play a licensing role for consonants that are not syllabified. This principle is founded in languages that show edge-effects, cf. Green (1997, 1998), to which Polish undoubtedly belongs by virtue of its abundant extrasyllabic consonants in word-initial and word-final position.

Rubach (1997) points out that an optimality account explains why the adjunction of extrasyllabic sonorants is to the prosodic word and not to the phonological phrase node. Since the constraint STRICT LAYER requires adjunction to the lowest available node and its violation should be minimal, the adjunction to the phonological phrase node "would incur an additional violation of STRICT LAYER by circumventing the PW node in addition to the syllable node," (Rubach 1997:568). Again, the constraint STRICT LAYER, based on the hierarchy of phonological constituents (syllables, feet, phonological words, etc.), requires extrasyllabic sonorants to be attached to the foot and not to the prosodic word.

In the following I propose that initial extrasyllabic sonorants are adjoined to the prosodic level immediately above the syllable, i.e. to the foot, and that noninitial sonorants are attached to the prosodic word. Similar to Rubach (1996, 1997), I assume that sonorants are specified neither for the laryngeal node nor for [+voice] underlyingly but that they receive the laryngeal node and the [+voice] specification either when they are syllabified or prosodified by the foot. I also assume that voicing assimilation requires adjacency of laryngeal nodes, which means that the extrasyllabic sonorant has to be transparent if the voicing assimilation is to take place or it has to be specified for voicing if assimilation is to be blocked.

In the selection of the optimal candidate constraints such as *Son⋣V and Layer are involved. An additional constraint, proposed in (201), distinguishes between sonorants that are specified and those that are not specified for voicing, according to their position in the prosodic representation. This constraint requires sonorants that are either syllabified or linked to the foot to be [+voice].

(201)

$\text{VOICE}_{\text{SON}}$: The only sonorants marked [+voice] are those belonging to a syllable or to a foot.

In (202) it is shown how the interaction of the constraints leads to the selection of the optimal representation.

(202)

r t e n $t^{ś}$	*Son↘V	VOICE_{SON}	Layer
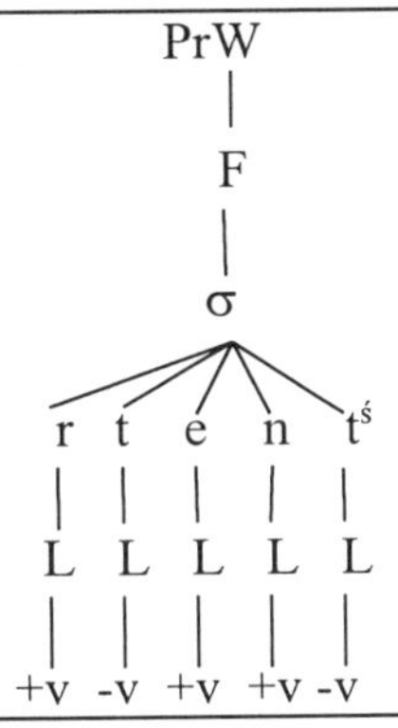	*!		
☞ 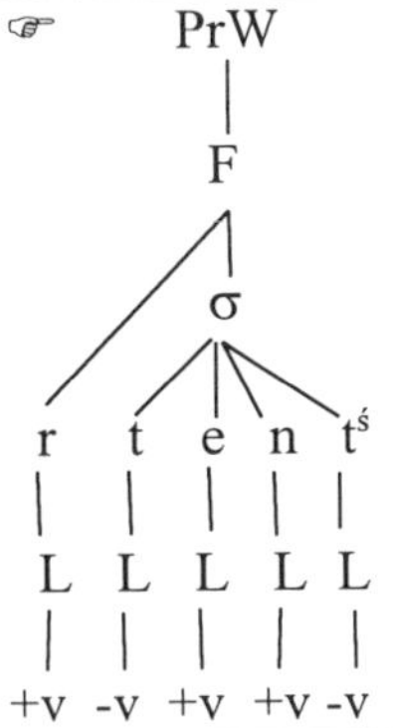			*
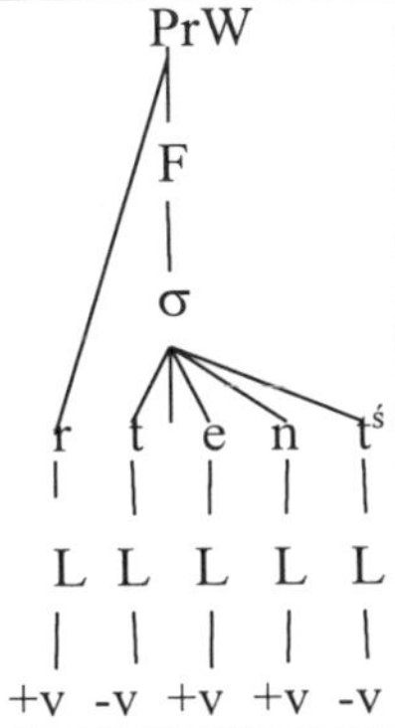	*!		

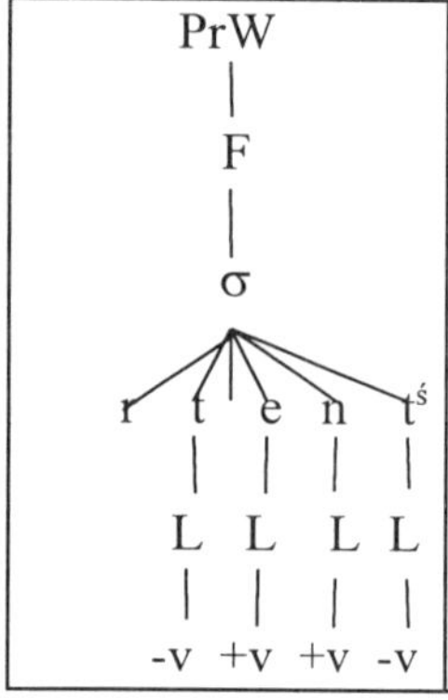	*!	*	

The second candidate emerges as optimal since it fully satisfies $VOICE_{SON}$ and *Son↘V. Its most serious competitor, the first candidate, violates *Son↘V by linking the sonorant to the syllable. The third candidate violates the high-ranking constraint $VOICE_{SON}$, since it assigns the voicing specification to a sonorant that is linked to the prosodic word. The last candidate is excluded from consideration because the sonorant is parsed into a syllable but remains without [+voice] specification. The winning candidate in (202) shows why voicing assimilation is blocked when a sonorant occurs in word-initial position; word-initial sonorants are already specified for voicing by being linked to a foot when the assimilation applies.

Leaving aside the constraints immediately responsible for the representational asymmetry between initial and noninitial sonorants, the ranking proposed in (202) also accounts for noninitial sonorants. They avoid [+voice] specification by being linked to the prosodic word; constraints responsible for voicing assimilation are not violated.

In sum, the voicing phenomena confirm that there is a clear asymmetry between initial and noninitial extrasyllabic consonants with respect to their respective representations. Initial sonorants, being linked to the foot, block voicing assimilation, while non-initial sonorants, being linked to the prosodic word, allow assimilation to apply between the obstruents. The representational asymmetry is shown in (203). Note that the representation of [p'osnka] does not violate No-Crossing Constraint because the constituents of the Prosodic Hierarchy are on different tiers.

(203)

a.

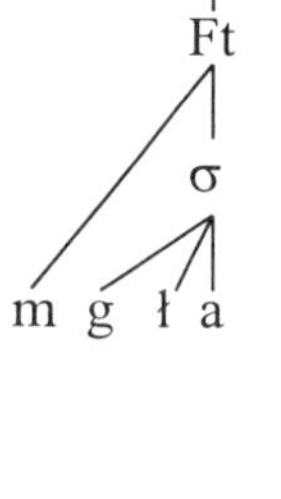

b.

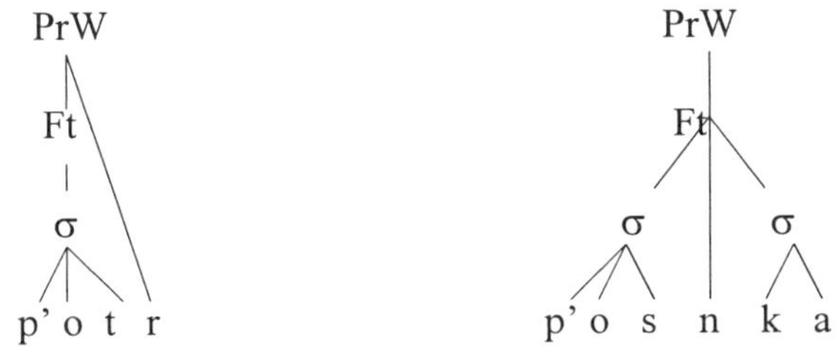

It is important to stress that Rubach (1997) rejects his optimality-theoretic account discussed above since it does not account for progressive assimilation, e.g. krwi→[krf]i 'blood' nom.sg., metr'e → metže → me[tš]e 'meter' loc.sg. It should be noted however that progressive assimilation is a totally different process than regressive assimilation, cf. also observation made by Bethin (1992:174). Progressive assimilation does not apply across word-boundaries and there are only two segments that undergo the assimilation, i.e. *v* and ž. Underlyingly, *v* and ž that undergo progressive assimilation are derived from sonorants *w* and *r'* respectively; they then obstruentize under the influence of the preceding obstruent. Although it would be beyond the scope of this subsection to analyze this process in detail, it has to be mentioned that the difficulty that arises with respect to progressive assimilation in a constraint-based approach is that the sonorant, e.g. *r* in /krwi/ 'blood' gen.sg. is not transparent assuming that it is attached to the foot (or to the syllable in Rubach's approach). This conflict can be presumably resolved with a high-ranked constraint that requires all sonorants trapped by obstruents to be transparent to voicing. The motivation for such a constraint is confirmed by the data presented thus far, cf. (190), since according to phonological studies, cf. Bethin (1992) the trapped sonorants are either voiced or devoiced depending on the voice specification of the surrounding obstruents. However, such a constraint requires phonetic as well as cross-linguistic evidence. Finally, it is conceivable that extrasyllabic sonorants which occur in absolute initial position, as e.g. *r* in rtęć 'mer-cury' nom.sg., have a diferent representation in word-initial clusters, as e.g. *r* in krtań 'larynx' nom.sg., do not have to be transparent since they are not affected by this con-straint.

The independent evidence supporting the representations in (203)b comes from the syllabification variation presented in 3.1.1, which shows that the sonorant in words like *piosnka* is neither linked to the syllable coda nor to the onset; speakers do not have any preferences if they are asked to syllabify words like ones in (190). *Piosnka* is syllabified either as *pios.nka* or as *piosn.ka*. In addition, word-medial sonorants are sometimes elided in fast speech, which indicates that they are not syllabified, since syllabified consonants are not apt to be deleted, cf. however discussion in chapter 5. Interestingly, not only medial but also word-final extrasyllabic sonorants are often deleted in fast speech. For example, wia[tr] 'wind' nom.sg. can be pronounced as wia[t] and przyja[śń] 'friendship' nom.sg. as przyja[ś].[79] In contrast to word-medial and word-final extrasyl-labic consonants, initial segments are always pronounced. These observations lead to

[79] These cases are discussed in chapter 5.

the conclusion that optional deletion processes affect only noninitial consonants, which provides an independent argument for the asymmetrical representation of initial and noninitial sonorants proposed in (203). Initial sonorants are linked to the foot, the level immediately above the syllable and are not deleted, while noninitial sonorants adjoining to the prosodic word can be deleted in fast speech.

3.3.2 Degemination

Degemination provides supporting evidence in favor of an asymmetrical representation of extrasyllabic consonants. It is namely only word-initial geminates that do not undergo degemination; medial and word-final geminates are degeminated without exception unless they occur in the intervocalic position. In contrast to the derivational approach, cf. Rubach and Booij (1990b:449-452), I will show that this asymmetry directly follows from constraints imposed on the representation of geminates.

In (204) word-initial geminates are provided. It is worth noting that (i) there is no morpheme-boundary between the identical consonants[80] and (ii) there are no identical sonorants attested in this position.

(204)

[d$^{\check{z}}$d$^{\check{z}}$]ownica	'worm' nom.sg.
[d$^{\check{z}}$d$^{\check{z}}$]ysty	'rainy' adj.nom.sg.masc
[ss]ak	'mammal' nom.sg.
[ss]ać	'to suck' nom.sg.
[t$^{\check{s}}$t$^{\check{s}}$]y	'empty' nom.sg.masc.

In word-medial position two identical consonants are pronounced if they occur intervocalically. In (205) words containing intervocalic geminates are shown. If geminates are adjacent to consonants they undergo deletion; examples are provided below in (209)b.

(205)

lass+o	la[s.s]o	'lasso' nom.sg.
mott+o	mo[t.t]o	'motto' nom.sg.
wann+a	va[n.n]a	'bath tub' nom.sg.
pann+a	pa[n.n]a	'unmarried woman' nom.sg.

All of the geminates in (205) are heterosyllabic, as indicated in the phonetic transcription. This invariability in syllabification is especially striking if one considers the fact that Polish allows variation in syllabification in a considerable number of cases, cf. 3.2.2. The heterosyllabification of geminates leads to the conclusion that they constitute neither true syllable onsets nor true syllable codas. This observation provides another important insight into the nature of the syllabification, which has to be determined by

80 As shown in 3.1.1.1 two identical obstruents can be also heteromorphemic.

an additional constraint prohibiting identical consonants in onsets and codas. The constraint *Son↘V, cf. (172) does not block the parsing of obstruent geminates into the same syllable since they do not violate *Son↘V by being equally sonorous.[81] In (206) the general formulation of the constraint prohibiting syllabification of geminates as well as its specific formulations with respect to the onset and the coda are given. Note that these constraints can be also replaced by those proposed in (174). Additionally, a constraint prohibiting identical obstruents in the syllable should be proposed.

(206)

*GEMINATE$_{SYLLABLE}$: Geminates are not parsed into the same syllable.
*GEM$_{ONSET}$: Geminates are prohibited in the onset.
*GEM$_{CODA}$: Geminates are prohibited in the coda.

The constraints in (206) were originally incorporated into the Obstruent Sequencing Constraint proposed by Rubach and Booij (1990a:124).[82] In the present study they are separated from *Son↘V in order to avoid contradictory statements: a sonority plateau is tolerated in obstruent sequences, and a sonority plateau is not tolerated in sequences of obstruents that are identical. In order to avoid this contradiction, I proposed separate constraints in (206) that are sensitive only to geminates. The role of *GEM is illustrated by the tableau in (207).

(207)

lasso	*Son↘V	*GEM$_{ONSET}$	*GEM$_{CODA}$
☞ las.so			
la.sso		*!	
lass.o			*!

The heterosyllabified word *las.so* 'lasso' nom.sg. emerges as optimal since it neither incurs a violation of *GEM$_{ONSET}$ nor *GEM$_{CODA}$. Other candidates must be excluded from consideration because they would syllabify geminates as onsets or as codas, which leads to the fatal violation of *GEM$_{ONSET}$ and *GEM$_{CODA}$, respectively.

Both constraints, *GEM$_{ONSET}$ and *GEM$_{CODA}$, are also sensitive to geminates occurring in all positions. The examples provided in (204) illustrate the word-initial geminates. *GEM$_{ONSET}$ prohibits both indentical segments from being syllabified. As a consequence, the first segment must be attached to a higher prosodic constituent. Since the foot is the next level up from the syllable in the prosodic hierarchy, the extrasyllabic consonants in (204) are linked to the foot in order to fulfill Layer, cf. (188), and not to allow geminates to be parsed into a syllable. Consider the tableau shown in (208).

81 *Son↘V forces however heterosyllabification of sonorant geminates.

82 Recall that Obstruent Sequencing Constraint says: "With non-identical obstruents there is no requirement of sonority distance", cf. Rubach and Booji (1990a:124).

(208)

ssak	*Son↘V	*GEM$_{ONS}$	Layer
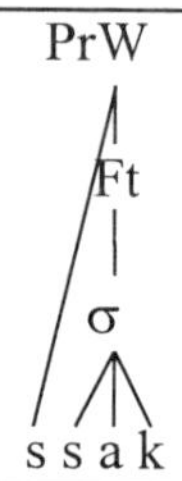			*!*
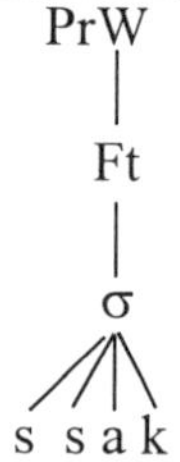		*!	
☞ 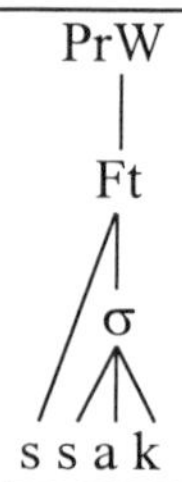			*

The tableau in (208) shows that the third candidate, which links the unsyllabified consonant to the foot, emerges as optimal. It fares better on the high-ranking *GEM$_{ONS}$ than the second candidate; it also satisfies Layer better than its most serious competitor, i.e., the first candidate.

Let us now proceed to the critical examples illustrating the discrepancy between intervocalic medial geminates and medial nonintervocalic geminates. In (209) the outputs of the suffixation of the adjectival suffix /n/ are shown.

(209)

a.			
diakon	diakon+ny	diako[nn]y	'deacon' noun nom.sg. /adj.nom.sg.masc.
płyn	płyn+ny	pły[nn]y	'liquid' noun nom.sg. /adj.nom.sg.masc.
obron+a	obron+ny	obro[nn]y	'defense' noun nom.sg. /adj. nom.sg. masc
koń	koń+ny	ko[nn]y	'horse' noun nom.sg. /adj.nom.sg.masc.
b.			
przyjaźń	przyjaźń+ny	przyja[zn]y	'friendship' noun nom.sg. / adj. nom.sg.masc.
piękn+o	piękn+ny	pię[kn]y	'beauty' noun nom.sg. / adj. nom.sg.masc.

The suffixation in the words provided in (209)a does not bear any influence on the final sonorant apart from its depalatalization, which is due to the Noncontinuant Depalatalization discussed in 4.2.5. In the examples shown in (209)b, on the other hand, the stem-final sonorant is deleted. If it were not deleted we would have a medial sequence consisting of an obstruent followed by two identical sonorants. Since the constraint $*GEM_{ONSET}$ disallows the parsing of the sonorants in the onset and *Son↘V prohibits their parsing into the coda, the medial sonorant cannot be syllabified. The ranking stated in (208) suggests that the offending sonorant is linked to the foot, cf. the representation in (210).

(210)

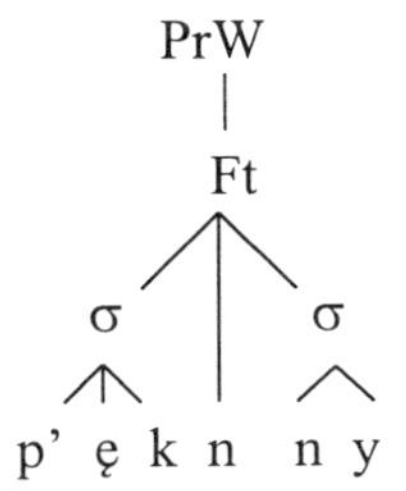

If this were indeed the case, then we would expect no difference between word-initial and word-medial geminates. But the crucial difference between the two is that the former are not deleted and the latter are. Hence, medial geminates must differ in their representation from word-initial geminates. This asymmetry can be expressed by linking the consonant to the next prosodic constituent, i.e., the prosodic word, cf. (211).

(211)

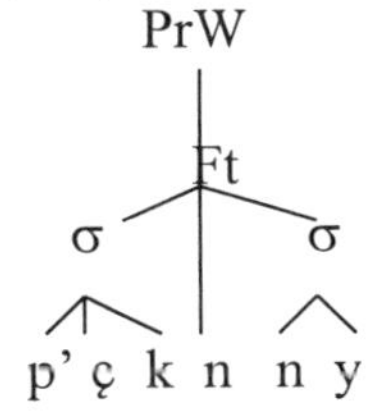

A similar pattern is seen in word-final geminates. The words provided in (212) show that the last consonant of geminates occurring word-finally is deleted.

(212)

bull+a	bull	bu[l]	'bull' nom.sg./gen.pl.
will+a	will	wi[l]	'residence' nom.sg./gen.pl.
idyll+a	idyll	idy[l]	'idyll' nom.sg./gen.pl.
sawann+a	sawann	sawa[n]	'savanna' nom.sg./gen.pl.
fontann+a	fontann	fonta[n]	'fountain' nom.sg./gen.pl.
nowenn+a	nowenn	nowe[n]	'novenna' nom.sg./gen.pl.
less+ow+y	less	le[s]	'loess' adj. nom.sg./ noun nom.sg.

Similar to medial geminates, they cannot be linked to the syllable or to the foot, but must be linked to the prosodic word, cf. (213).

(213)

Although the representations in (208), (211) and (213) display an asymmetry in the represenation, they do not show why the geminates in medial and final position are deleted. An additional constraint is responsible for the deletion of geminates. From examples presented above it follows that only geminates linked up to the foot level are prosodically licensed. If a part of a geminate is linked by a higher level than the prosodic foot, then it has to be deleted. This constraint will be not formally stated here as it requires cross-linguistic evidence. It has to be considered rather as a proposal of a constraint that is able to account for degemination in Polish.

In sum, there is a crucial asymmetry between extrasyllabic consonants in word-initial position on the one hand and in medial and word-final position on the other. This asymmetry directly follows from the behavior of these segments in voicing assimilations and degemination and is reflected in the representation of consonants; the former are linked to the foot and the latter to the prosodic word. An independent supporting evidence for a discrepancy between initial and noninitial extrasyllabic segments is provided by deletions founded in spontaneous speech: medial and word-final consonants being linked to the prosodic word are often elided, while the word-initial consonants which are linked to the foot are never deleted. This issue is discussed in detail in chapter 5.

4 CHAPTER FOUR: Palatalizations

This chapter is devoted to the further investigation of consonant clusters with respect to palatalization. Effects of palatalization on labials, coronals, and velars when followed by other consonants are analyzed. The study also includes an investigation of the influence of palatalization on all three natural classes when they occur as a single member of an onset or a coda.

The motivation for investigating palatalizations separately is at least two-fold. As it was shown in the previous chapter, the only dimension along which consonantal sequences agree is voicing. In light of this fact the question arises as to how palatalization – one of the main processes in Polish phonology – is manifested in consonant clusters. Furthermore, it is interesting to compare the effects of palatalization on consonant clusters and on consonants occurring in onset and coda positions, especially if consonants belonging to various natural classes are examined separately. Such an investigation allows one to draw conclusions on segmental markedness. Finally, the present study is important because previous analyses of Polish have not dealt with these markedness generalizations.

As the analyses provided below will show, palatalization manifests itself in various ways depending on both the articulatory complexity of the targets of palatalization and on the positions in which they occur. It will be argued that the underlying principle of such asymmetrical behavior is closely connected with the economy of articulation which depends inter alia on the number of articulatory gestures, the position of a target segment in a syllable/word and the kinds of adjacent segments.

Before we start our investigation, some introductory remarks concerning palatalization are in order. First, palatalization can be defined as a process in which either the front of the tongue raises towards the palate, while the same primary constriction is maintained, or as a process in which the whole constriction moves forward towards the palate. The first process is illustrated by the palatalization of a labial plosive /p/ to [p^j][83] and the second one by the palatalization of the dental plosive /t/ to the alveolo-palatal affricate [tɕ] (henceforth [t^ś]).[84] According to the working definition provided in (214), palatalization is characterized by different kinds of gestures.

---

83 In the present study the secondary palatalization will be marked by < ' >, which corresponds to IPA < ^{j} >.

84 Coronal Palatalization is discussed in 4.2.2 in detail.

(214)

> Palatalization:
> "(...) at least three distinct processes, namely tongue-fronting, tongue-raising, and spirantization which, occurring either individually or in different combinations, produce the effects that are generally denoted by the cover term, palatalization" (Bhat 1974: 47).

In light of this definition, some important questions may arise, namely what conditions cause palatalization and what kind of outputs are to be expected. As far as the first question is concerned, the environment that induces the change must be a 'palatalizing environment' such as a front vowel, a front semivowel or a palatal or palatalized consonant.[85] Concerning the second question, various kinds of outputs are to be expected. As it was mentioned above, the outputs of palatalization include segments that are articulated with a secondary articulation by maintaining the primary place of articulation, [p^j], or segments with a different place of articulation becoming, e.g., palatal, [c], or alveolo-palatal, [ɕ]. Further, as mentioned in (214), the manner of articulation can be changed from [-strident] to [+strident]. For example, the alveolar stops /t/ and /d/ are changed to alveolar [ts] and [dz] (henceforth [t^s] and [d^z]). However in most phonological studies this change is not considered to be a palatalization.

It is worth noticing that the same phoneme can display two or more different outputs depending on the palatalizing environment, e.g /k/→ [k'], /k/→ [tʃ], or /k/→ [tɕ].[86] Furthermore, the domain of palatalization is not necessarily restricted to a syllable or to a morpheme; rather it often applies over the boundaries of such units.

In this chapter examples of various kinds of palatalization attested in Modern Polish are provided. It is shown how the different outputs of palatalization can be accounted for in terms of articulatory economy. The chapter is outlined as follows. In 4.1 palatalized labials are investigated in different positions, i.e., when they occur as a single member of an onset, or a coda, and when they surface in consonant clusters. In addition, these positions are analyzed from a diachronic point of view; this analysis will illustrate the role of articulatory economy in the development of language. In 4.2 coronals, and in 4.3, velars are examined by using the same strategy as in the case of labials. Since coronals and velars are affected by various types of palatalizations only selected types of palatalizations will be considered.

The analyses proposed in this chapter are illustrated by means of constraints referring to different functions determining not only the phonetic component (PF) of a lexical entry (LE), but also its connections to other components, e.g., semantic form (SF), cf. 1.4.1. In particular, it will be shown that the connection between PF and SF can block the driving force of articulatory economy. In other words, the optimization of PF in terms of articulatory economy does not occur irrespective of other factors.

---

85 In phonological analyses it is claimed that palatalization is triggered by a single feature or features as e.g. [-back, +high] proposed in SPE, [-back] in Gussmann (1992) and Hall (1997), or [coronal] in Hume (1992), cf. also anayses in 4.2.3 and 4.2.4.

86 Palatalization of velars attested in Polish is discussed in 4.3.2.

4.1 Labials

The Polish consonantal inventory consists of the plain labials p, b, m, f, v and their palatalized counterparts p', b', m', f', v', respectively.[87]

Palatalized labials are articulated with a secondary articulation, while simultaneously maintaining the same primary place of articulation. The secondary articulation is commonly defined as an articulation of a lesser degree of stricture accompanying a primary articulation of a higher degree, cf. Ladefoged and Maddieson (1996:354). Hence, in the case of palatalized labials the secondary articulation is approximant-like as opposed to the labial closure or labio-dental constriction of a primary articulation. In the articulation of palatalized labials two independent articulators, the lips and the tongue, are involved. During the labial closure or labio-dental constriction the front of the tongue raises toward a high, front vowel position (approximately [i]). At the release of the primary constriction the approximant-like element appears. It is sometimes the case that the coarticulation of an approximant-like element with the following vowel results in two separate segments, i.e., a labial followed by the glide /j/. For example, piasek 'sand' nom.sg. may be pronounced not only as [p']asek but also [pj]asek, cf. 4.1.3.[88] The first variant is referred to as a 'synchronous' and the second as an 'asynchronous pronunciation', cf. Wierzchowska (1980:93ff). Thus, from the phonetic point of view both realizations differ primarily with respect to the synchrony of articulation. In the synchronous pronunciation, the tongue approaches the soft palate at the same time as the labial articulation, while in the asynchronous pronunciation, the positioning of the central part of the tongue toward the soft palate is not simultaneous with the labial articulation. As a consequence, palatalization is expressed as the glide [j]. Wierzchowska (1980:94) reports that the asynchronous pronunciation is found especially before vowels o, u, e, ę, and ą.

In Standard Polish, both pronunciation types, i.e. [p']asek and [pj]asek, are attested. In "Słownik wymowy polskiej" *The Dictionary of Polish Pronunciation* (Karaś and Madejowa 1977:LV) it is observed that the asynchronous variant occurs more frequently before back vowels,[89] while the synchronous articulation predominates before front vowels. Therefore, the first variant is more preferred over the second variant before back vowels, while the second variant is preferred over the first one before front vowels in Standard Polish. The asynchronous pronunciation is not grammatical in Standard Polish in cases when a labial is followed by the high front vowel /i/, i.e., sequences like [pji] are disallowed. In certain dialects, however, the secondary articulation might be reflected by an alveolo-palatal spirant, voiced or voiceless [ś, ź], depending on the voicedness or voicelessness of the preceding consonant. These cases are discussed in detail in 4.1.3.

---

87 For their exact featural content see 7.1 in the appendix.

88 Biedrzycki (1963) contends that the labial is followed by a glide in such words in the underlying representation. In the present study it is assumed that the glide in words like [pj]asek is not underlying, but instead is a result of a phonetic modification, cf. 4.2.8. Gussmann (1992a:11ff) provides some convincing arguments against a 'two-phoneme solution.'

89 Note that this statement is not in accordance with Wierzchowska's (1980) observations.

4.1.1 The asymmetric behavior of palatalized labials in onset and coda position

In Polish, palatalized labials occur in onset position followed by all vowels except for the high central vowel /ɨ/ that is restricted in its distribution to follow only 'hard' consonants. Palatalized labials in onset position are attested word-initially as well as word-internally. In both positions there are minimal pairs with non-palatalized counterparts. This is illustrated by the examples provided in (215)a and (215)b for word-initial and word-internal positions, respectively.

(215)

a. Onset: word-initially

[b']ały	'white' masc.nom.sg.	[b]ały	'to fear' 3ps.pl.past.non-virile
[b']erze[90]	'to take' 3ps.sg.pres.	[b]eże	'beige' nom.pl.
[b']el	'whiteness'nom.sg.	[b]el	'log' gen. pl.
[p']asek	'sand'nom.sg.	[p]asek	'belt' nom.sg.
[m']ała	'to have' 3ps.sg. past	[m]ała	'small' fem.nom.sg.
[m']otać	'to hurl' inf.	[m]otać	'to spool' inf.
[m']ej	'to have' imp.2ps.sg.	[m]ej	'my' fem.dat.sg.
[v']esz	'to know' 2ps.sg.pres.	[v]esz	'louse' nom.sg.
[v']ara	'faith' nom.sg.	[v]ara	'interj. 'Don't you dare'
ch[f']ała	'to stagger' 3ps.sg.past	ch[f]ała	'glory' nom.sg.

b.Onset: word- internally

ko[p']a	'copy' nom.sg.	ko[p]a	'stack' nom.sg.
kro[v']a[91]	'cow' adj.fem.nom.sg.	kro[v]a	'cow' nom.sg.
ko[p']arka	'copy machine' nom.sg.	ko[p]arka	'excavator' nom.sg.
kon[f']itury	'jam' nom.pl.		
ko[b']eta	'woman' nom.sg.		
ko[b']ałka	'chip basket' nom.sg.		
prze[m']ał	'grinding, grist' nom.sg.		

The examples provided in (215) indicate that palatalized labials are present in the phonetic representation in onset position. Since in present-day Polish, such palatalized labials cannot be derived from a phonological context and since there are minimal pairs with the corresponding nonpalatalized labials, they are uncontroversially considered to be phonemes.

In coda position, no palatalized labials are attested on the surface cross-lexically. Some examples of nouns and verbs ending just in plain labials are shown in (216).[92] [93]

---

[90] The letters rz and ż indicate the same fricative [ž].

[91] The palatalized labial in this example, as well as the one in ko[p']arka, are due to the palatalizing property of a suffix. Hence, [p'] is not present underlyingly. For different properties of suffixes cf. 4.2.2.

[92] Since adjectives and adverbs do not end in labials, they are omitted in the presentation.

(216)

a. Nouns

chło[p]	'farmer' nom.sg.
kra[p]	'shrimp' nom.sg.
gra[f]	'Count' nom.sg.

b. Verbs

ró[p]	'to do' 2ps.sg.imp.
ko[p]	'to kick' 2ps.sg.imp.
mó[f]	'to speak' 2ps.sg. imp.
tra[f]	'to hit' 2ps.sg. imp.

What can be gleaned from the examples in (216) is that (i) palatalized labials do not occur in coda position and (ii) only plain labials are present in the underlying representation. The reason (ii) is true for the nouns in (216) is that the final plain labials in these words do not alternate with the corresponding palatalized sounds. This is shown in (217).

(217)

chło[p]	chło[p]a	'farmer' nom.sg./gen.sg.
kra[p]	kra[b]a	'crab' nom.sg./gen.sg.
gra[f]	gra[f]a	'Count' nom.sg./gen.sg.

In light of these observations let us consider other examples with plain labials in word-final position and their alternants. In (218) nouns are presented in the nominative (the left-hand column) and genitive case (the right-hand column).

(218)

kar[p]	kar[p']a	'carp' nom.sg./gen.sg.
gołą[p]	gołę[b']a	'pigeon' nom.sg./gen.sg.
jastrzą[p]	jastrzę[b']a	'hawk' nom.sg./gen.sg.
pa[f]	pa[v']a	'peacock' nom.sg./gen. sg.

In (218) all stems show an alternation in the genitive case. What this observation suggest is that the alternating stems in (218) can either be analyzed with a final underlying palatalized sound that becomes depalatalized at the end of a word, or as an underlying plain labial that is palatalized by a following (palatalizing) suffix. Both possibilities are shown in (219)a and (219)b, respectively. ([PAL] denotes palatalizing property of a suffix, cf. 4.2.3).

(219)

(a) kar/p'/→ kar[p]	kar/p'/ + a → kar[p']a
(b) kar/p/→ kar[p]	kar/p/ + $^{[PAL]}$ a → kar[p']a

---

[93] In Polish there is a rule of final devoicing that operates in these and other examples.

In the following I will show that the underlying representation in (219)a is correct. I will argue that the suffix /a/ has no palatalizing properties and therefore that the alternative solution shown in (219)b must be excluded from consideration.

Considering the fact that many suffixes in Polish – even some suffixes that contain back vowels – have palatalizing properties,[94] we might assume that a suffix like /a/ triggers palatalization of the stem-final consonant, as in (219)b. If this were the case, then a problem arises as to labials which are not affected by palatalization resulting from suffixation by $^{[PAL]}$a, cf. (217). However, there are a few suffixes in Polish which palatalize only partially, i.e., they palatalize the stem-final consonant of some words but not others. As a consequence, the suffix -/a/, might be also considered to be a suffix which only palatalizes 'irregularly'. This assumption would lead again to the conclusion that only plain labials are present in the underlying representation, as in (219)b. On the other hand, we cannot exclude the possibility that the suffix -/a/ belongs to a group of suffixes which do not trigger palatalization at all. If this is true, then the final-labial in the words in (218) would be plain and the representation in (219)b would be correct. Thus, the question arises as to how can we get more insight into the input.

The answer is grounded on the implication that in Polish suffixes which never palatalize stem-final coronals never trigger the palatalization of stem-final labials either, cf. 4.2.2. Taking this implication into consideration we have to evaluate the properties of the suffix -/a/ with respect to stem-final coronals. Some examples are presented in (220).

(220)

tygry[s]	tygry[s]a	'tiger' nom.sg./gen.sg.
kaczo[r]	kaczo[r]a	'drake' nom.sg./gen.sg.
ko[t]	ko[t]a	'cat' nom.sg./gen.sg.
kormora[n]	kormora[n]a	'cormorant' nom.sg./gen.sg.
wó[ł]	wo[ł]a	'steer' nom.sg./gen.sg.
li[s]	li[s]a	'fox' nom.sg./gen.sg.

The examples in (220) show that the suffix -/a/ never palatalizes a stem-final coronal. Following the implication mentioned above we conclude that (i) the suffix -/a/ never triggers palatalization, and (ii) the palatalized labials in (218) are not underlyingly plain. As a consequence, only the underlying representation shown in (219)a is correct.

These conclusions are strongly confirmed by another declensional suffix, -/em/, which expresses the instrumental case of masculine and neutral nouns. In (221) it is shown how the suffix /em/ behaves with respect to stem-final coronals.

(221)

tygry[s]	tygry[s]em	'tiger' nom.sg./instr.sg.
kaczo[r]	kaczo[r]em	'drake' nom.sg./instr.sg.
kre[t]	kre[t]em	'mole' nom.sg./instr.sg.

[94] The properties of suffixes are extensively discussed in 4.2.2.

kormora[n]	kormora[n]em	'cormorant' nom.sg./instr.sg.
wó[ł]	wo[ł]em	'steer' nom.sg./instr.sg.
li[s]	li[s]em	'fox' nom.sg./instr.sg.

Like the cases presented in (220), the suffix -/em/ never palatalizes the stem-final coronal. As a consequence, the palatalization of final labials is not to be expected. This is indeed borne out by the following examples, cf. (222).

(222)

kra[p]	kra[b]em	'shrimp' nom.sg./instr.sg.
chle[p]	chle[b]em	'bread' nom.sg./instr.sg.
sno[p]	sno[p]em	'sheaf' nom.sg./instr.sg.
kra[m]	kra[m]em	'stall' nom.sg./instr.sg.
tra[f]	tra[f]em	'chance' nom.sg./instr.sg.
gra[f]	gra[f]em	'Count' nom.sg./instr.sg.

However, there are some examples in which palatalized labials surface after the suffixation of -/em/. These are exactly the same words that display palatalization before the suffix -/a/, cf. (218).

(223)

kar[p]	kar[p']em	'carp' nom.sg./instr.sg.
gołą[p]	gołę[b']em	'pigeon' nom.sg./instr.sg.
jastrzą[p]	jastrzę[b']em	'hawk' nom.sg./instr.sg.
pa[f]	pa[v']em	'peacock' nom.sg./instr.sg.

The examples in (223) clearly indicate the presence of palatalized labials in the underlying representation and confirm the conclusion that palatalized labials in Polish occur in the coda in the underlying representation, but they are neutralized on the surface to their plain counterparts, as in (219)a.

An independent piece of evidence supporting this conclusion comes from the formation of the imperative. In Polish, the imperative manifests itself phonetically in several different ways, cf. Rubach (1984: 85-93). Since an exhaustive presentation of the formation of the imperative is not important for our purposes, I restrict myself to only one relevant example, namely the palatalization of the stem-final consonant. This process is triggered either by an underlying jer[95] which is deleted after palatalization, or it is due to a [-back] feature, cf. Gussmann (1980), (1992). In (224) examples of imperative formation are presented. Note that the stem ends in a coronal.

(224)

plo[t]ę	ple[ć]	'to weave' 1ps.sg.pres./ 2ps.sg.imp.
nio[s]ę	nie[ś]	'to carry' 1ps.sg.pres./2ps.sg.imp.
wio[z]ę	wie[ś]	'to drive' 1ps.sg.pres./2ps.sg.imp.

[95] Gussmann (1980) assumes /ĭ/ (a jer) as an underlying representation of the imperative morpheme.

pio[r]ę	pie[š]	'to wash' 1ps.sg.pres./2ps.sg.imp.
pło[n]ę	pło[ń]	'to flame' 1ps.sg.pres./2ps.sg.imp.

What the examples in (224) show is that the imperative forms of stems ending in a coronal display a palatalizing effect on the consonant in coda position. This is in contrast to stems with final labials, which systematically reject palatalization. This is illustrated in (225).

(225)

ro[b']ę	ró[p]	'to do' 1ps.sg.pres./2ps.sg. imp.
ko[p']ę	ko[p]	'to kick' 1ps.sg.pres./2ps.sg.imp.
ku[p']ę	ku[p]	'to buy' 1ps.sg.pres./2ps.sg.imp.
mó[v']ę	mó[f]	'to say' 1ps.sg.pres./2ps.sg.imp.
ła[m']ę	ła[m]	'to break' 1ps.sg.pres./2ps.sg.imp.
tra[f']ę	tra[f]	'to hit' 1ps.sg.pres./2ps.sg.imp.
ło[v']ę	łó[f]	'to hunt' 1ps.sg.pres./2ps.sg.imp.

In sum, in Polish, there exists an asymmetry between plain labials and their palatalized counterparts. While plain labials occur in the onset and the coda, palatalized labials are attested exclusively in onset position. However, in a limited number of words palatalized labials are also present in the coda underlyingly but are neutralized to their plain counterparts on the surface.

4.1.2 Palatalized labials from a diachronic perspective

Labials present a very interesting issue from a diachronic point of view. They were palatalized allophonically in Late Common Slavic by front jers or front vowels. After the loss of jers[96] words with palatalized labials in the coda retained their palatalization until approximately the sixteenth century. It was after the sixteenth century that they started to be neutralized to their plain counterparts. There is direct support for this process in the orthography of manuscripts, in which the palatalization of labials, according to reports by several grammarians (cited in (228)), was marked by the diacritic ›'‹. In (226) some nouns excerpted from manuscripts are shown.

(226)

a. Kromer (1551-54). 'Rozmowy dworzanina z mnichem'. Bibljoteka pisarzów polskich. Wydawnictwo Akademji Umiejętności w Krakowie. Nr.70.

kilku ziem̓ p. 206 'some earth' gen.pl

b. Orzechowski (1562-63). 'Rozmowa albo Dialog około egzekucyjnej polskiej korony'. Bibljoteka pisarzów polskich. Wydawnictwo Akademji Umiejętności w Krakowie. Nr.70.

[96] Cf. the analyses presented in chapter 2.

Radoṁ	p.154	'Radom', city name, nom.sg.
cerkieẇ[97]	p. 40	'Orthodox Church' nom.sg.
kreẇ	p. 205	'blood' nom.sg.

Palatalized labials were also found in imperative forms. Here, the secondary articulation is a reflex of a high, front vowel /i/, which constituted an imperative allomorph in the fourteenth and fifteenth centuries, and eventually disappeared.

A piece of empirical evidence for this kind of development is provided again by manuscripts, some of which are cited in (227). In the documents from the fourteenth and fifteenth centuries imperative forms are marked by a vowel /i/, while imperatives found in manuscripts written from the sixteenth century on are distinguished from other forms solely by the palatalization of a final consonant. This is shown by the examples provided in (227)a through (227)c, respectively.

(227)

Imperative forms

a. Psałterz Floriański. (14th/15th). Florianesis partem polonicam ad fidem codicis recensuit. Wl. Nehring. (1883). Poznań.

odkupi	p.11, 25	'to buy (sth) off (sb)' 2ps.sg.imp.
wykupi	p. 118, 134	'to repurchase' 2ps.sg.imp.
wznowi	p. 11, 50	'to resume' 2ps.sg.imp.
zstępi	p. 6, 143	'to descend' 2ps.sg.imp.

b. Rej (1557). Postylla. Bibljoteka pisarzów polskich. Wydawnictwo Akademji Umiejętności w Krakowie.

odstęṗ	p. 8	'to leave' 2ps.sg.imp.

c. Orzechowski (1562-63). Rozmowa albo Dialog około egzekucyjnej polskiej korony. Bibljoteka pisarzów polskich. Wydawnictwo Akademji Umiejętności w Krakowie. Nr.74.

wątṗ	p.16	'to doubt' 2ps.sg.imp.
moẇ	p.114	'to tell' 2ps.sg.imp.
moẇże	p.114	'to tell+particle że' 2ps.sg.imp.
zostaẇmy	p. 225	'to leave' 1ps.pl.imp.
ośleṗ	p.239	'to blind' 2ps.sg.imp.
postąṗ	p.283	'to treat' 2ps.sg.imp.

Concluding this subsection, some interesting comments on palatalized labials are cited from various grammars, cf. (228).

[97] The letter ẇ denotes [v'].

(228)

a. Roter, J. (1616). Schlüssel zur polnischen und deutschen Sprache. Wrocław.

"ṁ ḃ und ẇ kommen gar selten vor, werden auch wenig von den meisten Polen observieret und in Acht genommen."

"The occurrence of m', ḃ and ẇ is very rare; they are also barely noticed and taken into consideration by most Poles."

b. Moneta, J. (1720). Enchiridion Polonicum oder Pohlnisches Handbuch. Breslau, Thorn, Leipzig (1753?). Biblioteka Jagiellonska 115400-401. p.1.

"Das b kommt mit dem Deutschen überein, ausser daß es zuweilen mit einen subtilen i bezeichnet wird, als Jedwaḃ 'die Seide', als Kiełḃ 'Gründling'."

"The b corresponds to the same letter in German, except that it is occasionally marked by a subtle i as in Jedwaḃ silk, Kiełḃ gudgeon."

c. Muczkowski, J. (1849). Mała gramatyka języka polskiego. Kraków. p.199-200.

"Na szczególną uwagę zasługują wargowe ḃ, f ', ṁ, ẇ, które wielu nie zawsze miękczy tam, gdzie z zasad języka miękczyć się powinny. W których imionach miękczyć je należy poznaje sie w rzeczownikach z dopełniacza (...). Lubo z ogólnej zasady należałoby te głoski miękczyć w sposobie rozkazujacym, jednakże je w mowie potocznej, szczególniej zaś w ḃ i ẇ powszechnie twardo wymawiamy."

"ḃ, f', ṁ, and ẇ deserve special attention. These consonants are not always pronounced soft by many people in cases where, according to grammatical principles, they should be. The genitive form reveals in which nouns they are to be pronounced soft (...). According to a general rule, such sounds should be soft in imperative forms, but in colloquial speech we generally pronounce them hard, especially ḃ and ẇ."

d. Małecki, (1879). Gramatyka historyczno- porównawcza języka polskiego. p. 79.

"Nikt nie mówi paẇ i droṗ, więc tak i pisać nie może i nie będzie.(...). Brzmienie wargowych miękkich nie jest tego rodzaju, żeby nawet na końcu wyrazu można było w nich schwycić uchem zmiękczenia."

"None says paẇ and droṗ, and therefore nobody can and will write them in that way. The sound of soft labials is not such that one can hear the softness at the end of a word."

e. Suchecki, (1873). Zwięzła gramatyka polska do użytku w szkołach. Wyd. 5. Tom I. p.163.

"Spółgłoski ṗ, ḃ, f ', ẇ, ṁ na końcu słowa należy pisać własnie tak, chociaż brzmią prawie twardo. "

"The consonants ṗ, ḃ, f ', ẇ, and ṁ are to be written precisely in that way at the end of a word, even if they sound almost hard."

f. Rozwadowski, J., Ułaszyn, H. (1923). Gramatyka języka polskiego. Kraków. p. 181.

"Oznaczanie miękkości wyszło z użycia dopiero pod koniec XIXw., chociaż w wymowie palatalizacja znikła już nieco wcześniej."

"The marking of softness became obsolete at the end of the nineteenth century, while palatalization in the spoken language had already disappeared somewhat earlier."

These comments indicate that palatalized labials were pronounced before the sixteenth century. The process of depalatalization most likely started in the sixteenth century. In the nineteenth century palatalized labials were pronounced only occasionally. Finally, by the end of the nineteenth century the secondary articulation had disappeared altogether. However, it continued to be represented orthographically for most of the nineteenth century.

This process shows that articulatory economy, which obviously disfavored not only the movements by independent articulators and the secondary articulation but also the realization of palatalization in coda position, turned out to be victorious over the faithful parsing of the underlying forms. The articulatory economy was even stronger than the surface manifestation of indicators of a grammatical modus (imperative) since the secondary articulation was also lost in imperative forms ending in labials, cf. (225).

4.1.3 The secondary articulation of labials in various Polish dialects

In the cases presented thus far, the palatalization of labials is phonetically expressed by a relatively short and approximant-like element following the labial, e.g. [p']. However, as mentioned in the introduction, the secondary articulation of labials can manifest itself in different ways. In this subsection, data from various Polish dialects provide an insight into the nature of labial palatalization. Different realizations of the secondary articulation indirectly corroborate our conclusions that palatalized labials are present in the underlying representation in onset and coda position and that they undergo various types of phonetic modification.

As mentioned in the introduction, palatalized labials are often pronounced as two separate segments, e.g. [p'] surfaces as [pj].[98] It is difficult to identify in which region exactly the [pj] variant occurs, since it can probably be found everywhere in Poland; typically, this variation is ascribed to the Warsaw dialect.[99] Such a wide-spread pronunciation can easily be explained from a phonetic point of view because /j/ is phonetically very similar to the approximant-like secondary articulation. The main output difference between both reflexes of palatalization is their duration, i.e., if the approximant-like secondary articulation is pronounced longer it changes to a segment /j/. This follows from the synchronous and asynchronous pronunciation described in the introduction. Consider the examples shown in (229).[100]

98 Recall that both pronunciation types are recognized as Standard Polish in "Słownik wymowy polskiej" *The Dictionary of Polish Pronunciation* (Karaś and Madejowa 1977:LV).

99 Stieber (1966:108), however, claims that in Warsaw the realization of a secondary articulation as /j/ like in e.g. [pj]es 'dog' nom.sg. is becoming less common.

100 Recall that according to Wierzchowska (1980:94) the asynchronous pronunciation is found especially before vowels *o*, *u*, *e*, ę, and ą.

(229)

/b'/ały	→	[bj]ały	'white' nom.sg.
/b'/erze	→	[bj]erze	'to take' 3ps.sg.pres.
/p'/asek	→	[pj]asek	'sand' nom.sg.
/m'/ara	→	[mj]ara	'measure' nom.sg.
/m'/otać	→	[mj]otać	'to hurl' inf.
/v'/osk	→	[vj]osk	'village' gen.pl.
/v'/esz	→	[vj]esz	'to know' 2ps.sg.pres.
o/f'/erze	→	o[fj]erze	'sacrifice' dat.sg.

In the north-eastern part of Poland[101] the secondary articulation is realized as a fricative, i.e. /ź/ or /ś/, depending on whether the preceding consonant is voiced or voiceless, respectively. Interestingly, as shown in (230)a and (230)b, this pronunciation occurs in both onset and coda positions.[102] Note that the secondary articulation is realized not only as an alveolo-palatal ś but also as a segment sometimes transcribed as š̀, which is a soft variant of š, (distinct from ś), cf. Dejna (1994:23). (I assume that š̀ is a palatalized retroflex= IPA [$ʂ^j$]).

(230)

a. Onset, cf. Dejna (1994:78)
p', b', f', v' → pś, bź, fś, vź/ σ[_ V
/p'/asek→ [pś]asek 'belt' nom.sg.
o/f'/ara/→ o[fś]ara 'sacrifice' nom.sg.

b. Coda,[103] cf. Dejna (1994:77)
p'→ pś/ _ #
p'→pš̀/_ #
kar/p'/→ kar[pś] 'carp' nom.sg.
gołą/p'/→ gołą[pš̀] 'pigeon' nom.sg.

Furthermore, the secondary articulation of palatalized labials can also be realized as a voiced or voiceless palatalized velar fricative whose voicing specification depends on the voice specification of the preceding consonant. The regions where such a pronunciation is attested are marked on the map in 7.2.1 in the appendix. Examples of the realization of a secondary articulation as velar friction are found in both positions, i.e. onset and coda, cf. (231)a and (231)b. (ẋ is a soft equivalent of x).

(231)

a. Onset, cf. Dejna (1994:78)
p', b', f', v' → pẋ, bɣ̇, fẋ, vɣ̇/ σ[_ V

[101] For the exact regions see the maps shown in 7.2.1 in the appendix.
[102] The featural content of most transcriptions is provided in 7.1 in the appendix.
[103] The examples provided here show labials in a word-final coda. If they occur word-medially, they are syllabified as the onset, e.g. kar[pś] → kar.[pś]a, cf. also discussion in 3.2.2.

/p'/asek → [pẋ]asek 'belt' nom.sg.
o/f'/ara/ → o[fẋ]ara 'sacrifice' nom.sg.
/v'/ara → [vẏ]ara 'faith' nom.sg.

b. Coda, cf. Dejna (1994:78)
p'→ pẋ/_ #
kar/p'/→ kar[pẋ] 'carp' nom.sg.
pa/f'/ → pa[f] → [paẋ] 'peacock' nom.sg.

If the consonant is a labial nasal /m/, then the feature [nasal] shows up in the secondary articulation, which is realized as alveolo-palatal ń (IPA [ɲ]). Relevant examples are shown in (232). A nasal reflex of palatalization is, however, found only in onset position.

(232)

a. Onset, cf. Dejna (1994:78)
m'→mń/ σ[_ V
/m'/asto → [mń]asto 'town' nom.sg.
/m'/ęso→ [mń]ąso 'meat' nom.sg.

Summing up, the data presented above show how secondary palatalization in Standard Polish is realized in various dialects. In contrast to Standard Polish, the dialects display a secondary articulation not only in onset position but also in coda position, where the palatalization can be manifested by a fricative element. This can be seen as indirect supporting evidence for the conclusion derived from the analysis in 4.1.1, that palatalized labials are present in the coda in the underlying representation in Standard Polish, although they do not manifest their secondary articulation in the surface representation.

4.1.4 An OT analysis

In this section, I propose an analysis of the facts presented in 4.1.1 and 4.1.2 within Correspondence Theory (McCarthy and Prince 1995), a modified version of Optimality Theory. For details see the introduction presented in 1.2.2.

As is required by the theoretical assumptions of this theory, I shall make use of faithfulness and universally motivated markedness constraints. Starting with faithfulness constraints, I propose IDENT [Lab, Pal], cf. (233), (Prince and Smolensky 1993:87), which requires the secondary articulation of palatalized labials to be retained in the output.

(233)

IDENT [Lab, Pal]:[104] The secondary articulation of underlying labials must be retained on the surface.

For notational convenience, I call a feature which expresses the secondary palatalization [Pal]. Following this assumption, it is possible to represent palatalized labials, palatalized coronals and palatalized velars in a homogeneous way. As will be shown below, this simplification bears no effect on the outcome of the analysis.

The faithfulness constraint IDENT [Lab, Pal] interacts with a markedness constraint to be posited below that bans structurally complex places of articulation. In phonological representations that mirror phonetic facts, complex places of articulation are manifested by branching under the PLACE node, in contrast to simple articulations represented by a nonbranching PLACE node. Compare the representations of plain labials in (234)a as opposed to the palatalized labials in (234)b, cf. Hume (1992). Similar branching representations for complex segments have been proposed by Sagey (1986), Clements (1991), and Lahiri and Evers (1991).

(234)

a. Simple articulations

```
PLACE
  |
C-Pl
  |
 Lab
```

b. Complex articulations

```
     PLACE
    /     \
C-Pl     V-Pl
  |        |
 Lab      Cor
```

Complex structures, such as the one presented in (234)b, are universally disfavored by a general markedness constraint NONCOMP that prohibits segments from having more than one place of articulation, cf. (235)a. Its specific instantiation, i.e. *[Lab, Pal], shown in (235)b, militates against palatalized labials, cf. Prince and Smolensky (1993:179ff).

(235)

a. A general constraint:
NONCOMP Do not have structurally complex places of articulation.

b. Specific instantiation:
*[Lab, Pal] Do not have palatalized labials.

---

[104] This constraint in its general form should be formalized as IDENT[Pal]. I have added Lab(=Labial) in order to express the fact that [Pal] is to be understood as a secondary palatalization of labials. This notational modification is important for the identification of labials in contrast to coronals and velars. In addition, [Pal] alone will not be analyzed as a secondary palatalization but as a palatalizing feature, cf. 4.2.4.

Since we analyze palatalized labials, we adopt the constraint presented in (235)b.[105] As is already known, in Polish palatalized labials surfaced in coda position until the sixteenth century. Thus, the faithfulness constraint IDENT [Lab, Pal] must have been ranked higher than the markedness constraint prohibiting them, namely *[Lab, Pal]. This ranking resulted in the emergence of the faithful parse as an optimal candidate. The implementation of a ranking IDENT[Lab,Pal]>> *[Lab, Pal] is illustrated by the tableau in (236).

(236)

until the 16 th C: Palatalized labials in coda position

gołą/b'/	IDENT [Lab, Pal]	*[Lab, Pal]
gołą[p]	*!	
☞ gołą[p']		*

The first candidate in (236), being an unfaithful parse, incurs a violation of IDENT [Lab, Pal] and is therefore immediately excluded. The second candidate, which retains the secondary articulation, fully satisfies IDENT [Lab, Pal] and is selected as optimal.

As stated in 4.1.2, the process of depalatalization most likely started in the sixteenth century. According to reports by various grammarians, cf. (228), until the nineteenth century both variants, i.e. with and without the secondary articulation, were attested. This is a clear example of the so-called variation stage, cf. 1.3.1. According to the model presented in 1.3.3 such a variation is expressed by the unranking of relevant constraints. In the case at hand it is IDENT [Lab, Pal] and *[Lab, Pal] that became unranked with respect to each other. The lack of a crucial ranking between IDENT [Lab, Pal] and *[Lab, Pal] led to the selection of two optimal candidates, namely gołą[p] and gołą[p']. This is illustrated by the tableau in (237).

(237)

from the 16 thC until the19th/beginning of the 20thC: both variants attested

gołą/b'/	IDENT [Lab, Pal]	*[Lab, Pal]
☞ gołą[p]	*	
☞ gołą[p']		*

What the tableau in (237) shows is that two candidates gołą[p] and gołą[p'] were attested at the same time in Polish.[106]

At the beginning of the 20th century the secondary articulation totally disappeared in coda position. Hence, the variation between gołą[p] and gołą[p'] was abandoned in favor of one optimal output, namely, gołą[p].

105 I assume that the constraint in (235)a as a 'general' constraint exists neither in Polish nor in the phonology of other languages. It has to be specified in every case according to sounds under consideration.

106 Note that the tableau is not intended to show what preferences speakers had in various contexts, cf. 1.3.3.

Note that a ranking in which IDENT [Lab, Pal] outranks *[Lab, Pal] would incorrectly predict the selection of gołą[p'] as an optimal form, cf. the tableau in (238) in which the sign ☜ indicates the selected candidate which is the unintended winner.

(238)

gołą/b'/	IDENT [Lab, Pal]	*[Lab, Pal]
gołą[p]	*!	
☜ gołą[p']		*

As proposed in the Free-Variationist model, cf. 1.3.1, sound change is accounted for by the reranking of relevant constraints. This means that gołą[p] can be selected as an optimal candidate if one reverses the ranking of IDENT [Lab, Pal] and *[Lab, Pal] in a way that the former is dominated by the latter. Let us consider what this strategy predicts for our data.

As the tableau in (239) illustrates, the low rank of IDENT [Lab, Pal] cannot stop the first candidate from surfacing as an optimal output. This candidate does not violate *[Lab, Pal] as opposed to its competitor gołą[p'], which is due to a violation of *[Lab, Pal].

(239)

nowadays: No palatalized labials in coda position

gołą/b'/	*[Lab, Pal]	IDENT [Lab, Pal]
☞ gołą[p]		*
gołą[p']	*!	

The analysis proposed in (239) seems to provide an adequate explanation of the facts. However, if we consider one of the most important premises of OT, namely its requirement of a unique, language specific constraint ranking, we encounter some problems.

As it was presented in the first subsection of the present chapter, in Polish there is only one position in which palatalized labials do occur on the surface. This is onset position, cf. the examples presented in (215). However, evaluating candidates with palatalized labials in the onset against the ranking proposed in (239) leads to the selection of an incorrect output, i.e., a form without the secondary articulation. This is illustrated by the tableau in (240).

(240)

/p'/asek	*[Lab, Pal]	IDENT [Lab, Pal]
☜ [p]asek		*
[p']asek	*!	

By adopting the ranking *[Lab, Pal]>> IDENT [Lab, Pal], the underlying form of a word like /p'asek/ emerges as [pasek]. The secondary articulation of palatalized labials is incorrectly deleted in such examples due to the high-ranked constraint *[Lab, Pal], which prohibits structurally complex places of articulation. The optimal output is unfortunately an unintended one. Even worse, it has a completely different meaning than the intended one, cf. [p]asek 'belt' nom.sg. vs. [p']asek 'sand' nom.sg. As shown in (215), minimal pairs of this kind abound in Polish. Despite the difference between two underlying forms constituting minimal pairs, the optimal output remains always the same, i.e. without the secondary articulation. This is demonstrated by the tableaux in (241).

(241)

/p'/asek	*[Lab, Pal]	IDENT [Lab, Pal]
☞ [p]asek		*
[p']asek	*!	
/p/asek	*[Lab, Pal]	IDENT [Lab, Pal]
☞ [p]asek		
[p']asek	*!	

What follows from the analyses in (241) is that the ranking proposed above in (239) requires further modification so as to allow palatalized labials to emerge in the onset on the one hand, and prohibit them in the coda on the other.

In the following, I will propose an additional constraint, which is universally well motivated. It directly refers to coda position as a position that is uncontroversially susceptible to different kinds of neutralizations, cf. e.g. Steriade (1995:129) and Beckman (1995: 19-24).

An example of a neutralization of place, manner and laryngeal features is attested in Korean. In this language there are also deletions of final segments, cf. Kim-Renaud (1974), Ahn (1985). In (242)a,b various types of neutralizations in coda position in Korean are shown, while in (242)c,d,e deletions are displayed, cf. Gebert (1994: 18).

(242)

	coda:		example:		
	underlyingly	surface	underlyingly	surface	
a.	t^h	t	pat^h	pat	'field'
	s	t	os	ot	'clothes'
	s'	t	is'-	it	'exist, stay'
	c	t	nac	nat	'daytime'
b.	c^h	t	$k'oc^h$	k'ot	'flower'
	p^h	p	ap^h	ap	'front'
	k^h	k	$pu\Lambda k^h$	puʌk	'kitchen'
	k'	k	pak'	pak	'outside'
c.	ps	p	kaps	kap	'price'
	ks	k	moks	mok	'share'
	ls	l	tols	tol	'cycle; postnatal year of age'
	lt^h	l	$halt^h$-	halt-	'lick, taste'

	nc	n	anc-	an-	'sit down'
d.	lk	k,l	talk	tak, tal	'chicken'
	lm	m,l	kulm-	kum-, kul-	'go without food'
	lp	p,l	palp	pap-, pal-	'tread on'
	lp^h	p,l	ɯlp^h-	ɯp-,ɯl-	'intone, chant'
e.	h	t; h	noh-	not-; noh-	'put'
	lh	l; lh	ilh-	il-; ilh-	'lose'
	nh	n; nh	k'ɯnh-	k'ɯn-; k'ɯnh-	'sever'

h aspiration
' fortis (tense)
, optional pronunciation
; depending on the following segment

Based on cross-linguistic generalizations we can formulate a constraint that prohibits marked structures in coda position. In the case at hand, this constraint bans palatalized labials in the coda, cf. (243), Smolensky (1993:8).

(243)

No palatalized labials in coda position.

Formally, such a constraint can be expressed by conjoining two constraints, namely *[Lab, Pal], which penalizes structurally complex palatalized labials, and NoCoda which prohibits codas, cf. (244), Prince and Smolensky (1993:34).[107]

(244)

NoCoda: Syllables do not have codas.

The conjunction of NoCoda and *[Lab, Pal] bans palatalized labials in coda position. In (245) its formal representation is shown, cf. Smolensky (1993:8). Note that the domain of the conjunction is a segment.

(245)

$[*[\text{Lab, Pal}]\&\text{NoCoda}]_{\text{SEGMENT}}$:[108] No palatalized labials in coda position.

The constraint in (245) will be integrated in the ranking proposed in (236), i.e., IDENT [Lab, Pal]>> *[Lab, Pal]. This is illustrated in the tableau in (246). Note that we reject the idea of the reversing of constraints since the ranking proposed in (238) predicts incorrect results, cf. also tableaux provided below.

[107] The strategy of conjoining constraints, the so-called Local Conjunction, is discussed in 1.2.4 in detail.

[108] When the conjunction is used in my analyses below, I refrain from mentioning the brackets, i.e. $[\ \ ]_{\text{SEGMENT}}$.

(246)

gołą/b'/	*[Lab, Pal]&No Coda	IDENT [Lab, Pal]	*[Lab, Pal]
☞gołą[p]		*	
gołą[p']	*!		*

The high-ranked conjunction *[Lab, Pal]&NoCoda excludes the unintended candidate, gołą[p'], from emerging as optimal. Instead, its competitor gołą[p], which satisfies the conjunction, is selected as the optimal output. The ranking in (246), contrary to the one proposed in (238), does not exclude palatalized labials in onset position, since the high-ranking *[Lab, Pal]&No Coda refers exclusively to codas. Consider the tableau in (247).

(247)

/p'/asek	*[Lab, Pal]&No Coda	IDENT [Lab, Pal]	*[Lab, Pal]
[p]asek		*!	
☞ [p']asek			*

The critical candidate, [p']asek, is selected as the optimal output because it fares better on IDENT [Lab, Pal] than its competitor [p]asek. This analysis clearly indicates that phonological change does not have to result in a reranking of constraints, although this seemed to be the case at first sight, cf. (239). Moreover, a reranking of constraints would predict incorrect results, cf. (240).

To conclude this subsection let us consider another language from the Slavic family, viz. Russian, in which secondary palatalizations are not neutralized in coda position. Russian, as opposed to other Slavic languages, has retained palatalized labials in coda position, cf. the tableau in (248), in which various Slavic languages are compared with respect to the occurrence of palatalized labials in different positions.

(248)

Palatalized labials in modern Slavic languages (Carlton 1990:162)

Proto-slavic	Russian	Ukrai-nian	Belo-russian	Polish	Upper Lusatian	Lower Lusatian	Slovak	Czek	Bulga-rian
v'	+	-	0	0	0	0	-	-	0
p'	+	-	0	0	0	0	-	-	0
b'	+	-	0	0	0	0	-	-	0
m'	+	-	0	0	0	0	-	-	0

+: still present in all environments
-: absent or phonologically irrelevant
0: restricted presence: only before vowels

One might indeed question the reasons for such aberrant behavior in Russian because secondary palatalization in coda position is a very costly gesture from an articulatory point of view. The answer to the unique behavior of Russian palatalized labials is probably based on semantics, or rather on the connections between PF with another component of Lexical Entry, i.e. SF (for details cf. 1.4.1.) As presented in (249), Russian has many minimal pairs which differ only in a secondary articulation of labials.

(249)

a.	грабь	gra[b̥’]	‘to steel’ 2ps.sg.imp.
	граб	gra[b̥]	‘hornbeam’ nom.sg.
b.	kровь	kro[v̥’]	‘blood’nom.sg.
	kров	kro[v̥]	‘shelter’ nom.sg.
c.	новь	no[v̥’]	‘new’ noun, nom.sg.
	нов	no[v̥]	‘new’ short form nom.sg.
d.	Обь	o[b̥’]	‘Ob’ proper name, nom.sg.
	об	o[b̥]	‘against’
e.	правь	pra[v̥’]	‘to govern’ 2ps.sg.imp.
	прав	pra[v̥]	‘to have a legar right to sth’ adj.masc.nom.sg.
f.	рябь	rja[b̥’]	‘ripples’ nom.sg.
	ряб	rja[b̥]	‘pock-marked’ adj.masc.nom.sg.

As the data in (249) indicate, the depalatalization of labials would lead to homophones, which are avoided by speakers. This conclusion provides evidence that the optimization of PF does not occur independently but is influenced and controlled by its connection to other components of Lexical Entry. However such an explanation is not completely satisfactory because Russian has homophones due to final devoicing (250).

(250)

под	po[t]	‘under’	пот	po[t]	‘sweat’ nom.sg.
код	ko[t]	‘code’ nom.sg.	кот	ko[t]	‘cat’ nom.sg.
muz	mu[s]	‘muse’ gen.pl.	mus	mu[s]	‘mousse’ nom.sg.

In other words, the question arises whether we can treat final devoicing and final depalatalization in the same way.

The Russian data differ clearly with respect to the Polish data. In Polish the depalatalization of labials in coda position led maximally to a few homonyms. In the same vein, the depalatalization of labials in the onset in Polish did not take place because the secondary articulation is the only distinctive feature which distinguishes words in minimal pairs. Interestingly, there are a few words in which the secondary articulation was deleted in onset position. For example, a[b]ecadło ‘alphabet’ nom.sg. used to be pronounced a[b’]ecadło in the 15th century, cf. Moszyńska (1975:84); [p]erła ‘pearl’ nom.sg. was pronounced as [p’]erła in the 16th century according to Brückner (1957:402); [v]esele ‘wedding’ nom.sg. and [v]esoły ‘joyful’ masc.nom.sg. were realized as [v’]esele and [v’]esoły, respectively, cf. Długosz-Kurczabowa and Dubisz (1993: 122) and finally, czer[v]ony ‘red’ masc.nom.sg. was pronounced as czer[v’]ony, cf. £oś (1922:161). However, there were no minimal pairs between these words and ones with plain labials, e.g. czer[v’]ony vs. czer[v]ony. It should be noted here that there are also many words which retained their secondary articulation despite the fact that they did not constitute minimal pairs, e.g. [p']es is still pronounced as [p']es. Hence, these words behave in a homogeneous way with the majority of words occurring in the Polish lexicon. [109]

Let us summarize the facts presented so far. In present-day Polish palatalized labials occur in the onset. If they occur in coda position in the underlying representation they are neutralized on the surface by constraints prohibiting palatalized labials in the coda. In the sixteenth century palatalized labials occurred in coda position but were gradually neutralized on the surface to their plain counterparts. Finally, at the end of the nineteenth century the secondary palatalization disappeared totally.

The secondary articulation in onset position did not disappear. As we saw in (215) secondary palatalization proves useful in distinguishing the semantics of single words which constitute minimal pairs with words containing plain labials. Thus, the connection between PF and SF seems to play an important role in language develop-ment. Finally, retaining a secondary articulation in the onset is not as costly in terms of articulatory effort as in the coda, because of the presence of a following vocalic element in the former in contrast to the latter.

4.1.5 Lexicon Optimization

> " 'Sound change' is unfortunately a very bad and misleading term for the phenomena to which it is supposed to refer for the simple reason that what really changes is not sounds but grammars."
>
> Postal (1968:270)

In this subsection it will be shown how the algorithm of Lexicon Optimization creates new underlying forms taking as its input 'new' surface forms which emerge after a sound change. A theoretical background of Lexicon Optimization is presented in 1.4.3.

The neutralization of palatalized labials in coda position seems to lead directly to the restructuring of underlying forms. For example, the neutralization in kar/p'/ → kar[p] 'carp' nom.sg. is expected to change the underlying form to kar/p/. Taking as a basis the ranking proposed thus far, cf. (247), the algorithm of Lexicon Optimization selects the optimal input-output pair which incurs the fewest and least significant violations, thereby identifying the optimal input without the secondary articulation, i.e. kar/p/. This is illustrated in (251).

---

[109] In cyclic phonology, cf. Rubach (1984), depalatalization in these cases is explained by the fact that at some point palatalization was no longer triggered by front vowels and applied only in a derived environment. Therefore "when morpheme internal sequences stopped being affected, some words retained the historical hard consonants while some others restructured assuming as underlying representations what used to be derivable outputs" Rubach (1984:68).

(251)

INPUT OUTPUT		*[Lab, Pal]& No Coda	IDENT [Lab, Pal]	*[Lab, Pal]
kar/p'/	☞ kar[p]		*	
	kar[p']	*!		*
☜ kar/p/	☞ kar[p]			
	kar[p']	*!	*	*

The algorithm of Lexicon Optimization chooses incorrectly kar/p/ as the best underlying form for kar[p]. It incurs fewer violations than its most serious contestant, kar/p'/, which is excluded due to a violation of IDENT [Lab, Pal]. This indicates that the restructuring of underlying forms took place and that the new input form, kar/p/, became the optimal underlying form. If this were indeed the case, then we would expect that the new underlying form holds not only for the nominative case but also for other cases of the same paradigm. This expectation follows from a morphological principle according to which there is one underlying form for one paradigm, i.e., the output forms do not differ with respect to a root which has to be homogeneous in all forms. This often invoked principle in the literature is formulated by Kenstowicz and Kissberth (1979: 199) in the following way, cf. (252).

(252)

> "The UR of a morpheme is identical with the alternant appearing in the greatest number of contexts" whereby "context refers to the number of different morphemes which can precede and follow the morpheme in question within the word."

In the following, we want to explore this issue by looking at different forms of the paradigms relevant for the subject under investigation. Since we already know that a secondary articulation of labials, although neutralized in the nominative case, shows up in the genitive case, cf. (218), let us consider the whole morphological paradigm of masculine nouns ending in palatalized labials. Generally in Polish, masculine nouns ending in a nonvelar consonant undergo either the so called 'soft' declension or 'hard' declension.[110] The criterion for their classification is the featural content of the stem-final consonant. Stems in which the last consonant is a palatalized one undergo the soft declension. This is illustrated in (253). It is worth noting that nouns undergoing the soft stem declension are by far in the minority.

(253)

Soft stem declension of masculine nouns in present-day Polish (e.g. paw 'peacock', cietrzew 'black-grouse', drop 'bustard', gołąb 'pigeon', jastrząb 'goshawk', karp 'carp', żółw 'tortoise', żuraw 'crane')

[110] It is beyond the scope of this subsection to present the very complex system of Polish noun declensions. For our purposes, it might suffice to restrict the presentation to two cases, the soft and hard declensions of masculine nouns ending in nonvelar consonants. This simplification bears no effect on the present analysis.

	Singular	Plural
Nom.	pa[f]	pa[v']e
Gen.	pa[v']a	pa[v']i
Dat.	pa[v']owi	pa[v']om
Acc.	pa[v']a	pa[v']e
Instr.	pa[v']em	pa[v']ami
Loc.	pa[v']u	pa[v']ach
Voc.	pa[v']u	pa[v']e

As follows from (253), in the soft stem declension all forms apart from the nominative case singular display the secondary articulation of labials, which, as was shown in 4.1.1, is a reflection of palatalized labials being present in the underlying representation. This conclusion is directly confirmed by the nonpalatalizing properties of declensional suffixes, cf. the desinences of soft stem declension are listed in tableau in (254), cf. Grzegorczykowa et al. (1984: 252).

(254)

	Singular	Plural
Nom.	- Ø	- e
Gen.	- a	- y /-i
Dat.	- owi	- om
Acc.	- a	- e
Instr.	- em	- ami
Loc.	- u	- ach
Voc.	- u	- e

The difference between the soft and hard stem declensions is not only different desinences but also the lack of the palatalization of the last consonant in the hard stem declension. The only exception here is found in the locative and vocative cases in the singular. This is illustrated in (255) on the basis of the declension of a hard stem /krab/ 'crab' nom.sg.

(255) Hard stem declension of masculine nouns in present-day Polish

	Singular	Plural
Nom.	kra[p]	kra[b]y
Gen.	kra[b]a	kra[b]ów
Dat.	kra[b]owi	kra[b]om
Acc.	kra[b]a	kra[b]y
Instr.	kra[b]em	kra[b]ami
Loc.	kra[b']e	kra[b]ach
Voc.	kra[b']e	kra[b]y

The palatalization of the last consonant in the locative and vocative case singular is due to the palatalizing properties of the declensional suffixes. In the tableau in (256) the properties of all declensional suffixes of a hard stem declension are summarized, cf. Grzegorczykowa et al. (1984:250).[111]

(256)

	Singular	Plural
Nom.	- Ø	- y
Gen.	- a	- ów
Dat.	- owi (u)	- om
Acc.	- a	- y
Instr.	- em	- ami
Loc.	- ‘e	- ach
Voc.	- ‘e	- y

The comparison of the declensions in (254) and (256) shows that the nouns deserving our interest undergo the soft declension, in which palatalization of labials shows up on the surface in every case but the nominative singular. This observation leads to a crucial revision of the tentative conclusion following from the tableau presented in (251). It is not the case that the neutralization of palatalization in the nominative case led to the restructuring of the underlying form. On the contrary, the underlying form, i.e. the root form, did not undergo any changes, which is due to a morphological principle requiring only one underlying root form for a whole paradigm, cf. (252).

In OT the selection of an appropriate underlying form of a paradigm is possible by evaluating all output forms of a given paradigm with possible underlying forms. The algorithm of Lexicon Optimization determines the optimal input-output pair by finding which one has the fewest violations. The underlying form of the selected pair is claimed to be the attested underlying representation. This is predicted in (257).

(257)

INPUT	OUTPUT		*[Lab, Pal]& No Coda	IDENT [Lab, Pal]	*[Lab, Pal]
kar/p/	kar[p] kar[p’]a kar[p’]owi kar[p’]a kar[p’]em kar[p’]u kar[p’]u	kar[p’]e kar[p’]i kar[p’]om kar[p’]e kar[p’]ami kar[p’]ach kar[p’]e		*!******** ****	

[111] As already mentioned, desinences of the hard stem declension presented here refer to stems which end in a hard nonvelar consonant. The difference between velar and nonvelar final stem consonants plays a role in the declensional system of Polish, but it is not relevant here.

☞ kar/p'/	kar[p]	kar[p']e		*	
	kar[p']a	kar[p']i			
	kar[p']owi	kar[p']om			
	kar[p']a	kar[p']e			
	kar[p']em	kar[p']ami			
	kar[p']u	kar[p']ach			
	kar[p']u	kar[p']e			

The second pair in (257) wins over the first one and the underlying form kar/p'/ is selected as optimal because it incurs only one violation of IDENT [Lab, Pal], due to the nominative form kar[p]. This form does not display secondary palatalization since the high-ranked constraint *[Lab, Pal]&No Coda leads to its neutralization in coda position, cf. (251). What this analysis reveals is the necessity of taking into consideration all forms of a paradigm by examining possible underlying forms. As was shown in (251) the evaluation of separate forms might lead to incorrect results.

Concluding this analysis we contend that the changes presented above did not contribute to the optimization of the lexicon because the underlying forms of many words remained the same. For example, as shown in (257) the root /karp'/ in Old Polish is the same as in Modern Polish.

Interestingly enough, there are some words attested which originally had soft stems and as a consequence belonged to the soft stem declension. But at some point they changed their declension class from a soft to a hard one. This change pertains to a small set of words. Examples are provided in (258), cf. Reichan (1974:229).

(258)

jarząb	'sorb' nom.sg.
jaw	only in the phrase 'wyjść na jaw' 'to become evident, 'to come out'
karm	'fodder' nom.sg.
muchodrzew	'Stellaria media' (plant) nom.sg.
skrzyp	'horsetail' nom.sg.

In order to account for the change in declensional classes we assume that (i) all palatalized labials were neutralized in the nominative case in which they occurred in coda position on the surface and (ii) other cases of a paradigm changed their forms in accordance with the nominative stem. This process is illustrated on the basis of the genitive case in (259), whereby the lack of palatalization is attested in other cases as well.

(259)

jarzą[b']a → jarzę[b]a	'sorb' gen.sg.
kar[m']a → kar[m]u	'fodder' gen.sg.
muchodrze[v']a → muchodrze[v]a	'Stellaria media' (plant) gen.sg.
skrzy[p']a → skrzy[p]u	'horsetail' gen.sg.

As already mentioned, the lack of palatalization in the genitive case indicates the change of the word from a soft to a hard declension. Hence, we assume that the oblique cases changed their forms by taking the nominative form as a basis. In Optimality

Theory such a relation is expressed as output-output correspondence evaluated by identity constraints. These constraints demand a perfect correspondence between related words.[112]

Accounting for this change by output-output constraints seems to be, however, very problematic for OT considering the fact that the majority of soft stems (still a small number in comparison with all stems in Polish) did not switch their declension, and remained in the soft stem declension. Seen in this light, the changes presented in (259) are to be fully justified because they clearly show the optimization of underlying forms by reducing additional place features. Moreover, they contributed to the unification of declension types as the overwhelming majority of nouns belong to the hard stem declension.

From a diachronic point of view, such a development can be interpreted as an optimization process in terms of the reduction of marked structures. It also supports the claim that language change should be considered as language improvement, cf. e.g. Vennemann (1993). But the problem of presenting the different types of changes by invariant ranking remains unresolved.

To make the situation worse, according to Reichan (1975:230), there are also cases attested in which the opposite changes took place, i.e., some hard stems originally belonging to the hard declension became soft stems. Examples are provided in (260).[113]

(260)

drób	'poultry' nom.sg.
jastrząb	'goshawk' nom.sg.
nów	'new moon' nom.sg.
ołów	'lead' nom.sg.
paw	'peacock' nom.sg.
tułów	'trunk' nom.sg.
złotogłów	'Lilium martagon', plant nom.sg.

The cases presented in (260) are problematic in at least two respects. First, they shed doubt on our expectations, since the changes they underwent did not contribute to the optimization of the lexicon at all. On the contrary, they require an increased number of

---

[112] The idea of Output-Output Correspondence is presented in 1.2.2.

[113] It is worth noting that there is also some variation of words of the soft stem declension attested which eventually did not result in the change of the declension type. The variation is directly mirrored in old documents in which the original soft stems are found with inflectional suffixes indicating the hard stem declension, cf. the following examples from Reichan (1974:228). In Modern Polish all forms undergo soft stem declension.

jedwab	jedwaby	'silk' nom.sg./nom.pl.
drop	dropa	'bustard' nom.sg./gen.sg.
ślep	ślepy	'eye' nom.sg./nom.pl.
cietrzew	cietrzewem	'black grouse' nom.sg./instr.sg.
czerw	czerwem	'grub' nom.sg./instr.sg.
modrzew	modrzewy	'larch' nom.sg./nom.pl.

representational features, and consequently, an increased number of articulatory gestures. Second, they posit a challenge for OT in terms of accounting for the changes by one invariant ranking. Even if we assume a variation stage at which different output forms are possible we expect that the reranking of constraints or the activation of new constraints leads to homogeneous results. This expectation is, however, far from reality. As shown in 2.3.2 and 2.3.3, after the changes affecting jers, there were some processes such as the epenthesis of a consonant or the metathesis of consonants that were found only in a very limited number of words. It is also commonly known that at the variation stage linguistic structures are susceptible to different kinds of changes because speakers are not aware of the direction along which the change will take place. As a consequence they may produce structures that are not in line with the main direction of a change. Therefore, phenomena diametrically opposed to those of the majority of structures may be attested. For example, in German verb system strong verbs (starke Verben) change their 'strong' inflection (starke Flexion) to a 'weak' one (schwache Flexion). From ca. 339 strong verbs in Middle High German (Mittelhochdeutsch), 67 are weak in New High German (Neuhochdeutch), cf. August (1975:255). According to Hempen (1988:286) the number of verbs that changed amounts to 86. There were however a handful of verbs in which the opposite change took place. For example, the Middle High German weak form *prîsen* 'to praise' was predominantly weak until the seventeenth century but the process of changing its inflection type to a strong one started in the fifteenth century, cf. Paul (1959:254). In New High German this verb displays exclusively a strong inflection type. Similarly, the Middle High German weak form *gelîchen* 'to be alike' is in New High German strong, for its development cf. Paul (1959:253f). An analogous conclusion can be drawn with respect to nouns, cf. Paul (1959:38-44). In Middle High German a considerable number of masculine nouns indicating inanimate objects as well as the names for fish which end in the nominative singular case with -e (the weak declension type) took the desinence -en thereby changing the declension type from a weak to a strong one, cf. *Balken* 'beam', *Garten* 'garden', *Karpfen* 'carp', *Kasten* 'box', *Roggen* 'rye'. In a handful of words the opposite change is attested, i.e., a few masculine change their declension type from a strong to a weak one, cf. Paul (1959: 42). For example, *Rabe* 'raven' goes back to Middle High German *Raben*; *Heide* 'heathen' and *Christe* 'Christian' are derived from nominalized Middle High German adjectives *heiden* and *kristen*, respectively. What these examples show is that the seemingly aberrant behavior of a few words in Polish that were not in accordance with the main direction of the attested changes is not surprising. On the contrary, they confirm that a linguistic change is a complex process in which 'unexpected cases' are to be expected.

I conclude my investigation of palatalized labials in Polish onsets and codas by returning to the point I made earlier that soft stems are not productive in present-day Polish. A piece of evidence supporting this observation is provided by relatively new borrowings, adopted previously from English, which end in a labial, and which always belong to the hard declension class. This is illustrated in (261).

(261)

	-a, gen.sg.	-em, instr.sg	
video-cli[p]	video-cli[p]a	video-cli[p]em	'video clip'
lap-to[p]	lap-to[p]a	lap-to[p]em	'laptop'
sze[f]	sze[f]a	sze[f]em	'boss'
pu[p]	pu[b]u	pu[b]em	'pub'

Additional evidence comes from proper names, which also inflect according to the hard stem declension without exception. Relevant examples are provided in (262).[114]

(262)

nom.	gen.	instr.
Abraha[m]	Abraha[m]a	Abraha[m]em
Bo[p]	Bo[b]a	Bo[b]em
Bornhol[m]	Bornhol[m]u	Bornhol[m]em
Willia[m]	Willia[m]a	Willia[m]em
Amsterda[m]	Amsterda[m]u	Amsterda[m]em

New abbreviations also join hard stem declension, cf. (263).

(263)

OBO[p]	OBO[p]u	OBO[p]em	'OBOP : Ośrodek Badania Opinii Publicznej'
PA[m]	PA[m]u	PA[m]em	'PAM: Pomorska Akademia Medyczna'
WO[p]	WO[p]u	WO[p]em	'WOP: Wojsko Ochrony Pogranicza'

All the examples above indicate that in present-day Polish soft stems are not productive. They occur only in a limited number of paradigms in which they reflect the palatalization of a stem-final labial.

In sum, in Polish palatalized labials are present underlyingly in coda position but neutralized on the surface. Their presence in the coda, found in a limited number of nouns, is a diachronic reflex preserved by a constraint requiring the underlying representation of a root of a paradigm to be homogeneous. Such paradigms are not productive any more, which is corroborated by the declensions of assimilated borrowings, proper names and abbreviations. They always assimilate to hard declension types. The observations presented here confirm one aspect of a markedness theory, according to which certain marked structures are apt to undergo changes or simplifications more readily than unmarked ones.

Finally, it has to stressed that the ranking proposed in (257) accounts for all the data presented above. However, it does not account for the aberrant behavior of the small number of nouns in (259) and (260). This is not unexpected since there are always

[114] Interestingly, I have observed that foreign learners of Polish cannot differentiate between the soft and hard declension unless they are explicitly taught it. Generally, they take the nominative case as a basis of a paradigm and then choose desinences according to the hard stem declension. Thus, they make use of Output-Output Correspondence constraints which do not affect underlying forms. In my opinion, this is the main source of their mistakes.

structures that behave differently than the majority. Thus, a question arises how we can express 'exceptions' in a grammar with a single invariant ranking. I leave this question open for further study.

4.1.6 The depalatalization of labials in consonant clusters

From an articulatory point of view palatalized labials are, as mentioned above, complex sounds because (i) they have two places of articulation (a primary one and a secondary one) and (ii) two independent articulators, the lips and the tongue front, are involved in their articulation. The markedness of palatalized labials is increased when they are followed by other consonants because palatalization, like labialization, is more apparent at the release than at the formation of a primary constriction. Thus, the presence of a vocalic element makes the realization of the secondary articulation easier. Consequently, the presence of a consonantal element, i.e., in cases in which a palatalized labial is followed by another consonant, imposes a serious burden on the realization of palatalization.

In the following, it will be shown how palatalized labials behave in consonant clusters in Polish. We begin our investigation with an alternation presented in (264). Here, palatalized labials occur in the nominative case (the left-hand column) and in the genitive case (the right-hand column) in which they are depalatalized after the loss of a vowel.[115]

(264)

[p']es	[p]sa	'dog', nom.sg./gen. sg.
[p']eń	[p]ńa	'trunk', nom.sg./gen. sg.
[v']eś	[v]si	'village', nom.sg./gen. sg.
o[v']es	o[v]sa	'barley', nom.sg./gen. sg.

As shown below, it is not obvious that palatalized labials are present in the underlying representation because there are arguments in favor of the form /p/es. In the following I will present and reject them for the reasons discussed below. I will claim that /p'/es and not /p/es is correct.

Since palatalized labials in (264) occur before the front vowel /e/, one may question the phonemic status of palatalization in the underlying representation. The objection becomes more serious if one considers the complete paradigms of the words presented in (264). They are exemplified in (265) on the basis of paradigms of *pies* [p'es] 'dog' nom.sg. and *owies* [ov'es] 'barley' nom.sg.

(265)

Nom.	pies+ø	owies+ø
Gen.	ps+a	ows+a

---

[115] Such vowels are treated as underlying jers which are reflexes of historical jers, see analyses in chapter 2.

Dat.	ps+u	ows+u
Acc.	ps+a	owies+ø
Instr.	ps+em	ows+em
Loc.	ps+'e	ows+'e
Voc.	pies+ø	owies+ø

Taking these paradigms into consideration, one can postulate an epenthetic vowel in nominative ([p'es]), accusative ([ov'es]) and vocative cases ([p'es],[ov'es]), which do not require any desinence. Without an epenthetic vowel, these forms would not be well-formed, i.e., in the case of *pies*, a degenerate syllable would be constituted such as [ps]. In the second case, *owies*, a consonant cluster which does not occur in Polish would emerge, i.e., /fs/ in coda position. Since neither possibility can be taken into consideration, a vowel is to be epenthesized. The same pertains to the other words shown in (264). Therefore, our tentative conclusion might be that plain labials occur in the underlying representation, and that they are palatalized after the insertion of an epenthetic vowel.

However, adopting this hypothesis leads to some serious problems. In Polish, there are other words displaying vowel-zero alternation that exhibit slightly different properties. Consider the examples provided in (266).

(266)

[b]ez	'lilac' nom.sg.
[m]ech	'moss' nom.sg.
[v]esz	'louse' nom.sg.

In (266) plain labials are followed by the vowel /e/. The paradigms of these words show a similar kind of alternation to those in (265) with the crucial difference that the vowel does not induce palatalization of the preceding labial. Consider the paradigms in (267).

(267)

Nom.	bez+ø	mech+ø
Gen.	bz+u	mch+u
Dat.	bz+u	mch+u
Acc.	bez+ø	mech+ø
Instr.	bz+em	mch+em
Loc.	bz+'e	mch+u
Voc.	bez+ø	mech+ø

If one postulates plain labials in the underlying representation one has to account for the palatalized of labials in (264) and plain labials in (266). In other words, it has to be stated in which words the epenthetic vowel /e/ causes the palatalization of the preceding consonant and in which does not. In order to avoid such arbitrariness, I posit palatalized labials in the underlying representation of the words in (264).

Let us look for independent evidence supporting this conclusion. Relevant examples are provided by morphologically complex words. The suffix -/ec/ (masc.nom.sg.) contains a fleeting vowel,[116] which does not surface in the genitive case. Relevant data are shown in (268).

(268)

a.

go[ń]ec	go[ń]ca	'courier' nom.sg./gen.sg.
ma[l]ec	ma[l]ca	'a little boy' nom.sg./gen.sg.

b.

kra[v']ec	kra[v]ca	'tailor' nom.sg./gen.sg.
ku[p']ec	ku[p]ca	'merchant' nom.sg./gen.sg.
chło[p']ec	chło[p]ca	'boy' nom.sg./gen.sg.
lata[v']ec	lata[v]ca	'kite' nom.sg./gen.sg.

Recall that suffixes in Polish display different properties with respect to the palatalization of the stem-final consonant, cf. the examples provided in 4.1.1. The cases presented in (268) clearly show that regardless of the property of the suffix, stem-final coronals remain soft as opposed to labials, which, without exception are depalatalized before the suffix -ca.

A similar situation occurs after the affixation of other suffixes, e.g. /stv/. This suffix, as postulated by Gussmann (1978:107), is represented underlyingly as /-ĭstv/, where ĭ is called a palatalizing jer. In the course of derivation the jer is deleted. Another solution, which I defend in 4.2.2 and 4.2.3, is to postulate a palatalizing floating feature, cf. also Gussmann (1992). Regardless of the suffix representation, the output of the suffixation process is a palatalized stem-final consonant, except when it is a labial. Relevant examples are provided in (269).

(269)

a.

pa/n/	pa[ń]stwo[117]	'lord' nom.sg./ 'nation' nom.sg.
aposto/ł/	aposto[l]stwo	'apostle' nom.sg./ 'apostleship' nom.sg.

b.

chło/p/	chło[p]stwo	'landlord' nom.sg./ 'country-folk' nom.sg.
hra/b'/a	hra[p]stwo	'Count' nom.sg./ 'county' nom.sg.
głu/p'/i[118]	głu[p]stwo	'foolish' adj.nom.sg./ 'nonsense'nom.sg.

The same scenario is repeated in (270), where the palatalizing suffix -sk- (adj.sg.masc.) palatalizes the coronal sonorants /ł/ and /n/,[119] cf. (270)a. Its ability to

[116] This is a diachronic reflex of a jer, cf. the cases presented in (265) and (267).

[117] If /n/ and /ł/ are palatalized, they emerge as [ń] (IPA [ɲ]) and [l], respectively, cf. 4.2.2.

[118] The stem of głupi ends in a palatalized labial, i.e głu/p'/. If it ended in a nonpalatalized labial, then we would expect the form głu[p]y, as in upar[t]y 'stubborn' masc.sg.nom. The desinence is dependent on the underlying representation of labials.

[119] The suffix - sk does not palatalize /r/. We will return to this issue in 4.2.5, when we discuss palatalization of coronals in clusters.

ca[r]	ca[r]ski	'tsar'noun/adj.

palatalize is consistently neutralized when the stem ends in a labial, cf. (270), cf. also Gussmann (1978: 105).

(270)

a.

anio/ł/	anie[l]ski	'angel' noun, nom.sg./adj. nom.sg.masc.
aposto/ł/	aposto[l]ski	'apostle' noun, nom.sg./adj. nom.sg.masc.
pa/n/	pa[ń]ski	'lord' noun, nom.sg./adj. nom.sg.masc.
Londy/n/	londy[ń]ski	'London' noun, nom.sg./adj. nom.sg.masc.

b.

Rado/m'/	Rado[m]	rado[m]ski	'Radom' noun, nom.sg./adj. nom.sg.masc.
zie/m'/a	zie[m']a	zie[m]ski	'earth' noun, nom.sg./adj. nom.sg.masc.
Ara/b'/a	Ara[b']a	ara[b]ski	'Arabia' noun, nom.sg./adj. nom.sg.masc.

All the examples presented above lead to the straightforward conclusion that the secondary articulation of palatalized labials is consistently neutralized when it is followed by another consonant. Since this conclusion derives direct support from the articulatory complexity of these sounds, which is crucially strengthened when they occur in clusters, it should be confirmed cross-linguistically.

The markedness of palatalized labials in clusters is confirmed by the rarity of their occurrence in consonant clusters in the languages of the world. This conclusion follows from my examination of many Indo- and non Indo-European languages. Even in the Caucasian family, cf. Colarusso (1988), languages like Anatolian Besleney, Kabardian, Bzhedukh or Georgian, which display different types of the secondary articulation in clusters, do not have any palatalized labials in clusters. Some of them allow, however, secondary palatalized coronal fricatives in clusters. The only languages I am aware of in which palatalized labials in clusters are attested are the Irish of Tourmakeady, co. Mayo examined by de Burca (1970) and Russian, cf. Zubritskaya (1994).

In (271) examples from Irish are provided, in which palatalized labials are attested. Words in which palatalized labials occur in consonant clusters are marked by bold letters.

(271)

The Irish of Tourmakeady, co. Mayo, cf. de Burca (1970: 23f.)

/b'/ b'o:, b'an, rib'ə, **b'l'ehux**, k'i:b', **b'r'ak**, b'alux, **b'r'i:vur**, **gam'b'i:n'**

/p'/ p'iən, **p'l'eb'**, sp'e:r', **p'r'ab**, p'e:r'ə, k'ip'in', p'akux, p'i:pə, sip'ər, sep'

/v'/ **siv'nux**, **dav's'e:rux**, **av'r'es**, **kiv'n'ə**, **v'r'ak**, riv'ə, riv', kriv', **g'iv'ru**, **kev'l'in't'**

/f'/ f'i: dor', **f'r'agurt'**, **af'l'iən'**, f'es't'u:, **d'ef'r'u:**, f'o:six'ə, **f'r'astul**, f'aru:l'

The second language in which palatalized labials occur in clusters is Russian. According to Zubritskaya (1994), at the beginning of the 20th century, a secondary palatalization assimilation in homorganic consonant clusters was a rule in Standard

gospoda[š]	gospoda[r]ski	'landlord' noun/adj.
kucha[š]	kucha[r]ski	'cook' noun./adj.

Russian. Hence, in labial/labial clusters the first consonant had to be palatalized. This is shown in (272).

(272)

lam'p'e	'lamp' dat.sg.
v' m'iske	'in dish'
v'b'ezat'	'run into' inf.perf.
bom'b'e	'bomb' dat.sg.

Furthermore, the secondary palatalization assimilation in Standard Russian was obligatory in some nonhomorganic clusters, e.g. labial-dorsal clusters. Examples are shown in (273), cf. Zubritskaya (1994: 337).

(273)

lap'k'i	'paw' nom.pl.
jub'k'i	'skirts' nom.pl.
ob'x'itrit'	'to outsmart' inf.perf.

Nowadays, however, Standard Russian palatalization is not a rule any more. Most clusters underwent depalatalization, although the secondary articulation still occurs as an optional process.

Hence, only the Irish of Tourmakeady is the only real exception I am aware of because it allows palatalized labials to be followed by other consonants.

In summary, I suspect that the markedness of palatalized labials in consonant clusters is a tendency that is true for many languages, which is resolved by disfavoring the secondary palatalization of labials in clusters. Therefore, I posit a markedness constraint which prohibits palatalized labials in clusters. It is formally expressed as in (274).

(274)

*[Lab, Pal]C: No palatalized labials are followed by another consonant.

The implementation of this constraint into the ranking proposed so far, cf. (247), leads to a straightforward selection of an optimal candidate. This is illustrated by the tableau in (275).

(275)

/p'sa/	*[Lab, Pal]C	Ident [Lab, Pal]	* [Lab, Pal]
[p']sa	*!		*
☞ [p]sa		*	

The optimal output [p]sa 'dog' gen.sg., whose secondary articulation is deleted, satisfies *[Lab, Pal]C, while its contestant, the faithful parse, is ruled out because it incurs a violation of the high ranked *[Lab, Pal]C.

To sum up, in Polish there are cases attested in which palatalized labials do not occur on the surface despite their presence in the underlying representation. Their secondary palatalization is neutralized due to a high ranked constraint, *[Lab, Pal]C, which prohibits palatalized labials when they are followed by other consonants. In this respect Polish clearly supports a cross-linguistic tendency that disfavors articulatory complex structures.

4.1.7 Palatalized labials in consonant clusters from a diachronic perspective

The emergence of consonant clusters in Polish was a consequence of the loss of jers.[120] Before they disappeared, they induced the palatalization of the preceding consonant. Hence, after their loss the palatalized consonant was followed by another consonant, i.e., a consonant from the coda of the same syllable or a consonant from the onset of the next syllable. Depending on the palatalized consonant the palatalization was either retained or lost. In the following, we will examine the development of palatalized labials in detail.

There is no consensus in the literature as to how long the secondary palatalization of labials in clusters had been retained. Some scholars, e.g., Carlton (1990:166), cf. (276)a, or Łoś (1922:144,160), cf. (276)b, do not even explicitly list this stage, although they occasionally mention it in passing.

(276)

a.

*mьgla → m'ьgla→ mgła	'mist' nom.sg.
*pьčela → p'ьčela → pčela	'bee' nom.sg.
*pьšenica → p'ьšenica → pšenica	'wheat' nom.sg.

b.

*glupьstvo → glup'ьstvo → glupstvo	'stupidity' nom.sg.
*potomьstvo → potom'ьstvo → potomstvo	'offspring' nom.sg.
*bьrati→ b'ьrati → brać	'to take'inf.imperf.

On the other hand, other scholars, e.g., Długosz- Kurczabowa and Dubisz (1993: 122), cf.(277)a, or Klemensiewicz, Lehr-Spławiński and Urbańczyk (1955:130, 137), cf. (277)b, explicitly state that a stage occurred in which palatalized labials were followed by other consonants.

(277)

a.

*chłopьca → chłop'ca → chłopca	'boy' gen.sg.
*gřebimy→ gřeb'my → gřebmy	'to grub' 1ps.pl.imp.
*mьgła → m'gła → mgła	'fog' nom.sg.
*ovьca → ov'ca → ovca	'sheep' nom.sg.

b.

*chłop'ca → chłopca	'boy' gen.sg.
*kupicie → kup'cie → kupcie	'to buy' 2 ps.pl.imp.
*mo(ł)wimy→ mo(ł)w'my →mówmy	'to talk' 1 ps.pl.imp.

[120] This process is extensively discussed in 2.1 and 2.2.

It would be too arbitrary to conclude that the secondary articulation was lost parallel to the loss of the palatalization of labials in coda position, cf. 4.1.2. Documents from the sixteenth century indicate that at that time the secondary palatalization was retained, at least orthographically. Examples are provided in (278).

(278)

Orzechowski, J. (1563, 1564). Polskie dialogi polityczne. Bibljoteka pisarzów polskich. Kraków: Wydawnictwo Akademji Umiejętności w Krakowie, nr 74.

mowẃże	p. 114	'to talk' 2ps.sg.imp.
mowẃmy	p. 135	'to talk' 1ps.pl.imp.
zostawẃmy	p. 225	'to leave' 1ps.pl.imp.

As presented in the previous subsection, in present-day Polish all these forms are pronounced without a secondary palatalization.

In the following we will account for the changes by means of constraint interaction. From the facts presented above it follows that the palatalization of labials was retained after the loss of jers[121] for some time. This leads to the conclusion that at that time *[Lab, Pal] was dominated by IDENT [Lab, Pal]. Further, there must have been a stage in which two variants were allowed, i.e. one with and one without secondary palatalization. Consequently, the crucial ranking between IDENT [Lab, Pal] and *[Lab, Pal] no longer existed. This stage is illustrated in the tableau in (279).

(279)

m'gła	IDENT [Lab, Pal]	*[Lab, Pal]
☞ m'gła		*
☞ mgła	*	

In the next stage the secondary articulation totally disappeared, which was due to the activation of a new conjunction of constraints, *[Lab, Pal]&*σ[CCC, which prohibits palatalized labials in clusters. Note that if this constraint existed at the time when the variation presented in (279) was attested, a 'tie' between the selected candidates would be impossible because *m'gła* but not *mgła* violates *[Lab, Pal]&*σ[CCC. In other words, *[Lab, Pal]&*σ[CCC did not exist in Polish when the variation stage existed but instead it was created in the latest stage of a variation stage when one variant took precedence over another. The formation of a new constraint was possible by conjoining two single constraints such as *[Lab, Pal] and *σ[CCC. While the former constraint prohibits palatalized labials, the latter militates against complex consonantal sequences in the onset. The conjunction *[Lab, Pal]&*σ[CCC is violated only if a palatalized labial occurs in a consonant cluster. The emergence of this conjunction led directly to the selection of one optimal input, cf. the tableau in (280).

[121] The first stage of this development, i.e. loss of jers, is analyzed in chapter 2.

(280)

m'gła	*[Lab,Pal] & *σ[CCC	IDENT [Lab, Pal]	*[Lab, Pal]
m'gła	*!		*
☞ mgła		*	

The first candidate in (280), *m'gła*, violates the conjunction *[Lab,Pal] & *σ[CCC since it contains not only palatalized labials but also a complex cluster. The second candidate, *mgła,* does not violate the high-ranked conjunction because it satisfies *[Lab,Pal].

In light of new outputs, the question arises as to what consequences this simplification had for the lexicon. Did the neutralization contribute to the optimization of a lexical entry? We have no reason to assume that it was not the case. On the contrary, since all forms of a paradigm systematically obey the constraint *[Lab,Pal] & *σ[CCC, we have to conclude that the neutralization was mirrored also in lexicon, cf. (281).

(281)

Nom.	[m]gła	[m]gły
Gen.	[m]gły	[m]g'eł
Dat.	[m]gle	[m]głom
Acc.	[m]głę	[m]gły
Instr.	[m]głą	[m]głami
Loc.	[m]gle	[m]głach
Voc.	[m]gło	[m]gły

The algorithm of Lexicon Optimization, which evaluates possible input-output pairs, straightforwardly selects the input /m/gła because it fares better on high-ranking constraints than its most serious competitor /m'/gła. As a consequence the restructuring of the input /m'/gła to /m/gła took place. This is shown in (282).

(282)

INPUT	OUTPUT	*[Lab, Pal] & *σ[CCC	IDENT [Lab, Pal]	*[Lab, Pal]
/m'/gła	[m]gła [m]gły [m]gły [m]g'eł [m]gle [m]głom [m]głę [m]gły [m]głą [m]głami [m]gle [m]głach [m]gło [m]gły		*!********* ****	

☞/m/gła	[m]gła [m]gły [m]gły [m]g'eł [m]gle [m]głom [m]głę [m]gły [m]głą [m]głami [m]gle [m]głach [m]gło [m]gły			

In sum, the cases presented above illustrate the depalatalization of labials in clusters from a diachronic point of view. They provide a convincing example of markedness reduction in terms of the neutralization of a secondary articulation. Moreover, this neutralization, in contrast to the depalatalization of labials in coda position, directly contributed to the optimization of the phonological representation of lexical entries in the lexicon.

4.1.8 Phrase-level palatalization

The last issue we want to discuss with respect to the palatalization of labials is the so called Phrase-level Palatalization, cf. Szpyra (1995).

Phrase-level Palatalization is by definition a phonetic process which adds a secondary palatalization to the final consonant in a syntactic phrase when the next word begins with /i/ or /j/. This phonetic process affects labials, coronals and velars in a similar way, i.e., all of them are pronounced with a secondary articulation. Some examples illustrating this point are provided in (283).

(283)

skle[p'] Ireny	'Irena's shop'
ko[p'] jeszcze	'dig more'
mó[f'] jasno	'speak clearly'
mło[t'] Jurka	'Jurek's hammer'
be[z'] incydentów	'uneventfully'
łu[k'] Indianina	'Indian's bow'

Phrase-level Palatalization is phonetically conditioned and therefore exceptionless, cf. Szpyra (1995: 195).

The data in (283) seem to be problematic with respect to our conclusion drawn so far. Recall that it was palatalized labials that do not occur in coda position even when they are present underlyingly, cf. 4.1.1. Yet Phrase-level Palatalization reveals that palatalized labials do occur in coda position if followed by a high front vowel or a palatal glide in the next word. In other words, palatalized labials are neutralized in coda position except when followed by i or j of the next word.[122]

[122] If palatalized labials occur word-medially they are syllabified as onsets, e.g. pa/v'+i/m → pa.[v'i]m 'peacock' adj.masc.instr.sg.

Now we are faced with the problem of how to account for the facts assuming one invariant ranking. Clearly, the ranking proposed thus far, cf. (284), does not lead to the selection of an optimal candidate.

(284)

grzyb jadalny	*[Lab, Pal] &No Coda	IDENT [Lab, Pal]	*[Lab, Pal]
grzyb'. ja.dal.ny.	*!		*
grzy.b'ja.dal.ny.			*!
☞grzy.b ja.dal.ny.			
☞grzyb.ja.dal.ny			

In order to account for Phrase-level Palatalization we need a constraint that shows the special status of palatalized labials in the coda, which is caused by the quality of a vowel of a next word. First, we have to postulate a constraint that prohibits resyllabification, i.e., a constraint which requires a stem to match to its final syllable. This is clearly a constraint belonging to the Align constraint family.[123] Formally, this constraint is formulated as in (285), cf. McCarthy and Prince (1993b: 116).

(285)

Align (Stem, R, σ, R) Align $]_{\text{STEM}} =]_{\sigma}$
ALIGN RIGHT; Aligh R: Every final stem-edge matches to a final syllable-edge.

ALIGN RIGHT quantifies universally over stems but existentially over syllables, in accordance with the definition of Generalized Alignment. Note that it does not demand that every syllable-edge coincide with a stem edge.

The tableau in (286) shows the implementation of the constraint into the ranking.

(286)

/grzyb jadalny/	Align R	*[Lab, Pal] &No Coda	IDENT [Lab, Pal]	*[Lab, Pal]
grzyb'. ja.dal.ny.		*!		*
grzy.b'ja.dal.ny.	*!			*
grzy.b ja.dal.ny.	*!			
☞grzyb.ja.dal.ny				

As expected, Align R does not directly lead to the selection of the optimal candidate, since it only prohibits resyllabification. Our optimal candidate should display a palatalization of the last consonant. Therefore, we need a constraint that forces the palatalization of consonants if they are followed by high, front vowels or by a glide /j/. Such a phonetically motivated constraint undoubtedly derives support from cross-linguistic data. Its formulation is proposed in (287), where C stands for a consonant and

---

123 Recall a general schema for Align (McCarthy and Prince (1993b:80), presented in 1.2.3.

/i/ for /i/ as well as /j/. This constraint ensures that a consonant is fronted before [i , j]. Thus, [p'i] is less marked cross-linguistically than [pi]. (One could argue that *Ci is a phonetic constraint because it captures coarticulation effects.)

(287)

*Ci: There are no plain consonants followed by i or j.[124]

In other words, the constraint in (287) requires every consonant followed by i or j to be palatalized in any position. The tableau in (288) illustrates that the high-ranking *Ci leads to the selection of the optimal candidate, cf. also the application of this constraint in 4.3.3.

(288)

/grzyb jadalny/	*Ci	Align R	*[Lab, Pal] & No Coda	IDENT [Lab, Pal]	*[Lab, Pal]
☞grzyb'. ja.dal.ny.			*		*
grzy.b'ja.dal.ny.		*!			*
grzy.b ja.dal.ny.	*!	*			
grzyb.ja.dal.ny	*!				

The high-ranking of *Ci leads straightforwardly to the selection of the first candidate as a winner, since it does not incur any violation of *Ci and Align R, as opposed to its contestants.

In sum, the ranking proposed in (288) explains why in Polish palatalized labials are neutralized in coda position except when they are followed by a high front vowel /i/ or a palatal glide /j/ in the next word.

4.2 Coronals

In Polish, coronals constitute the most diversified group of natural classes since sounds produced with the tongue blade (the corona) subsume several places and manners of articulation. Stops, fricatives, affricates, nasals, laterals, and the trill are produced at different places of articulation within the coronal range, all of which are phonemes of Polish. In (289) these sounds are systematized with regard to place and manner of articulation.[125] The exact featural content of the phonemes is presented in 7.1 in the appendix. Note that there are no phonemic coronals with a secondary articulation,

---

[124] This constraint alone does not predict that consonants followed by i or j have to be secondarily palatalized. Potentially, it is possible that Gen produces a consonant which is aspirated or labialized, i.e. C^h or C^w. However, such sequences cannot be selected as optimal because constraints prohibiting aspiration or labialization are very high-ranked in Polish. For this reason only secondarily palatalized consonants will be considered in the following analyses.

[125] Cf. also Rubach (1984:26).

although sounds like [t'] or [s'] surface as allophones of the corresponding plain segments, cf. (294) below.

(289)

	Dentals	Alveolars	Retroflexes (Postalveolars)	Alveolo-palatals (Prepalatals)
Stops	t d			
Fricatives		s z	š ž	ś ź
Affricates		t^{s} d^{z}	$t^{\check{s}}$ $d^{\check{z}}$	$t^{\acute{s}}$ $d^{\acute{z}}$
Nasals	n			ń
Laterals	ł	l		
Trill		r		

Some points require further clarification. First of all, all symbols used here belong to a transcription system which is typically used in the Slavic tradition. Therefore, in (290) the Slavic transcription symbols are compared with their IPA counterparts.[126]

(290)

Slavic	IPA	Slavic	IPA	Slavic	IPA
s	s	š	ʂ (ʃ)	ś	ɕ
z	z	ž	ʐ (ʒ)	ź	ʑ
c/t^{s}	ts	č/$t^{\check{s}}$	tʂ (tʃ)	ć/$t^{\acute{s}}$	tɕ
ʒ/d^{z}	dz	ǯ/$d^{\check{z}}$	dʐ (dʒ)	ʒ́/$d^{\acute{z}}$	dʑ
				ń	ɲ

In many studies on Polish phonology the sounds described in (289) as š ž $t^{\check{s}}$ $d^{\check{z}}$ are considered to be postalveolars, i.e. IPA [ʃ ʒ tʃ dʒ], cf. Rubach (1984) and Gussmann (1980). In other studies such as Chomsky and Halle (1968), Hume (1992), Hall (1997a) š ž $t^{\check{s}}$ $d^{\check{z}}$ are analyzed as retroflexes, i.e. IPA [ʂ ʐ tʂ dʐ]. Ladefoged and Maddieson (1996:154) take a position different from all the authors mentioned above in calling them 'flat postalveolars (retroflex)' sounds [ṣ ẓ].

The next remark refers to the dental, velarized lateral /ł/ (IPA [l̪ˠ]) which is present in the underlying representation but not on the surface. When /ł/ is phonologically palatalized, it emerges as [l]. When it is nonpalatalized, it undergoes a context-free shift to a glide [w], cf. Gussmann (1980a:15), Wierzchowska (1971:162). Various reasons for postulating the underlying /ł/ (e.g. phonotactics, morphological alternations and phonological rules) are discussed in Rubach (1976). In 4.2.2 it will also be shown that /ł/ undergoes Coronal Palatalization and therefore behaves as other dental/alveolar coro-nals and not as the glide [w].

As far as terminology is concerned, the term *palatalized* will be used with respect to coronals which change the feature [+back] in the underlying representation to [-back]

[126] The symbols used in the Slavic tradition are mainly derived from various Slavic spelling systems. The Slavic transcription and corresponding orthographic reflexes in Polish are provided in 0.3.

on the surface. In addition, this term will be referred to consonants which are specified as [-back] at a stage of a derivation in thc derivational approach to palatalization of coronals I discuss below.

4.2.1 Coronals in onset and coda positions

Coronals – with the exception of /ń/ – are not restricted with respect to a particular position within a word/syllable (/ń/ does not occur in absolute word-initial position.) Word-initially minimal- or near minimal pairs involve almost all coronals. Some of them are listed in (291).

(291)

[t]en	'this' masc.nom.sg.	[t^{s}]en	'price' gen. pl.
d[r]ew	'wood' gen.pl.	d[ž]ew	'tree' gen.pl.
[z]ąb	'tooth' nom.sg.	[ź]ąb	'cold' nom.sg.
[s]en	'dream' nom.sg.	[ś]eń	'entrance hall' nom.sg.
[d]en	'bottom' gen.pl.	[$d^{ź}$]eń	'day' nom.sg.
[t]en	'this' masc.nom.sg.	[$t^{ś}$]eń	'shadow' nom.sg.
[r]ok	'year' nom.sg.	[l]ok	'lock' nom.sg.

Coronals also occur frequently in word-internal onsets. Examples are provided in (292).

(292)

ko[t]a	'cat' gen.sg.
wo[d]a	'water' nom.sg.
ko[r]a	'bark' nom.sg.
bu[ź]a	'mouth' dim.nom.sg.
stru[ś]a	'ostrich' gen.sg.
ziar[n]o	'corn' nom.sg.
pa[l]ec	'finger' nom.sg.
ko[w]o	'circle' nom.sg.
ci[š]a	'silence' nom.sg.
ko[ń]a	'horse' gen.sg.
mo[ž]e	'sea' nom.sg.
ko[t^{s}]e	'blanket' nom.pl.

Since dentals/alveolars like /t, d/ are generally considered to be the most unmarked sounds, they should occur in coda position as well because unmarked sounds typically occur in syllable-final position. Indeed, they are frequently found in coda position, in which also marked coronals such as [ž], [š], [ś], [ź], [$t^{ś}$], [$d^{ź}$], [$t^{š}$], and [$d^{ž}$] occur. Consider the minimal pairs provided in (293).

(293)

pa[n]	'sir' nom.sg.	pa[ń]	'lady' gen.pl.
bro[n]	'harrow' gen.pl	bro[ń]	'weapon' nom.sg.
ma[s]	'mass' gen.pl.	ma[t]	'mat' gen.pl.
ko[š]	'basket' nom.sg.	ko[s]	'scythe' gen.pl.
pie[t^{s}]	'to bake'inf.	pie[s]	'dog' nom.sg.
klu[$t^{\check{s}}$]	'key' nom.sg.	klu[$t^{\acute{s}}$]	'to hatch' inf.
gło[ś]	'to announce' 2ps.sg.imp.	gło[s]	'voice' nom.sg.
wó[r]	'sack' nom.sg.	wó[w]	'bullock' nom.sg.

An interesting aspect pertaining to dentals/alveolars concerns the numerous words of foreign origin. Here coronals with a secondary palatalization are attested.[127] The secondary palatalization of coronals is also a critical feature for constituting minimal- or nearly minimal pairs with native words.[128] Examples are provided in (294). In addition, retroflexes [š], [ž], [$t^{\check{s}}$] and [$d^{\check{z}}$] are secondarily palatalized in some assimilated foreign words and proper names. For example, *Chile* is realized as [$t^{\check{s}}$']ile and *jeans* as [$d^{\check{z}}$']ins.

(294)

Borrowings		Native words	
[s']erra	'Sierra' nom.sg.	[s]era	'cheese' gen.sg.
[t']ara	'tiara' nom.sg.	[t]ara	'tare' nom.sg.
[t']ul	'tulle' nom.sg.	[t]ul	'to hug' 2ps.sg.imp.
[t']ik	'tic' nom.sg.	[t]yk	'stake' pl.gen.
[r']usza	'ruche' nom.sg.	[r]usza	'to touch' 3ps.sg.pres.
[r']asy	'rias' nom.pl.	[r]asy	'race' nom.pl.
[d']ariusz	'diary' nom.pl.(old P.)	[d]ariusz	'Dariusz' nom.sg.

Because secondarily palatalized coronals are present in the underlying representation and contrast with their nonpalatalized counterparts, substantial support for the phonemic status of these sounds can be made. On the other hand, this proposal can be questioned, since the sounds under consideration are attested only in foreign words. Moreover, as I pointed out in note 127, they are often pronounced as a sequence of a nonpalatalized coronal and a glide /j/, e.g. [tj]ara or [sj]erra.

That the secondary palatalization of coronals is generally avoided in Polish is expressed by a rule called *Retraction*, according to which [i] is turned into the high central unrounded vowel [ɨ], after hard dental/alvolar and retroflex consonants /t, d, s, z, t^{s}, d^{z}, r, š, ž, $t^{\check{s}}$, $d^{\check{z}}$/. For example, the nominative plural marker /i/ is changed to [ɨ] if the stem-

[127] As in the case of labials, cf. 4.1, the secondary articulation in the words in (294) is realized either as an approximant-like element or as a separate segment /j/, cf. also the analysis with underlying /j/ proposed by Rubach (1984:78).

[128] Plain dentals/alveolars are also attested in foreign words but they do not constitute minimal pairs with words containing secondarily palatalized coronals.

final consonant is a dental/alveolar or retroflex: *Holendr+i*[129] 'Dutchman' nom.pl. is pronounced as *Holend[žɨ]* and not **Holend[ži]*, while *chłop+i* 'farmer' nom.pl. is regularly realized as *chło[pi]*, cf. Rubach (1984:201-206). Interestingly, even some foreign words undergo Retraction, cf. (295)a, or they display an optional pronunciation, cf. (295)b.

(295)

a.

ins[tɨ]tucja		'institution' nom.sg.
ins[tɨ]tut		'institute' nom.sg.

b.

ma[ks'i]mum	ma[ksɨ]mum	'maximum' nom.sg.
[s'i]ngiel	[sɨ]ngiel	'single' nom.sg.
[d'i]sco	[dɨ]sco	'disco' nom.sg.

The fact that Polish employs Retraction as a strategy for avoiding secondarily palatalized coronals leads to the preliminary conclusion that these sounds are marked segments. Were Retraction not to apply, then the /i/ would cause the hard coronals to become secondarily palatalized by Surface Palatalization, cf. 4.3.

The markedness of secondarily palatalized coronals is further supported by other kinds of palatalizations which force coronals to change either their place of articulation or both the place and manner of articulation, thus creating new phonemes, cf. Coronal Palatalization discussed in 4.2.2.

In summary, all coronals in (289), except for /ń/, are attested in onset and coda position, where they constitute minimal- or nearly minimal pairs. They do not display a secondary articulation except in foreign words, which leads to the conclusion that these are 'marginal phonemes' in the Polish consonantal inventory.

4.2.2 Palatalization of coronals

This subsection is intended as a brief introduction to a process affecting Polish coronals that is referred to as Coronal Palatalization, cf. Rubach (1984:70), or alternatively as I-Anterior Palatalization, cf. Gussmann (1978:86). Coronal Palatalization converts //s z t d n ł r// into alveolo-palatals /ś ź $t^ś$ $d^ź$ ń l' ř'/ before suffixes beginning with front vowels /e/ and /i/, cf. (298) below.[130] The reason I discuss this process is that this type of palatalization directly shows the main differences between the behavior of coronals when they occur alone in the onset and the coda on the one hand, and in consonant clusters, on the other hand. In other words, it demonstrates that the way coronals under-

[129] The suffix -i causes the palatalization of the stem-final consonant, cf. 4.2.2. In Rubachs approach to cyclic phonology, Retraction applies after Coronal Palatalization, cf. Rubach (1984:201-206).

[130] Rubach (1984) differentiates between the underlying representation and the outputs of phonological rules by using forward slashes / / and double forward slashes // //, respectively. Brackets [ ] indicate phonetic outputs.

go palatalization depends on two factors, namely, their inherent properties as well as the positions they occupy in a syllable.

The present investigation also aims at showing that the account of Coronal Palatalization within Optimality Theory is more adequate than in rule-based frameworks, e.g. in the cyclic phonology model of Rubach (1984). It will be argued that Coronal Palatalization is not a regular rule applying in a derived environment but instead that it is triggered by the palatalizing properties of certain suffixes.

Before I propose my analysis let us consider main facts of Coronal Palatalization. In present-day Polish, Coronal Palatalization is not only related to the properties of the following vowel, in contrast to Common Slavic and Old-Polish, in which front vowels (i, e, ę, ě, ь) and /j/ always induced the palatalization of a preceding consonant morpheme-internally or across a morpheme boundary.[131] In Modern Polish, as already mentioned, palatalization does not affect morpheme-internal strings, i.e. morpheme-internal consonants do not undergo palatalization when followed by front vowels. Some examples are listed in (296).

(296)

[d]elfin	'dolphin' nom.sg.
d[r]ewno	'wood' nom.sg.
[t]eren	'ground' nom.sg.
[d]eptać	'to tread' inf.
[s]er	'cheese' nom.sg.
[s]eler	'celery' nom.sg.

When stems are followed by suffixes beginning with the front vowels /e/ or /i/, the palatalization of a stem-final consonant is induced. Examples are provided in (297), where the right-hand column illustrate the output of the palatalization of the underlying dental/alveolar coronals in the first column. The suffix triggering the palatalization is /e/, the locative singular marker.

(297)

gra/d/	gra[d^{ź}]e	'hail' nom.sg./loc.sg.
ko/t/	ko[t^{ś}]e	'cat' nom.sg./loc.sg.
mły/n/	mły[ń]e	'mill' nom.sg./loc.sg.
ko/r/a	ko[ž]e	'bark' nom.sg./loc.sg.
ko/ł/o	ko[l]e	'wheel' nom.sg./loc.sg.
ko/s/a	ko[ś]e	'scythe' nom.sg./loc.sg.
gru/z/	gru[ź]e	'rubble' nom.sg./loc.sg.

Within the framework of cyclic phonology, cf. Rubach (1984:70), this process is generally known as Coronal Palatalization. Formally, the rule is stated as in (298), cf. Rubach (1984:70).

[131] We will return to this topic when discussing the palatalization of coronals from a diachronic point of view.

(298)
Coronal Palatalization

$$\begin{bmatrix}\text{+anter}\\ \text{+coronal}\\ \text{-del rel}\\ \alpha\ \text{obstr}\end{bmatrix} \rightarrow \begin{bmatrix}\text{-back}\\ \text{+distr}\\ \text{+high}\\ \text{-anter}\\ \alpha\ \text{strid}\end{bmatrix} /\ \_\_\_ \quad \begin{bmatrix}\text{-cons}\\ \text{-back}\end{bmatrix}$$

Coronal Palatalization converts //s z t d n ł r// into alveolo-palatals /ś ź $t^{ś}$ $d^{ź}$ ń l' ř'/.[132] The [α obstr] feature guarantees that the [+obstr] sounds //t// and //d// are changed into the [+strid] /$t^{ś}$ $d^{ź}$/ affricates, while the [-obstruent] sounds //n ł r// become ([-strid]) /ń l' ř'/, cf. Rubach (1984:71). Note that retroflexes (postalveolars) and alveolo-palatals, which are themselves often derived (outputs of Coronal Palatalization), are not subject to Coronal Palatalization because they are [-anter] and the input to Coronal Palatalization is [+anter].

The final two segments, /l'/ and /ř'/, as opposed to /ś ź $t^{ś}$ $d^{ź}$ ń/, are 'abstract' in the sense that they do not surface as such. Therefore, additional Spell-out rules are needed. Rubach posits the Liquid Spell-out rule, presented in (299), which turns /l'/ to [l] and /ř'/ to [ř], cf. Rubach (1984:199).

(299)

Liquid Spell-out

$$\begin{bmatrix}\text{-anter}\\ \text{+sonor}\\ \text{+cons}\\ \text{-nas}\\ \alpha\text{cont}\end{bmatrix} \rightarrow \begin{bmatrix}\text{-high}\\ -\alpha\text{anter}\end{bmatrix}$$

The feature [αcont] in the input is necessary so that the [-cont] sound /l'/ becomes [+ant], i.e. [l], whereas the [+cont] segment /ř'/ shifts to the [-ant] [ř]. Since [ř] is not attested on the surface at all, additional r-Spell-out rules are needed in order to convert [ř] into [r] before a consonant and to [ž] elsewhere. Both rules are shown in (300), cf. Rubach (1984:200).

[132] Another rule accounting for the palatalization of anterior consonants (so-called I-Anterior Palatalization) was proposed earlier by Gussmann (1978:86). This rule converts the coronals /s z t d n ł r/ into their palatalized counterparts /s' z' t' d' n' l' r'/, which subsequently have to undergo various Spell-out rules such as Obstruent Spell-out /s' z' t' d'/ → [ś ź $t^{ś}$ $d^{ź}$], Nasal Spell-out /n/→[ń], r-Spell-out /r'/→[ž], and Lateral Spell-out /l'/→[l].

Evidently, there is a crucial difference between Coronal Palatalization proposed by Rubach (1984) and I-Anterior palatalization proposed by Gussmann (1978). The outputs of the latter are always secondarily palatalized consonants which additionally require Spell-out rules. The former is a one-stage process with respect to obstruents and /n/. As a consequence Coronal Palatalization dispenses with Nasal and Obstruent Spell-out rules.

(300)

r-spell-out	[+sonor, +cons, -anter, -high]	→	[+anter] / __ C	(a)
			[+obstr]	(b)

We will discuss both Liquid Spell-out and r-spell-out when we account for the palatalizations of coronals within OT, cf. 4.2.5.

It is also worth noting that Coronal Palatalization is a highly productive process in present-day Polish. It affects not only the native vocabulary but also borrowings and foreign proper names, cf. (301)a and (301)b, respectively. This phenomenon is consequently ascribed to properties of suffixes which begin with a front vowel. (Note again that in (301) a morpheme-internal /e/ does not trigger palatalization.)

(301)

a. Borrowings

bilar/d/	bilar[d^{ź}]e	'billiards' nom.sg./loc.sg.
elemen/t/	elemen[t^{ś}]e	'element' nom.sg./loc.sg.
fenome/n/	fenome[ń]e	'phenomenon' nom.sg./loc.sg.
kompute/r/	kompute[ž]e	'computer' nom.sg./loc.sg.
teni/s/	teni[ś]e	'tennis' nom.sg./loc.sg.

b. Proper names

Manfre/d/	Manfre[d^{ź}]e	'Manfred' nom.sg./loc.sg.
Gisber/t/	Gisber[t^{ś}]e	'Gisbert' nom.sg./loc.sg.
Stepha/n/	Stepha[ń]e	'Stephan' nom.sg./loc.sg.
Pete/r/	Pete[ž]e	'Peter' nom.sg./loc.sg.
Lar/s/	Lar[ś]e	'Lars' nom.sg./loc.sg.

In Polish, there is a considerable number of suffixes like the inflectional /e/ in (301), which trigger Coronal Palatalization. These are inflectional as well as derivational suffixes. Some of them are listed in (302), cf. also Rubach (1984: 64; 74).

(302)

-ist+ɨ	adjectival
-isk+o	augmentative
-ic+a	feminine
-in+a	pejorative
-i	nom.pl.masc.

Based on the examples presented thus far Coronal Palatalization is triggered by a suffix beginning with a front vowel. According to Rubach (1984:69) Coronal Palatalization is a cyclic rule.

In the reminder of this section it will be shown that Coronal Palatalization is not a 'regular' rule triggered by initial front vowels of suffixes.[133] Instead it will be argued that the palatalization of stem-final anterior consonants is due to inherent properties of certain suffixes. This proposal follows from the fact that (i) suffixes with initial front vowels often fail to palatalize the stem-final consonant, (ii) suffixes with initial back vowels sometimes induce palatalization, (iii) some suffixes have the same segmental exponents with different palatalizing properties, (iv) some suffixes that trigger palatalization have no segmental exponents, and (v) some suffixes with an initial consonant induce palatalization. Against this background it will be proposed in 4.2.3 that palatalization is triggered only by suffixes which contain a palatalizing floating feature in their underlying representations. (Rubach's explanation of the problematic suffixes is discussed below.)

Let us consider suffixes with an initial front vowel which fail to palatalize the preceding consonant. It has to be stressed that this restriction holds for stem-final coronals and labials, while velars undergo a separate rule of palatalization (i.e. Surface Velar Palatalization).[134] Examples of the suffixes are listed in (303).

(303)

-emu	dat. sg. masc.
-em	instr. sg. masc.
-ego	gen./acc. sg. masc.
-ej	gen. dat. loc. sg. fem. adj.
-e	nom. pl./acc.pl. nonmasc.
-ek	diminutive (variable)

The lack of palatalization of stem-final coronals is exemplified by the suffix -/em/ presented in (304).

(304)

bra/t/	bra[t]em	'brother' nom.sg./instr.sg.
kra/n/	kra[n]em	'tap' nom.sg./instr.sg.
chó/r/	chó[r]em	'choir' nom.sg./instr.sg.
wó/ł/	wo[w]em	'ox' nom.sg./instr.sg.
gło/s/	gło[s]em	'voice' nom.sg./instr.sg.

There are also suffixes with initial back vowels, i.e., [u], [o], [a], which trigger palatalization of coronals. These are illustrated on the basis of some selected examples in (305).

---

[133] The problematic aspects of Coronal Palatalization as a cyclic rule have been also discussed by Czaykowska-Higgins (1988), Szpyra (1989), Gussmann (1992), and Szpyra (1995).

[134] Surface Velar Palatalization is discussed in 4.3.2.

(305)

-och pejorative

tłus/t/y	tłuś[$t^{ś}$]och	'fat' nom.sg. masc. /'fatty' nom.sg.
czys/t/y	czyś[$t^{ś}$]och	'clear' nom.sg. masc./ 'stickler' for cleanliness' nom.sg.
zrzę/d/ny	zrzę[$d^{ź}$]och	'grumpy' nom.sg. masc./ 'grumbler' nom.sg.

-uch augmentative

ma/ł/y	ma[l]uch	'little' nom.sg. masc./ 'little boy' nom.sg.
upar/t/y	upar[$t^{ś}$]uch	'stubborn' nom.sg. masc./'a stubborn man' nom.sg.
natrę/t/ny	natrę[$t^{ś}$]uch	'intrusive' nom.sg. masc./ 'intruder' nom.sg.
niedba/ł/y	niedba[l]uch	'sloppy' nom.sg. masc./ 'bungler' nom.sg.

-ąt- ko diminutive

pie/s/	p[ś]ątko	'dog' nom.sg./ 'doggie' nom.ag.
tygry/s/	tygry[ś]ątko	'tiger' nom.sg./ 'little tiger' nom.ag.
ko/t/	ko[$t^{ś}$]ątko	'cat' nom.sg./ 'kitty' nom.ag.

Furthermore, some suffixes that have the same surface exponent display asymmetrical behavior, i.e., they sometimes do and sometimes do not induce palatalization. These are declensional as well as morphological suffixes. Compare the examples shown in (306)a and (306)b, where the suffix /e/ shows its different properties with respect to palatalization.

(306)

a. -e nom. pl.

frędze/l/	frędzle	'fringe' nom.sg./nom.pl.
kapse/l/	kapsle	'cap' nom.sg./nom.pl.
kręgie/l/	kręgle	'skittles' nom.sg./nom.pl.

b. -e loc.sg.

bra/t/	bra[$t^{ś}$]e	'brother' nom.sg./dat.sg.
siost/r/a	siost[š]e	'sister' nom.sg./dat.sg.
ść́a/n/a	ść́a[ń]e	'wall' nom.sg./dat.sg.

It is important to stress that in the examples in (306) the suffix /e/ encodes different morphological information. In (306)a it is the nominative plural desinence /e/ that does not affect the stem-final consonant, while in (306)b it is the dative singular /e/ which shows palatalizing properties. Nevertheless, there are suffixes attested which, on the one hand, encode the same information and on the other hand display different properties regarding palatalization. Their behavior is even asymmetrical with respect to the same kind of stem-final consonant. Consider the examples shown in (307)a and (307)b, in which the outputs of suffixation by the derivational suffix -/až/ (arz) expressing professions in the masculine are shown.

(307)

a.

sekre/t/ariat	sekre[t]arz	'office' nom.sg. /'secretary' nom.sg.
dygni/t/arski	dygni[t]arz	'dignity' adj. nom.sg./'official of high rank' nom.sg.
ślu/s/arski	ślu[s]arz	'metal work' adj.nom.sg /'metal-worker' nom.sg.
pi/s/ać	pi[s]arz	'to write' inf./ 'writer' nom.sg.

b.

pamfle/t/	pamfle[$t^{ś}$]arz	'lampoon' nom.sg./'lampooner' nom.sg.
nar/t/a	nar[$t^{ś}$]arz	'ski' nom.sg./ 'skier' nom.sg.
ochro/n/a	ochro[ń]arz	'protection' nom.sg./'body guard' nom.sg.
spadochro/n/	spadochro[ń]arz	'parachute' nom.sg./'parachutist' nom.sg.
ko/s/a	ko[ś]arz	'scythe' nom.sg./'mower' nom.sg.

The next argument that palatalization is not triggered by the properties of the initial segment of a suffix is provided by suffixes which do not display a segmental exponent on the surface at all. The presence of the suffixes in the underlying representation is signaled by a palatalization of a stem-final consonant. In the right-hand column in (308) the outputs of a denominal adjectivization are provided. Here all stem-final consonants are palatalized, although there is no segmental exponent available on the surface. Since the suffix -/a/ is only an inflectional suffix in both cases, the critical feature providing a distinction between words constituting 'minimal pairs' is the palatalization of the stem-final consonant.

(308)

mał/p/a	mał[p']a	'monkey' noun, nom.sg. fem./ adj. nom. sg. fem.
ry/b/a	ry[b']a	'fish' noun, nom.sg. fem./ adj. nom. sg. fem.
kro/v/a	kro[v']a	'cow' noun, nom.sg. fem./ adj. nom. sg. fem.
ku/r/a	ku[ž]a	'hen' noun, nom.sg. fem./ adj. nom. sg. fem.
ko/z/a	ko[ź]a	'goat' noun, nom.sg. fem./ adj. nom. sg. fem.

Finally, some suffixes with an initial consonant have a palatalizing effect on the stem-final consonant. Consider the outputs of suffixation by an adjectival suffix -/n/- shown in (309).[135] Recall that labials are always depalatalized when followed by another consonant, cf. 4.1.6.

(309)

a.

szko/ł/a	szko[l]ny	'school' noun, nom.sg./ adj.nom.sg.masc.
bana/ł/	bana[l]ny	'commonplace' noun, nom.sg./adj. nom.sg.masc.
la/s/	le[ś]ny	'wood' noun, nom.sg./ adj. nom.sg.masc.
wyra/z/	wyra[ź]ny	'word' nom.sg./ 'clear' nom.sg.masc.

[135] The inflection -y spelled out as the unrounded central high vowel [ɨ], derived from /i/, encodes nom.sg. of adjectives.

gło/s/	gło[ś]ny	'voice' nom.sg./ 'loud' nom.sg.masc.
b.		
mle/k/o	mle[č]ny	'milk' noun/ adj. nom.sg.masc.
dro/g/a	dro[ž]ny	'road' noun/ adj. nom.sg.masc.
brzu/ch/	brzu[š]ny	'abdomen' noun/ adj. nom.sg.masc.
sma/k/	sma[č]ny	'taste'/ 'tasty' nom.sg.masc.

In addition, there are a few stems that reject the palatalization of -/n/. They are presented in (310).[136]

(310)

żela/z/o	żela[z]ny	'iron' noun/adj. nom.sg.masc.
bezkre/s/	bezkre[s]ny	'immensity' noun/adj. nom.sg.mas
mię/s/o	mię[s]ny	'meat' noun/adj. nom.sg.masc.

The data presented above lead to the conclusion that there are some serious arguments against the claim that palatalization is a 'regular' rule in derived-environments triggered by suffixes with initial front vowels. They can be summarized as follows:

a. suffixes with initial front vowels that fail to palatalize the stem-final consonant

b. suffixes with initial back vowels that induce palatalization

c. suffixes of the same segmental exponents with different palatalizing properties

d. suffixes without segmental exponents that trigger palatalization

e. suffixes with an initial consonant that induce palatalization.

The different properties of various suffixes are summarized in the following tableau, cf. (311).

[136] Note that the words listed below contain -n in the root. Therefore, they cannot be considered here.

współczesn+ość	współczesn+y	'contemporary' noun/adj. nom.sg.masc.
powszechn+ość	powszechn+y	'generality' noun/adj. nom.sg.masc.
piękn+ość	piękn+y	'beauty' noun/adj. nom.sg.masc.

(311) The palatalizing properties of Polish suffixes. (Czaykowska-Higgins, 1988:185)

Type	Labials	Coronals	Velars	Morphemes
I	P	T	K	-ę, -av, -ov, -ač, -at, -liv-y
II	P	T	K'	-i/y, -ix/yx, -ego, -emu, -ej, -e, -em, -ego, -emu, -ej, -e, -em, $-iv/y_{vs}$
III	P'	T(ć)	K'	-iń-i/yń-i, ik/yk, -ist-a/yst-a
IV	P/P'	T/ć	K/č	-ak, -až, -arń, -an, -k, -in-a/yn-a, -izm/yzm
V	P'	ć	č	-ast, -c, -ik/yk, -izn/yzn, -ic/yc, -ist/yst,-y, - isk/ysk-o, -sk-i, -stv-o, -nik, -n-y, $-i_{vs}$, $-e_{vs}$, $-ej_{vs}$
VI	P'	ć	C	-i/y, -e

The alternations are specified in terms of the outputs of the underlying voiceless stops, which are held to be representative of the whole group to which they belong. ( )'s indicate that while this alternation occurs, it is not the primary alternation. The dash (/) indicates either that both illustrated alternations occur consistently, or that both surface forms of a morpheme are predictable. 'VS' indicates that the morpheme is a verbalizing suffix.

It is interesting to consider what strategies have been posited so as to account for the claim that Coronal Palatalization is a rule applying in a derived environment. For example, according to Rubach (1984) suffixes that do not cause any palatalization, although the derived environment condition is fulfilled, are represented with an abstract mid, back and unrounded vowel /γ/ in the underlying representation. The function of this vowel is simply to block palatalization. As a consequence "this analysis leads to the postulation of a postcyclic Vowel Spell-out rule which turns /γ/ to /e/" (Rubach 1984:126). Note that this solution requires inserting an abstract vowel into the vocalic inventory in order to rescue the Rubach's claim that Coronal Palatalization is a derived-environment rule.

In other cases palatalizing properties of suffixes are expressed by front high jers, e.g. the adjectival suffixes /sk/, /stv/, and /n/ are represented as /ĭsk/, /ĭstv/, and /ĭn/, respectively, where /ĭ/ is the segment responsible for palatalization, cf. Gussmann (1978: 105, 107, 109) and Rubach (1984:42). Positing a jer in the underlying representation was justified by Lower, a rule that accounts for the vocalization of jers.

Furthermore, suffixes that do not appear in the phonetic representation as a segment, cf. (308), are represented as /i/ in the underlying representation. For example, mał[p']a is represented as małp+i+a 'monkey' adj.nom.sg. fem, cf. Rubach (1984:101). After the palatalization of the stem-final consonant, the underlying segment /i/ is deleted.

Finally, in the case of suffixes displaying different effects on stems, Rubach (1984: 98) claims that these are cases of allomorphy. As a consequence, he argues that the nonpalatalizing suffix is encoded in the lexicon and its palatalizing counterpart is the result of an allomorphy rule which inserts /i/ into lexically governed contexts.

4.2.3 Towards a solution: floating features

In this subsection I will propose that Coronal Palatalization can be accounted for by means of a floating feature which is part of palatalizing suffixes and triggers palatalization. The floating feature is argued to be present only in palatalizing suffixes. This proposal is more economical than the other approaches described above since (i) the vocalic inventory is not enlarged by abstract vowels,[137] (ii) additional operations such as deletions of segments or additional rules such as Spell-out rules are avoided, (iii) an additional underlying node in the segmental representation of suffixes is dispensed with. The following account differs from previous ones, cf. Gussmann (1978), Rubach (1984), Gussmann (1992), Szpyra (1995), in that generalizations are made not by means of rules but with constraints holding for the surface representation. Details will be provided in the following section.

Accounting for palatalization with a floating feature is not an entirely new proposal. Gussmann (1992) has proposed the floating feature [-back], which accounts for Coronal Palatalization within the framework of rule-based phonology.

It is also worth noting that the account of palatalization as a floating feature was rejected by Czaykowska-Higgins (1988:191) for the following reason:

> "Floating or free autosegments, because they are not bound to a particular position, do not exhibit the kinds of local effects seen in the case of Polish palatalization but rather are free to associate wherever universal conventions will allow them to do so."

In the following I will show that Czaykowska-Higgins' objection is unfounded. First, let us have a look at floating features themselves. As it is generally assumed the presence of a root node is a necessary prerequisite for floating features (subsegments) to surface. Consequently, in the absence of a root node, floating features fail to be interpreted and are not visible for syllabification. They will also not be pronounced. According to Zoll (1996), who investigated floating features on the basis of many languages, a single representational distinction between full segments and all subsegments, i.e. latent segments[138] and floating features,[139] is the presence of a root node in the case of full segments. Therefore, Zoll (1996:48) proposes the following representational distinction between full segments on the one hand, and latent segments and floating (dependent)[140] features, on the other hand, cf. (312).

---

[137] Note that an abstract feature is more economical than an abstract vowel consisting of many features.

[138] Another term for *latent* segments is *ghost* segments.

[139] The only difference between latent segments and floating features is their realization. While the former associate with an epenthetic node inserted only in well-defined phonological contexts, the latter associate with an existing root node, cf. Zoll (1996:34).

[140] Since the realization of a floating feature is contingent upon an existing root node, floating features are also called *dependent* features in Zoll's study.

(312)

SURFACE	FULL SEGMENTS	LATENT SEGMENTS AND DEPENDENT FEATURES
UNDERLYING	Root | features	features

A generally accepted characteristic of floating features, as their name suggests, is their mobility, i.e. floating features are assumed not to have a fixed position with respect to the segmental string. For this reason Czaykowska-Higgins (1988:191) rejects floating features as a mechanism that accounts for Coronal Palatalization in Polish. However, as Zoll's extensive study (1996) shows, mobility might also be a property of segments or even strings of segments, cf. Tagalog-um-Infixation (McCarthy and Prince 1993:19). Moreover, the position to which floating features can dock is often fixed, which indicates the unreliability of mobility as a diagnostic for the underlying presence or absence of a root node, i.e. for a distinction between full segments and subsegments. For example, in Inor certain plural verb forms are marked by a palatalizing feature [-back], which can only dock at the right edge of a root. But if the root-final consonant is not a coronal obstruent, the feature [-back] will disappear, cf. Zoll (1996:21f). This behavior is very different from another process in Inor, i.e. labialization. Here, the floating feature morpheme [round] indicating masculine gender associates to the rightmost labializable segment, which is either a labial or a dorsal. If neither one is present, it fails to appear.[141] Hence, these cases show that the target of a floating feature is well-defined: the right or left edge of a stem, or a coronal or dorsal segment. Other examples discussed by Zoll also indicate that the targets of floating features are not arbitrary but strictly defined. What these observations reveal is that floating features might require a specific target that is directly governed by the language specific ranking. Zoll (1996:48) claims that various instances of subsegmental behavior must follow from options encoded in grammars and from consequences of the representations themselves.

The results of the investigation by Zoll have a direct application to Coronal Palatalization in Polish. They show that floating features can be bound to particular positions, which consequently leads us to reject Czaykowska-Higgins' objection to floating features.

[141] This kind of an asymmetrical behavior of floating features was captured by Archangeli and Pulleyblank (1994) by means of the following iteration parameter: non-iterative palatalization searches for a target only at the right edge and disappears if a target is not found, while iterative labialization continues to look for a place to dock if the final segment is not a licit target.

I claim that palatalization in Polish is induced by a floating feature, which will be dubbed henceforth [PAL].[142] This floating feature is a property only of those suffixes that induce palatalization, cf. (313).[143]

(313)

$^{[PAL]}$ ist+ɨ	adjectival
$^{[PAL]}$ isk+o	augmentative
$^{[PAL]}$ ic+a	feminine
$^{[PAL]}$ in+a	pejorative
$^{[PAL]}$ i	nom.pl.masc.

Consequently, nonpalatalizing suffixes such as *-emu* dat. sg. masc., *-em* instr. sg. masc., *-ego* gen./acc. sg. masc., and others presented in (303) do not contain [PAL].[144] Furthermore, suffixes that do not have segmental exponents such as mał/p/+i+a vs. mał[p']a 'monkey' adj. nom. sg. fem. or ry/b/+i+a vs. ry[b']a 'fish' adj. nom. sg. fem., cf. also (308), are represented as single floating features, i.e. $^{[PAL]}$, cf. (314).

(314)

mał/p/+$^{[PAL]}$+a	mał[p']a	'monkey' noun, nom.sg. fem./ adj. nom. sg. fem.
ry/b/+$^{[PAL]}$+a	ry[b']a	'fish' noun, nom.sg. fem./ adj. nom. sg. fem.
kro/v/+$^{[PAL]}$+a	kro[v']a	'cow' noun, nom.sg. fem./ adj. nom. sg. fem.

In cases in which stems show an asymmetrical behavior that does not depend on the quality of the final consonant, they are to be marked with an abstract feature in the lexicon as not palatalizable, cf. (310). For example, żela[z]o 'iron' nom.sg. is represented as żela[z]o$^{[-P]}$ where $^{[-P]}$ indicates 'not palatalizable.'[145] The list of marked stems must be longer in order to account for the behavior of stems as in (307)a.

---

142 [PAL] is to be considered as a shorthand for a palatalizing feature. Gussmann (1992) proposes that [PAL] contains a [-back] feature. In 4.2.4 I propose that [PAL] is interpreted as [+high, -back]. Cf. also the discussion on the palatalization feature by Hall (1997a:82ff).

143 It is important to stress that a floating feature might also project its own root node. For example, in Yowlumne a floating feature either moves to find a suitable docking site in the base or projects its own root node, cf. Zoll (1996:167ff). There are also cases in Polish where a floating feature might emerge as a segment. Traditionally such segments are represented as underlying abstract vowels called jers, which either disappear or are vocalized. Recent studies show that it is possible to represent jers in terms of features, cf. e.g. Szpyra (1992), Zoll (1993), Zoll (1996). Since this topic is not of primary interest to the present study, it will not be further developed here.

144 It should be noted that the palatalization of velars by suffixes such as those presented in (303), e.g. kro[k] vs. kro[k']em 'step' nom.sg./instr.sg., cannot be triggered by [PAL] but is triggered by Surface Velar Palatalization, discussed in 4.3.3.

145 Rubach (1984) does not account for such cases.

4.2.4 An OT analysis

In this subsection an OT account of Coronal Palatalization is proposed.

In a constraint ranking for Polish, there must be a constraint which prohibits the deletion of a floating feature present in the underlying representation. Recall that the constraint MAX-IO, presented again in (315), generally prohibits deletion of segments, i.e. structures having an underlying root node.

(315)

MAX-IO
Every segment in the input has a correspondent in the output.

As a consequence, MAX-IO, referring directly to segments, cannot evaluate the relation between the floating feature [PAL] and its correspondent in the output. Moreover, Ident [F] does not offer a solution either, since it deals only with features dominated by a root. The presence of [PAL] in the input is accounted for by Max(subsegment) proposed by Zoll (1996:59). This constraint requires every subsegment in the input to have a correspondent in the output, where a subsegment is equated with an undominated F-element, i.e. a floating feature. A general formulation of MAX(subsegment) is represented in (316)a, and its specific instantiation with respect to [PAL] is shown in (316)b.

(316)

a.
MAX (subseg) Every subsegment in the input has a correspondent in the output.
b.
MAX [PAL] Every [PAL] in the input has a correspondent in the output.

Furthermore, there must be an alignment constraint that has the power to bind the floating feature to the right edge of a stem since, as the examples presented above indicate, the target position of the floating feature [PAL] is always a stem-final consonant. Such a constraint, called No-Intervening, was proposed by Ellison (1995:2) and adopted by Zoll (1996:108). Its general formulation is cited in (317).[146] (ρ denotes an element e.g. a floating feature).

(317)

No-Intervening (ρ; E; D)
There is no material intervening between ρ and an edge E in domain D.

Each full segment that occurs between the element in question ρ and the edge of the domain violates No-Intervening in (317), cf. the explanations given below.

The specific instantiation of the constraint formulated for our purposes is demonstrated in (318).

[146] For the advantages of the No-Intervening constraint over an Align constraint, see Zoll (1996: 102-107).

(318)

No-Intervening ([PAL]; Right; Stem)[147]

The constraint in (318) forces the final segment of a stem to be a target of the floating feature [PAL], since it allows no intervening material between [PAL] and the right edge of a stem. The floating feature has to be associated with a segment on the surface, otherwise it does not surface. For this reason, '[PAL]' in (318) is actually to be understood as a segment in which [PAL] is realized. I assume that [PAL] contains features [+high, -back]. Therefore, I claim that if [PAL] is realized, the stem-final consonants change from dental/alveolar coronals /s z t d n ł r/ into alveolo-palatals [ś ź $t^{ś}$ $d^{ź}$ ń l' r̠']. [148] Note that the all outputs but r̠' are the same as outputs of Coronal Palatalization, cf. (298). I will return to this point when I discuss the palatalization of /r/.

As mentioned above, if there are other segments between the segment on which [PAL] is realized and the right edge of a stem, No-Intervening ([PAL]; Right; Stem) is violated. Note that one of the possible candidates produced by GEN might entirely reject the presence of [PAL]. In such a case the high-ranked constraint No-Intervening would be vacuously satisfied, and as a consequence this candidate could emerge as an optimal one besides the candidate that associates [PAL] to the last consonant of the stem and satisfies the constraint nonvacuously. Such a highly undesirable situation is prevented by Max [PAL], cf. (316), which forces [PAL] to emerge on the surface. In the tableau in (319) the interaction of the two constraints is shown on the basis of a root /sus/ 'leap' nom.sg. and a palatalizing suffix /e/ loc.sg.masc., which is represented with a floating feature [PAL]. In this example the segment /s/, to which [PAL] associates, is realized as [ś].

(319)

sus+[PAL]e	No-I([PAL];R)	MAX[PAL]
☞ suśe		
suse		*!
śuse	*!*	
śuśe	*!*	

The optimal candidate *suśe*, in which the last consonant of the root is palatalized, is selected as optimal. It perfectly satisfies both No-I([PAL];R) and Max [PAL]. Its most serious competitor, *suse*, in which [PAL] is not present at all, violates the high-ranked MAX [PAL]. This is exactly the critical candidate which could emerge as optimal by vacuously satisfying No-I([PAL];R). In the third candidate, *śuse*, [PAL] is associated with the initial consonant. Since two consonants intervene between this segment and the right edge of the stem, the candidate is penalized twice by No-I([PAL];R), once for

[147] I have replaced the original term 'root' with 'stem', because there are cases in Polish in which palatalization affects stems. Hence, 'stem' is to be understood as a cover term for roots and stems. In the following analyses this constraint will be abbreviated as No-I([PAL];R).

[148] All outputs of Coronal Palatalization are [-ant].

each segment. The fourth candidate, *śuśe*, similarly incurs two violation of No-I([PAL];R).

Let us account for the additional data presented in (309). Recall that the adjectival suffix -/n/ palatalizes stem-final consonants. Its underlying representation contains the floating feature [PAL], which is responsible for triggering the palatalization of the final consonant of the stem to which it attaches. The tableau in (320) illustrates how the constraint interaction predicts that the root gło/s/ 'voice' nom.sg. when combined with the suffix -/n/ emerges as *głośny*.

(320)

gło/s/+PALn+y	No-I([PAL];R)	MAX[PAL]
☞ głośny		
głosny		*!
gl'osny	*!*	

The first candidate, *głośny*, which incurs no violations of No-I([PAL];R) and MAX [PAL], emerges as the optimal one. The violation of MAX[PAL] by the second candidate, *głosny*, immediately eliminates it from consideration. The third candidate, *gl'osny*, violates No-I([PAL];R) twice, because the feature [PAL] is not realized on the root-final consonant but on the third consonant /l/ from the right edge of the root.

In summary, the rule usually referred to as Coronal Palatalization is captured by representing the relevant suffixes with the floating feature [PAL]. The high-ranking constraints No-I([PAL];R) and MAX[PAL] force the floating feature to dock onto the stem-final consonant. If [PAL] is realized on dental/alveolar coronals such as /s z t d n ł r/, they are changed into alveolo-palatals [ś ź $t^{ś}$ $d^{ź}$ ń l' r̠'].

4.2.5 The behavior of coronals in clusters

In this subsection we shall consider the asymmetrical behavior of coronals with respect to palatalization when they are followed by other consonants.

We shall start our investigation by discussing the aberrant behavior of the suffix -/n/ that mirrors the properties of coronals, cf. (320). It is namely sometimes the case that a stem-final consonant systematically rejects the palatalization power of -/n/. The coronal noncontinuants /t, d, n/ are not palatalized when followed by the suffix -/n/. Consider the examples presented in (321).

(321)

wo/d/+a	wo[dn]y	'water' nom.sg./ adj.masc.nom.sg.
groma/d/+a	grom[dn]y	'herd' nom.sg./ adj.masc.nom.sg.
obro/n/+a	obro[nn]y	'defense' nom.sg./ adj.masc.nom.sg.
rodzi/n/+a	rodzi[nn]y	'family' nom.sg./ adj.masc.nom.sg.
komple/t/	komple[tn]y	'complete (group)' nom.sg./ adj.masc.nom.sg.
prostoką/t/	prostoką[tn]y	'rectangle' nom.sg./ adj.masc.nom.sg.

Furthermore, alveolo-palatals /$t^{ś}$/, /$d^{ź}$/ and /ń/ are depalatalized before the suffix /n/. Relevant examples are shown in (322).

(322)

chę/$t^{ś}$/	chę[tn]y	'willingness' noun, nom.sg./adj.nom.sg.
wilgo/$t^{ś}$/	wilgo[tn]y	'moisture' noun, nom.sg./adj.nom.sg.
go/$d^{ź}$/en	go[dn]y	'worthy' (old P.) adj.nom.sg./adj.nom.sg.
jesie/ń/	jesie[nn]y	'autumn' noun, nom.sg./adj.nom.sg.
kamie/ń/	kamie[nn]y	'stone' noun, nom.sg./adj. nom.sg.

The noncontinuants /$t^{ś}$ $d^{ź}$ / are also depalatalized if they are followed by other coronal sonorants such as /ń/, /r/ or /ł/. In (323) examples are shown in which /$t^{ś}$/ and /$d^{ź}$/ are depalatalized after suffixation. Note that the vowel following alveolo-palatals is deleted.

(323)

kwie/$t^{ś}$/eń	(+a)	kwie[tń]a	'April' nom.sg./ gen.sg.
/$d^{ź}$/eń	(+a)	[dń]a	'day' nom.sg./ gen.sg.
wy/$d^{ź}$/er+am	(+ę)	wy[dr]ę	'to tear out' 1ps.sg.pres./ 1ps.sg.fut.
wy/$t^{ś}$/er+am	(+ę)	wy[tr]ę	'to rub out' 1ps.sg.pres./ 1ps.sg.fut.
ko/$t^{ś}$/oł	(+a)	ko[tw]a	'cauldron' nom.sg./ gen.sg.

The depalatalization of /$t^{ś}$/, /$d^{ź}$/, and /ń/ occurs without exception before coronal sonorants. In Rubach's (1984) approach to rule-based phonology this phenomenon is expressed with the rule shown in (324), cf. Rubach (1984: 101). Note that this rule occurs before the rule converting /ł/ into [w].

(324)

$$\begin{bmatrix} \text{+high} \\ \text{+coronal} \\ \text{-cont} \\ \text{-lateral} \end{bmatrix} \rightarrow \begin{bmatrix} \text{-high} \\ \text{-del rel} \\ \text{+anter} \end{bmatrix} / \_\_ \begin{bmatrix} \text{+cons} \\ \text{+coron} \\ \text{+sonor} \end{bmatrix}$$

The rule in (324) turns noncontinuant prepalatals such as /$t^{ś}$/, /$d^{ź}$/, and /ń/ into the corresponding dentals [t] [d] [n] before coronal sonorants. The feature [-cont] in the input is necessary because fricatives like /ś/ and /ź/ do not depalatalize, cf. also 4.2.6. It is worth noticing that the sonorant /r/ is not affected by this rule. (The data will be provided below.) There are at least two arguments against including /r/ in the natural class of segments that undergo this rule. Rubach (1984:106) points out correctly that it would be too arbitrary to assume that /r/ is a noncontinuant. Second, since /r/ is depalatalized before any coronal segment and not only before sonorants, its depalatalization should be expressed by a separate rule. We will return to this point below.

In cyclic-phonology the input for depalatalization is in many cases the output of Coronal Palatalization, cf. (298). For example, //t d n// are converted to /$t^{ś}$ $d^{ź}$ ń/ by Coronal Palatalization and then to [t d n] by Noncontinuant Depalatalization. A sample derivation is presented in (325), in which the palatalizing suffix -/n/ and a declensional suffix +/a/ are appended to the stem *przechod-*, which surfaces as przecho[dń]a 'passer-by' gen.sg., cf. Rubach (1984:103). (The derivation at cycle 1 is omitted in (325) since it is not relevant for the present discussion). Recall that ĭn is the representation of a palatalizing suffix in Rubach's treatment, where ĭ is a fronting jer inducing palatalization.

(325)

przecho[dń]a	przexod+ĭń+a	(-a gen.sg.)
UR	-xod+ĭń+a	
Cycle 2	-xod+ĭń	
	-xod^{ź}	Cor.Pal
	-	Lower[149]
Cycle 3	-xod^{ź} +ĭń+a	
	-	Cor.Pal
	-	Lower
Postcyclic	-xod^{ź} +ń+a	Yer Deletion
	-xod +ń+a	Noncontinuant Depalatalization

Noncontinuant Depalatalization also affects alveolo-palatal noncontinuants present underlyingly. For example, chę[t^{ś}] 'willingness' nom.sg. will be depalatalized to chę[tn]y 'willing' masc.nom.sg. after the suffix -/n/ is appended.

In what follows the process of Noncontinuant Depalatalization will be reanalyzed within the framework of Optimality Theory. It will be shown that the account for depalatalization of noncontinuants by means of constraints is more economical than the one presented in (325) since it avoids unnecessary generalizations and dispenses with steps in a derivation.

First, we have to infer from the examples already presented that in Polish grammar there must be a high-ranked constraint which prohibits the occurrence of alveolo-palatal noncontinuants when they are followed by coronal sonorants, i.e. liquids or nasals. We will formulate this constraint below.

Generally, a phonological rule like A→B/_C says nothing more than 'avoid AC by changing A to B.' This statement can be easily expressed by the ranking of a markedness and a faithfulness constraint. The first one prohibits the underlying structure AC, and it is higher ranked than the second one, which expresses faithfulness to the change under consideration. Schematically, the ranking is shown in (326).

(326)

rule:	constraint ranking:	
A→B/_C	*AC>>F(A→B)	AC is ruled out

[149] Lower is a rule that vocalizes jers in certain contexts. It does not affect the case presented here.

Consequently, a constraint that prohibits alveolo-palatals *[t^{ś} d^{ź} ń] followed by coronal sonorants can be stated as in (327).

(327)

$$* \quad \underset{\begin{bmatrix} +\text{high} \\ +\text{coronal} \\ -\text{ cont} \\ -\text{ later} \end{bmatrix}}{\text{A}} \quad \underset{\begin{bmatrix} +\text{cons} \\ +\text{coron} \\ +\text{sonor} \end{bmatrix}}{\text{C}}$$

In the following analyses, the constraint presented in (327) will be abbreviated as NonCONT, cf. (328).

(328)

NonCONT: *[t^{ś} d^{ź} ń]CorSoN
No prepalatal noncontinuants followed by coronal sonorants.

As already mentioned, the constraint that governs depalatalization (or rather nonpalatalization) in (328) must obviously be high-ranked in Polish grammar, otherwise palatalizing suffixes such as -/n/ would incorrectly cause alveolo-palatals to emerge before coronal sonorants. For exactly this reason NonCONT must be ranked higher than constraints forcing palatalization: No-I([PAL];R) and MAX[PAL]. The tableau in (329) illustrates the effect of implementing NonCONT into the ranking.

(329)

go[d]+PALn+y	NonCont	No-I([PAL];R)	MAX[PAL]
☞ go[d]ny		*	*
go[d^{ź}]ny	*!		

Although the optimal candidate *godny* 'worthy' masc.nom.sg. rejects palatalization, it emerges as optimal, since the violations of the lower ranked constraints are tolerable. This candidate fully satisfies the high-ranking NonCONT.

The constraint NonCont shows its effect also in cases in which alveolo-palatal noncontinuants are present underlyingly. As stated above, these segments also undergo depalatalization in stem-final position when they are followed by a suffix with the palatalizing floating feature. This is shown by the tableau in (330).

(330)

wilgo[t^{ś}]+PALn+y	NonCont	No-I([PAL];R)	MAX[PAL]
wilgo[t^{ś}]ny	*!		*
☞ wilgo[t]ny			*

Here, the candidate that satisfies NonCont, *wilgo[t]ny* 'moist' masc.nom.sg., is selected as the optimal one because it fares better on NonCont than its most serious competitor *wilgo[t^{ś}]ny*.

Now we are in a position to account for the slightly different behavior of /r/. Recall that Coronal Palatalization turns //r// to /ř'/, cf. (298). Since /ř'/ does not emerge on the surface, it requires two additional Spell-out rules: Liquid Spell-out rule that converts /ř'/ into [ř] and r-Spell-out rule that turns [ř] into [r] before consonants or to [ž] elsewhere, cf. Rubach (1984:199f). The rules are shown in (299) and (300).

Let us illustrate this process with some examples. Consider the words shown in (331) in which /ř'/, the output of palatalization by the palatalizing suffixes -/t^s/+/a/ and -/ł/+/a/,[150] is affected by a depalatalization rule which then derives [r]. The single stages of this process can be represented as /r/→ /ř'/→[r].

(331)

męd//r//+ca	męd/ř'/ca	męd[rt^s]a	'sage' gen.sg.
wzo//r//+ca	wzo/ř'/ca	wzo[rt^s]a	'pattern' gen.sg.
dwo//r//+ca	dwo/ř'/ca	dwo[rt^s]a	'railway station' gen.sg.
o//r//+ła	o/ř'/ła	o[rw]a	'eagle' gen.sg.
ka//r//+ła	ka/ř'/ła	ka[rw]a	'dwarf' gen.sg.

According to the predictions made in Rubach's (1984) treatment, exactly the same derivational steps are required in order to account for suffixation by the suffix -/n/. Consider the examples shown in (332), cf. (325).

(332)

poko//r//+ny	poko/ř'/ny	poko[rn]y	'humble' adj.nom.sg.
pa//r//+ny	pa/ř'/ny	pa[rn]y	'sultry' adj.nom.sg.
browa//r//+ny	browa/ř'/ny	browa[rn]y	'brewer's-' adj.nom.sg.
skwa//r//+ny	skwa/ř'/ny	skwa[rn]y	'sweltering' adj.nom.sg.
sono//r//+ny	sono/ř'/ny	sono[rn]y	'sonorant' adj.nom.sg.

In all of the cases presented in (331) and (332) the /r/ goes through an intermediate stage /ř'/. This abstract sound is postulated by Rubach in order to differentiate between words that undergo depalatalization as in (331) and (332) and words that contain /ž/ in their underlying representation that do not undergo depalatalization when they are followed by the same suffixes. In (333) examples of stems ending in /ž/ followed by the suffix -/t^s/+/a/ (genitive case), /ł/+/a/ and /n/+/ɨ/ are provided.

(333)

nosoro/ž/+ca	nosoro[žt^s]a	'rhino' gen.sg.
tę/ž/+ca	tę[žt^s]a	'tetanus' gen.sg.
wy/ž/+ła	wy[žw]a	'pointer' gen.sg.
podró/ž/+ny	podró[žn]y	'travelling-'adj.nom.sg.
orę/ž/+ny	orę[žn]y	'armed' adj.nom.sg.

---

[150] Both palatalizing suffixes -c and -ł emerge in the singular with a vowel -e, e.g. wzo[ž]ec 'pattern' nom.sg. and o[ž]eł 'eagle' nom.sg. Neither is productive in present-day Polish.

It is worth noting that the suffixation by -/tˢ/ and -/ł/ (the nominative case) results in the same output. The obstruent [ž] emerges on the surface regardless of its source, cf. męd/r/+ec → męd[ž]ec vs. nosoro/ž/+ec → nosoro[ž]ec.[151]

The examples presented in (331), (332) and (333) show why Coronal Palatalization must convert /r/ into an abstract /ř'/ followed by an additional Spell-out rule (i.e. /r/→ /ř'/→[r]). If the underlying /r/ were converted directly into [ž] by Coronal Palatalization, then the depalatalization rule would take [ž] as its input and turn it into [r]. More importantly, the depalatalization rule taking ž as its input would also affect the underlying /ž/, cf. (333). Hence, in order to distinguish between outputs of Coronal Palatalization and the underlying /ž/ an intermediate stage, i.e. /ř'/, differentiating between underlying /r/ and /ž/ is required, cf. (331) and (333). In other words, "if Cor. Pal. changed r to [ž] directly, there would be no way of recovering /r/ in the contexts where it undergoes depalatalization. Thus, for instance, *wierny* 'faithful' and *podróżny* 'journey' (Adj.) would have the same structure after Palatalization had applied: /ž+ĭn/"(Rubach (1984:72)).

Let us consider how the cases presented in (331), (332), (333) are evaluated by means of constraints. It seems that they are problematic for OT, which does not recognize intermediate stages in derivation and consequently is not able to account for the cases under consideration. In the following I will demonstrate that an OT account not only correctly predicts the attested candidates but also avoids abstract segments such as ř' by making use of universal markedness constraints.

The constraints triggering the palatalization of the stem-final consonant, No-I([PAL];R) and MAX[PAL], cause the palatalization of the final /r/ when it is followed by palatalizing suffixes. The floating feature [PAL] is realized if the stem-final /r/ changes to [r̠']. Consider the tableau in (334), in which the output *mie[r̠']e* 'measure' dat.sg., derived from *mia[r]a* 'measure' nom.sg., satisfies both No-I([PAL];R) and MAX[PAL] and therefore is incorrectly selected by Eval as optimal.

(334)

mia[r]+PALe	No-I([PAL];R)	MAX[PAL]
☞ mie[r̠']e		
mie[r]e		*!

Unfortunately, the candidate *mie[r̠']e*, is not an attested output in Polish. Thus, there must be another constraint in Polish which is responsible for the selection of the correct candidate *mie[ž]e*. Before stating the constraint let us consider the outputs of the palatalization of /r/ that have to be taken into consideration. In (335) six most important candidates are shown.

[151] It is interesting to note the spellings of the words under consideration. Words that do not undergo depalatalization and have /ž/ underlyingly like those in (333) are spelled with ż, e.g. nosorożec 'rhino' nom.sg., while words that evince palatalization and are later depalatalized are spelled with rz, e.g. mędrzec 'sage' nom.sg., cf. (331).

(335)

a. r → ř
b. r → ř’
c. r → r’
d. r → r̲’
e. r → ž
f. r → ž’

The matrices in (336) show how the sounds in (335) are represented in terms of features.

(336)[152]

	ř	ř’	r̲’	r’	ž	ž’
[cor]	+	+	+	+	+	+
[ant]	+	+	-	+	-	-
[dist]	+	+	-	-	-	-
[back]		-	-	-		-
[high]		+	+	+		+
[son]	-	-	+	+	-	-

From a cross-linguistic perspective the sound ř (ř’)[153] is more marked than r̲’, r’, ž’, and ž. While there are at least 15-20 languages attested with r̲’ and r’, cf. Hall (1999)[154] the fricative trill ř occurs only in Czech, cf. Hall (1999). Ladefoged and Maddieson (1996:229) observe that ř in Czech is a sequential combination of a trill and a fricative. For this articulatory reason ř is extremely marked cross-linguistically: languages have sounds that are either trills or fricatives but not both. Further, r̲’ and r’ are more marked than ž’ because they are palatalized trills while ž’ is a palatalized fricative. From a cross-linguistic perspective r’(r̲’) and ž’ are more marked than ž. Hall (1999) ascribes this discrepancy to a general tendency for languages to avoid palatalized apical sounds. R-sounds, being in most languages apical and not laminal, in contrast to sounds like t or d, are not stable hosts for palatalizations. He also observes that ř and ř’ are highly marked sounds because they are *laminal* trills.

In Polish of the six sounds in (336) only r’, ž’ and ž are attested. The first two sounds occur only in foreign words, e.g. [r’]iksza ‘ricksha(w)’nom.sg. or [ž’]iwago ‘proper name’ nom.sg. (and also across word-boundaries). In native vocabulary both r’ and ž’ are systematically avoided by constraints banning secondarily palatalized dental, alveolar, and retroflex consonants /t, d, s, z, t^s, d^z, r, š, ž, $t^{\check{s}}$, $d^{\check{z}}$/. As noted in 4.2.1, these sounds are also avoided in some foreign words. For example, [r’]iksza is also pronounced as [rɨ]ksza and [ž’]iwago as [žɨ]wago, cf. also Retraction in 4.2.1.

---

152 [-back, +high]= palatalized, [+back]=velarized, [0 back, 0 high]= neither palatalized nor velarized.

153 I am not aware of a language in which ř’ occurs. My suspicion is that ř’ is attested in Czech in cases in which ř is followed by i.

154 From the ariculatory point of view r̲’ seems to be more marked than r’ because the former is a *retroflex* palatalized trill.

All these observations allow us to posit universal markedness constraints which prohibit various outputs of palatalization: [r'], [r̠'], [ř], [ř'], [ž'], and [ž]. They are shown in (337).

(337)

*[ř]: [ř] is prohibited.
*[ř']: [ř'] is prohibited.
*[r̠']: [r̠'] is prohibited.
*[r']: [r'] is prohibited.
*[ž']: [ž'] is prohibited.
*[ž]: [ž] is prohibited.

In terms of features the six constraints in (337) can be collapsed into the constraints in (338). Note again that from the cross-linguistic perspective the constraints in (338)a and (338)b are higher ranked than the constraint in (338)c because the former two occur far less frequently in languages than the latter, cf. Hall (1997a, 1999).

(338)

(a) * [-dist, -back] (*[r'], *[r̠'], *[ž'])
(b) * [+dist, +rhotic] (*[ř], *[ř'])
(c) * [-dist, -ant] (*[ž])

Let us assume that MAX[PAL] is satisfied whenever the input /r/ changes its featural content and emerges as [ř], [ř'], [r̠'], [r'], [ž'], or [ž].[155] Implementation of the constraints in (337) into the Polish ranking leads to the selection of the attested candidate, mie[ž]e, which is the least marked output of the palatalization from a cross-linguistic point of view. Note that my analysis crucially depends on ranking *[ž] lower than other constraints in (337).

(339)

mia[r]+PALe	*[ř]	*[ř']	*[r̠']	*[r']	*[ž']	No-I([PAL];R)	MAX[PAL]	*[ž]
mie[ř]e	*!							
mie[ř']e		*!						
mie[r̠']e			*!					
mie[r']e				*!				
mie[ž']e					*!			
☞ mie[ž]e								
mie[r]e							*!	

[155] In this anlaysis I will abandon the preliminary assumption that [PAL] is only realized if the stem-final /r/ emerges as [r̠'] in order to show that the correct output does not have to follow from this assumption but can be selected by universal markedness constraints.

The candidate *mie[ž]e* is selected as optimal since it violates neither the high-ranking *[ř], *[ř'], *[ṟ'], *[r'], and *[ž'], nor MAX[PAL], in contrast to its competitors which violate one of them. The proposed analysis shows that the output of the palatalization of /r/ does not require one to posit a nonoccurring segment /ř'/ (or ṟ') and more importantly, it demonstrates that the attested output in Polish directly follows from high-ranked markedness constraints.

As mentioned above, the trill /r/ surfaces as [r] when it is followed by a suffix with an initial consonant such as -n, -ł or -c, (331) and (332). The ranking in (339), however, cannot predict that the stem-final /r/ emerges as [r] on the surface. For example poko-/r/+ny 'humble' adj.nom.sg. is incorrectly predicted to surface as poko[žn]y and pa/r/+ny 'sultry' adj.nom.sg. as pa[žn]y. This situation is shown in the tableau in (340), in which the candidate wie[ž]ny, which violates neither the high-ranking markedness constraints nor No-I([PAL];R)/ MAX[PAL], incorrectly emerges as optimal.

(340)

wie[r]+PALn+y	*[ř]	*[ř']	*[ṟ']	*[r']	*[ž']	No-I([PAL];R)	MAX [PAL]	*[ž]
wie[ř]ny	*!							
wie[ř']ny		*!						
wie[ṟ']ny			*!					
wie[r']ny				*!				
wie[ž']ny					*!			
☞ wie[ž]ny								*
wie[r]ny							*!	

Consequently, there must be a higher ranked constraint in the ranking in Polish grammar which prevents the candidate wie[ž]ny in (340) from surfacing. This constraint prohibits palatalization of /r/ if /r/ is followed by a consonant. Formally, this phenomenon can be expressed by a faithfulness constraint which bans any changes of the featural content of r when r is followed by a consonant, cf. (341). The application of this constraint in other languages requires further investigation.

(341)

Faith (rC) /r/ is not changed when followed by a consonant.

The constraint in (341) is violated if the featural content of r is changed. The tableau in (342) illustrates the effect of the implementation of the constraint Faith (rC) into the ranking.

(342)

wie[r]+PALn+y	Faith (rC)	*[ř]	*[ř’]	*[r̠’]	*[r’]	*[ž’]	No-I ([PAL]; R)	MAX [PAL]	*[ž]
wie[ř]ny	*!	*							
wie[ř’]ny	*!		*						
wie[r̠’]ny	*!			*!					
wie[r’]ny	*!				*				
wie[ž’]ny	*!					*			
wie[ž]ny	*!								*
☞ wie[r]ny								*	

The candidate *wie[r]ny* in (342) entails no violations of Faith (rC) and ultimately emerges as the optimal output, while other competitors are eliminated due to a violation of the high-ranking Faith (rC).

Let us proceed to the cases presented in (333), in which the underlying /ž/ is followed by a consonant-initial palatalizing suffix. Similar to the analysis presented in (342), I will propose a constraint that prohibits the palatalization of [ž]. Such a constraint was proposed in (337), i.e.*[ž’], and implemented into the ranking proposed thus far. In (343) it is shown how the optimal candidate is selected.

(343)

podró[ž]+PALn+y	*[ž’]	NoI([PAL];R)	MAX[PAL]	*[ž]
☞ podró[ž]ny			*	
podró[ž’]ny	*!			

Although [ž] in the first candidate in (343), *podró[ž]ny*, is not palatalized, it is selected as the optimal candidate since it does not violate the high-ranked *[ž’]. Due to a violation of this constraint its competitor, *podró[ž’]ny*, must be excluded from consideration.

As mentioned above retroflexes and alveopalatals as well as alveolars /t^{s}/ and /d^{z}/ do not undergo palatalization. Hence, a faithfulness constraint prohibiting any changes in the featural content of these sounds must be high-ranked in Polish. Consider the constraints shown in (344).

(344)

a. Ident (+high, -anterior, -back,+distributed): Faith (ś ź $t^{ś}$ $d^{ź}$ ń)
b. Ident (+back, -anterior, -distributed): Faith (š ž $t^{š}$ $d^{ž}$)
c. Ident (+back +anterior, -distributed, +del.release): Faith (t^{s} d^{z})

In (345) it is shown how the high-ranked Faith (ž) leads to the selection of the attested candidate.

(345)

podró[ž]+PALn+y	Faith [ž]	No-I([PAL];R)	MAX[PAL]	*[ž]
☞ podró[ž]ny			*	*
podró[ž']ny	*!			
podró[r']ny	*!			
podró[r]ny	*!			

The first candidate in (345), in which /ž/ surface as [ž], proves to be optimal. Its competitors do not emerge on the surface since they change the featural content of underlying /ž/. Note that this was the critical example in Rubach's approach for postulating an abstract segment /ř'/ as the output of Coronal Palatalization of //r//, cf. (298).

From the analyses presented above it directly follows that the palatalization of /r/ requires neither an intermediate stage, i.e. an abstract segment /ř'/, nor additional Spell-out rules. Instead constraints alone make a distinction between an underlying /ž/ and an underlying /r/, a potential input for palatalization. Accounting for these phenomena by means of constraints is more economical than by rules since constraints do not require a palatalization stage at all as opposed to a cyclic account, cf. (325). Consequently the name Noncontinuant Depalatalization holds only for the cyclic approach cf. Rubach (1984) and not for Optimality Theory, which systematically avoids palatalization in such cases.

4.2.6 Alveolar fricatives in consonant clusters

The alveolar fricatives /z/ and /s/ behave differently than other coronals with respect to palata-lization when they are followed by other consonants. In this subsection I discuss the behavior of these continuants in consonant clusters when they occur in a palatalizing environment. The following discussion, including the conclusions drawn in 4.2.5, leads to the systematization of coronals into four sets according to their behavior in clusters in various palatalizing contexts. The set can be ranked from the least marked to the most marked in the following way: /s/ /z/< /ł/< /t/ /d/ /n/< /r/.

As shown in the previous subsection, /t, d, n/ and /r/ do not undergo palatalization when the palatalizing suffix begins with a coronal sonorant. In other words, sequences such as [t^{ś}n], [d^{ź}n], [ńn], or [žn][156] are prohibited. In addition /r/ does not undergo palatalization before a consonant, cf. (341). The fricatives /s/, /z/ as well as the non-continuant /ł/ react in exactly the opposite way; they readily palatalize before a consonant. The examples are shown in (346).

[156] Only if [ž] comes from an underlying /ž/ is the sequence [žn] is allowed.

(346)

a.

bana/ł/	bana[l]+ny	'commonplace' noun/adj. nom.sg.masc.
wyra/z/	wyra[ź]+ny	'word'/ 'clear' nom.sg.masc.
la/s/	le[ś]+ny	'wood' noun/ adj. nom.sg.masc.
gło/s/	gło[ś]+ny	'voice'/ 'loud' nom.sg.masc.
szko/ł/a	szko[l]+ny	'school' noun/ adj.nom.sg.masc.

b.

wo/d/+a	wo[dn]y	'water' nom.sg./ adj.masc.nom.sg.
groma/d/+a	grom[dn]y	'herd' nom.sg./ adj.masc.nom.sg.
obro/n/+a	obro[nn]y	'defense' nom.sg./ adj.masc.nom.sg.
rodzi/n/+a	rodzi[nn]y	'family' nom.sg./ adj.masc.nom.sg.
komple/t/	komple[tn]y	'complete (group)' nom.sg./ adj.masc.nom.sg.
prostoką/t/	prostoką[tn]y	'rectangle' nom.sg./ adj.masc.nom.sg.
poko/r/+a	poko[rn]y	'humility' nom.sg./adj. nom.sg.
pa/r/+a	pa[rn]y	'steam' nom.sg./adj.nom.sg.

The examples in (346) indicate a crucial difference between /z, s/ and /ł/ on the one hand and /t, d, n, r/ on the other. While the first set undergoes palatalization when followed by a suffix with an initial sonorant, as in (346)a, the latter set remains unpalatalized, as in (346)b.

Further, alveolar fricatives sometimes assimilate their place of articulation to the place of articulation of the following consonant. Consider the examples shown in (347), in which the outputs of suffixation by -e (loc.sg.) are shown.

(347)

mia/st/o	mie[śt^{ś}]+e	'town' nom.sg./loc.sg.
mo/st/	mo[śt^{ś}]+e	'bridge' nom.sg./loc.sg.
ja/zd/a	je[źd^{ź}]+e	'travel' nom.sg./loc.sg.
/s/e/n/	[śń]+e	'dream' nom.sg./loc.sg.

What can be gleaned from the examples in (347) is that /s z/ assimilate to the place features of the following alveolo-palatal noncontinuant.

Another context in which the place assimilation of fricatives is attested is illustrated by the examples in (348). [157]

(348)

po/st/	po[št^{š}]+ę	'fast' nom.sg./'to fasten' 1ps.sg.pres.
chło/st/a	chło[št^{š}]+ę	'flogging' nom.sg./ 'to flog' 1ps.sg.pres.
mó/zg /	mó[žd^{ž}]+ek	'brain' nom.sg./'brain' dim.nom.sg.

[157] The final three examples in (348) end in an underlying /k/ or /g/ which are subject to First Velar Palatalization, presented in 4.3.2.

drobia/zg/	drobia[žd^{ž}]+ek	'trinket' nom.sg./'trinket' dim. nom.sg.
wrza/sk/	wrze[št^{š}]+ę	'scream' nom.sg./'to scream' 1ps.sg.pres.

The examples in (348) show that the fricatives /s/ and /z/ assimilate also to the place features of retroflex affricates. Although I will not discuss the data in (347) and (348) it has to be stressed that in contrast to data shown below they are not optional because they are result of palatalization by palatalizing suffixes.

There is only a handful of words which show that /t, d, n/ do not undergo palatalization when they are followed by another consonant in the same word. For example, motto 'motto' nom.sg. is pronounced as mo[tt^{ś}]e loc.sg., Wanda 'Wanda' nom.sg. as Wa[nd^{ź}]e loc.sg., pro[nt] as pro[nd^{ź}]e 'current' nom.sg., Budda 'Budda' nom.sg. as Bu[dd^{ź}]e loc.sg. All words, however, can be optionally pronounced as mo[t^{ś}t^{ś}]e, Wa[ńd^{ź}]e, pro[ńd^{ź}]e and Bu[d^{ź}d^{ź}]e, respectively.

The optional pronunciation of /t d/ is accounted for by a rule which affects alveolar strident coronals. The rule is called Strident Assimilation by Rubach (1994), cf. also Wierzchowska (1971). In (349) it is shown in which contexts alveolar strident coronals are optionally affected by Strident Assimilation, cf. Rubach (1994:137).

(349)

a. s z → š ž / __ š ž t^{š} d^{ž}
ś ź / __ ś ź t^{ś} d^{ź}

b. t^{s} d^{z} → t^{š} d^{ž} / __ š ž t^{š} d^{ž}
t^{ś} d^{ź} / __ ś ź t^{ś} d^{ź}

c. t d → t^{š} d^{ž} / __ š ž t^{š} d^{ž}
t^{ś} d^{ź} / __ ś ź t^{ś} d^{ź}

d. t d → t^{s} d^{z} / __ s z t^{s} d^{z}

All rules presented in (349) apply within and across word-boundaries.

Apart from the cases presented in (347) and (348), fricatives undergo palatalization when they are followed by other consonants than those presented above. In (350) examples are presented in which fricatives /s/ and /z/ change their place of articulation when they are followed by palatalized labials. Note that palatalization is induced by different palatalizing suffixes.

(350)

romanty[zm]	romanty[źm']+e	'Romanticism' nom.sg./ 'Romanticism' dat.sg.
uniwersali[zm]	uniwerali[źm']+e	'universalism' nom.sg./ 'universalism' dat.sg.
[sp]ać	[śp']+ący	'to sleep' inf. / 'sleepy' masc.nom.sg.
[sp]ać	[śp']+i	'to sleep' inf. / 'to sleep' 3ps. nom.sg. masc.
pi[sm]o	pi[śm']+e	'writing' nom.sg./ 'writing' loc.sg.

The behavior of the fricatives in (350) indicates that their primary place of articulation does not assimilate to the place of assimilation of the following consonant, e.g. /zm/→*[vm]. Instead they agree with the following consonant with respect to the palatalizing feature only. However, it has to be stressed that there exist words in which fricatives do not undergo palatalization. Consider the examples listed in (351).

(351)

i[zb]a	i[zb']e	'room' nom.sg./ 'room' dat.sg.
wy[sp]a	wy[sp']e	'island' nom.sg./ 'island' dat.sg.
za[sp]a	za[sp']e	'snow-drift' nom.sg./ 'snow-drift' dat.sg.
o[sp]a	o[sp']e	'chicken-pox' nom.sg./ 'chicken-pox' dat.sg.

The examples in (351) require further comment. As stressed earlier in this section, palatalization is not induced by front vowels or a glide /j/ in morpheme-internal position, as opposed to Old Polish, in which palatalization was triggered by front vowels and a glide /j/ regardless of their position.[158] In present-day Polish the outputs of diachronic palatalization processes, /ś/ and /ź/, are phonemic, i.e., they are underlying alveolo-palatal fricatives. For example, *siano* [ś]ano 'hay' nom.sg. is underlying /ś/ano and *ziemia* [ź]emia 'earth' nom.sg. is represented as /ź/emia. Alveolar fricatives cannot be posited here since palatalization, as already stated, is only triggered by suffixes that contain a palatalizing floating feature. Clearly, if /s/ or /z/ occur morpheme-internally in relatively new words or borrowings, these phonemes must remain as they are. This is supported by the pronunciation of the borrowings such as [sl]im-fast 'slim-fast' nom.sg. or [sl]ip 'marine railway' nom.sg., in which fricatives do not undergo palatalization.

In summary, the coronals in the examples provided in 4.2.5 and 4.2.6 behave differently with respect to palatalization. Although all of them undergo palatalization when they are followed by a palatalizing suffix with an initial vowel, only the fricatives /s/ /z/ are palatalized when they are followed by consonant-initial palatalizing suffixes. The fricatives /s/ /z/ change their place of primary articulation to [ś] and [ź] if the following consonant becomes an alveolo-palatal or to [ž] and [š] if the following consonant changes to a retroflex (postalveolar) as a result of palatalization. In contrast to the fricatives, the lateral /ł/ does not undergo palatalization in clusters as readily as the fricatives do. In some contexts it does not change its featural content even if it is followed by palatalizing suffixes. The noncontinuants /t, d, n/ do not palatalize when they are followed by laterals or nasals. In other words, the sequences of alveolo-palatal noncontinuants and coronal sonorants are avoided. The most marked segment is /r/, which does not palatalize before any consonants, cf. also Hall (1998), Walsh Dickey (1997). The results of the investigation lead to establishing a markedness hierarchy of coronals with respect to their behavior in different palatalizing contexts. The investigated segments can be ranked from the least marked to the most marked in the following way: /s/ /z/ < /ł/ < /t/ /d/ /n/ < /r/.

[158] This process is discussed from a diachronic point of view in 4.2.7.

4.2.7 Palatalization of coronals from a diachronic point of view

In Late Common Slavic coronals /t d n l r s z/ had begun to undergo palatalization in the environment of front vowels such as /i e ę ě ь/ and syllabic /r̥' l̥'/.[159] Palatalization manifested itself with a secondary articulation while keeping the primary place of articulation intact, i.e. the coronals under consideration were realized as [t'], [d'], [n'], [l'], [r'],[160][s'], and [z'], respectively.

However, after some vocalic changes went into effect, as e.g. a change from /e/ to /o/, from /ě/ to /a/ and from /ę/ to /ą/, the palatalized coronals occurred not only before front vowels but also before back ones. Examples are provided (352), cf. Stieber (1966:12f).

(352)

kos[t']el → kos[t']oł	'church' nom.sg./nom.sg.
[s']estrze → [s']ostra	'sister' dat.sg./nom.sg.,
[st']enie → [st']ana	'wall' dat.sg./nom.sg.
[n']esiesz → [n']osę	'to carry' 2ps.sg.pres./1ps.sg.pres.

After these changes the secondarily palatalized sounds became phonemes since they were not positionally conditioned. Thus, in the eleventh century the coronal consonantal inventory consisted of the set of coronals shown in (353), [161] cf. Stieber (1973: 33).

(353) The consonantal inventory of coronals in the eleventh century

t, t', d, d', t^{s}, d^{z}, $t^{š}$, ($d^{ž}$),[162] s, s', z, z', š, ž, n, n', r, r', l, l'

In the second half of the twelfth century the context-free change of the plosives /t'/, /d'/ to the affricates [$d^{ź}$] and [$t^{ś}$] had already started (d' t' → $d^{ź}$ $t^{ś}$). All instances of /r'/ (from Common Slavic *rj and from r followed by a front vowel) had begun to change to [ř]. This process seems to date from the thirteenth century, cf. Stieber (1973:49). It is, however, difficult to determine when the change from /s'/, /z'/ to [ś] and [ź] started. Generally, the variation in the pronunciation of various sounds occur from the second half of the twelfth century until the sixteenth century.

The consonants /š, ž, t^{s}, d^{z}, $t^{š}$, $d^{ž}$/, outputs of the first and the second velar palatalization, were also palatalized allophonically when they were followed by front vowels. This is confirmed by the spellings found in some manuscripts from the fourteenth and fifteenth centuries in which the palatalization of a consonant preceding a vowel is

---

[159] For the further development of /r̥' l̥'/ cf. Stieber (1966:52-60).

[160] According to Carlton (1991:113) d', t', n', l', r' had already existed as reflexes of the former clusters in Common Slavic, *tj, *dj, *nj, *lj, *rj. Cf. also Stieber (1973: 14)

[161] At that time reflexes of the first and the second velar palatalization, š, ž, t^{s}, d^{z}, $t^{š}$, $d^{ž}$, had already existed, cf. Rospond (1971:108).

[162] The occurrence of $d^{ž}$ was restricted to the context after ž. For this reason, Stieber (1973:15) does not assign it a phonemic status.

marked by the letter /y/. In "The Psalter of St. Florian" from the late fourteenth century, the forms *wprzyebytkoch* 'in sanctuaries' and *wewszyey szemy* 'all over the earth' are attested which directly indicate palatalization of /ž/ and /š/, cf. Stieber (1973:65). Since the spellings of palatalized /š, ž, t^{s}, d^{z}, $t^{š}$, $d^{ž}$/ in various manuscripts are inconsistent, we do not know exactly when the palatalization of these sounds disappeared. According to Stieber (1973:66) in the middle of the fifteenth century they had not yet lost their palatalization all over Poland, especially when followed by /i/.

The stable system of /s, ś, z, ź, š, ž, d^{z}, $t^{š}$, $d^{ž}$, $t^{ś}$/ was established not earlier than in the middle of the 16th century. At that time the consonantal system consisted of the coronals presented in (354), cf. Stieber (1996:62).

(354) The consonantal inventory of coronals in the mid-sixteenth century

t, d, t^{s}, d^{z}, $t^{š}$, $d^{ž}$, $t^{ś}$, s, ś, z, ź, š, ž, n, ń, r, ř, ł, l'

The changes presented above support the generalization that certain complex structures are prone to disappear earlier than other less complex ones. Since sounds which are pronounced with a secondary articulation are generally more marked than sounds produced at one place of articulation, the markedness of secondarily palatalized coronals was reduced by abandoning a secondary articulation. In many cases such a reduction led directly to the change of the main place of articulation, cf. (355)a, while in others (retroflexes and alveolar affricates) the secondary articulation was simply elided, cf. (355)b.

(355)

a. t' d' → $d^{ź}$ $t^{ś}$
s' z' → ś ź
r' → ř

b. š' ž' → š ž
t^{s}' d^{z}' → t^{s} d^{z}
$t^{š}$' $d^{ž}$' → $t^{š}$ $d^{ž}$

Phonologically, the markedness of secondary palatalized phonemes is represented by complex structures such as those presented in (356)a, cf. Hume (1992) or in (356)b, cf. Clements (1991).

(356)

a.

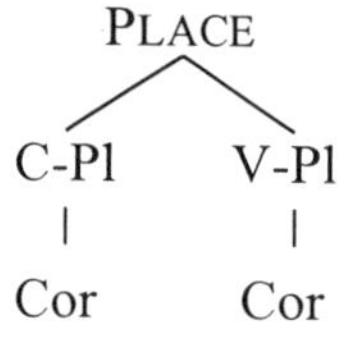

b.

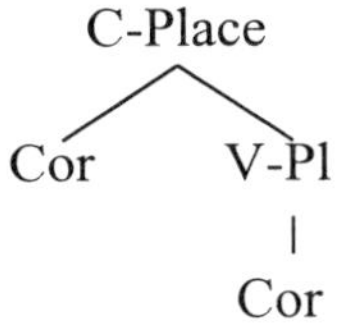

Accounting for the changes presented above in terms of constraints, we may posit a constraint that prohibits complex structures. Its general and specific formulation is given in (357), cf. Prince and Smolensky (1993:179ff).

(357)

a. A general constraint:
NONCOMP: Do not have structurally complex places of articulation.

b. Specific Instantiation:
*[Cor, Pal]: Do not have a secondarily palatalized coronal.

Since the following analyses concern *palatalized coronals*, we adopt the constraint presented in (357)b. A constraint that directly conflicts with *[Cor, Pal] is stated in (358). IDENT [Cor, Pal] requires a secondary articulation of palatalized coronals in the input to be faithfully parsed into the output.

(358)

IDENT [Cor, Pal]: A secondary articulation of coronals present underlyingly must be retained on the surface.

Both constraints, IDENT [Cor, Pal] and *[Cor, Pal], are directly responsible for processes sketched above. For example, the changes from /d'/, /t'/ to /d^{ź} /, /t^{ś}/ involve three stages, each of which shows a different constraint interaction. In the first stage the high-ranking constraint IDENT [Cor, Pal][163] is responsible for selecting the first candidate in (359) as the optimal one since it is the only output that does not incur any violation of IDENT [Cor, Pal]. The second candidate, in which coronals appear without a secondary articulation, is ruled out due to a violation of IDENT [Cor, Pal]. This is illustrated by the tableau in (359).[164]

[163] This is a general version of the Ident constraint forcing a faithful parse of a secondary articulation of coronals. Since the changes discussed above affected various coronals at different times, Cor should be specified for its featural content for every coronal segment.

[164] In the following tableaus only /d/ will be analyzed for reasons mentioned earlier. Note that n' is a secondarily palatalized (anterior) n while ń is an alveolo-palatal sound.

(359)

1st stage: until the second half of the twelfth century

d'en'	IDENT [Cor, Pal]	*[Cor, Pal]
☞ d'en'		*
$d^{ź}$eń	*!	

As already stated, from the second half of the twelfth century, the plosives /t'/ and /d'/ began to be pronounced as the affricates [$d^{ź}$] and [$t^{ś}$], respectively. According to Stieber (1973:48), "for a century or longer the sounds t' and $t^{ś}$ may have coexisted as optional variants of the phoneme t', as well as d' and $d^{ź}$ as variants of d." Hence, from the second half of the twelfth century to approximately the end of the thirteenth century, two variants of /t'/ and /d'/, namely [$d^{ź}$] and [$t^{ś}$], are attested. In terms of constraints, this is a consequence of a tie between IDENT [Cor, Pal] and *[Cor, Pal], a situation which is shown in (360).[165]

(360)

2nd stage: from the second half of the 12th century to the end of the 13 th century

d'en'	IDENT [Cor, Pal]	*[Cor, Pal]
☞ d'en'		*
☞ $d^{ź}$eń	*	

The lack of a crucial ranking between IDENT [Cor, Pal] and *[Cor, Pal] resulted in the optional pronunciation of /d'/: with a secondary articulation [d'], or as an affricate [$d^{ź}$].

At the end of the thirteenth century the affrication of secondarily palatalized plosives was accomplished. The constraint *[Cor, Pal], prohibiting a secondary articulation of coronals, became higher ranked than IDENT [Cor, Pal]. Therefore, complex sounds were not tolerable any longer and affricates always emerged as optimal. This is illustrated by the tableau in (361).

(361)

3rd stage: from the end of the 13th century

d'en'	*[Cor, Pal]	IDENT[Cor, Pal]
d'en'	*!	
☞ $d^{ź}$eń		*

Different coronals underwent depalatalization at different times. As mentioned earlier, /r'/ (from Common Slavic *rj and from r followed by a front vowel) had begun to change into [ř] in the thirteenth century, cf. Stieber (1973:49). The phoneme ř (also

165 The candidate *den* is not considered here, since it is immediately excluded due to a high-ranking constraint that prohibits nonpalatalized consonants followed by front vowels.

written as ŕ)[166] did not change its place of articulation until the eighteenth century, cf. Stieber (1966:69). Due to the different times in which changes under consideration were accomplished, a unified account of them is impossible. Therefore, *[Cor, Pal] is to be further specified in terms of its featural content as mentioned in note 163.

Some remarks concerning the historical development of palatalization of coronals in consonant clusters are in order. Recall that after the loss of jers, cf. the analyses in chapter 2, new consonant clusters were created. If a jer disappeared in the first syllable of a word, a new onset cluster arose. In cases in which a jer was lost in a noninitial or nonfinal syllable, a new consonant cluster was broken up by a syllable boundary. Finally, if a jer disappeared in the final syllable of the word, a new coda cluster emerged. Consider the examples shown in (362), which illustrate the outputs of palatalization of coronals in different positions in a word when followed by a front jer.[167] Most probably the consonants were not palatalized immediately but underwent the same development as coronals occurring in other positions, cf. also (359), (360), and (361).

(362)

* go/rь/ki → go[ř]ki	'bitter' masc.nom.sg.	£oś (1922: 171)
* gro/zь/ba → gro[ź]ba	'threat' nom.sg.	£oś (1922: 171)
* bole/st'ь/ → bole[śt^ś]	'pain' nom.sg.	£oś (1922: 207)
* prija/znь/ → przyja[źń]	'friendship' nom.sg.	£oś (1922: 207)
* /tь/ma→[t^ś]ma	'moth' nom.sg.	Długosz-Kurczabowa and Dubisz (1993:74)

As indicated in the examples *bole/st'ь/ → bole[śt^ś] and *prija/znь/ → przyja[źń] palatalization must have spread from the last palatalized coronal to the preceding

---

166 The development of r' (ŕ) from rj or r+ i, e, ě, ь, ę merits special attention. A secondary articulation of r' changes it into the fricative ž, hence r' was pronounced as r^ž (ř), cf. r'→r^ž. Furthermore the fricative secondary articulation gradually became stronger than the primary articulation. Finally the primary articulation was entirely abandoned and the sound was pronounced as ž, cf. Rospond (1971:115, 116). Schematically this change can be represented in the following way :

r'(ŕ)→ř(r^ž)→ž

According to Rospond (1971:116) r^ž was pronounced until the end of the eighteenth century. Finally, most probably in the first half of the nineteenth century, only ž was pronounced. Note that in Modern Czech ř(r^ž) exists as a phoneme.

Interestingly, these changes are mirrored in spellings in various manuscripts where /r^ž/ was rendered orthographically as rz and /ž/ as ż. The difference in spelling is also attested in Modern Polish, although there is no difference in the pronunciation. Consider the following examples:

	Pronunciation	Spelling	
zo[r^ž]e→	zo[ž]e	zorze	'dawn' nom.pl.
mo[ž]e →	mo[ž]e	może	'perhaps'
ko[r^ž]e →	ko[ž]e	korze	'bark' loc.sg.

167 Recall that palatalization was induced only by front jers, while back jers did not have any effect on the preceding consonant.

coronal fricative /s/ or /z/, cf. assimilation of fricatives in Modern Polish shown in (347).

Interestingly, /t d n/ and /r/ did not undergo palatalization after the loss of a front jer if the following consonant was a coronal sonorant. They simply lost their secondary palatalization. Additionally /r/ was depalatalized before any coronal consonant. Consider the examples shown in (363).

(363)

* věr'ьny → věr'ny → v'ěrny	'faithful' masc.nom.sg.	£oś (1922: 24)
* běr'ьny → běr'ny → běrny	'passive' masc.nom.sg.	£oś (1922: 33)
* t'ьnǫ → t'no̦ → t'nę	'to cut' 1ps.sg. pres.	Długosz-Kurczabowa and Dubisz (1993:122)
* d'ьne → d'ńe → dńe	'day' instr.sg.	Długosz-Kurczabowa and Dubisz (1993:122)

The examples presented in (363) also display an intermediate stage in which secondarily palatalized noncontinuant coronals existed before coronal sonorants.

Note that there is a crucial difference between the outputs of the change of /t'/, /d'/ when they are followed by sonorant consonants, and when they appear in other contexts. In the first case it is plain [t] and [d], cf. (363), while in the second it is [t^{ś}] and [d^{ź}], cf. t'en' → [t^{ś}eń], d'en' → [d^{ź}]eń. This process clearly resembles the depalatalization of noncontinuants, discussed in 4.2.5. In terms of constraints, we conclude that the high-ranking constraint NonCont, cf. (328), did not allow noncontinuants to be palatalized before coronal sonorants, while Faith (rC), cf. (341), prohibited palatalization of /r/ before sonorant coronals.

In summary, the palatalization of coronals from a diachronic point of view provides evidence for the claim that more complex structures, i.e. secondarily palatalized consonants, are reduced earlier than less complex ones. The loss of a secondary articulation is compensated in most cases with a change in place of articulation. Sounds such as /t, d, n, r/ do not undergo palatalization when they are followed by sonorant coronals. This is in contrast to the behavior of coronal continuants such as /s/ and /z/, which not only undergo palatalization in the context of front vowels but also assimilate to following alveolo-palatals with respect to palatalization.

4.2.8 Coronal fricatives and affricates in Polish dialects

The realization of coronal fricatives and affricates in various Polish dialects constitutes a very interesting issue with respect to markedness which shows that (i) the system of coronals is very complex and therefore avoided by speakers in various ways and (ii) some coronals are more marked than others in terms of their articulation.

Recall that the consonantal inventory of Modern Standard Polish consists of the following coronal fricatives and affricates, cf. (364).

(364)

	Alveolars	Retroflexes (Postalveolars)	Alveolo-palatals (Prepalatals)
Fricatives	s z	š ž	ś ź
Affricates	t^{s} d^{z}	$t^{š}$ $d^{ž}$	$t^{ś}$ $d^{ź}$

The system in (364) is, however, considerably reduced in various dialects in different ways. In the following, three manners of realization of this system are demonstrated.

In dialects spoken in Mazovia (except the extreme northeast), in Małopolska (except the areas between the rivers Wisłok i San, the Upper Wieprz and Bug) and in northern Silesia[168] all retroflexes (postalveolars) are realized as alveolars. The context-free historical change that converted retroflexes to the corresponding alveolars is illustrated in (365).

(365)

š ž $t^{š}$ $d^{ž}$ → s z t^{s} d^{z}

This phenomenon is one of the most important characteristics of the well-known *mazurzenie* [mazužeńe] 'Mazovianism', which derives its name from Mazovia, the area where the change is attested. Some examples illustrating *mazurzenie* are shown in (366).

(366)

Standard Polish	Mazovian	
[ž]yto	[z]yto	'rye' nom.sg.
[$t^{š}$]as	[t^{s}]as	'time' nom.sg.
[š$t^{š}$]ekać	[st^{s}]ekać	'to bark' inf.

There is no consensus in the literature as to when exactly this process has been started and accomplished. Stieber (1973: 60) claims that /š ž $t^{š}$ $d^{ž}$/ had already changed into /s z t^{s} d^{z}/ by the fifteenth century.[169] According to Brajerski (1954) the process dates back into the thirteenth century because the alveolo-palatals ś ź $t^{ś}$ $d^{ź}$ entered the dialect. The process was accomplished in the fifteenth century by depalatalization of sounds transcribed as / š́ ž́ $t^{š}$ $d^{ž}$ $t^{s'}$ $d^{z'}$/.[170] (It is difficult to determine what the symbols š ž $t^{š}$ $d^{ž}$ mean phonetically. They are commonly described as an intermediate stage between retroflexes and alveolo-palatals. I assume that they are palatalized retroflexes).

In addition, in the Kashubian dialect spoken in the northern part of Poland,[171] the alveolo-palatal fricatives and affricates of Standard Polish /ś ź $t^{ś}$ $d^{ź}$/ are realized as dentals, [s z t^{s} d^{z}], respectively. Consider the examples shown in (367).

---

168 The exact geographical areas are shown in 7.2.2 in the appendix.

169 Cf. also Kuryłowicz (1954), Rospond (1954), Taszycki (1954), who deal with various issues directly connected with *mazurzenie*.

170 Cf. also explanations given by Hall (1997b) for Sanscrit.

171 Cf. the maps in 7.2.2 in appendix.

(367)

Standard Polish	Kashubian[172]	
[śt^{ś}]ana	[st^{s}]auna	'wall' nom.sg.
[d^{ź}]ik	[d^{z}]ek	'boar' nom.sg.
[ś]miesznie	[s]misznie	'ridiculous'

From the diachronic point of view the change from /ś ź t^{ś} d^{ź} / to /s z t^{s} d^{z}/ never took place in Kashubian. It is commonly assumed that the secondarily palatalized /s' z' t' d'/, which in Standard Polish changed to /ś ź t^{ś} d^{ź}/, were at some point depalatalized in Kashubian, cf. Stieber (1973:140). If this is correct then it follows that there must have been a stage at which secondarily palatalized dental affricates [t$^{s'}$ d$^{z'}$], derived from /t'/ and /d'/, occurred. These sounds must have subsequently been depalatalized to [t^{s} d^{z}].

Finally, in the dialects spoken in the northeastern regions of Poland (around Malbork, Ostróda, Lubawa and eastern Warmia) and in the small area in the southern part of Poland (around Jabłonków)[173] neither retroflexes nor alveolo-palatal fricatives and affricates are attested. Both series, /š ž t^{š} d^{ž} / and /ś ź t^{ś} d^{ź}/, merged into an intermediate one. In the Polish literature the outputs of this merge are symbolized as š́ ž́ t$^{š́}$ d$^{ž́}$ (Dejna 1994:71), cf. (368).

(368)

š ž t^{š} d^{ž} →
š́ ž́ t$^{š́}$ d$^{ž́}$
ś ź t^{ś} d^{ź} →

In (369) relevant examples illustrating outputs of this merger are shown, cf. Dejna (1994:71).

(369)

Standard Polish	Jabłonków & Mazurian dialects	
[ž]yto	[ž́]yto	'rye' nom.sg.
[t^{š}]as	[t$^{š́}$]as	'time' nom.sg.
[š]are	[š́]are	'grey' neut.nom.sg.
[ś]ano	[š́]ano	'hay'nom.sg.

Interestingly, minimal pairs occurring in Standard Polish such as ka[š]a 'grits' nom.sg. vs. Ka[ś]a 'Katarzyna' proper name, dim.nom.sg. are most probably not distinguished in these dialects. If this is indeed the case then we are faced with a clear example of precedence of economy of articulation over other economies, cf. the discussion in 1.3.3.

172 The Kashubian dialect also underwent various vowel changes. They are described by Topolińska (1974) in detail.

173 Cf. maps in 7.2.2 in the appendix.

The facts presented above show that the system of coronal fricatives and affricates in Standard Polish is marked in terms of a high number of different phonemes realized at closely related places of articulation. Therefore, dialects dispense with this complicated system by reducing three sets to two sets. The most modified sounds are retroflexes which can be considered as indirect evidence that they are more marked than other coronals.

4.3 Velars

In contrast to coronals, the number of velars in the phonemic inventory of Polish is rather small, cf. 4.2. It consists of two velar plosives /k/ and /g/ and a velar fricative /x/. All three segments have secondarily palatalized counterparts, i.e. k', g', x', whose phonemic status is controversial. Some scholars like Laskowski (1975:20), and Rubach (1984:26) do not recognize secondarily palatalized velars as phonemes, while others, e.g., Sawicka (1974:67), Bethin (1992:19) and Szpyra (1995:185) assume just the opposite. An intermediate solution is proposed by Stieber (1966:114) and Bargiełówna (1950:3) who claim that k' and g' are phonemic as opposed to x', which is not. In the reminder of this section I discuss this controversy.

The lack of consensus regarding the phonemic status of secondarily palatalized velars is revealed by different kinds of arguments. According to Gussmann (1980a:12) the presence of palatalization is dependent on the context, i.e. velars undergoing a rule he calls Surface Level Palatalization are realized as [k'], [g'] and [x'], cf. Gussmann (1980a:12); Surface Level Palatalization invariably palatalizes /k/ and /g/ before /e i/ and the fricative /x/ before /i/, cf. (385). This rule does not apply across word-boundaries, cf. 4.3.2. Hence, k', g', x' are allophones and not phonemes.

Rubach (1984:35) claims that there is a cyclic rule called Labio-Velar Palatalization which inserts /j/ after noncoronals and before /e/. The outputs of this rule are later affected by a general late phonetic rule called Surface Palatalization which triggers the palatalization of any consonant inside words and across word boundaries before /i j/, cf. Rubach (1984:25). For illustration, consider the single steps in the derivation of /krok/+/em/ 'step' instr.nom. shown in (370), cf. Rubach (1984:175).

(370)

krok+em	
krok+jem	j-insertion
krok'+jem	Surface Palatalization
krok'+em	j-deletion (variable)[174]

In the same vein, stem-final /g/ and /x/ are palatalized via j-insertion and Surface Palatalization.

---

174 Since palatalized velars are pronounced either as [k'je] [g'je] or [k'e] [g'e] j-deletion is optional.

Native words which contain palatalized velars morpheme-internally, cf. (371), and therefore cannot be subject to the cyclic j-insertion, are claimed to have sequences of /kj/ and /gj/ in the underlying representation. Consequently, Rubach (1984) argues that palatalized velars are not part of the underlying inventory of Polish but are present only when they are followed by /j/ that occurs morpheme-internally or is inserted in the course of the derivation. Optionally, they can be pronounced as [kj].

(371)

[k']eszeń	'pocket' nom.sg.
[k']edy	'when'
[k']erować	'to direct' inf.

According to Stieber (1966:114) g' is phonemic because of its unpredictable occurrences in words like z[g']ąć 'to bend' inf. or wy[g']ąć 'to bend' inf.[175] Additionally, there are 'minimal pairs' like those in (372), which argue for the phonemic status of g' and k', cf. Stieber (1996:114) and Bargiełówna (1950:3).

(372)

dro[g]ę	dro[g']e	'way' acc.sg./ 'expensive' nom.pl.
Pols[k]ę	pols[k']e	'Poland' acc.sg./ 'Polish' nom.pl.

However, the lack of palatalization in the examples shown in the left-hand column in (372) can be accounted for by a general restriction in Polish according to which nasal vowels block palatalization. This objection was also taken into consideration by Stieber (1966:114), who defends the phonemic status of /k'/ and /g'/ in (372) by arguing that the nasal vowels are pronounced as oral ones, i.e. Pols[ke] 'Poland' acc.sg. and dro[ge] 'way' acc.sg. This pronunciation is, however, found mainly in dialects, cf. 4.3.5. More importantly, it will be shown that the palatalized velars in dro[g']e and pols[k']e in (372) are not underlying, but that their palatalization is triggered by the suffix /e/

---

[175] Both words are derived from *giąć* 'to bend.' Although they might be used in different contexts, they have nearly the same meaning.
This peculiar example is often explained by analogy to verb forms like piąć 'to climb up' and miąć 'to crumple.' From a diachronic point of view the verbs under consideration had the following forms:

*pьną:*pęti: *pęlъ	'to climb up' 1p.sg.pres./inf./3p.sg.past.masc.
*mьną:*męti: *męlъ	'to crumple' 1p.sg.pres./inf./3p.sg.past.masc.
*gъbną:*gъbnąti: * gъbnąlъ	'to bend' 1p.sg.pres./inf./3p.sg.past.masc.

Consequently, after the loss of jers and other changes discussed in chapter 2 the first two verbs showed up in the following forms:
pnę: piąć: piął
mnę: miąć: miął
From the structures of the third verb, forms such as gbnę: gbnąć: gbnął were expected. However, they changed to gnę: giąć: giął, which used to be explained by analogy to the first two forms, cf. Klemensiewicz at al. (1955:135). Additionally, this change might be accounted for by the tendency of monosyllabic words to avoid clusters in onsets by metathesis, cf. 2.3.2.

(nom.pl). Hence, the only argument for regarding g' as a phoneme is the single item z[g']ąć (wy[g']ąć) 'to bend' inf. A similar example with k' is, however, not attested.

According to Sawicka (1974:68), who recognizes the phonemic status of x', the motivation for postulating x' as a phoneme is that [x'] contrast with [x] in some assimilated foreign words, cf. herbata [xe]rbata 'tee' nom.sg. and hierarchia [x'e]rarchia 'hierarchy' nom.sg.

Szpyra (1995) provides a different argument in favor of the phonemic status of k', g', x'. She justifies the presence of underlying palatalized velars by morphological facts. She shows that the system of Polish inflection makes a distinction between hard and soft stems. This is illustrated by examples shown in (373)a and (373)b, in which the hard stems take the inflectional suffix -/e/, while the desinence -/i/ attaches to soft stems. Both desinences express the dative and locative case of singular feminine nouns, cf. Szpyra (1995:176).

(373)

a.

to[g]a	to[dz]e	'gown' nom.sg./loc.sg.
mą[k]a	mą[t^s]e	'flour' nom.sg./loc.sg.
mu[x]a	mu[š]e	'fly' nom.sg./loc.sg.

b.

biolo[g']a	biolo[g']i	'biology' nom.sg./loc.sg.
anar[x']a	anar[x']i	'anarchy'nom.sg./loc.sg.
autar[k']a	autar[k']i	'autarchy' nom.sg./loc.sg.

It should be pointed out that all words in (373)b are of foreign origin. Although they are assmilated to a native vocabulary, their phonemic status might still be questioned.

From the arguments presented above it follows that the status of k', g', and x' is by no means clear. For now, we leave the question of the phonemic status of palatalized velars open, but we will come back to this issue in 4.3.3.

4.3.1 The distribution of velar obstruents

In this subsection I discuss the distribution of velar obstruents in Modern Polish. It will be shown that there are plain velars attested in onsets, codas and consonant clusters, i.e. when they are followed by other consonants, while secondarily palatalized velars occur exclusively in onset position. This distribution is similar to the distribution of labials, cf. 4.1.1 and 4.1.6.

Plain velars as well as their palatalized counterparts occur widely in one-member onsets. They are found word-initially and word-internally, cf. (374)a and (374)b. The only context in which plain velar plosives are not attested is before the central high unrounded vowel [ɨ]; sequences of the type [kɨ] and [gɨ] are thus prohibited.[176] In native

[176] There exist two idiosyncratic exceptions to this statement, i.e. [kɨ]nologia, 'cynology'nom.sg. and the interjection [kɨ]sz 'away!'.

words palatalized velar plosives occur exclusively before /i/ and /e/. This is discussed in detail in 4.3.3. In a handful of foreign words palatalized velar plosives /k g/ are also found before other vowels than /i/ or /e/, e.g. [k']osk 'kiosk' nom.sg. or [g']aur 'giaour' nom.sg.

As far as the velar fricative /x/ is concerned, it has to be stressed that in native words only the plain [x] occurs in onsets, cf. (374a). As mentioned above, the palatalized velar fricative [x'] occurs exclusively in words of foreign origin, cf. (374b). For the development of [x'] from a diachronic point of view see 4.3.4.

(374)

a.

[k]aczka	'duck' nom.sg.
[k]oło	'circle' nom.sg.
[g]ołąb	'pigeon' nom.sg.
[g]ęś	'goose' nom.sg.
[x]ałas	'noise' nom.sg.
[x]ełm	'helmet' nom.sg.
mat[k]a	'mother' nom.sg.
dro[g]a	'way' nom.sg.
dru[x]a	'scout' gen.sg.

b.

[g']ełda	'stock-exchange' nom.sg.
[g']erka	'game' dim.nom.sg.
[k']edy	'when'
[k']eszeń	'pocket' nom.sg.
[x']acynt	'hyacinth' nom.sg.
[x']ena	'hyena' nom.sg.
mle[k']em	'milk' instr.sg.
brze[g']em	'shore' instr.sg.

Codas are exclusively occupied by plain velars while secondarily palatalized velars are not attested in these positions. In (375) examples are provided.

(375)

kro[k]	'step' nom.sg.
bra[k]	'lack' nom.sg.
móz/g/ móz[k]	'brain' nom.sg.
posa/g/ posa[k]	'dowry' nom.sg.
da[x]	'roof' nom.sg.
me[x]	'moss' nom.sg.

Stem-final velars undergo different types of palatalizations that in most cases result in a change of their place and manner of articulation, cf. 4.3.2. Only the outputs of Surface Velar Palatalization, cf. (385), are secondarily palatalized velars but they are resyllabified as onsets, e.g. kru[k] 'raven' nom.sg. vs. kru.[k']em 'raven' instr.sg. Hence, even in derived contexts no velars with a secondary palatalization are attested in coda position. The only case in which palatalized velars occur in the coda is Phrase-level Palatalization discussed in 4.3.3.

Plain velars also occur widely in consonant clusters. Interestingly, in cases when secondarily palatalized /k/ and /g/ are followed by other consonants they are never secondarily palatalized, cf. (376).

(376)

m[g']eł	m[g]ła	'fog' pl.gen./nom.sg.
i[g']eł	i[g]ła	'needle' pl.gen./nom.sg.
o[k']en	o[k]no	'window' pl.gen./ nom.sg.
[g']er	[g]ra	'play' pl.gen./ nom.sg.
[k']eł	[k]ła	'fang' sg.nom./gen.sg.
sz[k']eł	sz[k]ło	'glass' pl.gen./sg.nom.
jas[k']er	jas[k]ra	'buttercup' sg.nom./gen.nom.

The alternations in (376) suggests either (i) underlying palatalized velars that are depala-talized before a consonant, e.g. m/g'ł/a → [mgw]a, or (ii) underlying plain velars that palatalize before an epenthetic front vowel, e.g. m/gł/ → [mg'ew]. There are good reasons to believe that (ii) is correct.

The ad hoc conclusion that palatalized velars in (376) undergo depalatalization when they are followed by consonants is problematic. First, the context of occurrence of palatalized velars is restricted because all velars in (376) are invariably palatalized before a front vowel /e/. There are no plain velars followed by /e/ in alternations of this type which indicates that the palatalization is predictable. This observation suggests that the secondarily palatalized velars in (376) are plain underlyingly and since they are subject to Surface Velar Palatalization they do not undergo depalatalization when they are followed by consonants, as in the right-hand column in (376). It is also interesting to compare this alternation with the depalatalization of labials in clusters discussed in 4.1.6.

Before concluding this subsection let us consider a rule which is very important with regard to the issue just discussed, namely *Fronting*. This rule, shown in (377), derives [i] from /ɨ/ after velars, cf. Rubach (1984:153).[177]

(377)

ɨ → i /velar __

Condition: if /x/, then not in an inflectional morpheme

The motivation for the rule in (377) is found in the behavior of a considerable number of inflectional suffixes in which the underlying /ɨ/ is fronted to [i] after stem-final velar plosives. Consider the examples shown in (378), where in the right-hand column the

[177] In the cyclic approach Fronting applies after First Velar Palatalization in the cyclic-phonology, cf. (379).

nominative plural of masculine nonpersonal nouns is shown. The condition stated in (377) "if /x/, then not in an inflectional morpheme" is necessary because of the last two examples in (378b), in which *Fronting* does not apply since the vowel /ɨ/ is a part of the inflectional morpheme.

(378)

a.

grzy[b]	grzy[bɨ]	'mushroom' nom.sg./nom.pl.
gło[s]	gło[sɨ]	'voice' nom.sg./nom.pl.
to[r]	to[rɨ]	'track' nom.sg./nom.pl.
gła[z]	gła[zɨ]	'stone' nom.sg./nom.pl.

b.

kro[k]	kro[k'i]	'step' nom.sg./nom.pl.
brze[g]	brze[g'i]	'shore' nom.sg./nom.pl.
da[x]	da[xɨ]	'roof' nom.sg./nom.pl.
me[x]	m[xɨ]	'moss' nom.sg./nom.pl

In sum, plain velars widely occur in onsets, codas and consonant clusters. They are not found before the central high unrounded vowel [ɨ].

The presence of palatalized velars is attested only in (single-member) onsets where palatalized velar plosives are derived in the context of the following /i/ and /e/. If a velar is secondarily palatalized by an initial vowel of the suffix, it is resyllabified as an onset.[178] The palatalized velar fricative [x'] occurs only in foreign words, while in native words it is followed by the retracted vowel /ɨ/.

4.3.2 Three types of velar palatalization in present-day Polish

This subsection introduces various types of palatalization of velars in Polish. As already mentioned, velars are subject to different kinds of palatalization that depend on the context. Generally, three types of velar palatalization are attested, i.e., First Velar Palatalization, Second Velar Palatalization, and Surface Velar Palatalization. In the following, all of them are briefly presented.

First Velar Palatalization turns /k, g, x/ into postalveolars [$\mathrm{t}^{\check{s}}$, $\mathrm{d}^{\check{z}}$, š] in the context of following front vowels and glides, cf. Rubach (1984:112). Relevant examples are provided in (379), where stem-final velars are palatalized before a diminutival suffix -ek.

(379) First Velar Palatalization

człowie/k/	człowie[k]	człowie[$\mathrm{t}^{\check{s}}$]ek	'man' nom.sg./ dim.nom.sg.
ro/k/	ro[k]	ro[$\mathrm{t}^{\check{s}}$]ek	'year' nom.sg./dim.nom.sg.

178 This conclusion will be revised in the next subsection when Phrase-level Palatalization is discussed.

móz/g/	móz[k]	móż[$d^{\check{z}}$]ek	'brain' nom.sg./dim.nom.sg.
drobiaz/g/	drobiaz[k]	drobiaż[$d^{\check{z}}$]ek	'trinket' nom.sg./dim.nom.sg.
orze/x/	orze[x]	orze[š]ek	'nut' nom.sg./dim.nom.sg.
brzu/x/	brzu[x]	brzu[š]ek	'abdomen' nom.sg./dim.nom.sg.

First Velar Palatalization also changes the affricate [$d^{\check{z}}$], which is derived from the voiced plosive /g/, into the fricative [ž], if the plosive is preceded by a sonorant. This process is commonly known as Spirantization, cf. Rubach (1984:119). Consider the examples shown in (380).

(380)

brze/g/	brze[ž]ek	'shore'nom.sg./dim.nom.sg.
śnie/g/	śnie[ž]ek	'snow'nom.sg./dim.nom.sg.
ró/g/	ro[ž]ek	'horn' nom.sg./dim.nom.sg.
wil/g/otny	zwil[ž]yć	'moist' masc.nom.sg./ 'to moisten' inf.
skar/g/a	skar[ž]yć	'complaint' nom.sg./ 'to complain' inf.

In Rubach's derivational approach (1984: 110-115) First Velar Palatalization is regarded as a cyclic rule. In Optimality Theory an account of this process is provided by £ubowicz (1998).

Second Velar Palatalization takes place when stem-final velars are followed by front vowels in some grammatically specified contexts, i.e., before suffixes encoding the following properties: the nominal plural of masculine personal nouns and adjectives, the dative and the locative of singular feminine nouns and masculine nouns that have feminine declension, and adverbs, cf. Szpyra (1995: 191).

Second Velar Palatalization changes /k/ and /g/ into dental affricates [t^s] and [d^z]. The palatalization of the velar spirant /x/ is, however, indistinguishable from the results of the First Velar Palatalization, i.e. /x/ becomes /š/. In (381) outputs of the application of Second Velar Palatalization are illustrated.

(381) Second Velar Palatalization

dro[g]a	dro[d^z]e	'way' fem.nom.sg./dat.sg.
dro[g]i	dro[d^z]y	'dear' masc.nom.sg./masc.nom.pl.
wiel[k]a	wiel[t^s]e	'large' fem.nom.sg./ 'largely'
rze[k]a	rze[t^s]e	'river' nom.sg./dat.sg.
mu[x]a	mu[š]e	'fly' nom.sg./dat.sg.

Second Velar Palatalization as a cyclic rule is also regarded as a cyclic rule, cf. Rubach (1984:121-127). A detailed discussion of this process is irrelevant for the present study and therefore will be avoided here.

The last palatalization process affecting velars, the most important one for the purposes of the present study, is the so-called rule of Surface Velar Palatalization (SVP). According to Szpyra (1995:191) Surface Velar Palatalization turns plain velars into secondarily palatalized velars when they are followed by /i/ or /e/, cf. (382).

(382)

bru[k]	bru[k'i]	'pavement' nom.sg./nom.pl.
bra[k]	bra[k'i]	'lack' nom.sg./nom.pl.
kro[k]	kro[k'e]m	'step' nom.sg./instr.sg.
bie[g]	bie[g'e]m	'run' nom.sg./instr.sg.

Szpyra (1995:192) claims that the velar fricative /x/ does not undergo SVP because it is not found in contexts in which velar plosives undergo palatalization, cf. examples in (383) in comparison with those in (382).

(383)

podmu[x]	podmu[xɨ]	'breath' nom.sg./nom.pl.
brzu[x]	brzu[xɨ]	'abdomen' nom.sg./nom.pl.
śmie[x]	śmie[xe]m	'laughter' nom.sg./instr.sg.
me[x]	m[xe]m	'moss' nom.sg./instr.sg.

There are however suffixes with an initial high front vowel /i/ such as -iw, -ista, -izm, -ini which trigger the fronting of the velar fricative, cf. (384). Szpyra (1995:243) marks these cases as "positive exceptions to Surface Velar Palatalization."

(384)

sza[x']ista	'chess player' nom.sg.
monar[x']ista	'monarchist' nom.sg.
zdmu[x']iwać	'to blow away' inf.
nadsłu[x']iwać	'to prick up'inf.
kate[x']izm	'catechism' nom.sg.

Gussmann (1980:12) proposes that Surface Velar Palatalization applies to velar plosives before front vowels and to the velar fricative only before the front vowel /i/. In terms of Gussmann's features, this rule is stated as in (385).

(385)

$$\begin{bmatrix} \text{-anter} \\ \text{-coron} \\ \text{(+cont)} \end{bmatrix} \rightarrow \text{[-back]/} \_\_ \begin{bmatrix} \text{+syll} \\ \text{-back} \\ \text{(+high)} \end{bmatrix}$$

This rule accounts for the cases presented in (384), which no longer have to be treated as exceptions. Moreover, it also accounts for a considerable number of words in which a morpheme-internal fricative /x/ emerges as [x']. Its palatalization is predicted by the rule in (385). Relevant examples are shown in (386).

(386)

[x']ixot	'giggle' nom.sg.
[x']iny	'China' nom.pl.

[x’]istoria	‘history’ nom.sg.
[x’]igiena	‘hygiene’ nom.sg.

Nevertheless there are words which show an aberrant behavior, although they are subject to the rule in (385). Consider the examples are provided in (387).

(387)

a.	
[g]eneza	‘genesis’nom.sg.
[g]eniusz	‘genius’ nom.pl.
[k]efir	‘kefir’ nom.sg.
[k]elner	‘waiter’ nom.sg.
b.	
[g]ęsto	‘thickly’
[g]ęś	‘goose’ nom.sg.
[k]ęs	‘piece’ nom.sg.

Words in which velars are followed by the vowel /ę/ in (387)b are exempt from consideration since SVP is not conditioned by the nasal vowel, cf. examples in (372). The examples in (387)a do not undergo SVP because, according to Gussmann (1980), they are of foreign origin and “foreign words in general exhibit properties which very often serve to emphasize their foreignness” Gussmann (1980:12). We will postpone the discussion of this interesting issue to the next subsection.

Surface Velar Palatalization proposed by Gussmann does not apply across word-boundaries because word-final /k/ and /g/ are not palatalized before a word-initial /e/. The only context in which palatalized velars are found in word-final position is before the front vowel /i/ and the glide /j/ Consider examples shown in (388).

(388)

kro[k’] Jana	‘Jan’s step’
upade[k’] Ikara	‘Icharus’ fall’
twaró[g’] i mleko	‘cottage cheese and milk’
bie[g’] indywidualny	‘individual run’
nie[x’] idzie	‘she/he should go’

It is however not clear how Gussmann accounts for the data in (388). According to Rubach (1984:25) palatalization in (388) is due to Surface Palatalization as shown in (389) which palatalizes any consonant inside words and across word boundaries.

(389)

$$[+\text{cons}] \rightarrow \begin{bmatrix} +\text{high} \\ -\text{back} \end{bmatrix} \; / \; \_\_\_ \; ([-\ \text{seg}]) \begin{bmatrix} -\text{cons} \\ +\text{high} \\ -\text{back} \end{bmatrix}$$

Szpyra (1995:195) proposes Phrase-level Palatalization, which palatalizes all word-final consonants when the next word begins with i or j. This is discussed in 4.1.8.

Concluding this introduction, the outputs of different palatalization of velars are summarized in (390).

(390)

	1^{st}Vel	2^{nd}Vel	SVP
/k/	[$t^{š}$]	[t^{s}]	[k']
/g/	[$d^{ž}$/ž]	[d^{z}]	[g']
/x/	[š]		[x']

4.3.3 Nonpalatalization of velar plosives: an OT account

In this subsection we consider the problematic aspects of Surface Velar Palatalization mentioned in the previous subsection. These problems are of some interest, since they are pertinent to the ongoing process related to SVP in present-day Polish. It will be shown that velar plosives followed by /e/, which earlier underwent SVP, are not palatalized any longer.

The new nonpalatalized variant is generally attested in the pronunciation of younger generation speakers while the palatalized one is pronounced by older people. In a handful of native words palatalization is still attested.

In the following I claim that only plain velar plosives are attested underlyingly and that they are palatalized before /e/ inside words. The constraint responsible for their palatalization is *VELe, cf. (395); In the subsequent analyses this palatalization will be referred to as Surface Velar Palatalization.

In order to account for the fact that in some words of foreign origin velar plosives do not undergo palatalization before /e/ I propose to split faithfulness constraints into constraints that refer either to assimilated foreign words or to native words. In addition, I will show that the palatalization of all velars before /i/ and /j/ is triggered by a constraint *Ci, cf. (411).

Recall that according to Gussmann (1980:12) velar plosives are secondarily palatalized before /i/ and /e/ and the velar fricative before /i/, cf. (385). On this view, one would not expect nonpalatalized velar plosives to occur after front vowels. Words like [g]enerał 'general' nom.sg., [g]eniusz 'genius' nom.sg., [k]efir 'kefir' nom.sg., [k]elner 'waiter' nom.sg. in (387)a, were argued to be exempt from the rule because of their foreign origin.

In the following I argue that words like the ones in (387)a do not have to be treated as exceptions to SVP but can instead be seen as outputs of an ongoing process of nonpalatalization (depalatalization).[179] I support this claim with the following

[179] The term depalatalization is commonly used in this context. But if one assumes that palatalized velars do not occur underlyingly, the term nonpalatalization seems to be more adequate for describing the phenomenon under consideration.

arguments. First, in contrast to other processes, Surface Velar Palatalization as a phonetic process should not have exceptions, and therefore should apply in native as well as in foreign words. Second, the words in (387)a are of foreign origin but they show a high degree of assimilation in the native grammar. That they are indeed assimilated into Polish grammar is supported by the fact that they not only undergo different types of declensions, but also that they are the target for palatalizations, just as the native stems. For example, Coronal Palatalization, discussed in 4.1.2, affects final coronals of the stems under consideration in the regular way, cf.(391).

(391)

genera/ł/	genera[l]e	'general' nom.sg./loc.sg.
kefi/r/	kefi[ž]e	'kefir' nom.sg./loc.sg.
kelne/r/	kelne[ž]e	'waiter' nom.sg./loc.sg.
gene/z/a	gene[ź]e	'genesis' nom.sg./loc.sg.
ge/n/	ge[ń]e	'gene' nom.sg./loc.sg.

Finally, a considerable number of foreign words underwent Surface Velar Palatalization after they entered the Polish language, just as native words did. In my view this is a strong argument against their being marked as exceptions to the rule in (385). Selected examples are provided in (392).

(392)

[g']eografia	'geography 'nom.sg.
[g']ermanistyka	'German philology'nom.sg.
[g']enerał	'general' nom.sg.
[g']ermania	'Germany', old P. nom.sg.
[g']eometria	'geometry' nom.sg.
al[g']ebra	'algebra' nom.sg.
le[g']enda	'fable' nom.sg.

In the fifties some of the words which underwent SVP started to be pronounced without a secondary articulation. Others, however, are still pronounced with palatalized velar plosives. The first variant is preferred by the younger generation, while the second by the older generation, born before 1920, cf. Rubach (1984:175). The older generation, however, is gradually adopting the pronunciation without a secondary palatalization. The younger generation, on the other hand, rejects the 'palatalized' version and consistently tries to keep pronouncing plain velars. This change is illustrated in a simplified version in (393).

(393)

[g']eografia → [g]eografia	'geography' nom.sg.
[g']ermanistyka → [g]ermanistyka	'German philology' nom.sg.
[g']enerał → [g]enerał	'general' nom.sg.
al[g']ebra → al[g]ebra	'algebra' nom.sg.
le[g']enda → le[g]enda	'fable' nom.sg.

It is also worth noting that there are still a few words in which this variation is also attested in the pronunciation of younger Polish speakers, cf. (394).

(394)

ewan[g']elia → ewan[g']elia, ewan[g]elia	'gospel' nom.sg.
inteli[g']entny → inteli[g']entny, inteli[g]entny	'intelligent' nom.sg.
inteli[g']encja→ inteli[g']encja, inteli[g]encja	'the intellectuals' nom.sg.

From the facts presented above it is doubtless that we are faced with an ongoing nonpalatalization of velar plosives.

In the following we will account for this process by means of constraints. As diachronic investigations show, sequences like /ge/ and /ke/ were consistently pronounced as [g'e] or [k'e] over a hundred years ago, cf. e.g. Małecki (1863:391). Hence, a constraint against plain velar plosives followed by /e/ must have been high-ranked. Formally, it is stated as in (395).

(395)

*VELe: No plain velar plosives followed by the vowel /e/.

The constraint in (395) alone does not predict that velar plosives followed by the vowel /e/ have to be secondarily palatalized. It is possible that k emerges as k^h or k^w. However, as mentioned in the previous parts of this chapter, such sequences do not emerge in Polish because constraints prohibiting aspiration or labialization are very high-ranked in this language. For this reason only secondarily palatalized velars will be considered in the following analyses.

The constraint in (395) was in direct conflict with Ident [VEL], which forces a faithful parse of plain velars. In other words, Ident [VEL] prohibits the palatalization of plain velars. Since all sequences of velar plosives+/e/ were pronounced with a secondary articulation this constraint must have been low-ranked. The tableau in (396) illustrates the interaction of the two constraints under consideration.

(396)

kedy	*VELe	Ident [VEL]
☞ [k']edy		*
[k]edy	*!	

The optimal candidate [k']edy 'when' emerges as optimal because it avoids a faithful parse of the sequence /ke/ by satisfying *VELe. For this reason it incurs a violation of Ident[VEL] which is tolerable due to its low rank.

Since SVP affected the whole vocabulary, the underlying sequences /ke/ and /ge/ in foreign words were also subject to it, cf. (397).

(397)

geografia	*VELe	Ident [VEL]
☞ [g']eografia		*
[g]eografia	*!	

As mentioned above, we are now at the stage at which Polish speakers produce both variants, i.e. they either palatalize velar plosives before /e/ or they produce these sequences faithfully to the output i.e. without a secondary articulation. This is illustrated by the tableau in (398) in which *VELe and Ident[VEL] are unranked with respect to each other and therefore both candidates are selected as optimal.

(398)

[g]eografia	*VELe	Ident [VEL]
☞ [g']eografia		*
☞ [g]eografia	*	

Note that this tableau shows that two different outputs are *attested* in present-day Polish. It illustrates a general picture of a language with respect to the palatalization of velars. However, it does not show individual variation because every speaker clearly produces one of the two outputs presented in (398). Therefore, this illustration is to be considered as a small part of a ranking of Polish language which allows certain 'flexibility' between *VELe and Ident[VEL], in contrast to the ranking of an individual speaker, cf. discussion in 1.3.3. This 'flexibility' is, nevertheless, problematic with respect to Polish words which do not display variation at all. It is only foreign words that do not undergo SVP in present-day Polish. Hence, the unranking of the constraints in (398) predicts a situation which is not mirrored in the language. The problem is illustrated with a representative example in (399).

(399)

kedy	*VELe	Ident [VEL]
☞ [k']edy		*
☜ [k]edy	*	

One of the selected candidates in (399), [k]edy, is not attested in the language. Thus we are faced with a problem since velar plosives in some foreign words are not palatalized and velar plosives in words of Polish origin still undergo SVP.

In terms of constraints, it is obvious that Ident [VEL] is promoted over *VELe with respect to foreign words. But it is the high-ranked *VELe which is responsible for the palatalization of the sequences /ge/ /ke/ in native words. Thus, the question is how one invariant ranking is able to account for the phenomenon described above.

The only possibility is to postulate a split of the faithfulness constraint Ident[VEL], in two separate constraints i.e. Ident[VEL]-A and Ident[VEL]-P. Formally, both constraints are stated in (400).

(400)

Ident[VEL]-P: velar plosives are faithfully parsed into Polish native words.
Ident[VEL]-A: velar plosives are faithfully parsed into assimilated foreign words.

If Ident[VEL]-A outranks *VELe, no palatalization in foreign words is possible. If Ident[VEL]-P is outranked by *VELe, palatalization occurs only in native words. The tableau in (401) shows the selection of the optimal candidate, which is of foreign origin.

(401)

kelner	Ident[VEL]-A	*VELe	Ident[VEL]-P
[k']elner	*!		
☞ [k]elner		*	

The first candidate in (401) incurs a fatal violation of the high-ranked constraint Ident [VEL]-A, while the second candidate, which retains its input specification, proves as optimal. The violation of *VELe does not stop it from surfacing as an optimal candidate because *VELe is outranked by Ident[VEL]-A.

Recall that the nonpalatalization of foreign words is an ongoing process with variation. I interpret this as the lack of ranking between the constraints under consideration. Hence, Ident[VEL]-A and *VELe cannot be crucially ranked. This is illustrated in (402).

(402)

kelner	Ident[VEL]-A	*VELe	Ident[VEL]-P
☞ [k']elner	*		
☞ [k]elner		*	

In (402) both candidates, [k']elner and [k]elner are selected. But in contrast to the ranking in (399) the constraint interaction (402) predicts that native words are pronounced with a secondary articulation and foreign words without it. This is possible because of the high-ranked constraint Ident[VEL]-A and the constraint Ident[VEL]-P, which is ranked below *VELe. Consider the tableau in (403), in which the native word [k']edy, an attested output, emerges as optimal.

(403)

kedy	Ident[VEL]-A	*VELe	Ident[VEL]-P
☞ [k']edy			*
[k]edy		*!	

From the ranking established thus far it follows that the high-ranking constraint Ident[VEL]-A is not only responsible for the nonpalatalization of assimilated foreign words but that it also prohibits the palatalization in recent borrowings. Some of these borrowings are listed in (404).

(404)

[g]etr	'gaiter' nom.sg.
[g]etto	'ghetto' nom.sg.
[k]ebab	'kebab' nom.sg.
kra[k]ers	'crackers' nom.sg.
[k]etchup	'ketchup' nom.sg.
[k]emping	'camping' nom.sg.
wee[k]end	'weekend' nom.sg.

The promotion of Ident[VEL]-A over *VELe can be analyzed as a reduction of markedness because Ident[VEL]-A prohibits marked structures (velars with a secondary articulation) by requiring a faithful parsing of plain velars. We might expect a similar rejection of palatalization in a handful of native Polish words which exhibit a secondary articulation. Plain velars in these words are indeed attested in certain dialects, cf. 4.3.5.

Before we proceed to other cases let us consider how the process presented above is mirrored in various prescriptive studies of Polish pronunciation.

"Słownik języka polskiego" *Dictionary of Polish Language* (1900-1927) prescribes that words like *ewangelia* 'gospel' nom.sg. and *geografia* 'geography' nom.sg. are pronounced as *ewan[g']elia* and *[g']eografia*, respectively. Similarly, according to "Prawidła poprawnej wymowy polskiej" *The Rules of Correct Polish Pronunciation* (Klemensiewicz 1930) all foreign words are to be invariably palatalized. Interestingly, in 1936 Komitet Ortograficzny 'The Orthography Committee', recognizing the prevailing nonpalatalized variant in the pronunciation, changed the orthographic rules of many foreign words, i.e., the vowel /i/ following velar plosives, which indicated palatalization, was to be elided. For example, the spelling *ewangielia* was replaced by *ewangelia*. These rules are followed in Modern Polish as well. The Committee, however, considered the pronunciation of secondarily palatalized velars as an option in Standard Polish.

According to "Słownik wymowy polskiej" *Dictionary of Polish Pronunciation* (1977) variation in the pronunciation of words like *geografia*, *generał*, *geneza*, *gest* still occurs in Standard Polish. It is however noted that the nonpalatalized pronunciation variant is the recent one, cf. Karaś and Madejowa (1977: XLIII). Other words are pronounced according to their spellings: *kielich* 'cup' nom.sg., *kiermasz* 'fair' nom.sg., *kierat* 'horse gear' nom.sg. are prescribed to be pronounced with a palatalized k, while *keson* 'caisson' nom.sg., *kedyw* 'Khedive' nom.sg., *kelner* 'waiter' nom.sg., *kefir* 'kefir' nom.sg. with a plain k; a similar conclusion was drawn with respect to g: the velar plosive is palatalized in words such as *giełda* 'exchange' nom.sg., *giermek* 'squire' nom.sg., but not in *germanista* 'Germanist' nom.sg., *generał* 'general' nom.sg., *geologia* 'geology' nom.sg., cf. Karaś and Madejowa (1977: LVI).

Returning to the OT analysis presented above, we want to consider the proposed constraints with respect to other cases in which the palatalization of velar plosives occurs.

It is important to note that the ranking established for native words, i.e. *VELe>> Ident[VEL], also correctly predicts the secondary palatalization of velars when they are followed by suffixes with the initial /e/ like those presented in (405). As shown in 4.2.3 these suffixes do not trigger the palatalization of stem-final labials or coronals. Hence, they are 'neutral' and do not contain the palatalizing feature [PAL].[180]

(405)

-emu	dat. sg. masc.
-em	instr. sg. masc.
-ego	gen./acc. sg. masc.
-ej	gen. dat. loc. sg. fem. adj.
-e	nom. pl./acc.pl. nonmasc.

The following tableau demonstrates why the palatalization of /k/ in stem-final position occurs in a representative example like /krok+em/ 'step' instr.sg.

(406)

krok+em	Ident[VEL]-A	*VELe	Ident[VEL]-P
☞ kro[k']em			*
kro[k]em		*!	

Since the high-ranked constraint *VELe prohibits plain velar plosives followed by /e/, the first candidate satisfying this constraint with a secondary palatalization proves to be optimal; the second candidate is excluded from consideration due to a fatal violation of *VELe. Note that by adopting this solution the asymmetrical behavior of the suffixes with respect to stem-final consonants, presented in (405), is treated in a homogeneous way, i.e. by means of constraints which refer only to velars.

That the suffixes presented in (405) trigger the surface palatalization of velars is additionally confirmed by the secondarily palatalized final velars in proper foreign names. For example, Murmansk is pronounced in the instrumental case as Murman-s[k']em, Narvik as Narvi[k']em Xiang as Xian[g']em, etc.

Thus, from the ranking established thus far, it follows that the palatalization of k and g is expected to apply not only across morpheme-boundaries but also across word boundaries if the next word starts with the vowel /e/. This is, however, not the case. Consider the examples shown in (407).

(407)

kro[k] Edmunda	'Edmund's step' nom.sg.
bra[k] empirii	'the lack of empiricism' nom.sg.
móz/g/ móz[k] elektroniczny	'electronic brain'nom.sg.

[180] Recall that in order to account for these cases in Rubach's cyclic approach, a j-insertion rule was proposed.

The reason why the velars in the examples in (407) are not palatalized follows from the fact that /e/ does not trigger palatalization across word-boundaries. If it did, the potential palatalized velar would be in coda position, since resyllabification across word-boundaries is not allowed in Polish. Moreover, palatalized velars in coda position are generally prohibited in Polish, except when word-final velars are followed by word-initial /i/ or /j/, cf. the discussion below.

In the following we account for these generalizations by means of constraints. First, we posit a universal alignment constraint which prohibits resyllabification across word-boundaries. Such a constraint would require a stem to match to its final syllable. It was postulated in 4.1.8. and it is repeated in (408) for convenience, cf. McCarthy and Prince (1993b: 116).

(408)

Align (Stem, R, σ, R) Align $]_{\text{STEM}} =]_\sigma$
ALIGN RIGHT; Aligh R: Every final stem-edge matches to a final syllable-edge.

Furthermore, there must be a constraint which prohibits complex structures such as secondarily palatalized velars in coda position. Formally, such a constraint can be expressed by conjoining two constraints, namely NoCoda, which generally prohibits codas, and *[Vel, Pal] which penalizes structurally complex palatalized velars. The domain of the conjunction is a segment. In (409) the formal representation of the conjunction is shown. [181]

(409)

$[$*[Vel, Pal]&NoCoda$]_{\text{SEGMENT}}$ [182]: No palatalized velars in coda position.

Ranking Align R and the conjunction [[Vel, Pal]&NoCoda] above *VELe allows for the selection of the attested form as an optimal candidate. This is illustrated by the tableau in (410).

(410)

krok Edmunda	Align R	[[Vel, Pal] &NoCoda]	*VELe	Ident[VEL]-P
krok'. Edmunda		*!		*
kro.k' Edmunda	*!			*
kro.k Edmunda	*!		*	
☞krok. Edmunda			*	

The first candidate in (410) incurs a violation not only of *[Vel, Pal], but also of NoCoda and as a consequence it violates the conjunction [*[Vel, Pal]&NoCoda]].[183] The fourth candidate in (410) violates neither Align R nor [*[Vel, Pal]&NoCoda]] and therefore emerges as optimal.

[181] The background of Local Conjunction is presented in 1.2.4.

[182] The conjunction is used in the following analyses without the notation $[\ ]_{\text{SEGMENT}}$.

[183] Recall that Local Conjunction is violated only if both constraints are violated.

There is, however, a single attested case in which secondarily palatalized velars occur in coda position, i.e., when they are followed by word-initial /i/ or /j/, cf. examples in (388). This palatalization, called Phrase-level Palatalization, affects stem-final labials, coronals, and velars in a similar way. As in the previous parts of this chapter we account for the obligatory palatalization of a stem-final consonant before /i, j/ by positing an undominated constraint which does not allow consonants preceded by /i/ or /j/ to remain plain. This constraint is repeated below for convenience, cf. also 4.1.8.

(411)

*Ci: There are no plain consonants followed by i or j.

The implementation of this undominated constraint into the ranking results in selecting a candidate which has a palatalized velar in word-final position.[184] Consider the tableau in (412).

(412)

upadek Ikara	*Ci	Align R	[Vel, Pal] &NoCoda]	*VELe
☞upadek'. Ikara			*!	
upade.k' Ikara		*!		
upade.k Ikara		*!		*
upadek. Ikara	*!			*

The first candidate in (412) emerges as optimal since it fully satisfies the high-ranking constraints *Ci and Align R, as opposed to other candidates, which incur a violation of one of them.

Concluding this subsection we contend that velar plosives preceded by /e/, which historically underwent palatalization (SVP), systematically fail to undergo SVP in present-day Polish. This process affects assimilated foreign words. The new nonpalatalized variant is generally attested in the pronunciation of younger generation speakers while the palatalized one is pronounced by older people. In a handful of native words palatalization is still attested. It also occurred across a morpheme boundary. To account for such two-fold phenomenon in terms of an invariable ranking, the splitting up of faithfulness constraints is required. Palatalization across word-boundaries (Phrase-level Palatalization) affects all three velars (as well as labials and coronals) and it is exclusively triggered by i and j. This is the only case in which palatalized velars are attested in word-final position. Finally, it has to be stressed that the ongoing process described above is not blocked by the semantic component (SF) of a lexical entry, as it was in the case of labials, cf. 4.1.4.

[184] As mentioned above, constraints prohibiting aspiration, labialisation are high-ranked in Polish. They are omitted in this account.

4.3.4 Secondarily palatalized velars from a diachronic point of view

In this subsection we will consider the diachronic sources of secondarily palatalized velar plosives.

This process started relatively late, in the fifteenth century, cf. Klemensiewicz et al. (1955:135). Manuscripts from the fourteenth century like *Kazania Świętokrzyskie* 'Sermons of the Monastery of the Holy Cross', *Kazania Gnieźnieńskie* 'Sermons of Gniezno' did not contain any trace of palatalization at all, and the second script of *Psałterz Floriański* 'The Psalter of St. Florian', as well as *Żywot św. Błażeja* 'Life of St. Blasius', both probably from the early fifteenth century, generally display palatalization marks but not with respect to velars. The only exception found in *Psałterz Floriański* is the word *ludzskye* 'human' nom.pl., where the palatalization of /k/ is indicated by the letter < y >, cf. Stieber (1973:67f.). In *Psałterz Puławski* 'Psalter of Puławy', written presumably in the early sixteenth century, the marking of velar palatalization appears fairly regularly, e.g. *sznyegyem* 'snow' inst.sg., *yednakyego* 'equal' gen.sg., *takyesz* 'same' nom.pl., although there are also words which did not contain any mark of velar palatalization like *wszelkemu* 'any' dat.sg. or *apostolske* 'apostolic' nom.pl., cf. Stieber (1973:68).

The vowels /e/ and /i/, which triggered SVP, must have been derived from other sources than vowels which caused First and Second Palatalization.[185] In the following, the different contexts in which SVP took place will be presented.

First, in sequences like [kɨ], [gɨ], spelled as ky, gy, the high central unrounded vowel /ɨ/ changed to /i/, thereby causing palatalization of the preceding velars. The relevant examples are illustrated in (413). Note that the Polish vowel /ɨ/ comes originally from the back vowel /y/. It was the PIE long /u:/ which lost its length in Late Proto-Slavic and finally was changed to /y/, cf. Carlton (1991:148).

(413)

*kyjь→ [k']ij	'stick' nom.sg.	£oś (1922: 156)
*gybnąti →[g']inąć	'to vanish' inf.	£oś (1922: 156)
*kywati → [k']iwać	'to sway' inf.	Klemensiewicz at al. (1955:135)

[185] First Velar Palatalization took place from the third until fifth century when velars were followed by e, ę, i, ь, ě, j, cf. Carlton (1991: 115f.) and Długosz-Kurczabowa and Dubisz (1993:116). Consider the following examples:

* mo[g]+ete → mo[ž]ete	'to be able to' 2ps.pres.
* vъnu[k]+ę → vъnu[t^{s}]ę	'grandson' nom.sg.
* grě[x]+ьnikъ → grě[š]ьnikъ	'sinner' nom.sg.

Second Velar Palatalization took place from the sixth until seventh century before i, ě, which were derived from the diphthong ai̯, cf. Carlton (1991:120f.) and Długosz-Kurczabowa and Dubisz (1993:116). Consider examples shown below:

*kai̯nā → *kěna→[t^{s}]ena	'price'nom.sg.
*gai̯lo → *gělŏ → [d^{z}]elo	'work'nom.sg.

The same source of palatalization, i.e. /i/ derived from /ɨ/, is found in adjectives. Here, after the loss of jers, sequences like ъjь changed to /ɨ/ and further to /i/. In (414) stages of the whole process are illustrated with some selected examples.

(414)

*długъjь → długy → dłu[g']i	'long' nom.sg. £oś (1922: 31)
*głębokъjь → głęboky→ głębo[k']i	'deep' nom.sg. £oś (1922: 31)
*dalekъjь → daleky→dale[k']i	'distant' nom.sg. Klemensiewicz at al.(1955:135)
*gybъkъjь → gybky→gib[k']i	'nimble' nom.sg. Klemensiewicz at al. (1955:135)
*ubogъjь →ubogy→ubo[g']i	'poor' nom.sg. Klemensiewicz at al. (1955:135)

Furthermore, the palatalization of velar plosives was triggered by the vowel /e/, which was derived from a back jer /ъ/. This process is described in detail in chapter 2. In (415) the reconstructed words, marked by <*>, as well as their correspondents in present-day Polish are shown. Most probably, before the fifteenth century secondarily palatalized velars were realized as plain ones, cf. also examples in (376).

(415)

*kъlъ	[k']eł	'tusk'nom.sg.	Klemensiewicz et al. (1955:135)
*okъnъ	o[k']en	'window'gen.pl.	Klemensiewicz et al. (1955:135)
*chorągъvь	chorą[g']ew	'flag'nom.sg.	Klemensiewicz et al. (1955:135)
*gъrъ	[g']er	'game'gen.pl.	Klemensiewicz et al. (1955:135)
*gъzъ	[g']ez	'breeze'gen.pl.	Długosz-Kurczabowa and Dubisz (1993:120)

The vowel /e/, which triggered palatalization of the preceding velars, was not only derived from a back jer /ъ/, but also from the sequence -oje, and from the syllabic l̥ (l̥ → el). This is shown in (416)a and (416)b, cf. Długosz-Kurczabowa and Dubisz (1993:120).

(416)

a. oje →e

wysokoje→ wysoke → wyso[k']e	'high' nom.pl.
drugoje → druge → dru[g']e	'second' nom.pl.

b. l̥→ el

kl̥basa → kelbasa → [k']ełbasa	'sausage' nom.sg.
zgl̥kъ → zgelk → z[g']ełk	'noise' nom.sg.

The velar fricative [x] did not undergo surface palatalization in the way velar plosives did. In Old Polish words like [h']iszpan 'Spaniard' nom.sg. and [x']iny 'China' nom.pl. were pronounced as [hɨ]szpan and [xɨ]ny, respectively, cf. Długosz-Kurczabowa and Dubisz (1993:120). According to Stieber (1973:114) Poles familiar with foreign languages pronounced the original sequences /xi/ with a palatalized [x']. Such pronunciation was further extended to native verb forms. For example, wyma[xɨ]wać 'to wave' inf. started to be pronounced as wyma[x']iwać and podsłu[xɨ]wać 'to intercept' inf. as podsłu[x']iwać. But the variation in pronunciation was still attested in the nineteenth century. In Modern Polish they are pronounced consistently with [x'], cf. (384).

4.3.5 Secondarily palatalized velars in dialects

Velar plosives which are secondarily palatalized in Standard Polish are realized in dialects in a different way. Interestingly, speakers of some dialects reject the surface palatalization of velars and prefer plain velars before /e/, while others allow palatalization to proceed in a sense that instead of secondarily palatalized velar affricates are produced.

Let us illustrate these variants with some concrete examples. In a considerably large part of north-eastern of Poland, in the dialects of Malbork, Ostróda, Lubawa, Warmia, in the Mazovian Kurpie and in the Płock area[186] the palatalization of velar plosives is not regular and rarely occurs, cf. Dejna (1994:81), Stankiewicz (1956:522). The velars are palatalized slightly in comparison to palatalized velars in Standard Polish, or they are pronounced without a secondary articulation. Consider examples provided in (417), cf. Dejna (1994:81).

(417)

Standard Polish	dialect	
ta[k']e	ta[k]e	'such' nom.pl.
dro[g']e	dro[g]e	'expensive' nom.pl.
cu[k']erki	cu[k]erki	'bonbon' nom.pl.
ło[k']eć	ło[k]eć	'elbow' nom.pl.
dro[g']emu	dro[g]emu	'dear' instr.sg.

In the Pomeranian dialects of Krajna and Tuchola palatalized /k/ and /g/ are realized in the context of the following /e/ or /i/ as alveolopalatal affricates i.e. [$t^ś$] and [$d^ź$], respectively, cf. the map in 7.2.3 in the appendix. Relevant examples are shown in (418), cf. Klemensiewicz et al. (1955:135).

(418)

dłu[g']i	dłu[$d^ź$]i	'long'nom.sg.masc.
[g']ib[k']i	[$d^ź$]ib[$t^ś$]i	'nimble' nom.sg.masc.
[k']ij	[$t^ś$]ij	'stock' nom.sg.
[k']edy	[$t^ś$]edy	'when'
ta[k']i	ta[$t^ś$]i	'such' nom.sg.masc.
no[g']i	no[$d^ź$]i	'leg' nom.pl.

[186] Cf. the map in 7.2.3 in the appendix.

It is worth noting that alveopalatal affricates do not merge with the outputs of First and Second Velar Palatalization, cf. 4.3.2. As pointed out by Dejna (1994:20) the velars under consideration can be also realized as sounds which Dejna describes as [t^{š}] and [d^{ž}] in Kashubian dialects, cf. also the realization of coronals in these dialects shown in 4.2.8. Consider the examples shown in (419).

(419)

ta[k']i	ta[t$^{š́}$]i	'such' nom.sg.
[k']ij	[t$^{š́}$]ij	'stick' nom.sg.
bu[k']i	bu[t$^{š́}$]i	'shoe', nom.pl.
no[g']i	no[d$^{ž́}$]i	'leg' nom.pl.

In these dialects the velar fricative /x/ is realized either as [ś] or as [š́]. This is illustrated in (420), cf. Dejna (1994:20).

(420)

mar[x]ew	mar[š́]ew	'carrot' nom.sg.
mu[x]y	mu[š́]y	'fly' gen.sg.

Surprisingly, in a very small area in the northeastern corner of Mazowsze, east of Mrągowo and west of Olecko we observe the reverse process, i.e., velars which are realized as plain in Standard Polish display the secondary palatalization, cf. the map 7.2.3 in the appendix. This is shown in the examples in (421), cf. Stankiewicz (1956: 522).

(421)

cze[k]ać	cze[k']ać	'to wait' inf.
dro[g]a	dro[g']a	'way' nom.sg.
mu[x]a	mu[x']a	'fly' nom.sg.

Finally, it is also worth pointing out that in Wielkopolska, nasal vowels were denasalized, which in consequence led to the emergence of minimal pairs, cf. (422). Note that denasalization does not cause the palatalization of the preceding velar. (In Standard Polish the words in the first column in (422) are pronounced with a slight nasalisation: drogę, Polskę, szybkę.)

(422)

dro[g]e	dro[g']e	'way' acc.nom. / 'expensive' nom.pl.
Pols[k]e	pols[k']e	'Poland' acc.nom. / 'Polish' nom.pl.
szyb[k]e	szyb[k']e	'glass panel' acc.nom. / 'fast' nom.pl.

In sum, velars which are secondarily palatalized in Standard Polish are realized differently in the dialects. For the most part dialect speakers either reject palatalization or they let the palatalized velars undergo the next stage of palatalization and pronounce them as affricates. This might be taken as indirect evidence that secondarily palatalized sounds are marked and therefore avoided by speakers in different ways. An apparent counterexample is also attested, i.e., plain velars of Standard Polish are realized with a secondary palatalization in one dialect. This process, however, is found only in a very small area and would require further investigation, especially from the diachronic point of view.

5 CHAPTER FIVE: Optional Simplifications Of Consonant Clusters

In the first chapter of this thesis it was shown that variation is commonly considered to be an indicator of an ongoing change in language, cf. 1.3. This observation was confirmed by a considerable number of examples provided in chapter 4, in which palatalization phenomena were discussed. In the present chapter we will consider variant pronunciations of consonant clusters attested in present-day Polish. The reason why the processes are the subject of the present chapter is that they may indicate future development of clusters.

In the following three separate processes affecting complex clusters will be discussed: deletion, merger, and assimilation. It will be shown that the processes have a common denominator: they lead to a simplified structure from the articulatory point of view. A deletion involves a single segment or sequences of segments; a merger unites two segments into one; an assimilation makes one segment similar to another with respect to certain properties such as e.g. place of articulation. Hence, all of these processes are manifestations of the important force governing language, i.e., minimization of articulatory effort. For this reason the processes will be referred to as *simplification processes*.

In addition, it has to be stressed that simplifications of clusters are fairly common in spontaneous speech of present-day Polish. Although they are optional, they are not arbitrary and some generalizations concerning the processes described above may be established. As we will see below, it is not always the case that quantitative complexity leads to the deletion of consonants. For example, a segment in a two-member cluster can be deleted fairly regularly, while certain three- or four-member clusters are never simplified. This observation leads to the conclusion that quantitative complexity does not play a decisive role and more importantly, that there must be other explanations for the ongoing changes in clusters. This topic will be examined in the present chapter.

The chapter is organized as follows. First, I will discuss deletions of extrasyllabic sonorants as well as (non-extrasyllabic) obstruents. Second, I will examine the conditions under which the optional merger of consonants takes place. Finally, I will demonstrate what kind of optional assimilations occur in spontaneous speech. The simplification processes will also be discussed from the perspective of Standard Polish pronunciation. Three sources for the pronunciation of Standard Polish will be cited below: "Słownik wymowy polskiej" *The Dictionary of Polish Pronunciation* (Karaś and Madejowa 1977), "Prawidła poprawnej wymowy polskiej" *The Rules of Correct*

Polish Pronunciation (Klemensiewicz ^{8}1995)[187] and “Zasady współczesnej wymowy polskiej” *The Principles of Contemporary Polish Pronunciation* (Madejowa 1993).

The main criterion taken for establishing norms of Standard Polish pronunciation by all three sources is the frequency of attested variants in official style, i.e., pronunciation used in theaters, in television and radio, at universities and schools, and in official events.[188]

5.1 Optional deletions

In this subsection we will investigate what factors determine the deletion of consonants in clusters in spontaneous speech. We will start our investigation with sonorants and continue with the deletion of obstruents.

The deletion of sonorants is the most frequent kind of simplification of clusters. Obviously not all sonorants are elided in spontaneous speech. This implies that there are conditions under which sonorants may be deleted. The first refers to their extrasyllabic status. It is namely extrasyllabic sonorants, discussed in 3.3., that are often dropped by speakers. Additionally, their deletion is conditioned by their position in the word. There is a clear asymmetry between word-initial position on the one hand and word-medial and word-final position on the other hand, cf. 3.3.1 and 3.3.2.

Let us examine the behavior of extrasyllabic sonorants in word-medial position. Consider the examples provided in (423), where the underlying forms of three-member clusters in words in the first column are shown. In the second and in the third column their optional pronunciation attested in spontaneous speech is provided, cf. Dukiewicz and Sawicka (1995:139) and Benni (1959:48). Note that in some cases voicing assimilation occurs due to the high-ranking constraint in Polish that requires voicing agreement among obstruents belonging to the same cluster, cf. 3.2.1.

(423)

ja/błk/o	ja[pwk]o	ja[pk]o	‘apple’ nom.sg.
be/dłk/a	be[twk]a	be[tk]a	‘agaric’ nom.sg.
źdźe/błk/o	źdźe[pwk]o	źdźc[pk]o	‘a little’

[187] *Prawidła poprawnej wymowy polskiej* by Klemensiewicz (^{8}1995) is the eighth edition of *Prawidła poprawnej wymowy polskiej* published in 1930.

[188] The most recent study of Polish pronunciation is Madejowa (1993). She investigated the pronunciation of native speakers of Polish living in Warszawa, Kraków, Poznań and Wrocław. The investigated speakers had to speak Standard Polish. They were divided into four groups. To the first group belonged speakers between the ages 15 to 25, to the second speakers of 25 to 40, to the third speakers of 40 to 60, and finally to the fourth speakers who were over 60 years old. The study consisted of three parts. In the first part speakers read a prepared text. In the second part they were asked to retell the text they read before. Finally, they answered various questions whereby the answers were supposed to contain ‘*problematic words*’. In total about sixty thousand recordings were obtained and evaluated. On this basis Madejowa formulated *The Principles of Contemporary Polish Pronunciation* that will be systematically referred to in the course of the present chapter.

naumy/ślń/ie	naumy[ślń]ie	naumy[śń]ie	'purposely' adv.
rzemie/ślń/ik	rzemie[ślń]ik	rzemie[śń]ik	'artisan' nom.sg.
ga/rnk/ów	ga[rnk]ów	ga[rk]ów	'pot' gen.pl.
zia/rnk/o	zia[rnk]o	źa[rk]o	'grain' dim. nom.sg.
czo/snk/u	czo[snk]u	czo[sk]u	'garlic' gen.sg.

It has to be stressed that not all extrasyllabic sonorants in medial positions are deleted with equal frequency. Several authors – Dunaj (1985), Rubach (1977), Benni (1959), Dukiewicz and Sawicka (1995) – agree that some sonorants are deleted more readily than others. Most likely to undergo deletions are [w] and [l]. As will be shown below, [w] is the only sonorant elided when it is part of a well-formed syllable onset, i.e. in the context #Cw. Another segment that is often deleted, albeit not as readily as [w] or [l], is the nasal [n]. Interestingly, extrasyllabic [m] never undergoes deletions. Similarly immune to deletion is the trill [r]. Its deletion occurs fairly frequently only in the single item sre[brn]y 'silver' adj.masc.nom.sg. that is simplified to sre[bn]y. In contrast, the extrasyllabic /r/ in words such as mę[trt^s]a 'sage' gen.sg., mę[trk]a 'crafty person' nom.sg., or Ję[trk]a 'Jędrek' gen.sg. never deletes.

Word-medial position is not the only one in which the optional deletion of extrasyllabic sonorants takes place. It is fairly common that stray sonorants in word-final position are dropped. Relevant examples are shown in (424).

(424)

my/śl/	my[śl]	my[ś]	'thought' nom.sg.
czasopi/sm/	czasopi[sm]	czasopi[s]	'journal' gen.pl.
mężczy/zn/	mężczy[sn]	mężczy[s]	'man' gen.pl.
pie/śń/	pie[śń]	pie[ś]	'song' nom.sg.
pomy/sł/	pomy[sw]	pomy[s]	'idea' nom.sg.

Especially frequent is the deletion of a word-final extrasyllabic [w] if it is separated from the preceding consonant by a morpheme-boundary. This is the case when the past tense form (3 ps.sg.masc.), whose marker is the sonorant /ł/, is affixed to a verb stem. Verb forms provided in (425) illustrate this case.

(425)

rze/kł/	rze[kw]	rze[k]	'to say' 3ps.sg.masc.past
strze/gł/	strze[kw]	strze[k]	'to guard' 3ps.sg.masc.past
bie/gł/	bie[kw]	bie[k]	'to run' 3ps.sg.masc.past
wió/dł/	wió[tw]	wió[t]	'to lead' 3ps.sg.masc.past

Furthermore, if a suffix with an initial consonant is attached to the forms presented in (425), then [w] can also optionally delete. This is illustrated by the words presented in (426), in which the suffix -szy [šɨ] 'participle perfect' is attached to the stem.

(426)

rze/kłš/y	rze[kwš]y	rze[kš]y	'to say' participle perfect
strze/głš/y	strze[kwš]y	strze[kš]y	'to guard' participle perfect
bie/głš/y	bie[kwš]y	bie[kš]y	'to run' participle perfect
wió/dłš/y	wió[twš]y	wió[tš]y	'to lead' participle perfect
mó/głš/y	mó[kwš]y	mó[kš]y	'to be able' participle perfect

A similar observation can be made with respect to other grammatical forms. For example, the conjunctive forms display the same kinds of optionality as in (426): rze[gwb]ym 'to say' conj.1ps.sg. may be pronounced as rze[gb]ym, strze[gwb]ym 'to guard' 1ps.sg.conj. as strze[gb]ym, or bie[gwb]ym 'to run' 1ps.sg.conj. as bie[gb]ym, etc.

In the same vein, the deletion of extrasyllabic sonorants is often attested in imperative forms. In (427)a the imperative in singular is shown, while in (427)b the same verbs in plural are provided. The crucial difference between the verb forms presented above and the imperative forms is the lack of a morpheme-boundary in the latter. The optionally deleted segment in all cases is the liquid [l] that belongs to the stem.

(427)

a.			
mó/dl/ się[189]	mó[tl] się	mó[t] się	'to pray' 2ps.sg.imp
pomy/śl/	pomy[śl]	pomy[ś]	'to think' 2ps.sg.imp
b.			
mó/dlt^{ś}/e się	mó[tlt^{ś}]e się	mó[tt^{ś}]e się	'to pray' 2ps.pl.imp
pomy/ślt^{ś}/e	pomy[ślt^{ś}]e	pomy[śt^{ś}]e	'to think' 2ps.pl.imp

In light of these data it seems that the morpheme-boundary does not play a decisive role in the deletion of the extrasyllabic segments under consideration. It is rather the extrasyllabic status of the elided segments as well as their intrinsic properties that cause them to more readily delete in spontaneous speech than other sounds, cf. also observations made below.

The judgment on the correctness of the variations presented in (423) and (427) in Standard Polish is the following. Madejowa (1993:77) makes a crucial distinction between the pronunciation of verbs and nouns. She contends that in Standard Polish the past tense forms are correct also in the simplified version, cf. (425), but she prescribes all nouns to be pronounced with the final glide. A similar position is taken by the *The Dictionary of Polish Pronunciation* (1977:XXXVI), in which the loss of the sonorants I have analyze as extrasyllabic as e.g. [w] in ja[pwk]o 'apple' nom.sg. is recognized as correct. Klemensiewicz (^{8}1995:50) takes into consideration only past tense forms with final sonorants I have treated as stray. He prefers the nonsimplified form for the stage pronunciation, while allowing the simplified variant elsewhere.[190]

---

[189] The verb *modlić się* 'to pray' is reflexive in Polish and therefore marked with a reflexive particle *się*.

[190] It has to be stressed that the sources cited do not give an opinion on every occurring variant in (423)-(427). Therefore only judgments on selected variations can be provided here.

Let us examine word-initial extrasyllabic sonorants. As was mentioned before, there is a crucial asymmetry between extrasyllabic sonorants occurring in initial position and those in noninitial position in a word. In (428), examples are shown in which stray sonorants occur word-initially. None of the sonorants is directly parsed into a syllable, since they would lead to violation of basic requirements on the syllable structure, cf. discussion in 3.1.1. and 3.2.2.

(428)

/mž/yć	[mž]yć	'to drizzle'inf.
/mx/u	[mx]u	'moss' gen.sg.
/lv/a	[lv]a	'lion' gen.sg.
/rt/ęć	[rt]ęć	'mercury' nom.sg.
/rdz/a	[rdz]a	'rust' nom.sg.
/wb/a	[wb]a	'head' pej.gen.sg.
/wz/a	[wz]a	'tear' nom.sg.

In contrast to the examples discussed above the consonant clusters presented in (428) are not simplified in spontaneous speech. Extrasyllabic sonorants are faithfully pronounced without exception. The only difference between extrasyllabic sonorants that are optionally deleted and those that are not deleted in spontaneous speech is their position in the word. In other words, word-initial position has a 'special' status in the sense that it is immune to deletions. The privileged status of initial position is indeed widely supported by the fact that languages typically allow a greater number of contrasts among phonemes word-initially than in other positions, cf. e.g. Beckmann (1995) and Takatori (1997).

The asymmetry between word-initial and other positions might also follow from the prosodic incorporation of the segments. In chapter 3 it was shown that extrasyllabic sonorants occurring word-initially are incorporated into a foot and noninitial ones into a prosodic word. Such representations follow from the ranking of constraints imposed on syllable structure as well as from the behavior of the consonants in the degemination and voicing assimilation processes discussed in 3.3.1 and 3.3.2. Consider the representations shown in (429)a and (429)b.

(429)

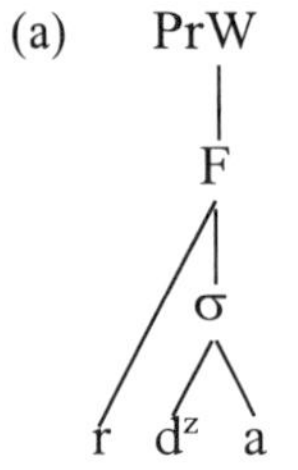

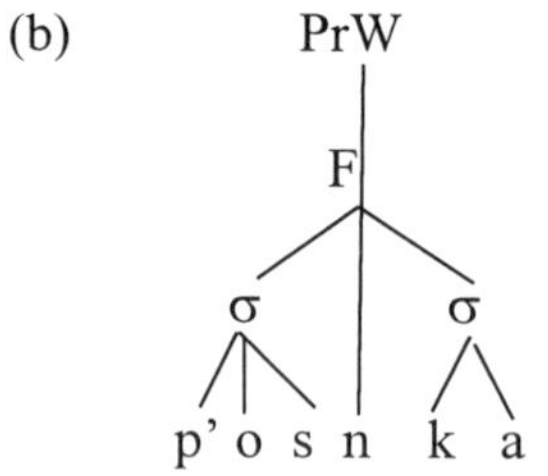

The two contrasting representations in (429) suggest that the optional deletion or nondeletion of extrasyllabic sonorants can be predicted from their respective prosodic representations. Segments that are linked to a foot are never deleted, while segments that are incorporated into a prosodic word are often elided in spontaneous speech. This explanation does not conflict with the solution described above, according to which word-initial position is more privileged than other positions. On the contrary, it provides supporting evidence for the existing discrepancy between segments occurring in initial and noninital positions.

Let us conclude our investigation of extrasyllabic sonorants by examining examples in which the stray sonorant is the second member of a word-initial cluster. Consider the data presented in (430).

(430)

/drg/ać	[drg]ać	'to twitch' inf.
/drž/eć	[drž]eć	'to tremble' inf.
/drv/ić	[drv']ić	'to deride' inf.
/trv/oga	[trf]oga	'fear' nom.sg.
/brn/ąć	[brn]ąć	'to wade' inf.
/brv/i	[brv']i	'eyebrow' nom.pl.
/zmń/ejszyć	[zmń]ejszyć	'to diminish' inf.
/plv/ać	[plf]ać	'to spit' inf.

None of the medial segments in the word-initial clusters in (430) is optionally dropped in spontaneous speech. However, optional deletion is found in two words that were not presented in (430), i.e. [pwt^{ś}]i 'gender' gen.sg. and [pwt^{ś}]owy 'sexual' masc.nom.sg. Significantly, these are the only two words in Polish beginning with the sequence consonant+[w]+consonant. Since it is only the sonorant [w] that undergoes deletion, it seems that this segment constitutes an exception in comparison with other sonorants. Its deletion in spontaneous speech does not follow from word-initial position and consequently, it is not mirrored in its prosodic representation. Hence, the explanation of the aberrant behavior of [w] must be sought elsewhere.

Interestingly, the glide [w] behaves also differently from other sonorants when it occurs as the second member of a word-initial cluster that is well-formed with respect to the Sonority Hierarchy for Polish, cf. 3.1.1. The data provided in (431) provide examples of clusters which contain the glide as well as their simplification in spontaneous speech, cf. Dunaj (1985:31).

(431)

/gł/upi	[gw]upi	[g]upi	'stupid' masc.nom.sg.
/dł/ugo	[dw]ugo	[d]ugo	'long' adv.
/sł/uchaj	[sw]uchaj	[s]uchaj	'to hear' 2ps.sg.imp.
/gł/ówny[191]	[gw]ówny	[g]ówny	'main' adj.nom.sg.

The examples in (431) show that the glide [w] may be optionally deleted even if it is a part of a well-formed onset. The glide does not violate the Sonority Hierarchy and it is parsed into a syllable together with the preceding obstruent. Furthermore, it occurs in

[191] In Polish orthographic ó is pronounced as [u].

the privilege word-initial position in which no other sonorants or obstruents are dropped, cf. (430). Additionally, the syllable in which [w] occurs is the head of a foot and therefore it bears stress.[192] It seems, however, that the asymmetry of stressed vs. unstressed syllables does not play a crucial role in simplifications. This is confirmed by examples provided below.

Interestingly, there are words, in which the glide [w] is never elided. Examples are provided in (432).

(432)

/kł/aść	[kw]aść	'to put' inf.
/kł/os	[kw]os	'sike of corn' nom.sg.
/gł/osić	[gw]osić	'to announce' inf.
/gł/az	[gw]az	'stone' nom.sg.

In light of these examples the question arises as to what is the source of the unique behavior of the glide [w]. A possible answer to this question lies in phonetics. It seems that the exceptional behavior of [w] is due to its articulatory properties, i.e. the involvement of labial and dorsal articulators, as well as the environment in which it surfaces. All data in (431) have a common denominator: [w] is followed by a vowel [u]. In the words in (432), in which the glide followed by a vowel other than [u], the glide is never optionally dropped. Hence, the transition from [w] to [u] appears to be difficult for speakers to the extent that they often drop the glide.[193] However, Dunaj (1985:31) observes that the simplification of the cluster consonant+[w] followed by other vowels than [u] is also possible in a very limited number of words. They are listed in (433), cf. Dunaj (1985:31).

(433)

/vł/aśnie	[vw]aśnie	[v]aśnie	'exactly'
/$t^{š}$ł/owiek	[$t^{š}$w]owiek	[$t^{š}$]owiek	'man' nom.sg.
/vł/aściwie	[vw]aściwie	[v]aściwie	'just; as a matter of fact'

Dunaj (1985:31) ascribes the simplification of the words in (433) to their high frequency.

In light of the facts presented above it is worth noting that the articulatory difficulty of the glide [w] is confirmed by acquisition data. £obacz (1996:63), citing Zarębina (1980), shows that even three-year old Polish children are not able to pronounce consonant clusters in which the second member is the glide [w]. For example, [vw]oski 'italian' masc.nom.sg. is systematically pronounced as [v]oski. More importantly, the acquisition of [w] generally occurs later in comparison with other sounds; in earlier stages of acquisition [w] is replaced by [l] or [j], sometimes even by [r]. These facts provide supporting evidence for the articulatory complexity of [w] that may be directly responsible for the deletion of the glide by adult speakers.

---

192 Recall that Polish has a regular trochaic foot.

193 This directly influences a listener who starts to pronounce the given forms in a way he/she hears them. For the role of speaker-hearer interaction in sound change cf. Holt (1997) and Ohala (1981).

Let us summarize the main observations concerning the optional deletion of sonorants. First, word-initial extrasyllabic sonorants are never deleted. In their prosodic representation these sonorants are linked to a foot, as in (429)a. Word-medial and word-final extrasyllabic sonorants are often dropped in spontaneous speech. Prosodically they belong to a prosodic word, as in (429)b. The asymmetrical behavior of sonorants shows that word-initial position has a privileged status in contrast to other positions in the word. Second, the fact that optional deletions of the glide [w] occur irrespective of the position it occupies in a syllable and in a word indicate that the phonetic markedness of [w] is more decisive than other requirements. Finally, it has to be stressed that the frequency of occurrence of words in which deletions are attested is one of the important instances triggering deletions of sounds, cf. also examples discussed below.

In the following, we will discuss the optional deletion of the fricative [f] in spontaneous speech. We start our investigation with simplifications which are attested very frequently in spontaneous speech. In (434), it is shown that the three-member cluster [fsk] may be simplified to a two-member cluster [sk]. The initial fricative [f], which is represented as /v/ underlyingly, is often elided in spontaneous speech. It has to be stressed that there is a morpheme-boundary between /v/ ([f]) and the remaining consonants, e.g. krako/v+sk/i. (Monomorphemic clusters /vsk/ are not attested.)

(434)

krako/vsk/i	krako[fsk]i	krako[sk]i	'Cracow's' masc.nom.sg.
warsza/vsk/i	warsza[fsk]i	warsza[sk]i	'Warsaw's' masc.nom.sg.
króle/vsk/i	króle[fsk]i	króle[sk]i	'king's' masc.nom.sg.
ojco/vsk/i	ojco[fsk]i	ojco[sk]i	'paternal' masc.nom.sg.
syno/vsk/i	syno[fsk]i	syno[sk]i	'son's' masc.nom.sg.

The optional simplification of words presented in (434) is so frequent that it is recognized as correct in Standard Polish. *The Dictionary of Polish Pronunciation* (1977:XXXV) prescribes both variants, krako[fsk]i and krako[sk]i, although it prefers the not simplified form to the simplified one. The same position is taken by (Klemensiewicz 1995:50) and Madejowa (1993:79).

In the same vein, fricatives occurring in four-member clusters are very often simplified to three-member clusters by eliding the first fricative /v/. Relevant examples are provided in (435). Again, there is a morpheme-boundary between /v/ and the suffix -/stv/. (The monomorphemic cluster /vstv/ is not attested.)

(435)

zna/vstv/o	zna[fstf]o	zna[stf]o	'expertness' nom.sg.
terenozna/vstv/o	terenozna[fstf]o	terenozna[stf]o	'topography' nom.sg.
kulturozna/vstv/o	kulturozna[fstf]o	kulturozna[stf]o	'cultural studies' nom.sg.
rzeczozna/vstv/o	rzeczozna[fstf]o	rzeczozna[stf]o	'oratory' nom.sg.
marnotra/vstv/o	marnotra[fstf]o	marnotra[stf]o	'waste' nom.sg.
krasomó/vstv/o	krasomó[fstf]o	krasomó[stf]o	'oratory' nom.sg.

Interestingly, *The Dictionary of Polish Pronunciation* (1977:XXXV) provides two words: myśli[stf]o 'shooting' nom.sg. and ojco[stf]o 'fatherhood' nom.sg., in which only the simplified form is prescribed in Standard Polish. Forms such as myśli[fstf]o and ojco[fstf]o are disqualified as hypercorrect. Since *The Dictionary of Polish Pronunciation* takes 'linguistic reality' as a criterion for correct pronunciation, it seems that the nonsimplified versions of these two words are not attested. This is directly mirrored in the orthography, since both words are written as *myślistwo* and *ojcostwo*, respectively. In their adjective forms, however, the fricative /v/, which is represented by the letter *w*, is retained: *myśliwski* and *ojcowski.*

In light of the data presented above the question arises whether we can formulate a generalization with respect to fricatives that are systematically dropped in spontaneous speech. The words provided in (434) and in (435) display at least three similarities. First, the deleted fricative is a stem-final segment, i.e., it is separated from the suffix by a morpheme-boundary. Second, it is always the labio-dental voiceless fricative [f] followed by the alveolar fricative [s] that is dropped. Third, the fricative [s] is part of a cluster and it is followed by a plosive.

Unfortunately, if we consider cases like kró[fsk]o 'cow' augm.nom.sg., tra[fsk]o 'grass' augm.nom.sg. or pi[fsk]o 'beer' augm.nom.sg., in which the [f] is never deleted in spontaneous speech, cf. Rubach (1977:126), none of the observations listed above can be used in formulating a generalization about optional deletions of fricatives; exactly as in words shown in (434) a morphological boundary separates [f] from the following two consonants, e.g. kró[f+sk]o or tra[f+sk]o. Furthermore, [f] is followed by the fricative [s] as well as the plosive [k]. This indicates that neither the phonological environment nor the presence of a morphological boundary contributes to the simplification of the cluster. It seems, rather, that two well-defined sets of words are affected by the optional deletion in pronunciation, i.e., adjectives with the desinence -/sk/, as in (434), and nouns with the suffix -/stv/, as in (435).

Finally, it has to be stressed that fricatives are never deleted in word-initial position when they occur in a similar context as the items provided in (434) and (435). Relevant examples are provided in (436). In all items there is a morphological boundary between the initial fricative that constitutes a prefix, and the following consonants that belong to a stem.

(436)

/vsk/azać	[fsk]azać	'to indicate' inf.
/vsk/órać	[fsk]órać	'to attain' inf.
/vsk/oczyć	[fsk]oczyć	'to jump in' inf.
/vskr/oś	[fskr]oś	'through'

There are two possible interpretations of the examples in (436). First, one might conclude that the deletion of fricatives depends neither on the following clusters nor on the presence of a morphological boundary. Second, the lack of the deletion of [f] in (436) may be explained by the privileged status of word-initial position. Both interpretations, however, do not conflict with the conclusion drawn thus far that optional deletions may affect only well-defined sets of words, i.e., they are independent of the complexity of consonants, prosodic requirements, and the presence of a morphological boundary.

Let us proceed to optional affricate and stop deletions. In (437) it is shown that the affricate [t^{ś}] is often deleted in word-final position in spontaneous speech.

(437)

wolno/śt^{ś}/	wolno[śt^{ś}]	wolno[ś]	'liberty' nom.sg.
powie/śt^{ś}/	powie[śt^{ś}]	powie[ś]	'novel' nom.sg.
ko/śt^{ś}/	ko[śt^{ś}]	ko[ś]	'bone' nom.sg.
miło/śt^{ś}/	miło[śt^{ś}]	miło[ś]	'love' nom.sg.
go/śt^{ś}/	go[śt^{ś}]	go[ś]	'guest' nom.sg.

Although deletions in spontaneous speech are mainly found in word-final position, we cannot consider this environment as the only reason for deletion of [t^{ś}] because there are words such as płaci[t^{ś}] 'to pay' inf or gołole[t^{ś}] 'glaze' nom.sg., in which the affricate is never dropped. These data lead to the conclusion that the deletion is conditioned by the presence of a preceding obstruent.[194] In every case it is always the alveolo-palatal [ś] that precedes the affricate; (there are no other word-final two-member clusters with [t^{ś}] as the second member.)

If the affricate is preceded by /r/, no deletion occurs. Consider the examples provided in (438).

(438)

sta/rt^{ś}/	sta[rt^{ś}]	'scuffle' gen.pl.
zwar/rt^{ś}/	zwar[rt^{ś}]	'short-circuit' gen.pl.
ćwie/rt^{ś}/	ćwie[rt^{ś}]	'quarter' nom.sg.
pe/rt^{ś}/	pe[rt^{ś}]	'mountain path' nom.sg.

In summary, the affricate [t^{ś}] is often optionally deleted when it occurs in the word-final [śt^{ś}] cluster. In case when it is preceded by the sonorant /r/ no deletion takes place. Besides, it has to be stressed that the cluster [śt^{ś}] occurring in word-initial position is never deleted, e.g., /śt^{ś}/ana 'wall' nom.sg. and /śt^{ś}/erać 'to rub (sth) off' inf are always pronounced as [śt^{ś}]ana and [śt^{ś}]erać, respectively.

As far as word-medial position is concerned, drastic simplifications of clusters containing affricates and fricatives are attested. The deletion of word-medial sounds is however limited to one grammatical category, i.e., numerals. For example, /dvad^{ź}eśt^{ś}a/ 'twenty' nom. is pronounced as [dvad^{ź}eśt^{ś}a] or in the most simplified version as [dvaeśt^{ś}a] or [dvaśt^{ś}a]. In the pronunciation of another numeral, i.e. /p'ɛ̃t^{ś}d^{ź}eśãt/ 'fifty' nom., the simplified variant such as [p'ɛ̃ńt^{ś}d^{ź}eśɔnt] is more frequently attested than the nonsimplified one, i.e. [p'ɛ̃ńd^{ź}eśɔnt]. The medial affricate [t^{ś}] is also dropped in /šeśt^{ś}d^{ź}eśɔnt/ 'sixty' nom.. Similary, /d^{ź}evięt^{ś}d^{ź}eśãt/ 'ninety' nom. is reduced in the pronunciation to [d^{ź}evieńd^{ź}eśɔnt]. Klemensiewicz (1995:50) considers all variants as

[194] Note again that foot structure (prominence vs. nonprominence or stressed vs. unstressed) does not play a role here, since both positions in which [t^{ś}] deletes or not are unstressed word-final syllables.

correct forms in Standard Polish. He also recognizes [šejset], the totally simplified form of /šeśt^{ś}set/ 'six hundred' nom. as a correct variant.

Deletions in numerals is not a Polish-specific phenomenon; words belonging to this category undergo also various simplifications in other languages. For example, German numerals ending in *zehn* [t^{s}e:n] 'ten' may be pronounced as [t^{s}n] and those ending in *zehnhundert* [ze:nhundɐt] 'ten hundreds' may be even spoken as [t^{s}ɐt] "as long as the word refers to a year and *hundert* is not stressed" Kohler (1998:27).

Plosives are also deleted in spontaneous speech. One of the most frequent deletions is the loss of the plosive [t] in word-final position. This is illustrated by the words provided in (439), cf. Dunaj (1985:40).

(439)

atrame/nt/	atrame[nt]	atrame[n]	'ink' nom.sg.
proce/nt/	proce[nt]	proce[n]	'percentage' nom.sg.
eksperyme/nt/	eksperyme[nt]	experyme[n]	'experiment' nom.sg.
mome/nt/	mome[nt]	mome[n]	'moment' nom.sg.
preze/nt/	preze[nt]	preze[n]	'gift' nom.sg.

What the data presented in (439) have in common is the final homorganic cluster consisting of the nasal [n] followed by the plosive [t]. As reported by Dunaj (1985:40), there is a significant difference between the loss of the final [t] in nouns, cf. (439), and in numerals such as pięćdziesio[nt] 'fifty' nom, sześćdziesio[nt] 'sixty' nom, siedemdziesio[nt] 'seventy' nom, etc. The clusters occurring in numerals are simplified more frequently than the ones in the nouns in (439). However, the same clusters in pronouns, cf. sko[nt] 'from where', sto[nt] 'from here', doko[nt] 'where', doto[nt] 'up to here', are not simplified. These observations lead to the conclusion that deletions of consonants are dependent on the grammatical category of the words they belong to. What remains to be examined is the relation between the grammatical category of words under consideration and their frequency of occurrence in every-day usage.

A final [t] also deletes after [s]. Consider the examples shown in (440).

(440)

je/st/	je[st]	je[s]	'to be' 3 ps.sg. pres.
natomia/st/	natomia[st]	natomia[s]	'however'
natychmia/st/	natychmia[st]	natychmia[s]	'immediately'
wyja/zd/	wyja[st]	wyja[s]	'departure' nom.sg.
u/st/	u[st]	u[s]	'mouth' gen.pl

It is worth noting that the loss of the [t] in the word je[st] 'to be' pres.3 ps.sg. occurs much more frequently than in the other words in (440), cf. Dunaj (1985:36-37). Undoubtedly, this asymmetry is due to the high frequency of occurrence of the former word as opposed to the latter ones. The examples presented above indicate that there is a difference between the affricate [t^{ś}] and the coronal plosive [t]. While the former is optionally deleted when it is preceded by a fricative [ś], the latter is elided after the fricative [s] and the sonorant [n]. In all of these deletions the consonants [t^{ś}] and [t] are homorganic with the preceding segments. As in the cases discussed earlier the frequency of occurrence contributes to the deletion of segments in spontaneous speech.

Let us proceed to other positions in which plosives are deleted. In (441) it is shown that the plosive [d] is deleted if it occurs between nasals. The preceding nasal but not necessarily the following one is always homorganic with the plosive [d]. As the example indicate, it is not only the plosive that deletes but in the most simplified version it is the last nasal in the cluster that may also delete.

(441)

porzo/ndn/y	porzo[ndn]y	porzo[nn]y	porzo[n]y	'solid' masc.nom.sg.
urze/ndń/ik	urze[ndń]ik	urze[ńń]ik	urze[ń]ik	'clerk' nom.sg.
wzgle/ndn/y	wzgle[ndn]y	wzgle[nn]y	wzgle[n]y	'relative' masc.nom.sg.
podrze/ndn/y	podrze[ndn]y	podrze[nn]y	podrze[n]y	'subordinate' masc.nom.sg.

The environment for the optional deletion of [d] is, however, not only between two nasals. In (442) words are provided in which the medial stops are optionally dropped in spontaneous speech, cf. (Rubach 1977:132).

(442)

przyje/zdn/y	przyje[zdn]y	przyje[zn]y	'visiting' masc.nom.sg.
gwi/zdn/ąć	gwi[zdn]ąć	gwi[zn]ąć	'to whistle' inf.
chrze/stn/y	chrze[stn]y	chrze[sn]y	'godfather' nom.sg.
po/stn/y	po[stn]y	po[sn]y	'meagre' masc.nom.sg.
a/stm/a	a[stm]a	a[sm]a	'asthma' nom.sg.
napa/stl/iwy	napa[stl]iwy	napa[sl]iwy	'aggressive' masc.nom.sg.
denty/stk/a	denty[stk]a	denty[sk]a	'dentist' fem.nom.sg.
zachły/stn/ąć	zachły[stn]ąć	zachły[sn]ąć	'to choke' inf.
bezszele/stn/y	bezszele[stn]y	bezszele[sn]y	'noiseless' masc.nom.sg.

In all the examples presented in (442) the plosive is a medial segment in a cluster and it is preceded by a homorganic fricative [s] or [z] depending on the voicing specification of the following plosive. The segment following the deleted [d] is either [n, m, l] or [k].

According to Rubach (1977: 132) there are no simplifications in mnó[stf]o 'many', pań[stf]o 'state' nom.sg., or mu[štr]a 'military training' nom.sg., since the stop is followed by a continuant. At the same time he observes that the deletion of [t] is possible in words such as wa[rstf]a 'stratum' nom.sg., głu[pstf]o 'nonsense' nom.sg., leka[rstf]o 'medicine' nom.sg., brate[rstf]o 'brotherhood' nom.sg., and others. Rubach (1997) captures all of these examples by a rule that deletes the plosive if it is preceded by an obstruent and followed by a consonant. When the consonant is a continuant, then the plosive must preceded by a sequence of two obstruents. The rule is shown in (443), cf. Rubach (1977:133).

(443)

$$\begin{bmatrix}-\text{cont}\\-\text{del rel}\\+\text{coron}\\+\text{anter}\end{bmatrix} \rightarrow \varnothing \quad / \quad \langle C\rangle \begin{bmatrix}+\text{obstr}\\+\text{coron}\end{bmatrix} \quad — \quad \begin{bmatrix}+\text{cons}\\\langle+\text{contin}\rangle\end{bmatrix}$$

Although simplifications captured by the rule in (443) are in common, *The Principles of Contemporary Polish Pronunciation* prescribe only the nonsimplified variant in (441) and (442) in Standard Polish, cf. Madejowa (1993:79f).

Another context in which coronal plosives are deleted in word-medial position is when they are followed by an affricate. In (444) examples are shown in which the plosive [t] is deleted before [t^s].

(444)

ra/dt^s/a	ra[tt^s]a	ra[t^s]a	'adviser' nom.sg.
wła/dt^s/a	wła[tt^s]a	wła[t^s]a	'ruler' nom.sg.
dowó/dt^s/a	dowó[tt^s]a	dowó[t^s]a	'commander' nom.sg.
ma/tt^s/e	ma[tt^s]e	ma[t^s]e	'mother' dat.sg.
cio/tt^s/e	cio[tt^s]e	cio[t^s]e	'aunt' dat.sg.
kur/tt^s/e	kur[tt^s]e	kur[t^s]e	'jacket' dat.sg.

The deletion of a plosive does not only occur when it is followed by an alveolar affricate. For example, oświa/dt$^{\check{s}}$/enie 'assertion' nom.sg., is pronounced as either oświa[tt$^{\check{s}}$]enie or oświa[t$^{\check{s}}$]enie. In *The Dictionary of Polish Pronunciation* (1977:LIX) both variants in (444) are recognized as correct forms in Standard Polish. The second variant, however, is more common and therefore it is preferred to the nonsimplified one. Similarly, Madejowa (1993:75) acknowledges the attested variations as correct in Standard Polish although she does not make any distinction with respect to which is the preferred pronunciation.

In sum, medial coronal plosives /t/ and /d/ may be deleted in spontanteous speech in well-defined contexts. The environment for deletion is constituted by nasals, cf. (441), or by coronal continuants and the following noncontinuants, cf. (442). When the plosive is followed by a continuant, it may only be deleted if two additional segments in the initial position of the cluster occur. Another deletion context is constituted by affricates that follow plosives, cf. (444).

Let us examine how velar plosives are simplified in spontaneous speech. In (445) it is shown that a velar plosive (voiced or voiceless) may be deleted if it is preceded by [ŋ].

(445)

pielęgniarka	piele[ŋgń]arka	pielę[ŋń]arka	'nurse' nom.sg.
ścięgno	ście[ŋgn]o	ście[ŋn]o	'sinew' nom.sg.
punktualny	pu[ŋkt]ualny	pu[ŋt]ualny	'punctual' masc.nom.sg.
punkcja	pu[ŋkt^{s}j]a	pu[ŋt^{s}j]a	'puncture' nom.sg.

All velars shown in (445) that are optionally elided occupy the medial position in a cluster. The segment preceding [g] is always a homorganic nasal. If the plosive is voiced, i.e. [g], it must be followed by a nasal and if it is voiceless, i.e. [k], it has to be followed by an obstruent. Hence, there are no deletions in pie[ŋkn]ość 'beauty' nom.sg. or ba[ŋkn]ot 'banknote' nom.sg. because, as Rubach (1977:136) observes, the deletion is conditioned by an agreement in voicing between the velars and the following segment apart from the presence of the nasal.

Let us proceed to other cases in which velar plosives may be optionally deleted if they occur in clusters. Consider the examples shown in (446).

(446)

obśli/zgn/ąć	obśli[zgn]ąć	obśli[zn]ąć	'to slide down' inf.
umi/zgn/ąć	umi[zgn]ąć	umi[zn]ąć	'to court' inf.
bry/zgn/ąć	bry[zgn]ąć	bry[zn]ąć	'to splash' inf.
blu/zgn/ąć	blu[zgn]ąć	blu[zn]ąć	'to gush' inf.

The examples presented in (446) show a straightforward simplification of the cluster [zgn]. The simplification has gone to the extent that it is beginning to be mirrored in the orthography. "Słownik poprawnej polszczyzny" *The Dictionary of Correct Polish Usage* (Doroszewski 1982) accepts *obślizgnąć* and *obśliznąć* as well as *umizgnąć* and *umiznąć* as correct in Standard Polish, while *bryzgnąć* and *bluzgnąć* are recognized as rare forms.

Rubach (1977:137) points also out that a similar deletion as in (446) takes place when a voiceless velar plosive is preceded by a fricative and followed by a nasal. As an example illustrating this generalization he provides a deletion in tę/skń/ć 'to miss' inf. that can be pronounced as tę[sń]ć. I will not deny this example, however, I will also not consider this single item as basis for generalizations. According to my observations, voiceless velar plosives are not as readily dropped as voiced velars are. It might be that the condition for deleting velar plosives is blocked by the same condition as for cases presented in (445). There is however no counterevidence available showing that velars are deleted if they are followed by voiceless segments.

Finally, it has to be stressed that the clusters /zgn/ and /skn/ are never simplified in word-initial position, e.g. /zgn/usnieć is pronounced as [zgn]usnieć 'to grow listless' inf and /skn/ocić as [skn]ocić 'to bungle' inf. Again, these example provide supporting evidence for the special status of word-initial position.

In sum, velar plosives are elided in spontaneous speech if they occur in medial position of a non-initial cluster. Their loss is determined by the segments that precede and follow them. Voiceless velars do not undergo deletions as readily as voiced velars do.

The last group to be discussed are labials. The deletion of labial plosives in contrast to coronal and velar plosives or labio-dental fricatives occurs extremely rarely in spontaneous speech. There is not enough evidence available that would allow one to state any generalizations. Wierzchowska (1971:206) reports that the word *przeste-[mpstf]o* 'crime' nom.sg. can be simplified to *przeste[mstf]o* or *przeste[msf]o*. She ascribes this change simply to the quantitative complexity of clusters, i.e., clusters consisting of four or five members. Further examples are not available.

In sum, the examples presented above show that certain consonants in two-, three-, and four-member clusters are dropped in spontaneous speech. Their deletion is not arbitrary but depends on various factors such as the position in the word, extra-syllabicity, presence of a morphological boundary, phonetic properties of deleted sounds and of their environment, the grammatical categories of words in which they occur, as well as the frequency of occurrence of simplified items. In some cases the interaction of some factors may contribute to the loss of a segment.

Since the deletion is attested only in certain clusters, it is difficult to state firm generalizations. It seems that extrasyllabic sonorants are most likely to be elided. Among fricatives it is [f] that is often deleted. As far as plosives are concerned, it appears that coronal plosives are more readily deleted in spontaneous speech than velar plosives. Deletions of labial plosives are extremely rare.

5.2 Merger and assimilation

In this subsection we will examine another simplification process, i.e., the merger of two consonants into one (i.e. $C_aC_b \rightarrow C_c$ where $c \neq a, b$). That this process is an example of optimization follows not only from the fact that a consonant cluster is simplified but also from the properties of the output segment, which is in every case an existing segment in the Polish consonantal inventory. Otherwise, if an entirely new segment were created, the simplification in terms of optimization would have to be questioned.

Before we proceed to concrete examples, let us observe that there is a crucial difference in pronunciation between a cluster consisting of a plosive and a fricative such as [tš] and an affricate such as [$t^{š}$]. More importantly, the difference in pronunciation provides a distinction between words such as [tš]ech 'three' gen.pl. and [$t^{š}$]ech 'Czech' nom.sg. or [tš]y 'three' nom.pl. and [$t^{š}$]y 'whether'.

Another point that requires clarification is the fact that the merger is closely connected with assimilation. It is often the case that the variants of the same word are results either of assimilation or the merger. Therefore, I will consider both variants simultaneously. In addition, in the final part of this subsection assimilations of different types are discussed.

Let us examine the data. In (447) examples are provided that show three pronunciation variants of the cluster [dž] and its voiceless counterpart [tš]. Apart from the faithful pronunciation, i.e. [dž] and [tš], both clusters are often pronounced as a sequence of an affricate and a fricative such as [$d^{ž}$ž] and [$t^{š}$š], respectively. This means that a plosive assimilates to the following fricative with respect to the place of articulation, and in addition it gains the [+cont] part of the affricate. The most reduced variant is the merger of the plosive with the following fricative that results in affricates [$d^{ž}$] and [$t^{š}$]. One may characterize the last case as deletion rather than merger. This interpretation is, however, possible only from a derivational point of view, which is abandoned in this thesis.

(447)

a.

/dž/azga	[dž]azga	[d$^{\check{z}}$ž]azga	[d$^{\check{z}}$]azga	'splinter' nom.sg.
/dž/wi	[dž]wi	[d$^{\check{z}}$ž]wi	[d$^{\check{z}}$]wi	'door' pl.tantum
/dž/ewo	[dž]ewo	[d$^{\check{z}}$ž]ewo	[d$^{\check{z}}$]ewo	'tree' nom.sg.

b.

/tš/eba	[tš]eba	[t$^{\check{s}}$š]eba	[t$^{\check{s}}$]eba	'it is necessary'
/tš/miel	[tš]miel	[t$^{\check{s}}$š]miel	[t$^{\check{s}}$]miel	'bumble bee' nom.sg.
/tš/ysta	[tš]ysta	[t$^{\check{s}}$š]ysta	[t$^{\check{s}}$]ysta	'three hundred' nom.

Although all variations provided in (447) are attested in spontaneous speech only two of them are recognized as correct in Standard Polish. *The Dictionary of Polish Pronunciation* (1977 : LVIII) gives priority to the pronunciation of the type *[d$^{\check{z}}$ž]azga* and *[t$^{\check{s}}$š]eba* since it is the most widespread formal variant. The faithful pronunciation, i.e. *[dž]azga* and *[tš]eba*, is also accurate but less common. The most reduced variant, i.e. *[d$^{\check{z}}$]azga* or *[t$^{\check{s}}$]eba*, is disqualified and considered as 'substandard' since it "is exclusive to folk dialects and city dialects; it is also heard in the cultural dialect of Cracow and western Małopolska" (*The Dictionary of Polish Pronunciation* 1977: LVII). Similarly, in the most recent edition of *The Rules of Correct Polish Pronunciation* (Klemensiewicz 1995:50) the last variant is considered as unacceptable in Standard Polish. Interestingly, Madejowa (1993:81) considers only forms with the initial [dž] and recognizes all of them as correct. She claims that the most simplified variant, [d$^{\check{z}}$], is correct since "this realization is the most frequent one in literary present-day Polish" (Madejowa 1993:81). Variants with affricates are preferred in borrowings such as *jam*, *jazz* or *judo*. According to *The Dictionary of Polish Pronunciation* (1977:LVIII) the correct pronunciation of these words in Standard Polish is [d$^{\check{z}}$]em, [d$^{\check{z}}$]azz, or [d$^{\check{z}}$]udo, albeit at least the first item is often pronounced as [dž]em or [d$^{\check{z}}$ž]em. What these examples show is an understandable movement in the language, namely, the adjustment of borrowings to native words in the pronunciation. Since the native words display optional variants in pronunciation, borrowings with similar properties tend to be pronounced in the same way.

What is particularly striking about the examples discussed above is the fact that it is precisely word-initial position in which changes are taking place. In light of other examples presented thus far we may hypothesize that since the variation takes place in word-initial position that is principally reluctant to changes, it is to be expected via implication that simplifications in noninitial positions may occur. This is indeed the case. In (448) it is shown what kinds of variations are heard in spontaneous speech if the cluster [tš] occurs word-finally.

(448)

pa/tž/	pa[tš]	pa[t$^{\check{s}}$š]	pa[t$^{\check{s}}$]	'to look' imp.2ps.sg.
wewną/tž/	wewną[tš]	wewną[t$^{\check{s}}$š]	wewną[t$^{\check{s}}$]	'intra-' pronoun
mi/stž/	mi[stš]	mi[st$^{\check{s}}$], mi[št$^{\check{s}}$š]	mi[št$^{\check{s}}$]	'master' nom.sg.

Note that in the last case the fricative /s/ that precedes the affricate assimilates to its place of articulation. Assimilations of this type will also be provided below.

Processes of a similar type are also attested in word-medial positions. In (449) examples are shown in which the medial cluster [stš] may be optionally pronounced as [št^{š}š] or [št^{š}]. Note that adjectives and nouns are treated separately in order to stress the difference between different processes in various word classes. In the former case it is the formation of the comparative, while in the latter it is the locative case of the noun paradigm that is created. The locative desinence -/e/ has palatalizing properties that trigger the palatalization of the stem-final consonant, cf. 4.2.2. In (449)b it is the trill /r/ that undergoes palatalization and becomes [ž]. Since [ž] occurs in cluster and segments constituting clusters agree with respect to voicing, the voiced [ž] becomes [š], cf. 3.2.1.

(449)

a. adjectives				
pro/stš/y	pro[stš]y	pro[št^{š}š]y	pro[št^{š}]y	'easy' comp.masc.nom.sg.
tłu/stš/y	tłu[stš]y	tłu[št^{š}š]y	tłu[št^{š}]y	'fat' comp.masc.nom.sg.
gę/stš/y	gę[stš]y	gę[št^{š}š]y	gę[št^{š}]y	'thick' comp.masc.nom.sg.
b. nouns loc.sg.				
lu/str/e	lu[stš]e	lu[št^{š}š]e	lu[št^{š}]e	'mirror' nom.sg.
pla/str/e	pla[stš]e	pla[št^{š}š]e	pla[št^{š}]e	'plaster' nom.sg.
torni/str/e	torni[stš]e	torni[št^{š}š]e	torni[št^{š}]e	'satchel' nom.sg.

It is worth noting that in all clusters presented in (449) the cluster [tš] is preceded by [s]. The presence of another segment seems to be a condition for the simplification of the following cluster. If the same cluster is preceded by a vowel in word-medial position, no simplification occurs. For example mło/dš/y 'jung' comp.masc.nom.sg. is pronounced exclusively as mło[tš]y or mło[t^{š}š]y; kró/tš/y 'short'comp.masc.nom.sg. may be pronounced either as kró[tš]y or as kró[t^{š}š]y. On the other hand, no alternate pronunciations for the two words mło[t^{š}]y or kró[t^{š}]y are attested.

A similar conclusion can be drawn from the words presented in (450).

(450)

po/dź/emny	po[dź]emny	po[d^{ź}ź]emny	'underground' adj.masc.nom.sg.
na/dz/ór	na[dz]ór	na[d^{z}z]ór	'inspection' nom.sg.
o/dž/ut	o[dž]ut	o[d^{ž}ž]ut	'recoil' nom.sg.
o/dž/ywka	o[dž]ywka	o[d^{ž}ž]ywka	'nutrient' nom.sg.

Note that the affricate has the same place of articulation as the following fricative. It seems that this variant is simpler from the articulatory point of view and is therefore preferred by speakers.

Finally, we consider assimilations. As it was shown in 4.2.6, alveolar fricatives such as /z/ and /s/ assimilate their place of articulation to the place of articulation of the following affricate. Consider the options provided in (451).

(451)

/zd^{ź}/wić	[zd^{ź}]wić	[źd^{ź}]wić	'to surprise' inf
/zd^{ź}/erać	[zd^{ź}]erać	[źd^{ź}]erać	'to tear (sth) off' inf.
ro/zd^{ź}/ał	ro[zd^{ź}]ał	ro[źd^{ź}]ał	'chapter' nom.sg.
ro/zd^{ź}/więk	ro[zd^{ź}]więk	ro[źd^{ź}]więk	'dissonance' nom.sg.
ro/zś/adać	ro[sś]adać	ro[śś]adać	'to sit down' inf.
ro/zś/ewać	ro[sś]ewać	ro[śś]ewać	'to sow' inf.

In all forms presented in (451) there is a morpheme boundary between the prefix /z/ or /roz/ and the following stem. As expected, assimilation occurs in words without a morpheme-boundary, such as [zd^{ź}]sław 'Zdźsław' nom.sg. that is pronounced either as [zd^{ź}]sław or as [źd^{ź}]sław.

Rubach (1994:137) proposes an optional rule that he dubs 'Strident Assimilation'. The rule applies also across word-boundaries and affects the changes presented in (452), cf. also 4.2.6.

(452)

a. s z → š ž / __ š ž t^{š} d^{ž}
ś ź / __ ś ź t^{ś} d^{ź}

b. t^{s} d^{z} → t^{š} d^{ž} / __ š ž t^{š} d^{ž}
t^{ś} d^{ź} / __ ś ź t^{ś} d^{ź}

c. t d → t^{š} d^{ž} / __ š ž t^{š} d^{ž}
t^{ś} d^{ź} / __ ś ź t^{ś} d^{ź}

d. t d → t^{s} d^{z} / __ s z t^{s} d^{z}

Examples of the rules in (452) are provided in (453), cf. Rubach (1994:138).

(453)

a. ro/zš/erzyć → ro/šš/erzyć	'broaden' inf
b. o/t^{s}t^{ś}/e → o/t^{ś}t^{ś}/e	'vinegar' loc.sg.
c. świa/dt^{š}/yć → świa/t^{š}t^{š}/yć	'witness' inf
d. o/dt^{s}/edzić → o/t^{s}t^{s}/edzić	'drain' inf

In sum, only alveolar fricatives and plosives are apt to undergo assimilation. Retroflexes and alveolo-palatal coronals systematically resist assimilations, e.g., mu/št^{s}/e is pronounced invariably as mu[št^{s}]e. This observation independently confirms that certain sounds undergo changes more readily than others. Generally, it appears that alveolar coronals undergo most changes; rules presented in (452) show that the subset of alveolar fricatives and plosives is changed in spontaneous speech more readily than other coronals.

Summary

In this chapter optional processes affecting consonant clusters in spontaneous speech were presented. It was shown that consonantal sequences occurring in present-day Polish undergo systematic changes such as deletion, merger, and assimilation. Evidently, the processes affect only certain clusters that are not necessarily complex with respect to the segments they consist of. The investigation of the attested variations indicates that there are various instances triggering the ongoing changes in clusters. The most important factors are: position in the word, extrasyllabicity, presence of a morphological boundary, phonetic properties of deleted sounds and of their environment, grammatical categories of words in which they occur, as well as the frequency of occurrence of simplified items. In many cases it is the interaction of some factors that leads to the emergence of the variation.

The table in (454) gives an overview of ongoing optional deletions in spontaneous speech. Generally, extrasyllabic sonorants and coronal plosives that are either the last member of a cluster (word-final position) or a medial one (word-medial position) are elided most frequently in spontaneous speech. Their deletion is obviously constrained by the environment in which they occur; for other deletions cf. (455).

(454) Deletions

Cluster	Position	Example	Word
obstruent+sonorant + obstruent	word-medial	/płk/, /dłk/, /ślń/, /rnk/, /snk/, /kłš/, /głš/, /dłš/, /dlt^{ś}/, /ślt^{ś}/;	ja[pwk]o → ja[pk]o
obstruent+sonorant	word-final	/śl/, /sm/, /zn/, /śń/, /kł/, /gł/, /dł/, /dl/;	my[śl] → my[śl]
płt^{ś}	word-initial	płt^{ś}	[płt^{ś}]owy → [pt^{ś}]owy
obstruent+ł+u	word-initial	/gł/, /tł/, /dł/, /sł/;	[gw]upi → [g]upi
v+sk$_{[SUFFIX]}$	word-medial	/v+sk/	krako[fsk]i → krako[sk]i
v+stv$_{[SUFFIX]}$	word-medial	/v+stv/	zna[fstf]o → zna[stf]o
śt^{ś}	word-final	/śt^{ś}/	wolno[śt^{ś}]→ wolno[ś]
śt^{ś}d^{ź}	word-medial	/śt^{ś}d^{ź}/	/šeśt^{ś}d^{ź}eśąt/ → [šeśd^{ź}eśɔnt]
nt	word-final	/nt/	atrame/nt/ → atrame[n]
st	word-final	st	je[st] → je[s]
ndn	word-medial	/ndn/	porzo[ndn]y → porzo[n]y
obstruent+plosive+ noncontinuant	word-medial	/zdn/,/stn/, /stm/, /stl/, /stk/, /stn/;	przyje[zdn]y → przyje[zn]y
obstruent+sonorant+ plosive+continuant	word-medial	/rstv/, /pstv/;	wa[rstf]a → wa[rsf]a
dt^{s}, tt^{s}	word-medial	/dt^{s}/, /tt^{s}/;	ma[tt^{s}]e → ma[t^{s}]e

nasal+voiced (voiceless) velar plosive+nasal	word-medial	/ngn/,/nkt/,/nkt^{s}/;	pu[ŋkt]ualny → pu[ŋt]ualny
zgn	word-medial	/zgn/	obśli[zgn]ąć → obśli[zn]ąć

The table in (455) summarizes the results of other processes affecting clusters, i.e., merger and assimilation. The target of the attested changes are alveolar fricatives, plosives or affricates.

(455) Merger and assimilation

Cluster	Position	Word
/dž/, /tš/	word-initial	[dž]azga → [d^{ž}ž]azga → [d^{ž}]azga
/tž/	word-final	pa[tš] → pa[t^{š}š] → pa[t^{š}]
/stš/	word-medial	pro[stš]y → pro[št^{š}š]y → pro[št^{š}]y
/dź/	word-medial	po[dź]emny → po[d^{ź}ź]emny
/zd^{ź}/	word-initial	[zd^{ź}]wić → [źd^{ź}]wić

Although deletion, merger, and assimilation drastically differ from each other as processes per se they lead to a homogeneous result, i.e., to a simplified articulatory structure. This opens a perspective for further development of clusters: it seems that the complex consonantal sequences will be further simplified. This hypothesis arises an important question as to what extent such optimization is possible. The answer will be provided by the future.

6 Summary

The present study is an examination of the development of Polish consonant clusters. The theoretical underpinnings, as outlined in the first chapter and built upon in chapters two through four, are those of Optimality Theory.

I started my investigation by examining the loss of 'semi-vowels', jers, which began in the tenth century. I showed that the loss of jers resulted in the emergence of complex consonantal sequences. However, the driving force behind this change had an exclusively prosodic character. It was in fact the tendency for the strengthening of a prominent position within a foot that had a crucial influence on the asymmetrical development of jers. Evidently, this tendency conflicted with the tendency to reduce the number of syllables in the word. As a consequence, jers were either reinforced to full vowels or they disappeared. I interpreted this asymmetry, predicted by Havlik's Law, as an interaction of both prosodic as well as segmental constraints. I showed that it was the loss of jers that directly caused the emergence of consonant clusters while the driving force behind this process was of prosodic character.

Further, I examined the consequences of these changes along phonological and morphological dimensions. I showed, for example, that output-output constraints requiring a homogeneous root for all forms of an inflectional paradigm took precedence over a phonological markedness constraint prohibiting complex codas. In other words, morphology was more influential than phonology. More importantly, the morphological constraint was directly influenced by a constraint requiring a minimal number of syllables in a word. Therefore the genitive case, whose root consisted of one syllable, served as a basis for a paradigm leveling as opposed to a bisyllabic nominative case. In some instances, however, this argument was unsatisfactory since there was no difference with respect to the number of syllables in the nominative and the genitive (or other) cases. I account for this peculiarity proposing that the genitive case was taken as a basis for a paradigm leveling in order to avoid vowel-zero alternation. Otherwise, the vowel-zero alternation would result in highly complex clusters prohibited by another constraint. As expected, the avoidance of vowel-zero alternations conflicted with a constraint minimizing the number of syllables in a word but on the other hand it satisfies a high-ranking constraint (at that time) prohibiting complex consonant clusters. This observation has a more general application: reductions (minimizations) on one level lead to increased complexity on another level. The degree of complexity is, however, limited. For this reason minimization is possible only to some extent. In the case at hand, the reduction of syllables was blocked by the increasing complexity of consonant clusters. Language economy decided not to admit the complex consonantal sequences by favoring paradigms with two consonants in the coda that block vowel-zero alternation and its undesired effects. This conclusion is directly supported by the seemingly exceptional development of jers. In some cases jers were reinforced to full vowels although the positions in which they occur predicted their disappearance. Again, I ascribed this peculiarity to the high-ranking constraint prohibiting clusters. In the same vein, processes of simplifications of clusters were accounted for. Finally, I also presented irregular, sporadic, and rather unexpected changes affecting the clusters, such as epenthesis of a consonant in the existing clusters. What these cases confirmed is the fact that the development of language cannot be encapsulated in systematic schemes. Rather, there are always various irregularities attested with respect to the main direction of development. They underline individual dynamics of linguistic structures which were strongly evidenced by the Period of Trial and Error.

In the third chapter I examined consonant clusters of present-day Polish. I provided a detailed presentation of word-initial and word-final clusters by grouping them into sets of two-, three-, four-, and five-member clusters. The systematization was also based on sonority distinctions: attested combinations of obstruents and sonorants were presented. In the case of word-initial clusters I also provided a number of lexical items in which the given cluster is attested.

Taking into consideration sonority distinctions, the number of possible consonant sequences in single sets(obstruent+obstruent, sonorant+sonorant, etc.), the frequency of occurrence of single clusters, as well as syllabifications provided by native speakers, I made some generalizations concerning Polish syllable structure. In other words, I tried to draw as many conclusions as possible from the facts referring to the surface. Based on this surface representation I investigated how this construct relates to phonological processes.

The main difference between my approach and previous accounts which I also presented in chapter three is that I consider the syllable as a surface construct. The earlier analyses, cf. Rubach and Booij (1990a,b), Gussmann (1991), Bethin (1992), assume abstract levels of derivation and create 'abstract' syllables by virtue of rules. The 'abstract' syllables are changed into surface syllables by later rules. In addition, rules are determined by constraints in order to prohibit the emergence of undesired structures. In my approach I assumed a single (concrete) level of representation. Instead of abstract rules I made use of constraints applying on the surface representation. The constraints, as opposed to rules, are violable which enables one to account for variations in syllabification within one invariable model of grammar.

The examination of clusters led to the conclusion that sonority plays a crucial role in the organization of Polish syllables. However, the sonority scale which holds for Polish considerably differs from that proposed by Selkirk (1984) or Vennemann (1988a). Similar to Rubach and Booij (1990a,b) I proposed that the sonority hierarchy for Polish has the following shape: obstruents < nasals < liquids < glides < vowels. Thus Polish treats obstruents regardless of their manner of articulation or voicing specifica-tions in a unified way; it allows sequences of plosives and fricatives in onsets and codas in either order. As far as sonorants are concerned it appears that the requirement of increasing sonority is fulfilled in the Polish syllable onset; of no relevance is the condi-tion for the coda in which sequences of two or more sonorants are prohibited.

Another important observation concerning Polish syllable structure is that it does not tolerate decreasing sonority from its edges towards its peak. This conclusion relies on the sonority hierarchy proposed above. While there is less evidence that sonorants violating the proposed sonority scale do not belong to a syllable, it is more than evident that the first member of sequences of sonorant+obstruent(s) in prevocalic position or the last member of sequences of obstruent(s)+sonorant(s) in postvocalic position is not parsed into a syllable. In other words, sonority violations are prohibited in the domain of a syllable. In light of this observation the question arises as to how the consonants that are not parsed into a syllable are to be represented. Since they are not subject to Stray Erasure, cf. Steriade (1982), I argued that extrasyllabic consonants are licensed by higher prosodic constituents such as a foot or a prosodic word. While word-initial segments are incorporated into a foot, word-medial and word-final extrasyllabic consonants are attached to a prosodic word. This asymmetry directly follows from investigation of processes such as voicing assimilation and degemination. In the first process it is only word-initial extrasyllabic sonorants that block voicing assimilation between obstruents, while noninitial sonoronts are permanently transparent to voicing. A similar asymmetry is attested in degemination: the only place in which geminates occur is in word-initial position; their presence in word-medial or word-final position is not allowed unless they are intervocalic. Furthermore, the proposed asymmetrical representation of extrasyllabic segments is supported by the phenomena attested in spontaneous speech: word-initial extrasyllabic consonants are never elided, while the deletion of medial and word-final extrasyllabic segments occurs fairly often in spontaneous speech.

Finally, the account I proposed shows that grammars of individual speakers, i.e. individual rankings, mostly allow only minimal variation, while a general ranking of a language mirrors all attested variations. The cornerstone of this idea is that a general ranking captures all possible syllabification patterns by resolving crucial rankings between some constraints. This flexibility, however, is possible only to some extent as it mirrors the plasticity found in individual grammars.

In the fourth chapter I focused my investigation on a phonological process which undoubtedly belongs to the most important processes in Polish (and Slavic) phonology, i.e., palatalization. I analyzed the effects of palatalization on labials, coronals, and velars, when followed by other consonants. For comparison purposes I also examined how the same natural classes react to palatalization when they occur in other positions such as onset and coda positions. In this chapter I also presented the main stages of palatalization processes from a diachronic point of view, which paves a better way to understanding the determining role of various functions (especially articulatory economy) in the development of language. Finally, I demonstrated the realization of palatalization in different dialects.

The investigation of labials showed that palatalized labials behave in an asymmetrical manner. First, they are present in the onset and the coda in the underlying representation but on the surface they occur only in the former and never in the latter position. If labials are followed by other consonants they are not palatalized. In other words, it is only when a labial is followed by a vowel that its secondary articulation is realized. Such a behavior is closely connected with economy of articulation: the best environment for the realization of a secondary approximant-like articulation is a vocalic element following the palatalized sound. If the palatalized segment is followed by another consonant or by a pause as in utterance(word)-final position, the realization of a secondary articulation is considerably impeded. The markedness of a secondary articulation is directly mirrored in the development of palatalized labials. The present study demonstrates that palatalized labials were pronounced in coda position until the sixteenth century when the speakers started to drop the secondary articulation in the pronunciation. At the end of the nineteenth century the process of neutralization was accomplished and the palatalization totally disappeared. This process, however, did not contribute to the optimization of Phonetic Form of Lexical Entries. In other words, the restructuring of the underlying representation did not take place. This was due to a high-ranking constraint requiring all forms of the same paradigm to have the same root. Interestingly, the secondary articulation was maintained in coda position in dialects in which it have been realized in various ways, e.g. as a fricative element. A different situation is attested in clusters. Most probably, there was a stage in which the secondary articulation was pronounced when a labial was followed by another consonant. In this case, however, the deletion of a secondary articulation was accomplished very quickly which confirms the articulatory markedness of these forms. More importantly, the markedness of palatalized labials in consonant clusters is strongly supported by a cross-linguistic tendency for disfavoring a secondary articulation in clusters: from a considerable amount of investigated languages only in one, i.e. Irish of Tourmakeady, co. Mayo, palatalized labials followed by a consonant are attested. In contrast to neutralization in coda position, the deletion of a secondary articulation in consonant clusters contributed to the optimization of underlying forms; there is no evidence available on the surface indicating the presence of palatalized labials in the underlying representation.

The next group I examined were coronals. The investigation shows that while plain coronals are widely attested in different positions, their secondarily palatalized counterparts are attested exclusively in onsets of foreign words. They do however constitute near 'minimal pairs' with native words which raises a question as to what their status in the Polish consonantal inventory is. In order to account for data requiring the rule usually referred to as Coronal Palatalization I showed that the palatalization of stem-final coronals is due to a floating feature [PAL] present in the underlying representation of the palatalizing suffixes. I argued that the account for nonpalatalization of noncontinuants by means of constraints is more adequate than one using rules since it avoids unnecessary generalizations and dispenses with non-existing derivational steps. For example, cyclic Coronal Palatalization requires an intermediate stage in which underlying /r/ and /ž/ are differentiated in order to account for the behavior of words that contain /ž/ in their underlying representation and do not undergo depalatalization when they are followed by palatalizing suffixes. If underlying /r/ were converted into [ž] directly, then the depalatalization rule would also affect the underlying /ž/. In Optimality Theory this stage is entirely avoided with the help of faithfulness constraints, which due to their highly-ranked status, prohibit the palatalization of retroflexes and alveolopalatals. Accounting for these phenomena by means of constraints seems to be more economical than by means of rules since constraints do not require a palatalization stage. Consequently the name Noncontinuant Depalatalization holds only in cyclic phonology and not in Optimality Theory which does not permit palatalization in such cases.

Furthermore, I examined the behavior of coronals in clusters with respect to palatalization. I showed that there exists a crucial asymmetry between coronals. While fricatives /s/ and /z/ always undergo palatalization when they are followed by a palatalizing suffix with a consonant, the lateral /ł/ does not change its featural content when it is followed by certain palatalizing suffixes. Noncontinuants systematically reject palatalization when the palatalizing suffix starts with laterals or nasals. In other words, sequences of alveolopalatal noncontinuants and coronal sonorants are avoided. The most marked segment seems to be /r/, which rejects palatalization before all consonants. The results of this investigation lead to a general systematization of coronals into four sets according to their behavior in different palatalizing contexts. The investigated segments can be ranked from the least marked to the most marked in the following way: /s/ /z/ < /ł/ < /t/ /d/ /n/ < /r/.

From a diachronic point of view in Late Common Slavic palatalization of coronals constitutes a very interesting issue with respect to markedness. The changes which coronals underwent undoubtedly support the generally accepted statement that marked structures are prone to disappear earlier than unmarked ones. Generally, in Late Common Slavic the palatalization of coronals was manifested by a secondary articulation in the environment of front vowels such as /i, e, ę, ě, ь/. Since sounds which are pronounced with a secondary articulation are far more marked than sounds produced at one place of articulation, the markedness of secondarily palatalized coronals was reduced by abandoning a secondary articulation. In many cases such a reduction led directly to the changing of the main place of articulation. In the second half of the twelfth century coronals started to change their place and/or manner of articulation. For example, the plosives /t'/, /d'/ started to be pronounced as affricates [$d^{ź}$] and [$t^{ś}$]. The obstruent system of /s, ś, z, ź, š, ž, d^{z}, $t^{š}$, $d^{ž}$, $t^{ś}$/ in the pronunciation of Polish people came into existence not earlier than in the middle of the 16th century. It has been still present in Modern Polish. What this study shows is that the secondary articulation is a very marked instance from an articulatory point of view. It is avoided by speakers in at least two-ways: they either use the strategies mentioned above – changing the place of articulation and/or manner of articulation of palatalized coronals – or they simply reject the palatalization as it was shown in the case of Kashubian dialects in which the secondarily palatalized /s', z', t', d'/, which in Standard Polish changed to /ś, ź, $t^{ś}$, $d^{ź}$/, were at some point depalatalized. The investigation of dialects also reveals that the system of coronal fricatives and affricates in Polish is marked in terms of a high number of different phonemes realized at closely neighboring places of articulation. Therefore, dialects dispense with this complicated system by reducing three sets to two sets. The most modified sounds are retroflexes which can be considered as indirect evidence that they are more marked than other coronals.

In the investigation of velars the focus was placed on secondarily palatalized velars. The study shows that the velars under consideration are attested only in onsets in which palatalized velar plosives are derived in the context of the following /i/ and /e/. If a velar occurring in the coda is secondarily palatalized by an initial vowel of the suffix it is invariably resyllabified as an onset. The palatalized velar fricative [x'] occurs only in foreign words while in native words it is followed by the retracted vowel [ɨ]. In addition, all velars are palatalized when they are followed by /i/ or /j/.

Furthermore, I concentrated on an ongoing process in present-day Polish which confirms the markedness of secondarily palatalized segments. Although the process is exclusively attested in foreign (albeit assimilated) vocabulary, it is of crucial importance for the present study. It shows that the secondary articulation of segments occurring even in onsets is disfavored by speakers. Velar plosives followed by /e/, which earlier underwent palatalization (SVP), are palatalized in present-day Polish rather sporadically. The palatalized variant is especially preferred by the older generation of speakers, while other speakers systematically reject it by producing a nonpalatalized variant. In the pronunciation of a handful of native words palatalization is still the only attested variant. In order to account for this discrepancy in terms of an invariable ranking I proposed to split appropriate faithfulness constraints into constraints that refer either to assimilated foreign words or to native words.

The examination of secondarily palatalized velars in dialects shows that dialect speakers either reject palatalization or they let the palatalized velars undergo the next stage of palatalization and realize them as affricates. Again, in light of the facts presented above this might be taken as indirect evidence that secondarily palatalized sounds are marked and are therefore avoided by speakers by using different strategies.

In summary, the investigation of labials, coronals and velars with respect to palatalization leads to some important conclusions. First, it shows that maintaining articulatory reflexes of palatalizations depends on some factors such as intrinsic properties of the target, the position in which the target segment occurs in a syllable/word, and the kinds of adjacent segments.

If palatalization manifests itself as a secondary articulation its survival chance is small in consonant clusters and in word-final position in comparison to prevocalic position. But if palatalization is reflected as a change in a place or manner of articulation (or both) its stability is to be expected. Again, this is dependent on the position in which the target of palatalization occurs. As far as the targets themselves are concerned it appears that the most reluctant to undergo palatalization are segments occurring in clusters (especially plosives) although some of them (coronal continuants) are still readily palatalized. That segments with a secondary articulation are generally disfavored in codas and clusters is confirmed by diachronic developments of these structures. Their intrinsic articulatory complexity is demonstrated by the nonpalatalization of velars occurring in onset position.

In the last chapter of my thesis I discussed potential future developments of clusters. The data show variations attested in spontaneous speech that are commonly considered to be indicator of ongoing changes in language. Pursuing this line I described processes that clusters optionally undergo in present-day Polish such as deletions, mergers, and assimilations. The investigation of the attested variations indicates that there are various instances triggering the ongoing changes in clusters. The most important factors include: position in the word, extrasyllabicity, presence of a morphological boundary, phonetic properties of deleted sounds and of their environment, grammatical categories of words in which they occur as well as the frequency of occurrence of simplified items. In most cases it is the interaction of some of these factors that leads to the emergence of variation.

As far as segments are concerned the present investigation reveals that extrasyllabic sonorants and coronal plosives that are either the last member of a cluster (word-final position) or a medial one (word-medial position) are dropped most frequently in spontaneous speech.

Furthermore, the study leads to the conclusion that although deletions, mergers, and assimilations differ from each other as processes per se they lead to a homogeneous result, i.e., to a simplified articulatory structure. This conclusion opens a perspective for further development of clusters, namely, it is highly probable that the complex consonantal sequences will be further simplified. The general application of this hypothesis is that the optimization of the segmental level proceeds.

6.1 Final conclusions

The present study is intended to be a contribution to a broad research project entitled "Economy and complexity in language." The questions of main interest for the present investigation are how the complexity of linguistic structures relates to economy of elements and principles in the organization of language and what role this relation plays in language development.

The present study demonstrates that there are various competing forces determining linguistic structures. Although the focus of the investigation was clearly placed on the phonetic component of lexical entries, the invocation of other components, such as grammatical or semantic, was in some cases indispensable. This fact reveals that the phonetic component, which undergoes its own principles, is connected with other components, which influence its development. In terms of constraints the complexity of the system can be expressed by constraints which exclusively refer to a phonetic, semantic, or grammatical component of LE and additionally to connections between them. Hence, the attested linguistic structures are dynamic outcomes of multiple and often conflicting promotions which determine language components.

The present investigation of principles determining the phonetic component shows that one of the underlying forces of PF is the tendency to economize (optimize) linguistic forms which manifests itself in various ways, e.g., minimization of articulatory effort is mirrored in minimization of articulatory gestures, minimization of segments, minimization of syllables, etc.

But as the study shows economization is possible only to some extent; complex linguistic structures such as Polish consonant clusters are a by-product of optimization (economy) at the prosodic level and optimization is possible only to the extent allowed by the increasing complexity of the segmental level.

The investigation also shows that the linguistic structures cannot be successfully affected by all minimization functions simultaneously. Since the minimization of elements/instances at one level leads to the increasing complexity on the other level it indicates that the improvement of one dimension leads to the worsening of the other. This conclusion suggests that there is a close connection between complexity and economy. The latter is in a sense contingent upon the former, i.e., whenever economy becomes visible, complexity does not remain silent. This inseparability let us to view optimization of linguistic outputs as products of local economies applying to separate dimensions/levels of language.

In light of these observations a plausible question arises as to whether global economy of language exists. The present longitudinal study leads to a conclusion that global economy is to be understood in terms of the shortening of the speech signal. The significant reduction of syllables resulting in complex clusters and the further permanent simplifications of consonantal sequences indicate that the Phonetic Form of Lexical Entries become shorter. The plausibility of this conclusion is in accordance with a linear representation of a Phonetic Form.

But again global economy is to be interpreted as a result of the interaction of local economies positing conflicting demands on linguistic structures. And the optimization strive is often blocked. Therefore the direct proofs of global economy in synchronic investigations are rather sporadic; they are visible from a longitudinal perspective. The optimal outputs are a kind of compromise between competing demands determining language. For this reason language cannot become better in all its dimensions.

This leads us again to the central concept of the thesis: *optimality*. As was mentioned in the first chapter the terminus *optimality* is closely connected with an 'optimism' idea developed by Gottfried Wilhelm Leibniz in the Theodicee (1702).[195] His optimism manifests itself in the belief that our world is the best of all possible worlds. However, while he did not intend to maintain that one cannot imagine a better one, he considered our world to be the best *realizable* one. Leibniz fought for a NECESSARY REALIZATION (Notwendige Realisierung) in this world which is the best because it does not stop to posit new tasks to be realized. Translating this idea to language it seems that Leibniz 'optimism' expresses, in a certain sense, the never-ending strive for optimization in language development strongly confirmed in this study. The ultimate optimization will probably never be achieved since a better system always remains to be realized.

[195] The main ideas of 'Theodizee' were most probably developed during Leibniz' stay in Berlin in 1701/1702 where he had discussions with Sophie Charlotte. Therefore, it is often contended that Sophie significantly influenced ideas presented in 'Theodizee'.

7 Appendix

7.1 Polish Consonant Features

	p	*p'*	*b*	*b'*	*f*	*f'*	*v*	*v'*	*m*	*m'*	*w*	*t*	*tš*	*d*	*dž*	*s*	*ś*
[cons]	+	+	+	+	+	+	+	+	+	+	-	+	+	+	+	+	+
[son]	-	-	-	-	-	-	-	-	+	+	+	-	-	-	-	-	-
[cont]	-	-	-	-	+	+	+	+	-	-	+	-	-/+	-	-/+	+	+
[voice]	-	-	+	+	-	-	+	+	+	+	+	-	-	+	+	-	-
[nasal]	-	-	-	-	-	-	-	-	+	+	-	-	-	-	-	-	-
[labial]	+	+	+	+	+	+	+	+	+	+	+						
[coronal]												+	+	+	+	+	+
[anter]											-	+	-	+	-	+	-
[distr]												-	+	-	+	-	+
[lateral]																	
[dorsal]																	
[high]	-	+	-	+	-	+	-	+	-	+	+	-	+	-	+	-	+
[back]	+	-	+	-	+	-	+	-	+	-	+	+	-	+	-	+	-

	z	*ź*	t^s	d^z	*n*	*ń*	*ł*	*l*	*r*	*j*	*š*	*ž*	*tš*	*dž*	*k*	*g*	*x*
[cons]	+	+	+	+	+	+	+	+	+	-	+	+	+	+	+	+	+
[son]	-	-	-	-	+	+	+	+	+	+	-	-	-	-	-	-	-
[cont]	+	+	-/+	-/+	-	-	-	-	+	+	+	+	-/+	-/+	-	-	+
[voice]	+	+	-	+	+	+	+	+	+	+	-	+	-	+	-	+	-
[nasal]	-	-	-	-	+	+	-	-	-	-	-	-	-	-	-	-	-
[labial]																	
[coronal]	+	+	+	+	+	+	+	+	+	+	+	+					
[anter]	+	-	+	+	+	-	+	+	+	-	-	-	-	-			
[distr]	-	+	-	-	-	+	-	-	-	+	-	-	-	-			
[lateral]							+	+									
[dorsal]															+	+	+
[high]	-	+	-	-	-	+	+	-	-	+	+	+	+	+	+	+	+
[back]	+	-	+	+	+	-	+	+	+	-	+	+	+	+	+	+	+

7.2 Charts: Palatalizations in various Polish dialects

7.2.1 Labials

ONSET

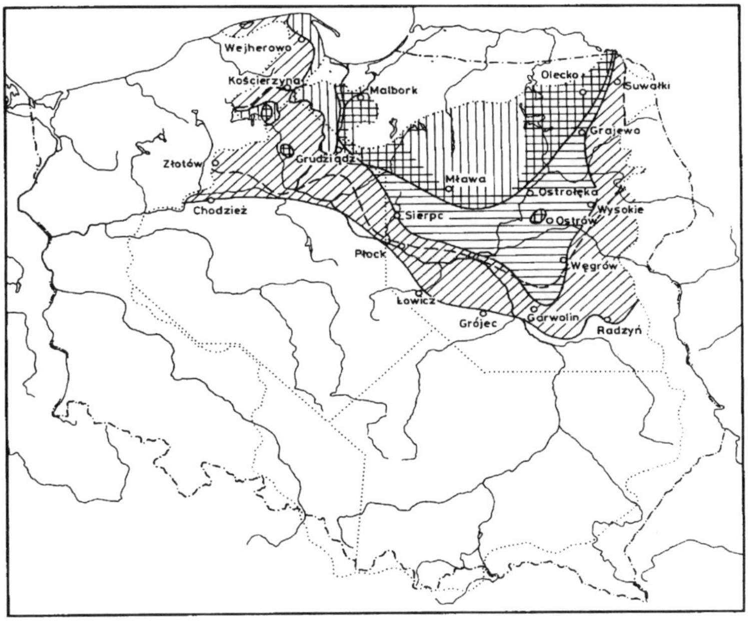

 p’, b’, f’, v’ → pś, bź, fś, vź (pš́ bž́ fš́ vž́) [pś]asek, o[fś]ara

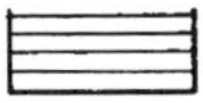 p’, b’, f’, v’ → px́, bɣ́, fx́, vɣ́ [px́]asek, o[fx́]ara, [vɣ́]ara

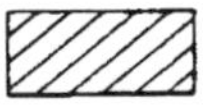 p’, b’, f’, v’, m’→ pj, bj, fj, vj, mj [bj]ały, [mj]asto

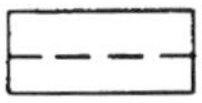 m’→mń [mń]asto, [mń]ąso

Labials

Coda

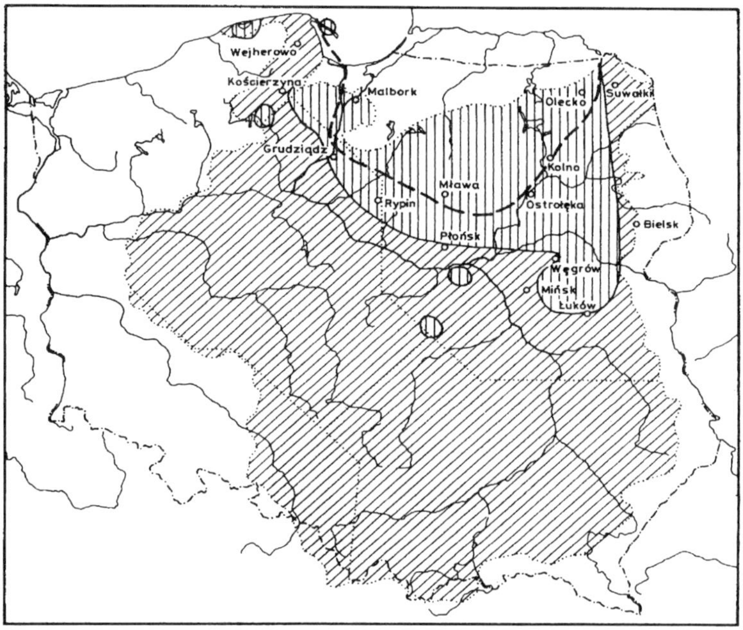

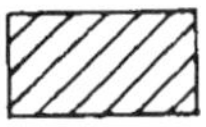 p’→ p / _ #   kar[p], pa[f]

 p’→pś, px̀/ _ #   kar[px̀],

 line separating p’→ pś, pš́ / _ #

from p’→ px́ / _ # (karp[ś], gołą[pš́]) vs (kar[px́])

7.2.2 Coronals

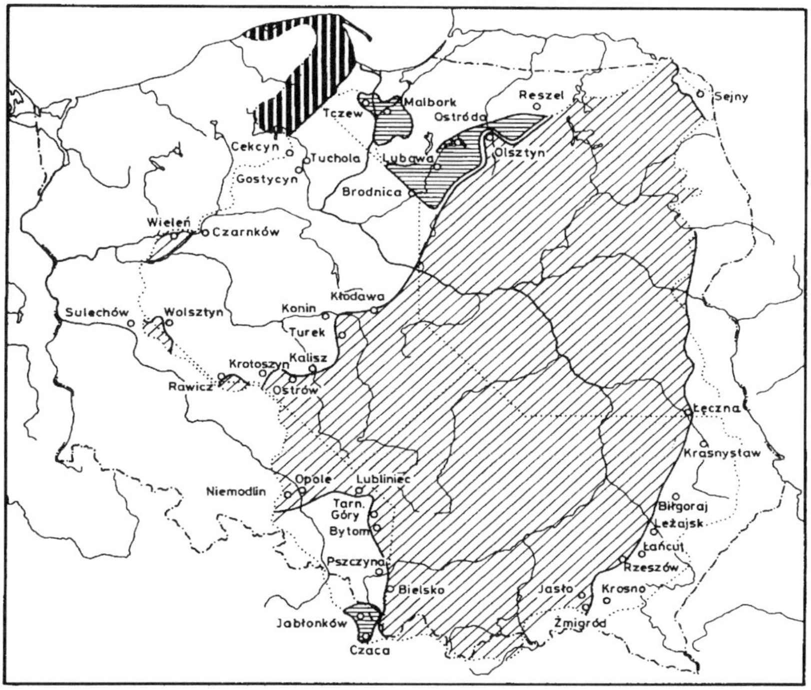

(diagonal hatching) $\check{s}\ \check{z}\ t^{\check{s}}\ d^{\check{z}} \rightarrow s\ z\ t^{s}\ d^{z}$ [z]yto, [s]yja

(horizontal hatching) $\check{s}\ \check{z}\ t^{\check{s}}\ d^{\check{z}}$ / $\acute{s}\ \acute{z}\ t^{\acute{s}}\ d^{\acute{z}}$ → $\acute{\check{s}}\ \acute{\check{z}}\ t^{\acute{\check{s}}}\ d^{\acute{\check{z}}}$ [š́]are, [š́]ano

(vertical hatching) $\acute{s}\ \acute{z}\ t^{\acute{s}}\ d^{\acute{z}} \rightarrow s\ z\ t^{s}\ d^{z}$ [s]ostra, se[d^{z}]e[t^{s}]

7.2.3 Velars

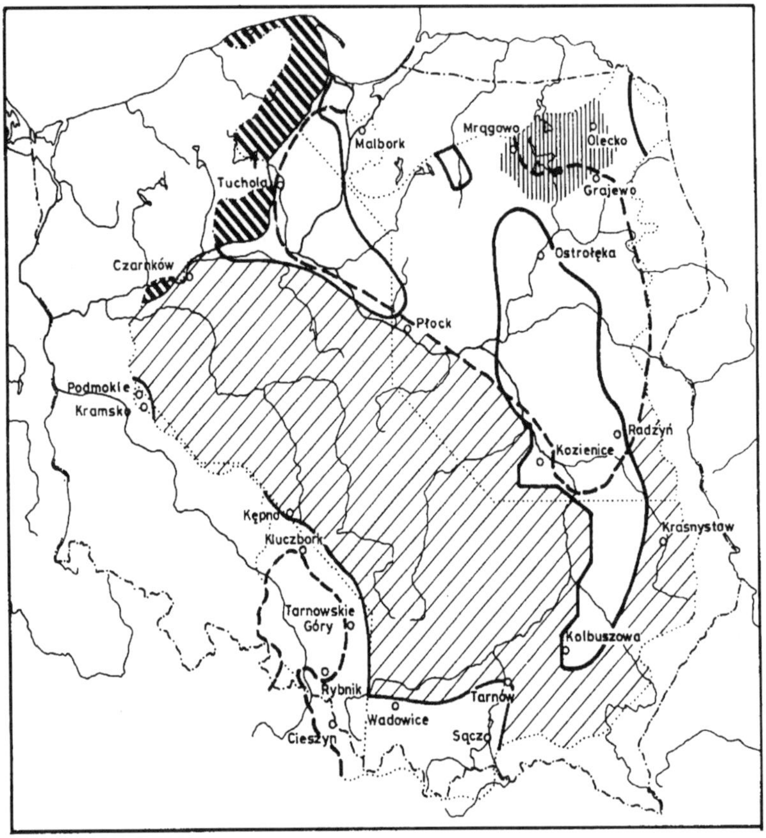

(dashed line) not regular palatalization or its lack ta[k]e, dro[g]e, cu[k]erki

(heavy hatching) k' g' x' → $t^{ś}$ $d^{ź}$ ś [$d^{ź}$]ib[$t^{ś}$]i, [$t^{ś}$]ij, dłu[$d^{ź}$]i

→ $\acute{t}^{š}$ $\acute{d}^{ž}$ $\acute{š}$ ta[$\acute{t}^{š}$]i, no[$\acute{d}^{ž}$]i, mu[$\acute{š}$]y

(light hatching) denasalization of nasal vowels Pols[k]e, dro[g]e, szyb[k]e

(vertical hatching) k g x → k' g' x' cze[k']ać, dro[g']a, mu[x']a

7.3 Consonant clusters

7.3.1 Word-initial clusters

TWO-MEMBER CONSONANT CLUSTERS

A OBSTRUENT+SONORANT

pn$_2$	pnącze	‘creeper’ nom.sg.
*pn	pneumatyczny	‘pneumatic’ nom.sg.
pń$_1$	pniak	‘stump’ nom.sg.
pl	pleśń	‘mould’ nom.sg.
pl’	plik	‘bundle’ nom.sg.
*pl’	pliocen	‘Pliocene’
pr	próba	‘trial’ nom.sg.
*pr	premia	‘bonus’ nom.sg.
*pr’$_2$	priorytet	‘priority’ nom.sg.
pw	płot	‘fence’ nom.sg.
tń	tnie	‘to cut’ 3ps.sg.pres.
tl$_1$	tlen	‘oxygen’ nom.sg.
tl’$_1$	tlić	‘to smoulder’inf.
tr	trep	‘clog’ nom.sg.
*tr	tradycja	‘tradition’
tw	tło	‘background’ nom.sg.
km’$_3$	kmieć	‘peasant’ nom.sg.
kn	knuć	‘to plot’ inf.
*kn	knajpa	‘pub’ nom.sg.
kń	knieje	‘forest’ nom.pl.
*kń	kniaź	‘Ukrainian prince’ nom.sg.
kl	klucz	‘key’ nom.sg.
*kl	klaser	‘stamp-album’ nom.sg.
*kl’	klimat	‘climate’ nom.sg.
kr	kruk	‘raven’ nom.sg.
*kr	kredo	‘credo’ nom.sg.
*kr’$_1$	krio-	‘crio-’
kw	kłos	‘ear of corn’ nom.sg.
bl	blok	‘block’ nom.sg.
br	brud	‘uncleanness’ nom.sg.
*br’	briologia	‘briology’ nom.sg.
bń$_1$	bniec	‘melandrium’ nom.sg.
bw	błysk	‘flash’ nom.sg.
dm$_1$	dmuch	‘blast’ nom.sg.

dn_1	dno	'bottom' nom.sg.
dl_3	dla	'for' prep.
dr	drut	'wire' nom.sg.
*dr'	driada	'dryad' nom.sg.
dw	dług	'debt' nom.sg.
gm_3	gmach	'building' nom.sg.
gm'_1	gmina	'community' nom.sg.
gn	gnać	'to speed' inf.
*gn	gnejs	'gneiss' nom.sg.
gń	gniew	'anger' nom.sg.
gl	gleba	'soil' nom.sg.
*gl	glon	'alga' nom.sg.
gr	grom	'thunderclap' nom.sg.
gr	gram	'gram'nom.sg.
gw	głos	'voice' nom.sg.
t^sm_2	cmokać	'to smak' inf.imperf.
t^sn_1	cnota	'virtue' nom.sg.
t^sw_1	cło	'customs duty' nom.sg.
$t^{š}m_1$	czmychnąć	'to flee' inf.perf.
$t^{š}w_3$	człon	'element' nom.sg.
$t^{ś}m_1$	ćma	'moth' nom.sg.
$t^{ś}m'_1$	ćmić	'to dim' inf.
v+m	wmówić	'to persuade' inf. perf.
vn	wnuk	'grandson' nom.sg.
v+n	wnosić	'to carry in' inf.
vń	wniosek	conclusion' nom.sg.
v+ń	wnieść	'to carry in' inf. perf.
vl	wlec	'to draw'inf.perf.
v+l	wlać	'to pour' inf. perf.
v+l'	wliczać	'to recon' inf.imperf.
vr	wrak	'wreck' nom.sg.
v+r	wrastać	'to strike root' inf. imperf.
vw	włos	'hair' nom.sg.
v+w	włazić	'to get into' inf. perf.
*fl	fleksja	'inflexion' nom.sg.
*fr	frak	'dress coat' nom.sg.
sm	smycz	'leash' nom.sg.
sn	snop	'sheaf' nom.sg.
*sl	slumsy	'slums' nom.pl.
*sj	sjesta	'siesta' nom.sg.
sr	sroka	'magpie' nom.sg.

sw	słoń	‘elephant’ nom.sg.
šm	szmata	‘rag’ nom.sg.
*šm	szmaragd	‘emerald’ nom.sg.
šm’	szminka	‘lipstic’ nom.sg.
*šn$_3$	sznur	‘line’ nom.sg.
šl	szloch	‘sob’ nom.sg.
*šl	szlauch	‘rubber pipe’ nom.sg.
*šl’$_2$	szlif	‘cut (of a gem)’ nom.sg.
šr	szron	‘hoar-frost’ nom.sg.
šw	szła	‘to go’ past 3ps.sg.
śm’	śmiech	‘laughter’ nom.sg.
śń	śnieg	‘snow’ nom.sg.
śl	śledź	‘herring’ nom.sg.
śl’	śliwka	‘plum’ nom.sg.
śr	śruba	‘screw’ nom.sg.
zm	zmrok	‘dusk’ nom.sg.
z+m	zmoknąć	‘to get wet’ inf.
zm’	zmiana	‘change’ nom.sg.
z+m’	zmiąć	‘to crumple’ inf. perf.
zn	znak	‘sign’ nom.sg.
z+n	znosić	‘to wear out’ inf. perf.
zń	zniewaga	‘insult’ nom.sg.
z+ń	zniszczyć	‘to devastate’ inf.perf.
zl	zlew	‘sink’ nom.sg.
z+l	zlecieć	‘to fly down’ inf.perf.
z+l’	zliczyć	‘to count’ inf.perf.
*z+l’	zliberalizować	‘to liberalize’ inf.perf.
z+r	zrosnąć	‘to fuse’ inf.perf.
zj	zjawisko	‘phenomenon’ nom.sg.
z+j	zjeść	‘to cat’ inf.pcrf.
zw	złość	‘anger’ nom.sg.
z+w	złamać	‘to break’ inf.perf.
žm$_1$	żmudny	‘arduous’ adj.masc.nom.sg.
žm’	żmija	‘viper’ nom.sg.
žń$_1$	żniwo	‘harvest’ nom.sg.
žl$_1$	żleb	‘gully’ nom.sg.
žr$_1$	żreć	‘to bite’ inf.
žw$_2$	żłób	‘manger’ nom.sg.
źl	źle	‘bad’adv.
źr	źrebak	‘colt’ nom.sg.
xm$_3$	chmura	‘cloud’ nom.sg.

xm'_1	chmiel	'hop' nom.sg.
xl	chleb	'broad' nom.sg.
*xl	chlor	'chlorine' nom.sg.
xl'	chlipać	'to snivel' inf.perf.
xr	chrapać	'to snore' inf.imperf.
*xr	chrom	'chrome' nom.sg.
xw	chłop	'peasant' nom.sg.

B. OBSTRUENT+OBSTRUENT

pt_1	ptak	'bird' nom.sg.
*pt	pterozaur	'pterosaurian' nom.sg.
*pt'_2	ptialina	'ptyalin' nom.sg.
ps_3	psota	'prank' nom.sg.
*ps	psalm	'psalm' nom.sg.
pš	przewód	'pipe' nom.sg.
$pś_3$	psioczyć	'to grumble' inf.
px_1	pchać	'to push' inf.
tk_2	tkać	'to weave' inf.
$tt^{š}_1$	Tczew	'Tczew' proper name
tš	trzask	'roar' nom.sg.
tf	twardy	'hard' masc.nom.sg.
tf'	twierdzić	'to maintain' inf.
tx	tchawica	'trachea' nom.sg.
$t^{s}f_2$	cwaniak	'cunning man' nom.sg.
*$t^{s}f_1$	cwibak	'zwieback' nom.sg.
$t^{š}t_1$	cztery	'four' nom.
$t^{š}t^{š}_1$	czczy	'empty' masc.nom.sg.
$t^{š}t^{ś}_2$	czcić	'to worship' inf. imperf.
$t^{š}f_1$	czwarty	'the fourth' masc.nom.sg.
$t^{š}k_1$	czkać	'to hiccup' inf.
$t^{ś}p_1$	ćpać	'to gobble' inf.
$t^{ś}f'$	ćwiczyć	'to exercise' inf.
kp'_1	kpić	'to mock' inf.
kt	kto	'who' nom.
$kt^{ś}_1$	kciuk	'thumb' nm.sg.
kf	kwoka	'hen' nom.sg.
kf	*kwant	'quantum' nom.sg.
kf'	kwiat	'flower' nom.sg.
*ks	ksero	'xero-'
kś	księga	'book' nom.sg.
kš	krzak	'bush' nom.sg.

bz_2	bzu	'lilac' gen.sg.
$bź_1$	bzik	'craze' nom.sg.
bž	brzuch	'abdomen' nom.sg.
db_1	dbać	'to take care' inf.
dv_3	dwa	'two' nom.
dv'_1	dwie	'two' fem.pl.
dž	drzewo	'tree' nom.sg.
d^zv_1	dzwonek	'call-bell' nom.sg.
d^zb_1	dzban	'pitcher' nom.sg.
$d^źg_1$	dźgać	'to prod' inf.
$d^źv'_1$	dźwięk	'sound' nom.sg.
$d^žd^ž_2$	dżdżownica	'earth-worm' nom.sg.
gb_1	gbur	'churl' nom.sg.
gd	gdy	'when'
$gd^ź_1$	gdzie	'where'
gv	gwara	'dialect' nom.sg.
gv'	gwiazda	'star' nom.sg.
gz	gzowy	'of the gadfly' adj.masc.nom.sg.
*gz	gzyms	'mould' nom.sg.
$gź_3$	gzić	'to run wild' inf.
gž	grzecznie	'politely'
f+p	wpadać	'to fall' inf.
f+p'	wpiąć	'to stick' inf.
fk	wkoło	'round'
f+k	wkuć	'to fix' inf.
fs	wsad	'batch' nom.sg.
f+s	wsadzać	'to put sth somewhere' inf
f+ś	wsiać	'to saw(in)' inf
fš	wszak	'however'
f+š	wszyć	'to sew' inf.
ft	wtedy	'then'
f+t	wtopić	'to set (sth in sth)' inf.
ft^s	wcale	'at all'
$f+t^s_3$	wcementować	'to embed (sth) in concrete' inf.
$f+x_1$	wchodzić	'to enter' inf.
$ft^ś$	wciąż	'constantly'
$f+t^ś$	wciąć	'to incise' inf.
$ft^š$	wczasy	'holiday' nom.pl.
$f+t^š$	wczołgać się	'to crawl in' inf.
sp	spacer	'walk' nom.sg.
*sp	sputnik	'sputnik' nom.sg.

s+p	spadać	'to fall (dawn)' inf.
sp'	spinka	'clasp' nom.sg.
*sp'	spiker	'speaker' nom.sg.
s+p'	spisać	'to write down' inf.
sk	skok	'step' nom.sg.
*sk	skala	'scale' nom.sg.
sk'	skinąć	'to nod' inf. perf.
s+k'	skiwnąć	'to sway' inf.perf.
s+s	zsypać	'to pour' inf.
s+š	zszargać	'to bedraggle' inf.imperf.
st	stan	'condition' nom.sg.
*st	studio	'studio' nom.sg.
s+t	stopić	'to melt' inf.perf.
st^{s}	scyzoryk	'penknife' nom.sg.
$*st^{s}$	scena	'stage' nom.sg.
$s+t^{s}$	scedzić	'to decant' inf.perf.
$s+t^{š}$	sczepiać	'to link' inf. imperf.
sf	swat	'matchmaker' nom.sg.
s+f	sfrunąć	'to flay away' inf.perf.
s+ś	zsiąść	'to alight' inf.perf.
sx	schab	'joint of pork' nom.sg.
*sx	scheda	'heritage' nom.sg.
s+x	schodzić	'to come down' imperf.
*sx'	schizma	'schism' nom.sg.
*s+x'	zhierarchizować	'to hierarchize' inf.perf.
šp	szpak	'starling' nom.sg.
šp'	szpik	'marrow' nom.sg.
št	sztywny	'stiff' nom. sg.
*št	sztaba	'bar' nom.sg.
$št^{š}$	szczaw	'sorrel' nom.sg.
šk	szkapa	'jade' nom.sg.
šk'	szkic	'sketch' nom.sg.
šf	szwalnia	'sewing work-room' nom.sg.
$śt^{ś}$	ściana	'wall' nom.sg.
$ś+t^{ś}$	ściec	'to flow down' inf.perf.
śp'	śpiew	'singing' nom.sg.
śf'	świadek	'witness' nom.sg.
v+b	wbudować	'to build in' inf.perf.
$v+b'_{2}$	wbić	'to beat (sth) into' inf.perf.
vd	wdech	'inspiration' nom.sg.
v+d	wdać się	'to intervene' inf.perf.

$vd^{ź}$	wdzięk	'charm' nom.sg.
$v+d^{ź}$	wdziać	'to make an irruption' inf.perf.
$v+g'_1$	wgiąć	'to bend in' inf.perf.
$v+g_1$	wgonić	'to drive in' inf.perf.
$v+v_1$	wwalać	'to chuck sth into sth' inf.imperf.
v+v'	wwieźć	'to convey' inf.perf.
vz	wzajemnie	'reciprocally'
$v+z_3$	wzuć	'to put on (one's shoes)' inf.perf.
vź	wziąć	'to take' inf.perf.
v+ź	wzionąć	'to inhale' inf.perf.
vž	wrzask	'scream' nom.sg.
$v+ž_3$	wżyć się	'to familliarize oneself' inf.perf.
zb	zbawienie	'salvation' nom.sg.
z+b	zbudować	'to build' inf.perf.
zb'	zbierzność	'convergence' nom.sg.
z+b'	zbić	'to throw (sth) down' inf.perf.
zd	zdarzenie	'event' nom.sg.
z+d	zdecydować	'to decide' inf.perf.
$źd^{ź}_1$	źdźebko	'a little'
$z+d^{ź}$	zdziałać	'to achieve' inf.perf.
z+g	zgadnąć	'to guess' inf.perf.
zg	zgaga	'hangover' nom.sg.
z+g'	zgięcie	'(a) bend' nom.sg.
z+ž	zrzeszyć	'to unite' inf.perf.
zv	zwać	'to call' inf.imperf.
z+v	zwalczać	'to fight (against sb, sth)'
z+v'	zwierać	'to close' inf.imperf.
zz_2	zza	'from behind (sb, sth)'
$z+ź_3$	zziajany	'out of breath' adj. masc. nom.sg.
z+ž	zżąć	'to mow' inf. perf.
žg	żgać	'to stab' inf.imperf.
xf	chwała	'glory' nom.sg.
xf'	chwila	'moment' nom.sg.
xt^{s}_2	chcieć	'to want' inf.imper.
xš	chrzest	'baptism' nom.sg.

C SONORANT+OBSTRUENT

mg'_1	mgieł	'mist' nom.sg.
mž	mżyć	'to drizzle' inf.
mš	msza	'mass' nom.sg.
mx_1	mxu	'moss' gen.sg.

lv$_1$	lwa	‘lion’ gen.sg.
lv’$_1$	lwi	‘lion’s’ adj.masc.nom.sg.
lž$_2$	lżej	‘lightly’ comp.
rt$_1$	rtęć	‘mercury’ nom.sg.
rd$_1$	rdest	‘water-papper’ nom.sg.
rd$^z{}_2$	rdza	‘rust’ nom.sg.
rv$_3$	rwać	‘to tear’ inf.
rž$_2$	rżnąć	‘to cut (sth) up’
wk$_1$	łkać	‘to sob’ imperf.
wb$_1$	łba	‘head’ gen.sg.
wg$_1$	łgać	‘to lie’ imperf.
wz$_1$	łza	‘tear’ nom.sg.

D SONORANT+SONORANT

mn$_3$	mnogość	‘multiplicity’ nom.sg.
mń	mniej	‘less’
ml	mleko	‘milk’ nom.sg.
mr	mrok	‘darkness’ nom.sg.
mw	młot	‘hammer’ nom.sg.
ln$_2$	lnu	‘flax’ gen.sg.
lń$_1$	lnisko	‘flax field’ nom.sg.
Optional:		
*lj	liana	‘liana’ nom.sg.

THREE-MEMBER CLUSTERS

A OBSTRUENT+SONORANT + OBSTRUENT/SONORANT

plf$_1$	plfać	‘to spit’ inf.
pwt$^ś{}_1$	płciowy	‘sexual’ masc.nom.sg.
*prj$_1$	priorytet	‘priority’ nom.sg.
*trj	triada	‘triad’ nom.sg.
trf$_2$	trwać	‘to stay’ inf.imperf.
kln$_2$	klnę	‘to swear’ 1ps.sg.pres.
klń$_1$	klnie	‘to swear’ 3ps.sg.pres.
krf’$_1$	krwi	‘blood’ gen.sg.
krf$_1$	krwawo	‘bloody’ adv.
krt$_1$	krtań	‘larynx’ nom.sg.
krn$_1$	krnąbrny	‘restive’ masc.nom.sg.
*krj$_1$	kriolit	‘cryolite’ nom.sg.
brn$_1$	brnąć	‘to wade’ inf.imperf.
brd$_1$	Brda	‘Brda’ a proper name, nom.sg.
brv’$_1$	brwi	‘eyebrow’ nom.pl.

brń$_1$	brnie	‘to wade’ 3ps.sg.pres.
*brj$_1$	briolgia	‘briology’ nom.sg.
*drj	driada	‘dryad’ nom.sg.
drv$_1$	drwal	‘lumbermann’ nom.sg.
drv’$_1$	drwina	‘sneer’ nom.sg.
drž$_1$	drżeć	‘to tremble’ inf.imperf.
drg	drgać	‘to twitch’ inf.imperf.
grd$_1$	grdyka	‘Adam’s apple’ nom.sg.
zmr$_1$	zmrok	‘darkness’ nom.sg.
z+mr$_2$	zmrozić	‘to freeze’ inf.imperf.
z+mń$_1$	zmniejszyć	‘to diminish’ inf.perf.
smr$_2$	smród	‘stink’ nom.sg.
Colloquial:		
z+mn$_1$	zmnożyć	‘to multiply’ inf.perf.
z+mw$_1$	zmłócić	‘to thresh’ inf.perf.
Optional:		
dvj$_1$	dwie	‘two’ fem.
kmj$_1$	kmieć	‘serf’ nom.sg.
knj$_3$	kniaź	‘Ukrainian prince’ nom.sg.
gvj$_1$	gwiazda	‘star’ nom.sg.
zmj	zmiana	‘change’ nom.sg.
z+mj	zmierzać	‘to aim (at sth)’ inf. imperf.
śmj	śmiech	‘laughter’ nom.sg.
xmj$_1$	chmiel	‘hop’ nom.sg.
t^{ś}mj$_1$	ćmienie	‘eclipse’ nom.sg.

B OBSTRUENT+OBSTRUENT+OBSTRUENT/SONORANT

pxw$_1$	pchła	‘flea’ nom.sg.
pxl’$_1$	pchli	‘flea’ adj.masc.nom.sg.
pxn$_1$	pchnąć	‘to give (sb, sth) a push’ inf.perf.
pxń$_1$	pchnięcie	‘push’ nom.sg.
pšt$^{š}{}_1$	pszczoła	‘bee’ nom.sg.
pšt$_1$	przytykać	‘to fillip’ inf. iperf.
tkn$_1$	tknąć	‘to touch’ inf.perf.
tkń$_1$	tknięcie	‘touch’ nom.sg.
tkf’$_1$	tkwić	‘to be stuck in (sth)’ inf. imperf.
tkl’$_1$	tkliwy	‘loving’ masc.nom.sg.
txn$_1$	tchnąć	‘to breathe’ inf.imperf.
txń$_1$	tchnienie	‘breath’ nom.sg.
džv’$_1$	drzwi	‘door’ pl.tantum
tšp’$_2$	trzpiot	‘fribble’ nom.sg.

tšt$^{ś}_{1}$	trzcina	'reed' nom.sg.
tšm'$_{1}$	trzmiel	'bumble-bee' nom.sg.
tšn	trznadel	'yellow-hammer' nom.sg.
kšt$_{2}$	kształt	'shape' nom.sg.
bzd$_{2}$	bzdura	'nonsense' nom.sg.
bžd$_{2}$	brzdąc	'dot' nom.sg.
bžm'	brzmienie	'sound of (sth)' nom.sg.
gžm$_{1}$	grzmot	'thunder' nom.sg.
gžm'$_{1}$	grzmieć	'to thunder' inf. imperf.
gžb'$_{1}$	grzbiet	'back of (sth)' nom.sg.
gžd$_{1}$	grzdykać	'to gobble' inf.imperf.
t^{s}kl'$_{1}$	ckliwy	'mawkish' masc.nom.sg.
t^{š}kn$_{1}$	czknąć	'to hiccup' inf. perf.
t^{š}kń$_{1}$	czknięcie	'hiccup' nom.sg.
d^{ź}gn$_{1}$	dźgnąć	'to prod' inf.perf.
d^{ź}gń$_{1}$	dźgnięcie	'prod' nom.sg.
f+pw$_{3}$	wpłynąć	'to swim into (sth)' inf.perf.
f+pl$_{1}$	wpleść	'to plait' inf.perf.
f+pr	wpraszać się	'to invite oneself to (sth)'
f+pš$_{2}$	wprzęgać	'to harness' inf.imperf.
fsp	wspak	'backwards'
f+s+p	wspomóc	'to help' inf.perf.
f+s+p'$_{2}$	wspiąć	'to ascend' inf.perf.
f+st	wstawać	'to get up' inf.imerf.
f+sk	wskoczyć	'to jump onto (sth)' inf.perf.
f+s+x$_{1}$	wschodzić	'to rise' inf.imperf.
f+sw	wsławiać	'to become famous' inf.imperf.
f+sn$_{1}$	wsnuć	'to spin' inf.perf.
fšt^{š2}	wszcząć	'to begin' inf.perf.
f+śl$_{1}$	wśliznąć	'to creep' inf.perf.
fśr$_{1}$	wśród	'among'
f+śr	wśrubować	'to screw (sth) in'
fśt$^{ś}_{3}$	wściec	'to madden (sb)' inf.perf.
f+tw	wtłoczyć	'to grout' inf.perf.
f+tr	wtrącić	''to throw in' inf.perf.
fkw	wkład	'contribution (to sth)' nom.sg.
f+kw	wkłuć	'to stab' inf.perf.
fkl$_{1}$	wklęsły	'concave' masc.nom.sg.
f+kl	wkleić	'to insert' inf.perf.
f+kr	wkroczyć	'to enter' inf. perf.
f+xw$_{1}$	wchłonąć	'to soak in' inf.perf.

vbr	wbrew	'in defiance'
v+dr$_3$	wdrążyć	'to crush (sth) in' inf.perf.
v+dm	wdmuchnąć	'to blow (into sth)' inf.perf.
v+gw	wgłębić	'to hollow out' inf.perf.
vgl$_1$	wgląd	'insight' nom.sg.
v+gr$_1$	wgryźć	'to penetrate' inf.perf.
v+gń$_1$	wgnieść	'to press (sth) in' inf.perf.
v+z+l$_1$	wzlecieć	'to fly up' inf.perf.
vzr$_3$	wzrok	'eyesight' nom.sg.
v+z+r	wzróść	'to grow' inf.perf.
v+z+n$_3$	wznowić	'to renew' inf.perf.
v+zń$_3$	wznieść	'to raise' inf.perf.
vzm'$_1$	wzmianka	'notice' nom.sg.
v+zm	wzmocnić	'to strengthen' inf.perf.
v+zb	wzburzyć	'to agitate' inf.perf.
v+zb'$_2$	wzbierać	'to swell' inf.imperf.
v+zv$_2$	wzwyż	'upwards'
vzg$_2$	wzgórze	'hill' nom.sg.
v+zd$_2$	wzdąć	'to inflate' inf.perf.
vžd$_1$	wżdy	'nevertheless'
s+pw	spłacać	'to pay off' inf.imperf.
s+pl	spleść	'to plait' inf.perf.
*spl	splendor	'splendour' nom.sg.
*spl'	splin	'spleen' nom.sg.
s+pl'	splisować	'to pleat' inf.perf.
spr	sprawa	'matter' nom.sg.
s+pr	sprać	'to wash (sth) off' inf.perf.
s+ps$_1$	spsocić	'to play a prank' inf.perf.
spš	sprzeczka	'quarrel' nom.sg.
s+pš	sprząć	'to connect' inf.perf.
s+tw	stłamsić	'to crush' inf.perf.
s+tl	stlić	'to burn' inf.perf.
str	strażnik	'guard' nom.sg.
s+tr	stracić	'to lose' inf.perf.
s+tf	stworzyć	'to create' inf.perf.
s+tf'	stwierdzić	'to ascertain' inf.perf.
*st^{s}j	scjentyzm	'scientism' nom.sg.
stš	strzał	'shot' nom.sg.
s+tš	strzaskać	'to shake sth down' inf.perf.
s+tx	stchórzyć	'to take fright' inf.perf.
skw	składnia	'syntax' nom.sg.

s+kw	skłamać	'to lie' inf.perf.
skr	skrawek	'cutting' nom.sg.
s+kr	skropić	'to sprinkle' inf.perf.
skl	sklep	'shop' nom.sg.
s+kl	skleić	'to stick' inf.perf.
skn	sknera	'miser' nom.sg.
sk+n_2	sknocić	'to bungle' inf.perf.
skf	skwar	'swelter' nom.sg.
s+kf	skwasić	'to sour' inf.perf.
skf'	skwierczeć	'to sizzle' inf.imperf.
skš	skrzydło	'wing' nom.sg.
sk+š	skrzyczeć	'to shout (at sb)' inf.perf.
s+st	zstąpić	'to descend' inf.perf.
s+fl	sflaczały	'flabby' masc.nom.sg.
s+fr	sfrunąć	'to fly away' inf.perf.
s+xw_2	schłodzić	'to cool' inf.perf.
s+xl	schlebiać	'to adulate' inf.imperf.
s+xr	schrupać	'to munch' inf.perf.
s+xn_1	schnąć	'to dry' inf.imperf.
sxń	schnięcie	'to become dry' nom.sg.
s+xf	schwycić	'to grasp' inf.perf.
*špr_3	szprycha	'spoke' nom.sg.
*štr_1	sztruks	'ribbed velveteen' nom.sg.
škw_1	szkło	'glass' nom.sg.
škl_1	szklanka	'glass' nom.sg.
škf_1	szkwał	'flaw' nom.sg.
škl'$_1$	szkliwo	'glaze' nom.sg.
š$t^š$f	szczwany	'cunning' masc.nom.sg.
xš$t^ś{}_1$	chrzcić	'to baptize' inf.imperf.
xš$t^š{}_1$	chrzczenie	'baptism' nom.sg.
z+bw	zbłądzić	'to lose one's way' inf.perf.
z+bl	zblednąć	'to pale' inf.perf.
z+br	zbratać się	'to make friends' inf.perf.
z+bź$_1$	zbzikować	'to go crazy' inf.perf.
z+bž$_2$	zbrzydnąć	'to become fed up with (sth)' inf.perf.
zdj_2	zdjęcie	'photo' nom.sg.
z+dw_1	zdławić	'to stifle' inf.perf.
zdr	zdrada	'treason' nom.sg.
z+dr	zdrapać	'to scrape (sth) off' inf.perf.
z+dm_1	zdmuchnąć	'to blow (sth) away' inf.perf.
z+dv_1	zdwoić	'to double' inf.perf.

z+dž$_1$	zdrzemnąć	‘to have a nap’ inf.perf.
z+gw	zgłosić	‘to apply’ inf.perf.
zgl$_2$	zgliszcza	‘smouldering ruin’ nom.pl.
zgr	zgrabnie	‘neatly’
z+gr	zgrabić	‘to rake up’ inf.perf.
z+gn$_3$	zgnuśnieć	‘to grow sluggish’ inf.perf.
z+gń	zgnieść	‘to crumple’ inf.perf.
z+gv	zgwałcić	‘to rape’ inf.perf.
z+gž	zgrzać	‘to heat’ inf.perf.
zgž	zgrzyt	‘gride’ nom.sg.
z+vw	zwłóczyć	‘to drag’ inf.imperf.
z+vl	zwlekać	‘to pull off’ inf.perf.
z+vr	zwrócić	‘to turn’ inf.perf.
źgn$_1$	źgnąć	‘to stab’ inf.perf.
źgń$_1$	źgnie	‘to stab’ 3ps.sg.pres.
žgn$_1$	żgnąć	‘to stab’ inf.perf.
žgń$_1$	żgnie	‘to stab’ 3ps.sg.pres.
Colloquial:		
f+tš	wtrząsnąć	‘to give (sb) a beating’inf.perf.
s+pś$_1$	spsieć	‘to become impoverished’ inf.perf.
s+xš$_1$	schrzaniać	‘escape’ inf.imperf.
C SONORANT+OBSTRUENT+SONORANT		
lgn$_1$	lgnąć	‘to cling’ inf.imperf.
lgń$_1$	lgnie	‘to cling’ 3ps.sg.pres.
lśń$_1$	lśnić	‘to sparkle’ inf.imperf.
mdl$_1$	mdleć	‘to faint’ inf.imperf.
mdl’$_1$	mdlić	‘to nauseate’ inf.imperf.
mdw$_1$	mdło	‘nauseatingly’
mgl’$_1$	mglisto	‘foggily’
mgw$_1$	mgła	‘fog’ nom.sg.
mgń$_1$	mgnienie	‘flicker’ nom.sg.
mkn$_1$	mknąć	‘to speed’ inf.imperf.
mkń$_1$	mknie	‘to speed’3ps.sg.pres.
mkl’$_1$	mklik	‘Ephestia’ nom.sg.
mśt$^{ś}_{1}$	mścić	‘to avenge’ inf.imperf.
ržn$_1$	rżnąć	‘to cut’ inf.imperf.
ržń$_1$	rżnie	‘to cut’ 3ps.sg.pres.
FOUR-MEMBER CLUSTERS		
drgń$_1$	drgnienie	‘tremor’ nom.sg.

$drgn_1$	drgnąć	'to budge' inf.perf.
$pstr_3$	pstry	'speckled' masc.nom.sg.
$pstš_1$	pstrzyć	'to variegate' inf.imperf.
s+trf	strwożyć	'to frighten' inf.perf.
$s+krf_1$	skrwawić	'to bleed' inf.perf.
$źd^{ź}bw_1$	źdźbło	'stalk' nom.sg.
$fstr_1$	wstręt	'repugnance' nom.sg.
$f+s+tš_3$	wstrzymać	'to suspend' inf. perf.
$f+s+kš_1$	wskrzesić	'to resuscitate' inf.perf.
$fskr_1$	wskroś	'through'
$vzdw_1$	wzdłuż	'along'
$vzdr_3$	wzdrygać się	'to shudder'inf.imperf.
$vzgl_2$	wzgląd	'regard' nom.sg.

7.3.2 Word-final clusters

TWO-MEMBER CLUSTERS

A OBSTRUENT+ SONORANT

pń	wapń	'calcium' nom.sg.
pr	Cypr	'Cyprus' nom. sg.
p+w	oziębł	'to cool' 3ps.sg.past
pn	wapn	'lime' gen.pl.
tm	rytm	'rhythm' nom.sg.
tr	wiatr	'wind' nom.sg.
t+w	szedł	'to go' 3ps.sg.past
$t^{ś}m$	zaćm	'cataract' gen.sg.
tl	módl się	'to pray' 2ps.sg.imper.
$t^{š}m$	karczm	'inn' gen.pl.
$t^{ś}m$	wiedźm	'witch' gen.pl.
kl	spektakl	'performance' nom.sg.
kr	ikr	'spawn' gen.pl.
k+w	mógł	'to be able to' 3ps.sg.past
*km	syntagm	'syntagmatic structure' gen.pl.
*kn	malign	'malignant fever' gen.pl.
*fl	trefl	'club' nom.sg.
*fr	manewr	'manoeuvre' nom.sg.
fn	drewn	'wood' gen.pl.
sm	rękopism	' manuscript' gen.pl.
śń	pieśń	'song' nom.sg.
śl	myśl	'thought' nom.sg.

śm	taśm	'tape' gen.pl.
sw	pomysł	'idea' nom.sg.
šm	jarzm	'yoke' gen.pl.
šn	jałmużn	'alms' gen.pl.
xr	ochr	'ochre' gen.pl.
x+w	zdechł	'to die' pej. 3ps.sg.past
*xm	drachm	'drachma' gen.pl.
xn	coróchn	'daughter' dim.gen.pl.

B OBSTRUENT+OBSTRUENT

*pt	szept	'whisper' nom.sg.
pt^{š}	szepcz	'to whisper' 2ps.sg.imper.
pt^{ś}	babć	'grandmother' gen.pl.
ps	klaps	'smack' nom.sg.
pš	pieprz	'pepper' nom.sg.
tf	kuropatw	'partridge' gen.pl.
tš	wnętrz	'(the) inside' gen.pl.
kt	akt	'act' nom.sg.
kf	pigw	'quince' gen.pl.
*ks	fuks	'fluke' nom.sg.
t^{ś}p	swadźb	'matchmaking' nom.sg.
t^{š}p	liczb	'number' gen.pl.
t^{š}t	uczt	'feast' gen.pl.
št^{š}	wieszcz	'prophet' nom.sg.
ft	haft	'embroidery' nom.sg.
ft^{s}	szewc	'shoemaker' nom.sg.
ft^{ś}	Stefć	'Stefcia' gen.pl.
sp	osp	'smallpox' gen.pl.
st	gwizd	'whistle' nom.sg.
sk	mózg	'brain' nom.sg.
sf	nazw	'name' gen.pl.
šp	świerzb	'itch' nom.sg.
*št	maszt	'mast' nom.sg.
šx	wierzch	'top' nom.sg.
śp	próśb	'request' gen.pl.
śt^{ś}	ugość	'to treat (sb) to (sth)' 2ps.sg.imperf.
śf	orzeźw	'refresh' 2ps.sg.imperf.
ft	prawd	'truth' gen.pl.
xt	klechd	'folk story' gen.pl.
xt^{ś}	ciuchć	'dolly' gen.pl.
xf	lichw	'usury' gen.pl.

xš	wichrz	'to dishevel'2ps.sg.imp.

C SONORANT+OBSTRUENT

*mp	jamb	'iambus' nom.sg.
mt^{ś}	mamć	'mummy' gen.pl.
*mf	nimf	'nymph' gen.pl.
*ms	giemz	'chamois' gen.pl.
mš	komż	'surplice' gen.pl.
mś	tłamś	'to smother' 2ps.sg.imp.
nt	student	'student' nom.sg.
nk	bank	'bank' nom.sg.
nt^{s}	brzdąc	'sprat' nom.sg.
nt^{ś}	Wandź	'Wandzia' gen.pl.
*nt^{š}	lunch	'lunch' nom.sg.
*nf	kanw	'ground-work' gen.pl.
*ns	sens	'sense' nom.sg.
*nš	branż	'trade' gen.pl.
ńp	hańb	'disgrace' gen.pl.
ńt^{š}	kończ	'to finish' 2ps.sg.imp.
ńt^{ś}	mamuńć	'mummy' gen.pl.
ńt^{s}	słońc	'sun' gen.pl.
lp	strzelb	'rifle' gen.pl.
lt	szyld	'sign' nom.sg.
lk	wilk	'wolf' nom.sg.
lt^{s}	walc	'waltz' nom.sg.
*lf	golf	'golf' nom.sg.
lx	olch	'alder' gen.pl.
rf	torf	'peat' nom.sg.
rp	skarb	'treasure' nom.sg.
rt	akord	'chord'nom.sg.
rk	chirurg	'surgeon' nom.sg.
rt^{s}	serc	'heart' gen.pl.
rt^{š}	skurcz	'contraction' nom.sg.
rt^{ś}	ćwierć	'quarter' nom.sg.
rf	torf	'peat' nom.sg.
rs	mors	'walrus' nom.sg.
rš	oberż	'tavern' gen.pl.
rś	pierś	'chest' nom.sg.
rx	parch	'scab' nom.sg.
jp	łajb	'boat' gen.pl.
jt	rajd	'rally' nom.sg.

*jk	strajk	'strike' nom.sg.
jt^{s}	lejc	'reins' gen.pl.
$jt^{š}$	pejcz	'riding-whip' nom.sg.
$jt^{ś}$	wejdź	'to come in' 2ps.sg.imp.
jf	sejf	'safe' nom.sg.
*js	rejs	'voyage' nom.sg.
jš	spójrz	'look' 2ps.sg.imp.
jś	czyjś	'somebody's'
wp	kiełb	'gudgeon' nom.sg.
wt	kształt	'shape' nom.sg.
wk	czołg	'tank' nom.sg.
$wt^{š}$	miaucz	'miaow'2ps.sg.imp.
$wt^{ś}$	żółć	'gall' nom.sg.
wf	żółw	'tortoise' nom.sg.
ws	zołz	'shrew'gen.pl.
wš	małż	'mollusc' gen.pl.

D SONORANT+SONORANT

*jl	koktajl	'cocktail' nom.sg.
ml	Kreml	'Kreml' nom.sg.
*wl	crawl	'crawl' nom.sg.
rw	żarł	'to gobble' 3ps.sg.past.
rl	rozperl	'pearl' 2ps.sg.imp.
jm	ujm	'discredit' gen.pl.
lm	bielm	'leucoma' gen.pl.
wm	hełm	'helmet' nom.sg.
rm	pokarm	'food' nom.sg.
jn	kombajn	'combine harvester' nom.sg.
mn	hymn	'hymn' nom.sg.
rn	urn	'urn' gen.pl.
rm	oferm	'muff' gen.pl.
lń	pralń	'laundry' gen.pl.
rń	cierń	'thorn' nom.sg.
wń	spełń	'to fulfil' 2ps.sg.imp.

THREE-MEMBER CLUSTERS

A OBSTRUENT+OBSTRUENT+OBSTRUENT/SONORANT

psk	babsk	'hag' gen.pl.
*kst	tekst	'text' nom.sg.
$t+^{s}tf$	bogactw	'wealth' gen.pl.

stm	astm	'asthma' gen.pl.
str	sióstr	'sister' gen.pl.
+stf	ojcostw	'fatherhood' gen.pl.
stš	ostrz	'to sharpen' 2ps.sg.imp.
štr	musztr	'drill' gen.pl.
št^{š}p	wieszczb	'prophecy' gen.pl.
xtr	blichtr	'glare' nom.sg.

B SONORANT +OBSTRUENT+ OBSTRUENT/SONORANT

mpt	asumpt	'inducement' nom.sg.
mpr	prekambr	'Pre-Cambrian era' nom.sg.
*mpl	ansambl	'ensemble' nom.sg.
mst	zemst	'vengeance' gen.pl
ntš	pnącz	'creeper' nom.sg.
ntf	mątw	'cuttle-fish' gen.pl
ntn	piętn	'mark' gen.pl.
nks	sfinks	'sphinks' nom.sg.
nkt	punkt	'point' nom.sg.
ntr	kontr	'contra' gen.pl.
nkr	wągr	'comedo' nom.sg.
nkf	makolągw	'linnet' gen.pl.
nšt	kunszt	'art' nom.sg.
ńt^{ś}p	gędźb	'tale' gen.pl.
ń+sk	wińsk	'wine' augm.gen.pl.
ńśt^{ś}	pięść	'fist' nom.sg.
ltr	filtr	'filter' nom.sg.
lšt^{š}	spolszcz	'to polonize' 2ps.sg.imp.
lśń	pilśń	'felt' nom.sg.
rpt^{s}	kierpc	'moccasin of Tatra mountaineers' gen.pl.
rst	wiorst	'verst' gen.pl.
rsk	parsk	'laughter' nom.sg.
ršt	herszt	'chieftain' nom.sg.
ršt^{š}	barszcz	'borsch' nom.sg.
rśt^{ś}	sierść	'animal's hair' nom.sg.
jst^{s}	miejsc	'place' gen.pl.
jśt^{ś}	pojść	'to go' inf.perf.
jsk	wojsk	'army' gen.pl.

FOUR-MEMBER CLUSTERS

A OBSTRUENT+OBSTRUENT+OBSTRUENT+OBSTRUENT

p+stf	hrabstw	‘county’ gen.pl.
$t^{ś}$+stf	uchodźstw	‘emigration’ gen.pl.
f+stf	terenoznawstw	‘topography’ gen.pl.

B SONORANT+OBSTRUENT+OBSTRUENT+OBSTRUENT

mp+sk	kępsk	‘tuft (of grass)’gen.pl.
m+stf	kłamstw	‘lie’ nom.sg.
n+stf	męstw	‘courage’ nom.sg.
n+t^{s}tf	dyletanctw	‘dilettantism’ nom.sg.
ń+stf	panieństw	‘maidenhood’ nom.sg.
l+stf	opieszalstw	‘laziness’ nom.sg.
r+stf	łgarstw	‘lie’ nom.sg.
j+stf	dobrodziejstw	‘benefit’ nom.sg.

FIVE-MEMBER CLUSTERS

mp+stf	skąpstw	‘parsimony’ nom.sg.

* word of foreign origin
+ morpheme boundary

8 References

Abbreviations used:

CLS	Papers from the Regional Meeting of the Chicago Linguistic Society
FAS	Forschungsschwerpunkt Allgemeine Sprachwissenschaft
GSLA	Graduate Linguistic Student Association
NELS	Annual Meeting of the North East Linguistics Society
PAN	Polska Akademia Nauk
ROA	Rutgers Optimality Archive http://ruccs.rutgers.edu/roa.html
SOAS	School of Oriental and African Studies

Abernathy, R. 1956. The Fall Of The Jers: A Statistical Interpretation. In: Halle, M., Lunt, H. G., McLean, H. and C. H. van Schooneveld (eds.) (1956). *For Roman Jakobson. Essays On The Occasion Of His Sixtieth Birthday*. The Hague: Mouton. 13-18.

Abondolo, D. (ed.) 1998. *The Uralic Languages*. London, New York: Routledge.

Ahn, S.-C. 1985. *The Interplay of Phonology and Morphology in Korean*. Ph.D. dissertation, University of Illinois at Urbana.

Alderete, J. 1997. Dissimilation as Local Conjunction. In: Kusumoto, K. (ed.). *Proceedings of the NELS 27*, 17-32. Amherst, MA: GSLA.

Anttila, A. 1995. Deriving variation from grammar: a study of Finnish genitives. ROA-63-0000.

Archangeli, D. and D. Pulleyblank 1994. *Grounded Phonology*. Cambridge, Mass.: MIT Press.

Archangeli, D. and D. T. Langendoen (eds.) 1997. *Optimality Theory*. An Overview. Oxford: Blackwell.

Auer, P. 1994. Einige Argumente gegen die Silbe als universale prosodische Hauptkategorie. In: Ramers at al. 1994. 55-57.

August, G. 1975. *Untersuchungen zum Morpheminventar der deutschen Gegenwarts-sprache*. Tübingen: Narr.

Bailey, C.-J. N. 1973. *Variation and Linguistic Theory*. Arlington: Center for Applied Linguistics.

Bargiełówna, M. 1950. Grupy fonemów spógłoskowych współczesnej polszczyzny kulturalnej. *Biuletyn Towarzystwa Językoznawczego 10*, 1-25.

Baumann, M. 1995. *The production of syllables in connected speech*. Nijmegen: Benda drukkers.

Beckman, J. N. 1995. Shona height harmony: Positional identity and markedness. In: J. N. Beckman, L. W. Dickey and S. Urbanczyk (eds.). *University of Massachusetts Occasional* Papers *18*, 53-75.

Béland, R. and Y. Favreau 1991. On The Special Status Of Coronals In Aphasia. In: Paradis, C. and J.-F. Prunet (eds.) 1991. 201-221.

Bell, A. 1978. Syllabic consonants. In: Greenberg, J. H. (ed.) 1978b. 156-201.

Benni, T. 1931. *Palatogramy polskie*. Kraków, Warszawa: Gebethner and Wolff.

Benni, T. 1959. *Fonetyka opisowa języka polskiego*. Wrocław: Zakład Narodowy imienia Ossolińskich.

Benua, L. 1995. Identity effects in morphological truncation. In: J.N. Beckman, L. W. Dickey and S. Urbanczyk (eds.). *University of Massachusetts Occasional Papers 18*, 77-136.

Benua, L. 1997. *Transderivational Identity: Phonological Relations Between Words*. Ph.D. dissertation, University of Massachusetts. ROA-259-0498.

Berg, T. 1992. Umrisse einer psycholinguistischen Theorie der Silbe. In Eisenberg et al. (1992). 45-99.

Bermúdez-Otero, R. 1996. Stress and quantity in Old and early Middle English: Evidence for an optimality-theoretic model of language change. ROA-136-0996.

Bethin, Ch. Y. 1992. *Polish Syllables. The Role of Prosody in Phonology and Morphology*. Columbus, Ohio: Slavica Publishers.

Bethin, Ch. Y. 1993. Neo-Acute Length in the North Central Dialects of Late Common Slavic. *Journal of Slavic Linguistics 1(2)*, 219-50.

Bethin, Ch. Y. 1998. *Slavic Prosody. Language change and phonological theory*. Cambridge: Cambridge University Press.

Bhat, D. N. S. 1974. A General Study of Palatalization. In Greenberg, J. H. (ed.) 1978b, 47-92.

Biedrzycki, L. 1963. Fonologiczna interpretacja polskich głosek nosowych. *Biuletyn Polskiego Towarzystwo Językoznawczego 22*, 25-45.

Bierwisch, M. 1996. Lexikon und Universalgrammatik. In: Weber, N. (ed.). *Semantik, Lexikographie und Computeranwendungen*. Sonderdruck aus Sprache und Information 33. Tübingen: Niemeyer.

Bierwisch, M. 1997. Lexical Information from a Minimalist Point of View. In: Wilder, C., Gärtner, H.-M. and M. Bierwisch (eds.) 1997. *The role of economy principles in linguistic theory*. Berlin: Akademie Verlag. 227-266.

Bittner, A. 1996. *Starke ‚schwache' Verben schwache ‚starke' Verben. Deutsche Verbflexion und Natürlichkeit*. Studien zur deutschen Grammatik 51. Tübingen: Stauffenburg Verlag.

Blevins, J. 1995. The syllable in phonological theory. In: J. A. Goldsmith (ed.) 1995. *The Handbook of Phonological Theory*. Oxford: Blackwell. 206-244.

Bluhme, H. 1971. Notes On Polish Phonotactics. *Linguistics 69*, 5-23.

Błaszczak, J. and M. Rochoń 1998. Some Remarks on Minimality and Optimality, not only in Language. *Kwartalnik Neofilologiczny XLV*, 255-273.

Boersma, P. 1997a. The Elements of Functional Phonology. ROA-173-0297.

Boersma, P. 1997b. Inventories in Functional Phonology. ROA-232-1197.

Boersma, P. 1998. *Functional Phonology. Formalizing the interactions between articulatory and perceptual drives*. The Hague: Holland Academic Graphics.

Bogusławski, A. 1985. Sylaba a system fonologiczny. *Prace filologiczne 32*, 59-65.

Booij, G. and J. Rubach, 1984. Morphological and prosodic domains in Lexical Phonology. *Phonology Yearbook 1*, 1-27.

Brajerski, T. 1954. Jak mogło powstać polskie mazurzenie. In: *Biuletyn Polskiego Towarzystwa Językoznawczego 13*, 1-7.

Brückner, A. 1957a. *Słownik etymologiczny języka polskiego*. Warszawa: Państwowe Wydawnictwo Naukowe.

Brückner, A. 1957b. *Początki i rozwój języka polskiego*. Warszawa: Państwowe Wydawnictwo Naukowe.

Buttler, D., Kurkowska, H. and H. Satkiewicz 1971. *Kultura języka polskiego*. Warszawa: Państwowe Wydawnictwo Naukowe.

Carlton, T. R. 1991. *Introduction To The Phonological History of The Slavic Languages*. Columbus, Ohio: Slavica Publishers.

Chitoran, I. 1994. Acoustic investigation of Georgian harmonic clusters. *Working Papers of the Cornell Phonetics Laboratory 9*, 27- 65.

Cho, Y. Y. 1995. Language change as reranking of constraints. Paper presented at the International Conference of Historical Linguistics in Manchester.

Chomsky, N. 1986. *Knowledge of Language: Its Nature, Origin, and Use*. New York: Praeger.

Chomsky, N. 1991. *Lectures in government and binding*. Dordrecht: Foris.

Chomsky, N. 1993. A minimalist program for linguistic theory. In Hale K. and S. J. Keyser 1993. *The view from Building 20*. Cambridge, Mass.: MIT Press.

Chomsky, N. 1995. *The Minimalist Program. Cambridge*, Mass.: MIT Press.

Chomsky, N and M. Halle 1968. *The Sound Pattern of English*. New York: Harper and Row.

Clements, G. N. 1988. Towards a Substantive Theory of Feature Specifications. *Proceedings of the NELS 18*, 79-93.

Clements, G. N. 1990. The role of the sonority cycle in core syllabification. In: Kingston, I. and M. Beckmann (eds.). *Papers in Laboratory Phonology I: Between the grammar and physics of speech*. Cambridge: Cambridge University Press. 283-333.

Clements, G. N. 1991. Place of articulation in consonants and vowels: a unified theory. *Working Papers of the Cornell Phonetics Laboratory 5*, 77-123.

Clements, G. N. and S. J. Keyser 1983. *CV phonology: a generative theory of the syllable*. Cambridge, Mass.: MIT Press.

Colarusso, J. 1988. *The Northwest Caucasian Languages. A Phonological Survey*. New York, London: Garland Publishing.

Comrie, B. and G. G. Corbett (eds.) 1993. *The Slavonic Languages*. London, New York: Routledge.

Cyran, E. and E. Gussmann 1999. Consonantal clusters and governing relations: Polish initial consonant sequences. In Hulst, H. and N. Ritter (eds.) 1999. *The syllable: views and facts*. Berlin: Mouton de Gruyter.

Czaykowska-Higgins, E. 1988. *Investigations into Polish Morphology and Phonology*. Ph.D. dissertation, MIT.

De Búrca, S. 1970. *The Irish of Tourmakeady, Co. Mayo: A Phonemic Study*. Dublin: Dublin Institute for Advanced Studies.

Dejna, K. 1994. *Atlas Polskich Innowacji Dialektalnych*. Warszawa, £ódź: Państwowe Wydawnictwo Naukowe.

Długosz-Kurczabowa, K. and S. Dubisz 1993. *Gramatyka historyczna języka pol-skiego*. Warszawa: Wydawnictwa Uniwersytetu Warszawskiego.

Dłuska, M. 1983. *Fonetyka polska. Artykulacje głosek polskich*. Warszawa, Kraków: Państwowe Wydawnictwo Naukowe.

Dobrogowska, K. 1990. Word Internal Consonant Clusters In Polish Artistic Prose. *Studia Phonetica Posnaniensia 2*, 43-67.

Dobrogowska, K. 1992. Word Initial And Word Final Consonant Clusters In Polish Popular Science Texts And In Artistic Prose. *Studia Phonetica Posnaniensia 3*, 47-121.

Doroszewski, W. 1958-1969. *Słownik języka polskiego*. Warszawa: Państwowe Wydawnictwo Naukowe.

Doroszewski, W. 1982. *Słownik poprawnej polszczyzny*. Warszawa: Państwowe Wydawnictwo Naukowe.

Dressler, W. U. 1982. On word formation in Natural Phonology. *Wiener Linguistische Gazzette 26*, 3-14.

Dressler, W. U. 1985. Typological aspects on Natural Morphology. *Acta Linguistica Academiae Scientarium Hungaricae 35*, 51-70.

Dressler, W. U., Mayerthaler, W., Panagl, O. and W. U. Wurzel 1987. *Leitmotifs in Natural Morphology*. Amsterdam: Benjamins.

Dukiewicz L. and I. Sawicka 1995. *Fonetyka i fonologia*. Kraków: Instytut Języka Polskiego PAN.

Dunaj, B. 1985. Grupy spółgłoskowe współczesnej polszczyzny mówionej (w języku mieszkańców Krakowa). Zeszyty naukowe Uniwersytetu Jagiellońskiego. *Prace Językoznawcze 83*.

Durand, J. and F. Katamba (eds.) 1995. *Frontiers of Phonology: Atoms, Structures, Derivations*. Harlow: Longman.

Dziubalska-Kołaczyk, K. 1993/1994. Acquisitional Evidence Against The Phonological Syllable. *Wiener Linguistische Gazette 48-50*, 145-160.

Dziubalska-Kołaczyk, K. 1995. *Phonology Without The Syllable. A Study In The Natural Framework*. Poznań: Motivex.

Eisenberg, P. 1991. Syllabische Struktur und Wortakzent. Prinzipien der Prosodik deutscher Wörter. *Zeitschrift für Sprachwissenschaft 10*, 37-64.

Eisenberg, P. 1993 Suffixreanalyse und Syllabierung. Zum Verhältnis von phonolo-gischer und morphologischer Segmentierung. *Folia Linguistica Historica XIII/1-2*, 93-113.

Eisenberg, P., Ramers, K. H. and H. Vater (eds.) 1992. *Silbenphonologie des Deutschen*. Tübingen: Narr.

Ellison, T. M. 1995. Phonological Derivation in Optimality Theory. Ms, University of Edinburgh.

Feynman, R. P., Leighton, R. B. and M. Sands (eds.) 1964. The Feynman lectures of physics, vol. 1. Addison-Wesley.

Fikkert, P. 1994. *On the Acquisition of Prosodic Structure*. Dordrecht: ICG Printing.

Fukazawa, H. 1997. A Correspondence Approach to Japanese Vocabulary Strata. *Proceedings of Mid-America Linguistics Conference 1997*, 47-58.

Fukazawa, H. and V. Miglio 1996. Restricting Conjunction to Constraint Families. *Proceedings from Western Conference on Linguistics 1996*, 102-117.

Fukazawa, H., Kitahara, M. and M. Ota 1998. Lexical Stratification and Ranking Invariance in Constraint-based Grammars. ROA-267-0698.

Gebert, P. 1994. Aspects of Korean Phonology from a Prosodic Licensing perspective. MA Thesis, University of Konstanz.

Gnanadesikan, A. E. 1995. Markedness and faithfulness constraints in child phonology. ROA-67-0000.

Goldsmith, J. A. 1976. *Autosegmental phonology*. Ph.D. dissertation., MIT. 1979 New York: Garland Press.

Goldsmith, J. A. 1990. *Autosegmental and Metrical Phonology*. Oxford: Blackwell.

Goldsmith, J. A. 1995 (ed.). *The Handbook of Phonological Theory*. Oxford and Cambridge, Mass.: Blackwell.

Golston, C. 1996. Direct Optimality Theory: Representation as Pure Markedness. *Language 72*: 713-748.

Golston, C and H. G. van der Hulst (to appear). Stricture is Structure. To appear in: Hermans, B. and M. van Oostendorp (eds.). *The derivational residue*. Dordrecht: Reidel.

Gorecka, A. 1988. Ephenthesis and the coda constraint in Polish. Ms, MIT.

Green, A. 1997. The Prosodic Structure of Irish, Scots Gaelic, and Manx. Ph.D. dissertation, Cornell University. ROA-196-0597.

Green, A. 1998. Extrasyllabic Consonants and Onset Well-Formedness. Ms, ZAS, Berlin. To appear in: Féry, C. and R. van de Vijver (eds.). *The Syllable in Optimality Theory*. Cambridge: Cambridge University Press.

Greenberg, J. H. 1978a. Some Generalizations Concerning Initial and Final Consonant Clusters. In: Greenberg, J. H. (ed.) 1978b. 243-79.

Greenberg, J. H. (ed.) 1978b. *Universals of human language*, vol. 2: Phonology. Standford: Standford University Press.

Grimshaw, J. 1994. Projection, Heads, and Optimality. ROA-68-0000.

Grzegorczykowa, R. and J. Puzynina 1973. *Index a tergo*. Warszawa: Państwowe Wydawnictwo Naukowe.

Grzegorczykowa, R., Laskowski, R., Puzynina, J., and H. Wróbel 1984. *Morfologia*. Warszawa: Państwowe Wydawnictwo Naukowe.

Gussmann, E. 1978. *Contrastive Polish-English Consonantal Phonology*. Warszawa: Państwowe Wydawnictwo Naukowe.

Gussmann, E. 1980a. *Studies in Abstract Phonology*. Cambridge, Mass: MIT Press.

Gussmann, E. 1980b. The Phonological Structure of the Polish Imperative. *Studia Gramatyczne 3*, 33-46.

Gussmann, E. 1991. Polish syllable structure: a hypothesis and its problems. In: Grochowski, M. and D. Weiss (eds.). *Words are physicians for an ailing mind*. Munich: Sagner. 207-213.

Gussmann, E. 1992a. Back to front: Non-linear palatalisation and vowels in Polish. In: Fisiak, J. and S. Puppel (eds.) 1992. *Phonological Investigations*. Amsterdam: Benjamins. 5-66.

Gussmann, E. 1992b. Resyllabification and Delinking: The Case of Polish Voicing. *Linguistic Inquiry 23*, 29-56.

Gussmann, E. and J. D. Kaye 1993. Polish notes from a Dubrovnik café. I: the yers. *SOAS Working Papers in Linguistics and Phonetics 3*, 427-462.

Hall, T.A. 1992. *Syllable Structure and Syllable-Related Processes in German*. Tübingen: Niemeyer.

Hall, T.A. 1997a. *The Phonology of Coronals*. Amsterdam: Benjamins.

Hall, T.A. 1997b. The Historical Development of Retroflex Consonants in Indo-Aryan. *Lingua 101*, 203-221.

Hall, T.A. 1999. Typological generalizations concerning secondary palatalization. Paper presented at the 31st Poznań Linguistic Meeting in Poznań, Poland on May 1, 1998. To appear in *Lingua*.

Hammond, M. 1995. There is no Lexicon. ROA-43-0195.

Harris, J. 1973. On the order of certain phonological rules in Spanish. In: Anderson, S. and P. Kiparsky (eds.). *A Festschrift for Morris Halle*. New York: Holt, Reinhart and Winston.

Harris, J. 1992. Licensing Inheritance. *UCL Working Papers in Linguistics 4*, 359-406.

Harris, J. and G. Lindsey 1995. The elements of Phonological Representation. In: Durand, J. and F. Katamba (eds.). *Frontiers in Phonology: Atoms, Structures, Derivations*. Harlow, Essex: Longmann. 33-79.

Havlík, A. 1889. K otázce jerové v staré češtine. *Listy filologické 16*, 45-51, 106-116, 248-258, 342-353, 436-445.

Hempen, U. 1988. *Die starken Verben im Deutschen und Niederländischen. Diachrone Morphologie*. Tübingen: Niemeyer.

Hermann, E. 1929. Lautveränderungen in der Individualsprache einer Mundart. *Nachrichten der Gesellschaft der Wissenschaften zu Göttingen 9*, 195-214.

Hewitt, M. and M. Crowhurst 1995. Conjunctive Constraints and Templates in Optimality Theory. *Proceedings of the NELS 26*, 101-116.

Hock, H. H. 1973. Exceptions and synchronic analogy in Sanskrit. *Studies in the Linguistic Sciences 3*, 81-101.

Hock, H. H. 1991. *Principles of Historical Linguistics*. Berlin, New York: Mouton de Gruyter.

Hock, H. H. and Joseph, B. D. 1996. *Language History, Language Change, and Language Relationship. An Introduction to Historical and Comparative Linguistics*. Berlin, New York: de Gruyter.

Holt, D. E. 1997. *The Role Of The Listener In The Historical Phonology Of Spanish And Portuguese: An Optimality-Theoretic Account*. Ph.D. dissertation, Georgetown University. ROA-278-0898.

Hooper, J. B. 1976. *An Introduction to Natural Generative Phonology*. New York: Academic Press.

Hulst, H. G. van der 1994a. An Introduction to Radical CV Phonology: In: Shore, S. and M. Vilkuna (eds.) 1994. *Yearbook of the Linguistic Association of Finland 1994*, 23-56.

Hulst, H. G. van der 1994b. Radical CV Phonology: The Locational Gesture. *University College London Working Papers in Linguistics 7*, 439-478.

Hulst, H. G. van der 1995. Radical CV Phonology: the categorial Gesture. In: F. Katamba and J. Durand (eds.) *Frontiers in Phonology: Atoms, Structures, Derivations*. Harlow, Essex. Longmann. 80-116.

Hulst, H. G. van der (in prep). Principles of Radical CV Phonology. Ms, University of Leiden.

Hume, E. 1992. *Front Vowels, Coronal Consonants and their Interaction in Non-linear Phonology*. Ph.D. dissertation, Cornell University, Ithaca, New York.

Hurch, B. 1988. *Über Aspiration. Ein Kapitel aus der natürlichen Phonologie*. Tübingen: Gunter Narr Verlag.

Isačenko, A.V. 1970. East Slavic Morphophonemics and The Treatment Of The Jers in Russian: A Revision Of Havlík's Law. *International Journal of Slavic Linguis-tics and Poetics 13*, 73-124.

Itô, J. 1986. *Syllable Theory in Prosodic Phonology*. Ph.D. dissertation, University of Massachusetts, Amherst.

Itô, J. and A. Mester 1995. The Core-Periphery Structure of the Lexicon and Constraints on Ranking. In: J.N. Beckman, L. W. Dickey and S. Urbanczyk (eds.). *University of Massachusetts Occasional Papers 18*, 181-209.

Itô, J. and A. Mester 1998. The Phonological Lexicon. ROA-256-0498.

Itô, J., Mester A. and J. Padgett 1995. Licensing and Underspecification in Optimality Theory. *Linguistic Inquiry 26*, 571-613.

Jakobson, R. 1971. *Studies in Child Language and Aphasia*. The Hague: Mouton.

Jespersen, O. 1904. *Lehrbuch der Phonetik*. Leipzig: B. G. Teubner.

Karaś, H. 1994. *Gramatyka historyczna języka polskiego. Materiały do ćwiczeń*. Warszawa: Wydawnictwa Uniwersytetu Warszawskiego.

Karaś, M and M. Madejowa. 1977. *Słownik wymowy polskiej. Warszawa*: Państwowe Wydawnictwo Naukowe.

Kaye, J. D. 1989. *Phonology: a cognitive view*. Hillsdale: Lawrence Erlbaum Associates.

Kaye, J. D. 1990. 'Coda' licensing. *Phonology 7*, 301-330.

Kaye, J. D. 1992. Do you believe in magic? The story of s+C sequences. *SOAS Working Papers in Linguistics and Phonetics 2*, 293-313.

Keen, P. G. W. 1977. The evolving concept of optimality. In M. K. Starr and M. Zeleny (eds.) 1997 TIMS (Total Information Management Solutions) *Studies in Management Science, vol. 6: Multiple Criteria Decision Making*. New York: North-Holland.

Kenstowicz, M. and Ch. Kissberth 1979. *Generative Phonology. Description and Theory*. New York, San Francisco, London: Academic Press.

Kim-Renaud Y.-K. 1974. *Korean Consonantal Phonology*. Ph.D. dissertation, University of Hawaii.

Kiparsky, P. 1973. Abstractness, Opacity, and Global Rules. In Fujimura, O. (ed.) (1973). *Three Dimensions in Phonological Theory*. Tokyo: TEC Company. 57-86.

Kiparsky, P. 1982a. From Cyclic to Lexical Phonology. In: Hulst, H. van der and N. Smith (eds.) (1982). *The Structure of Phonological Representations*. Dordrecht: Foris. 131-175.

Kiparsky, P. 1982b. Lexical phonology and morphology. In: Yang I.S. (ed.). *Linguistics in the Morning Calm*. Seoul: Hanshin. 3-91.

Kirchner, R. 1995. Contrastiveness is an Epiphenomenon of Constraint Ranking. ROA-51-0295.

Kirchner, R. 1996. Synchronic Chain Shifts in Optimality Theory. *Linguistic Inquiry 27* (2), 341-350.

Klemensiewicz, Z. 1964. *Gramatyka historyczna języka polskiego*. Warszawa: Państwowe Wydawnictwo Naukowe.

Klemensiewicz, Z. 1995. *Prawidła poprawnej wymowy polskiej*. Eight edition. Kraków: Wydawnictwo Baran i Suszczyński.

Klemensiewicz, Z., Lehr-Spławiński, T. and S. Urbańczyk 1955. *Gramatyka historyczna języka polskiego*. Warszawa: Państwowe Wydawnictwo Naukowe.

Klemensiewicz-Bajerowa, I. 1953. Z historii grup spółgłoskowych. *Biuletyn Towarzystwa Językoznawczego 12*, 129-149.

Kohler, K. J. 1998. The disappearance of words in connected speech. *ZAS Papers in Linguistics 11*, 21-33.

Kraska-Szlenk, I. 1995. *The Phonology of Stress in Polish*. Ph.D. dissertation, University of Illinois, Urbana-Champaign.

Kuraszkiewicz, W. 1972. *Gramatyka historyczna języka polskiego*. Warszawa: Państwowe Zakłady Wydawnictw Szkolnych.

Kuryłowicz, J. 1952. Uwagi o polskich grupach spółgłoskowych. *Biuletyn Polskiego Towarzystwa Językoznawczego 19* [1960], 221-232.

Kuryłowicz, J. 1954. Uwagi o mazurzeniu. *Biuletyn Polskiego Towarzystwa Języko-znawczego 13*, 9-19.

Labov, W. 1972. *Sociolinguistic patterns*. Philadelphia: University of Pennsylvania Press.

Ladefoged, P. and I. Maddieson 1996. *The Sounds of the World's Languages*. Cambridge, Mass.: Blackwell.

Lahiri, A. and Evers, V. 1991. Palatalization and Coronality. In Paradis, C. and J-F. Prunet (eds.). 79-100.

Laskowski, R. 1972. *Polnische Grammatik*. Leipzig: VEB Verlag Enzyklopädie.

Laskowski, R. 1975. *Studia nad morfonologią współczesnego języka polskiego*. Wrocław: Ossolineum.

Lehr-Spławiński, T. 1978. *Język polski. Pochodzenie, powstanie, rozwój. Warszawa*: Państwowe Wydawnictwo Naukowe.

Levin, J. 1985. A metrical theory of syllabicity. Ph.D. dissertation, MIT.

Liberman, M. and A. Prince 1977. On Stress and Linguistic Rhythm. *Linguistic Inquiry 8*, 249-336.

Löhken, S. 1995. Vowel weakening and vowel deletion in German: a constraint-based analysis. *FAS Working Papers in Linguistics 2*, 77-94.

Löhken, S. 1997. *Deutsche Wortprosodie. Abschwächungs- und Tilgungsvorgänge*. Studien zur deutschen Grammatik 56. Tübingen: Stauffenburg Verlag.

£obacz, P. 1996. *Polska fonologia dziecięca. Studia fonetyczno-akustyczne*. Warszawa: Energeia.

£oś, J. 1922. *Gramatyka polska. Głosownia historyczna*. Lwów, Warszawa, Kraków: Wydawnictwo Zakładu Narodowego imienia Ossolińskich.

£oś, J. 1925. *Gramatyka polska. Słowotwórstwo*. Lwów, Warszawa, Kraków: Wyda-wnictwo Zakładu Narodowego imienia Ossolińskich.

£ubowicz, A. 1998. Derived Environment Effects in OT. ROA-239-0198.

Madejowa, M. 1980. *Współczesna polszczyzna mówiona. Zagadnienia normy językowej*. Ph.D dissertation, Jagiellonian University, Kraków.

Madejowa, M. 1987. Współczesna norma jezykowa w zakresie wymowy samogłosek. *Studia Phonetica Posnaniensia 1*, 31-56.

Madejowa, M. 1990. Modern Polish Linguistic Norm With Special Reference To The Pronunciation Of Consonants. *Studia Phonetica Posnaniensia 2*, 69-105.

Madejowa, M. 1993. Normative Rules Of Modern Polish Pronunciation. *Studia Phonetica Posnaniensia 4*, 19-30.

Mascaró, J. 1976. *Catalan Phonology and the Phonological Cycle*. Ph.D. dissertation, MIT.

Mayerthaler, W. 1981. *Natürliche Morphologie*. Wiesbaden: Athenaion.

McCarthy, J. J. 1996. Process-Specific Constraints in Optimality Theory. ROA-114-0000.

McCarthy, J. J. 1997. Prosodic Morphology in Optimality Theory (Notes from class). Linguistic Institute. Cornell University, Ithaca, New York.

McCarthy, J. J. 1998. Sympathy and Phonological Opacity. ROA-252-0398.

McCarthy, J. J. and A. S. Prince 1993a. Prosodic Morphology I. Constraint Interaction and Satisfaction. Ms. University of Massachusetts and Rutgers University.

McCarthy, J. J and A. S. Prince 1993b. Generalized alignment. *Yearbook of Morpho-logy 1993*, 79-153.

McCarthy J. J. and A. S. Prince 1994. The Emergence of the Unmarked. Optimality in Prosodic Morphology. *Proceedings of the NELS 24*, 333-379.

McCarthy, J. J and A. S. Prince 1995. Faithfulness and Reduplicative Identity. In: J. N. Beckman, L. W. Dickey and S. Urbanczyk (eds.). *University of Massachusetts Occasional Papers 18*, 249-372.

Mhac an Fhailigh, É. 1968. *The Irish of Erris, Co. Mayo: A Phonemic Study*. Dublin: Dublin Institute for Advanced Studies.

Miglio, V. 1996. Mantuan Vowel Shifts. *University of Maryland Working Papers in Linguistics 4*, 103-124.

Mikoś, M. J. 1977. *Problems in Polish Phonology*. Ph.D. dissertation, Brown University. Providence, Rhode Island.

Morelli, F. 1998a. Markedness Relations and Implicational Universals in the Typology of Onset Obstruent Clusters. ROA-251-0398.

Morelli, F. 1998b. The Onset /Coda Asymmetry in Obstruent Clusters. Paper presented at the Conference 'The Syllable: Typology and Theory'. University of Tübingen.

Moszyńska, D. 1975. *Morfologia zapożyczeń łacińskich i greckich w staropolszczy-źnie*. Wrocław: Ossolineum.

Müller, M. 1892. *Die Wissenschaft der Sprache*. Vol 1. Leipzig: Klinkhardt.

Murray, R. and T. Vennemann 1983. Sound change and syllable structure in Germanic phonology. *Language 59*, 514-528.

Musan, R. 1994. On the Structure of the Coda and Voicing Phenomena in Polish. *MIT Working Papers in Linguistics 21*, 143-172.

Nespor, M. and I. Vogel 1986. *Prosodic Phonology*. Dordrecht: Foris.

Ohala, J. J. 1981. The listener as a source of sound change. In Masek, C. S., Hendrick, R. A. and M. F. Miller (eds.). *Papers from the Parasession in Language and Behavior*. Chicago: Chicago Linguistic Society. 178-203.

Ohala, J. J., Fischer-Jørgensen, E., Kohler, K. and L. Goldstein 1984: Phonetic Explanation in Phonology. *Proceedings of the Tenth International Congress of Phonetic Sciences*, 175-182.

Padgett, J. 1995a. Stricture and Nasal Place Assimilation. *Natural Language and Linguistic Theory 12*, 465-513.

Padgett, J. 1995b. Partial Class Behavior and Nasal Place Assimilation. Proceedings of the Arizona Phonology Conference Workshop on Features in Optimality Theory. ROA-113-0000.

Paradis, C. 1988. On constraints and repair strategies. *The Linguistic Review 6*, 71-97.

Paradis, C. and J.-F. Prunet (eds.) 1991. *Phonetics and Phonology. The Special Status of Coronals. Internal and External Evidence*. New York: Academic Press.

Paul, H. 1959. *Deutsche Grammatik. Teil III: Flexionslehre*. Vol. 2. Halle (Saale): Niemeyer.

Paul, H. 1966. *Prinzipien der Sprachgeschichte*. Tübingen: Niemeyer.

Pesetsky, D. 1997. Optimality Theory and Syntax: Movement and Pronunciation. In: Archangeli and Langendoen (eds.) (1997). 134-170.

Pompino-Marschall, B. 1990. *Die Silbenprosodie. Ein elementaler Aspekt der Wahrnehmung von Sprachrhythmus und Sprechtempo*. Tübingen: Niemeyer.

Pompino-Marschall, B. 1993. Die Silbe im Deutschen - gesprochen, geschrieben, beschrieben. In: Baurmann, J., Günther, H. and U. Knoop (eds.) *homo scribens*. Perspektiven der Schriftlichkeitsforschung. Tübingen: Niemeyer. 43-65.

Pompino-Marschall, B. 1995. *Einführung in die Phonetik*. Berlin, New York: de Gruyter.

Popowska-Toborska, H. 1993. *Wczesne dzieje Słowian w świetle ich języka*. Warszawa: Slawistyczny Ośrodek Wydawniczy.

Postal, P. 1968. *Aspects of Phonological Theory*. New York: Harper and Row.

Prince, A. 1990. *Quantitative Consequences of Rhythmic Organization*. In: Ziolkowki, M., Noske, M. and K. Deaton (eds.). *CLS 26 (2)*, 355-398.

Prince, A. and P. Smolensky. 1993. Optimality Theory. Constraint Interaction in Generative Grammar. Ms, Rutgers University and University of Colorado at Boulder.

Prince, A. and P. Smolensky. 1997. Optimality: From Neural Networks to Universal Grammar. *Science 275*, 1604-1610.

Pulleyblank, D. 1986. *Tone in Lexical Phonology. Studies in Natural Language and Linguistic Theory*. Dordrecht: Kluwer.

Pulleyblank, D. 1997. Optimality Theory and Features. In: Archangeli and Langendoen (eds.). 59-101.

Raffelsiefen, R. 1995. Conditions for stability: the case of schwa in German. In: *Theorie des Lexikons*. Arbeiten Sonderforschungsbereichs 282 (69). Heinrich-Heine-Universität, Düsseldorf.

Ramers, K. H., Vater H. and H. Wode (eds.) 1994. *Universale phonologische Strukturen und Prozesse*. Tübingen: Niemeyer.

Reichan, J. 1975. *Zmiany we fleksji rzeczowników męskich zakończonych pierwotnie na spółgłoski wargowe palatalne*. Wrocław, Warszawa, Kraków, Gdańsk: Zakład Narodowy imienia Ossolińskich, Wydawnictwo Polskiej Akademii Nauk.

Reynolds, W. T. 1994. *Variation and phonological change*. Ph.D. dissertation, University of Pennsylvania.

Rice, K. 1992. On Deriving Sonority: A structural account of sonority relationships. *Phonology 9*, 61-99.

Roca, I. (ed). 1997. *Derivations and Constraints in Phonology*. Oxford: Clarendon Press.

Rochoń, M. 1999a. Application of Universal Constraints in Polish: Palatalized Labials. To appear in: Lingustica Silesiana. Katowice, Warszawa: University of Silesia, Polska Akademia Nauk.

Rochoń, M. 1999b. An OT Approach to Coronal Palatalization. In: Böttger, K., Giger, M. und B. Wiemer (eds.) Die Welt der Slaven. Beiträge der Europäischen Slavistischen Linguistik. POLYSLAV 2. München: Otto Sagner Verlag. 244-253.

Rochoń, M. und B. Pompino-Marschall 1999. *The Articulation of Secondarily Palatalized Coronals in Polish. Proceedings of XIVth International Congress of Phonetic Sciences, San Francisco*. 1897-1900.

Rospond, S. 1954. Palatalizacja, dyspalatalizacja a tzw. mazurzenie. *Biuletyn Polskiego Towarzystwa Językoznawczego 13*, 21-50.

Rospond, S. 1971. *Gramatyka historyczna języka polskiego*. Warszawa: Państwowa Akademia Nauk.

Rowicka, G. 1994. Polish Palatal Assimilation in Prefixed Words. In: Bok-Bennema, R. and C. Cremers (1994). *Linguistics in the Netherlands 1994*. Amsterdam and Philadelphia: John Benjamins Publishing Company.

Rowicka, G. 1999. *On Ghost Vowels. A Strict CV Approach*. The Hague: Holland Academic Graphics.

Rowicka, G. and J. van de Weijer 1994. Prosodic constraints in the lexicon of Polish: The case of Derived Imperatives. *The Linguistic Review 11*, 49-76.

Rozwadowski, J. 1909. Bulla z r. 1136 jako najstarszy zabytek języka polskiego. *Materiały i Prace Komisji Językowej IV*, 432-482.

Rozwadowski, J. 1915. Historyczna fonetyka czyli głosownia języka polskiego. In: *Encyklopedya polska 2*. Kraków: Polska Akademia Umiejętności. 289-422.

Rubach, J. 1976. The Concept of an Underlying Representation. *Biuletyn Polskiego Towarzystwa Językoznawczego 34*, 101-109.

Rubach, J. 1977. *Changes of Consonants in English and Polish. A Generative Account*. Prace Językoznawcze 87. Wrocław, Warszawa, Kraków, Gdańsk: Zakład Narodowy imienia Ossolińskich, Wydawnictwo PAN.

Rubach, J. 1981. *Cyclic Phonology And Palatalization In Polish And English*. Warszawa: Wydawnictwa Uniwersytetu Warszawskiego.

Rubach, J. 1984. *Cyclic and lexical phonology: The structure of Polish*. Dordrecht: Foris.

Rubach, J. 1992. Abstracts vowels in three dimensional phonology: the yers. In: Fisiak, J. and S. Puppel (eds.) 1992. *Phonological Investigations*. Amsterdam, Philadelphia: John Benjamins Publishing Company.

Rubach, J. 1994. Affricates as Strident Stops in Polish. *Linguistic Inquiry 25*, 119-143.

Rubach, J. 1996. Nonsyllabic Analysis of Voice Assimilation in Polish. *Linguistic Inquiry 27*, 69-110.

Rubach, J. 1997. Extrasyllabic Consonants in Polish: Derivational Optimality Theory. In: Roca (ed.), 551-581.

Rubach, J. and G. E. Booij 1985. A Grid Theory Of Stress In Polish. *Lingua 66*, 281-319.

Rubach, J., and G. E. Booij 1990a. Syllable Structure Assignment in Polish. *Phonology 7*, 121-158 and 1988 *Vrije Universiteit Working Papers in Linguistics 32*, 1-59;

Rubach, J. and G. E. Booij 1990b. Edge of Constituent Effects in Polish. *Natural Language and Linguistic Theory 8*, 427-463.

Russell, K. 1995. Morphemes and Candidates in Optimality Theory. ROA-44-0195.

Russell, K. 1997. Optimality Theory and Morphology. In: Archangeli and Langendoen (eds.) 1997. 102-133.

Sagey, E. 1986. *The Representation of Features and Relations in Non-Linear Phonology*. Ph.D. dissertation, MIT.

Sawicka, I. 1974. *Struktura grup spółgłoskowych w językach słowiańskich*. Monografie Slawistyczne 27. Wrocław, Warszawa, Kraków, Gdańsk: Zakład Narodowy imienia Ossolińskich, Wydawnictwo PAN.

Schoemaker, P. J. H. 1991. The quest for optimality. A positive heuristic of science? *Behavioral and Brain Sciences 14*, 205-215.

Schuchardt, H. 1885. *Über die Lautgesetze: gegen die Junggrammatiker*. Berlin: Oppenheim.

Selkirk, E. 1984a. On the Major Class Features and Syllable Theory. In: Arnoff , M. and R. T. Oehre (eds.). 1984 *Language Sound Structure*. Cambridge, Mass.: MIT Press. 107-136.

Selkirk, E. 1984b. *Phonology and Syntax: The Relation Between Sound and Structure*. Cambridge: MIT Press.

Selkirk, E. 1995. The Prosodic Structure of Function Words. In: J. N. Beckman, L. W. Dickey and S. Urbanczyk (eds.). *University of Massachusetts Occasional Papers 18*, 439-469.

Shevelov, G. 1964. *The Prehistory of Slavic*. New York: Columbia University Press.

Siatkowski, J. 1965. *Bohemizmy fonetyczne w języku polskim*. Część I. Wrocław: Ossolineum.

Sievers, E. 1901. *Grundzüge der Phonetik*. Leipzig: Breitkopf und Härtel.

Smolensky, P. 1993. Harmony, Markedness, and Phonological Activity. Paper presented at Rutgers Optimality Workshop 1. ROA-87-0000.

Smolensky, P. 1996. On the Comprehension/Production Dilemma in Child Language. ROA-118-0000.

Smolensky, P. 1997. Constraint Interaction In Generative Grammar II: Local Conjunction (or, Random Rules in Universal Grammar). Paper presented at Hopkins Optimality Theory Workshop, University of Maryland.

Speas, M. 1997. Optimality Theory and Syntax: Null pronouns and Control. In: Archangeli and Langendoen (eds.) 1997. 171-199.

Stampe, D. 1972. *How I Spent my Summer Vacation*. Ph.D dissertation, Ohio State University.

Stankiewicz, E. 1956. The Phonemic Patterns of the Polish Dialects. A Study in Structural Dialectology. In: Halle, M., Lunt, H. G., McLean, H. and C. H. van Schooneveld (eds.) (1956). *For Roman Jakobson. Essays On The Occasion Of His Sixtieth Birthday*. The Hague: Mouton. 518-530.

Starr, M. K. and M. Zeleny, M. (eds.) 1977. *TIMS (Total Information Management Solutions) Studies in Management Science. Multiple Criteria in Decision Making*. Vol. 6. New York: North-Holland.

Steele, R.D. 1973. *The Segmental Phonology of Contemporary Standard Polish*. Ph.D. dissertation, Harvard University.

Steffen, W. 1982. Rozwój p̍, b̍ i v̍, f' w dialekcie warmińskim. *Język polski LXII*, 24-26.

Stemberger, P. and C. Stoel-Gammon 1991. The Underspecification of Coronals: Evidence From Language Acquisition And Performance. In: Paradis, C. and J.-F. Prunet (eds.) 1991. 181-199.

Steriade, D. 1982. *Greek Prosodies and the Nature of Syllabification*. Ph.D. dissertation, MIT.

Steriade, D. (1987). Redundant rules. *CLS 23*, 339-362.

Steriade 1993. Positional neutralization. Paper presented at *NELS 24*. University of Massachussets, Amherst.

Steriade, D. 1995. Underspecification and Markedness. In: Goldsmith, J. A. (ed.) 1995. 114-175.

Stieber, Z. 1958. *Rozwój fonologiczny języka polskiego*. Warszawa: Państwowe Wydawnictwo Naukowe.

Stieber, Z. 1966. *Historyczna i współczesna fonologia języka polskiego*. Warszawa: Państwowe Wydawnictwo Naukowe.

Stieber, Z. 1969. *Zarys gramatyki porównawczej języków słowiańskich. Fonologia*. Warszawa: Państwowe Wydawnictwo Naukowe.

Stieber, Z. 1973. *A Historical Phonology of the Polish Language*. Heidelberg: Carl Winter Universitätsverlag.

Sturtevant, E. H. 1907. *Linguistic change*. Chicago: University Press.

Szpyra, J. 1989. *The Phonology-Morphology Interface. Cycles, levels and words*. London and New York: Routledge.

Szpyra, J. 1992. Ghost Segments in Nonlinear Phonology: Polish Yers. *Language 68 (2)*, 277-312.

Szpyra, J. 1995. *Three Tiers in Polish and English Phonology*. Lublin: Wydawnictwo Uniwersytetu Marii Curie-Skłodowskiej.

Szymczak 1995. *Słownik Języka Polskiego*. Warszawa: Państwowe Wydawnictwo Naukowe.

Takatori, Yuki 1997. *A Study of Constraint Interaction in Slavic Phonology*. Ph.D. dissertation, Yale University.

Taszycki, W. 1954. Nowy argument za późnością mazurzenia. *Biuletyn Polskiego Towarzystwa Językoznawczego 13*, 51-56.

Tesar, B. and P. Smolensky 1996. Learnability in Optimality Theory. ROA-156-1196.

Timberlake, A. 1983. Compensatory lengthening in Slavic: conditions and dialect geography. Markov, V. and Worth, D. S. (eds.) 1983. *From Los Angeles to Kiev. Papers on the occasion of the Ninth International Congress of Slavists*. Columbus, OH: Slavica, 207-35.

Topolińska, Z. 1961. Z historii akzentu polskiego od wieku XVI do dziś. *Prace Językoznawcze 27*. Lwów, Warszawa, Kraków: Wydawnictwo Polskiej Akademii Nauk.

Topolińska, Z. 1968. Zakres i chronologia tzw. wzdłużenia zastępczego w językach zachodniosłowiańskich. In: Fasske, H. and R. Lötzsch, (eds.). *Přinoski k serbskemu rečespytej*. Bautzen: VEB Domowina. 77-83.

Topolińska, Z. 1974. *A Historical Phonology Of The Kashubian Dialects Of Polish*. The Hague: Mouton.

Trask, R. L. 1996. *A Dictionary of Phonetics and Phonology*. London and New York: Routledge.

Trubetzkoy, N. S. 1931. Die phonologischen Systeme. *Travaux du Cercle Linguistique de Prague 4*, 96-116.

Tyszyński, A. 1837. *Amerykanka w Polsce*. Petersburg: Drukarnia Karola Kraya.

Ultan, R. 1978. A typological view of metathesis. In Greenberg, J.H. (ed.) 1978b. 367-402.

Ułaszyn, H. 1956. *Uwagi o polskich grupach spółgłoskowych*. Wrocław: Zakład imienia Ossolińskich, Wydawnictwo PAN.

Vennemann, T. 1983. Causality in language change: Theories of linguistic preference as a basis for linguistic explanations. *Folia Linguistica Historica 6*, 5-26.

Vennemann, T. 1986. *Neuere Entwicklungen in der Phonologie*. Berlin: de Gruyter.

Vennemann, T. 1988a. *Preference Laws for Syllable Structure and the Explanation of Sound Change. With special Reference to German, Germanic, Italian, and Latin*. Berlin, New York, Amsterdam: de Gruyter.

Vennemann, T. 1988b. The rule dependence of syllable structure. In: Duncan-Rose, C. and T. Vennemann (eds.) 1988. *On language: Rhetorica, Phonologica, Syntactica: A Festschrift for Robert P. Stockwell from his friends and colleagues*. London: Routledge. 257-283.

Vennemann, T. 1993. Language change as language improvement. In: Charles, J. (ed.) 1993. *Historical Linguistics*. London: Longman.

Vennemann, T. 1994. Universelle Nuklearphonologie mit epiphänomenaler Silben-struktur. In: Ramers et al. 1994. 7-54.

Verhijde, M. M. 1995. Multiple constraint rankings in Polish. *FAS Working Papers in Linguistics 2*,176-211.

Vrtel-Wierczyński, S. 1963. *Wybór tekstów staropolskich. Czasy najdawniejsze do roku 1543*. Warszawa: Państwowe Wydawnictwo Naukowe.

Walczak, B. 1995. *Zarys dziejów języka polskiego*. Poznań: Kantor Wydawniczy SAWW.

Walsh Dickey, L. 1997. *The phonology of liquids*. Ph.D. dissertation. University of Massachusets, Amherst.

Warner, M. (ed.) 1996. *International Encyclopedia of Business and Management*. London and New York: Routledge. 3767-3781.

Weinreich, U., Labov, W. and M. I. Herzog 1968. Empirical foundations for a theory of language change. In Lehmann, W. and Y. Malkiel (eds.) 1968. *Directions for historical linguistics*. Austin: University of Texas Press.

Wierzchowska, B. 1971. *Wymowa polska*. Warszawa: Państwowe Zakłady Wydaw-nictw Szkolnych.

Wierzchowska, B. 1980. *Fonetyka i fonologia języka polskiego*. Wrocław, Warszawa, Kraków, Gdańsk: Zakład Narodowy imienia Ossolińskich, Wydawnictwo PAN.

Wilbur, R. 1973. *The Phonology of Reduplication*. Ph.D. dissertation, University of Illinois, Urbana-Champaign.

Wurzel, W. U. 1984. *Flexionsmorphologie und Natürlichkeit*. Berlin: Akademie Verlag.

Wurzel, W. U. 1998. On Markedness. *Theoretical Linguistics 24*, 53-71.

Zarębina, M. 1980. *Język polski w rozwoju jednostki. Analiza tekstów dzieci do wieku szkolnego. Rozwój semantyczny języka dziecka*. Kraków: Wydawnictwo Naukowe Wyższej Szkoły Pedagogicznej.

Zec, D. 1988. *Sonority Constraints on Prosodic Structure*. Ph.D. dissertation, Standford University. [1994]. New York: Garland.

Zec, D. 1998. Prosodic weight. Paper presented at the Conference 'The Syllable: Typology and Theory'. University of Tübingen.

Zoll, Ch. 1993. Ghost segments and Optimality. *The proceedings of the twelfth West Coast Conference on Formal Linguistics,* 183-199.

Zoll, Ch. 1996. Parsing below the Segment in a Constraint-Based Framework. Ph.D. dissertation, University of California. ROA-143-0996.

Zubritskaya, K. 1994. Sound change in Optimality Theory and constraint tie CLS 23(2) 335-349.